# HOW HITLER COULD HAVE WON WORLD WAR II

**Other Books by Bevin Alexander**

*Korea: The First War We Lost*

*The Strange Connection: U.S. Intervention in China 1944–1972*

*Lost Victories: The Military Genius of Stonewall Jackson*

*How Great Generals Win*

*The Future of Warfare*

*Robert E. Lee's Civil War*

# HOW HITLER COULD HAVE WON WORLD WAR II

*The Fatal Errors
That Led to Nazi Defeat*

Bevin Alexander

KONECKY&KONECKY

Konecky & Konecky
72 Ayers Point Rd.
Old Saybrook, CT 06475

This edition published by special arrangement with Crown Publishers

Photograph on page xiv: Adolf Hitler walks up stairs at Nazi rally
in Germany prior to the war. (*Topham/The Image Works*)
Design by Leonard W. Henderson

Maps by Jeffrey L. Ward

ISBN: 1-56852-615-6

Printed in the U.S.A.

# Contents

List of Maps . . . . . . . . . . . . . . . . . . . . . . . . . . . . . . . . . . . . . . . . . . .vii

Introduction . . . . . . . . . . . . . . . . . . . . . . . . . . . . . . . . . . . . . . . . . . .ix

1. Germany's Opportunity for Victory . . . . . . . . . . . . . . . . . . . . . . .1

2. The Campaign in the West: 1940 . . . . . . . . . . . . . . . . . . . . .9

3. The Defeat of France . . . . . . . . . . . . . . . . . . . . . . . . . . . . . .17

4. Hitler's First Great Error . . . . . . . . . . . . . . . . . . . . . . . .36

5. The Fatal Turn to the East . . . . . . . . . . . . . . . . . . . . . . .45

6. Attacking the Wrong Island . . . . . . . . . . . . . . . . . . . . . .61

7. Rommel's Unappreciated Gift . . . . . . . . . . . . . . . . . . . .71

8. Barbarossa . . . . . . . . . . . . . . . . . . . . . . . . . . . . . . . . . . .81

9. Falling Between Two Stools . . . . . . . . . . . . . . . . . . . . . .92

10. Failure Before Moscow . . . . . . . . . . . . . . . . . . . . . . . . . .100

11. To and Fro in the Desert . . . . . . . . . . . . . . . . . . . . . . . .110

12. No Change in Strategy . . . . . . . . . . . . . . . . . . . . . . . . . .126

13. The Drive to El Alamein . . . . . . . . . . . . . . . . . . . . . . . .131

14. Stalingrad . . . . . . . . . . . . . . . . . . . . . . . . . . . . . . . . . . . .145

15. Manstein Saves the Army . . . . . . . . . . . . . . . . . . . . . . . .156

16. The Western Allies Strike . . . . . . . . . . . . . . . . . . . . . . .165

17. Kasserine and the End in Africa . . . . . . . . . . . . . . . . . . . . . . . .180

18. The Invasion of Sicily . . . . . . . . . . . . . . . . . . . . . . . . . . . . . . .194

19. The Citadel Disaster . . . . . . . . . . . . . . . . . . . . . . . . . . . . . . . .204

20. The Assault on Italy . . . . . . . . . . . . . . . . . . . . . . . . . . . . . . . .214

21. Normandy . . . . . . . . . . . . . . . . . . . . . . . . . . . . . . . . . . . . . . .233

22. The Liberation of France . . . . . . . . . . . . . . . . . . . . . . . . . . . .254

23. The Battle of the Bulge . . . . . . . . . . . . . . . . . . . . . . . . . . . . . .276

24. The Last Days . . . . . . . . . . . . . . . . . . . . . . . . . . . . . . . . . . . . .290

Notes . . . . . . . . . . . . . . . . . . . . . . . . . . . . . . . . . . . . . . . . . . . . . .304

Selected Bibliography . . . . . . . . . . . . . . . . . . . . . . . . . . . . . . . . .324

Index . . . . . . . . . . . . . . . . . . . . . . . . . . . . . . . . . . . . . . . . . . . . . .329

# List of Maps

Conquest of the Low Countries and France, 1940   18

Battle of Britain, 1940   39

Conquest of Yugoslavia and Greece, 1941   58

Capture of Crete, May 20–June 1, 1941   66

The Crusader Battles, November 1941   74

War in the Desert, 1941–42   75

The Gazala Battles, May–June 1942   75

Barbarossa, 1941   85

Stalingrad, 1942   148

Landings in North Africa, November 8–15, 1942   168

Tunisia, 1943   182

Conquest of Sicily, July 10–August 17, 1943   198

Retreat in Russia, 1943   206

48th Panzer Corps in Citadel, July 7–12, 1943   210

Salerno Landings, September 9–16, 1943   216

Invasion of Italy, September 1943   217

Normandy and the Liberation of France, 1944   244

Battle of the Bulge, December 16–25, 1944   282

The Last Days, 1945   292

# Introduction

AROUND 400 B.C. THE GREAT CHINESE STRATEGIST SUN TZU BRUSHED IN THE characters for the most profound sentence ever written about warfare: "The way to avoid what is strong is to strike what is weak."

Adolf Hitler knew nothing of Sun Tzu. But for the first seven years of his dictatorship of Germany, from 1933 to 1940, he avoided strength, struck at weakness, and achieved such stunning success that he was on the threshold of complete victory.

After 1940, however, Hitler abandoned a course of action that would have completed his victory. He attacked frontally into the strength of the Soviet Union, allowed Britain and the United States time to build immense military power, and was unable to prevent them from striking into Germany's weakness. The collision of the Allies and Germans brought on the most titanic clash in history. But the outcome had already been foreshadowed by Hitler's fatal mistakes in 1940 and thereafter. By 1945 Germany was shattered and Adolf Hitler dead.

Hitler was one of the most evil monsters the world has ever known. But he was also a skilled politician. His political mastery boosted him into power and allowed him to hide his wickedness behind great economic, territorial, and military advances that he gained for Germany. Hitler did not seek rational goals, however. His aims were those of a maniac. He believed he could elevate the German people into a "master race" through restriction of marriages and sexual relations only among "Aryans," refusing to recognize that Europeans had been interbreeding for a millennium and there could be no such thing as a pure "race" of Aryans or anything else. He wanted to gain *Lebensraum,* or living space, for the German people in Russia and Ukraine, and intended to kill or starve millions of Slavs living in those lands. Beyond this Hitler wanted to kill whole categories of people—Jews, Gypsies, persons with mental and physical disabilities, and anyone who objected to his desires.

Hitler possessed great skill in spotting and exploiting the vulnerabilities of opponents. Using these gifts, Hitler gained an unparalleled string of victories that commenced with his installation as German chancellor in January 1933 and ended in the summer of 1940, when his victory over France convinced him he was an infallible military genius. He did not see that the victory came not from his own vision, but from that of two generals, Erich von Manstein and Heinz Guderian.

Believing Britain would no longer be a major problem, Hitler turned his attention to killing Jews and other peoples he despised, and to the destruction of the Soviet Union.

From this point on, these twin drives—war against Soviet Russia and perpetration of the Final Solution—consumed most of Hitler's attention and the vast bulk of the resources and manpower of the German Reich.

This course led straight to his destruction. It did not have to be. Hitler's strategy through mid-1940 was almost flawless. He isolated and absorbed state after state in Europe, gained the Soviet Union as a willing ally, destroyed France's military power, threw the British off the Continent, and was left with only weak and vulnerable obstacles to an empire covering most of Europe, North Africa, and the Middle East. This empire not only would have been unassailable from the outside, but would have put him into the position, in time, to conquer the world.

This did not happen. Hitler's paranoias overwhelmed his political sense. He abandoned the successful indirect strategy of attacking weakness, which he had followed up to the summer of 1940, and tried to grab *Lebensraum* directly and by main strength. He was unable to see that he could achieve these goals far more easily and with absolute certainty by indirection—by striking not what was strong but what was weak.

Even after Hitler invaded the Soviet Union in June 1941, he might have gained a partial victory if he had not possessed two more lethal defects—insistence on offensive solutions to military problems when his strength was inadequate, and attempting to keep all the territory he had seized when retreat would have preserved his forces. These failings led to disastrous offensives—Stalingrad, Tunisia, Kursk, the Bulge—and "no retreat" orders that destroyed huge portions of his army.

The way to victory was not through a frontal attack on the Soviet Union but an indirect approach through North Africa. This route was so obvious that all the British leaders saw it, as did a number of the German leaders, including Alfred Jodl, chief of operations of the armed forces; Erich Raeder, commander of the German Navy, and Erwin Rommel, destined to gain fame in North Africa as the Desert Fox.

After the destruction of France's military power in 1940, Britain was left with only a single armored division to protect Egypt and the Suez Canal. Germany had twenty armored divisions, none being used. If the Axis— Germany and its ally Italy—had used only four of these divisions to seize the Suez Canal, the British Royal Navy would have been compelled to abandon the Mediterranean Sea, turning it into an Axis lake. French North Africa—Morocco, Algeria, and Tunisia—could have been occupied, and German forces could have seized Dakar in Senegal on the west coast of Africa, from which submarines and aircraft could have dominated the main South Atlantic sea routes.

With no hope of aid, Yugoslavia and Greece would have been forced to come to terms. Since Hitler gained the support of Hungary, Romania, and Bulgaria, Germany would have achieved control of all southeastern Europe without committing a single German soldier.

Once the Suez Canal was taken, the way would have been open to German armored columns to overrun Palestine, Transjordan, the Arabian peninsula, Syria, Iraq, and Iran. This would have given Germany unlimited supplies of the single commodity it needed most: oil.

As important as oil was for the conduct of modern war, the greatest advantages of German occupation of the Arab lands and Iran would have been to isolate Turkey, threaten British control of India, and place German tanks and guns within striking distance of Soviet oil fields in the Caucasus and along the shores of the Caspian Sea. Turkey would have been forced to become an ally or grant transit rights to German forces, Britain would have had to exert all its strength to protect India, and the Soviet Union would have gone to any lengths to preserve peace with Germany because of its perilous position.

Germany need not have launched a U-boat or air war against British shipping and cities, because British participation in the war would have become increasingly irrelevant. Britain could never have built enough military power to invade the Continent alone.

Unless the strength of the Soviet Union were added, the United States could not have projected sufficient military force across the Atlantic Ocean, even over a period of years, to reconquer Europe by amphibious invasion in the face of an untouched German war machine. Since the United States was increasingly preoccupied with the threat of Japan, it almost certainly would not have challenged Germany.

Thus, Germany would have been left with a virtually invincible empire and the leisure to develop defenses and resources that, in time, would permit it to match the strength of the United States. Though Britain might have refused to make peace, a de facto cease-fire would have ensued. The United States would have concentrated on defense of the Western Hemisphere and the Pacific. Even if the United States had proceeded with development of the atomic bomb, it would have hesitated to unleash it against Germany.

This book is about the opportunities Hitler possessed that might have led to victory. But such was not to be, because of his inability to see the indirect way to victory, and his fixation on frontal assault of the Soviet Union.

# HOW HITLER
# COULD HAVE WON
# WORLD WAR II

# 1 GERMANY'S OPPORTUNITY FOR VICTORY

EARLY ON THE MORNING OF MAY 10, 1940, THE GREATEST CONCENTRATION OF armor in the history of warfare burst across the eastern frontiers of Belgium and Luxembourg. In four days, 1,800 tanks in seven panzer, or armored, divisions broke through the French main line of resistance on the Meuse River. Seven days later they reached the English Channel 160 miles away and cut off the most powerful and mobile of the French and British forces, who were now in Belgium. Those Allied soldiers who did not surrender were forced to evacuate by sea at Dunkirk.

A month later France capitulated, and the British were thrown onto their islands with few weapons and only twenty-one miles of the Channel to keep them from being conquered as well.

Germany had achieved the most spectacular, rapid, and overwhelming military victory in the twentieth century. It dominated Europe from the North Cape of Norway to the Mediterranean Sea and from Poland to the Atlantic. Victory lay within the grasp of the German dictator, Adolf Hitler.

Yet at this moment of his greatest success—with only feeble barriers remaining before he could create a virtually invincible empire embracing Europe, North Africa, and the Middle East—Hitler turned away and embarked on a course that led to the destruction of the "Thousand-year Reich" in only five years.

A number of high-command German officers saw the opportunities open in 1940 and urged Hitler to seize them. Hitler considered them, but in the end turned them down. After the victory over France, Hitler focused his attention on destruction of the Soviet Union and carrying forward his schemes to destroy the Jews and other peoples he hated.

Hitler came to this decision by an incredibly convoluted and illogical process. Since Britain refused to sign a peace treaty, and since invading Britain would be extremely hazardous given the strength of the Royal Navy and the weakness of the German navy, Hitler concluded that the only way to overcome Britain would be to destroy the Soviet Union. Hitler decided that Russia was Britain's chief remaining hope for assistance, its "continental dagger," and once the Soviet Union was destroyed, the British would see reason and give in.

This, of course, was entirely wrong. The British were relying on the United States, not Russia, for their salvation. "I shall drag the United States in," British Prime Minister Winston Churchill told his son after France fell. And the American president, Franklin D. Roosevelt, was doing everything he could to help. But Roosevelt had to play a cagey game. A majority of the American electorate was deathly afraid of getting into another war in Europe, and wanted to isolate the country behind its two oceans. Only a minority recognized the terrible danger of Adolf Hitler and realized the United States would have to enter the war if Nazi Germany was to be defeated.

Perhaps Hitler was engaging in wishful thinking in turning toward the Soviet Union, concocting a theory of the close connection of Britain to Russia to justify what he wanted to do anyway. He hated Communism, feared the growth of a powerful industrial state that was proceeding apace under Joseph Stalin, and wanted to seize a large segment of Russia and Ukraine. Besides, he could *reach* the Soviet Union, while he couldn't reach Britain.

Actually, Hitler did *not* want to destroy Britain, and this played a role in his decision to turn eastward. He admired the British Empire and wanted to reach an understanding with it. However, Hitler's conditions were that Britain would keep its empire while Germany would have a free hand on the Continent. Britain could never accept such a settlement, however, because it could not survive as an independent power if Germany controlled the European continent.

Hitler would listen to no criticism. His senior advisers knew the war in the west had been only half-won, and few thought it could be finished on the plains of Russia in the east. The Soviet Union was so vast that a war there could expand into limitless space—placing potentially impossible demands on the German war machine. A war against Russia would be nothing like the war in the west, where distances were limited, populations concentrated, objectives close, and the Atlantic Ocean a finite boundary.

On the advice of General Erich von Manstein, Hitler had changed the *Schwerpunkt*—or main weight—of the attack from northern Belgium to the Ardennes, when the top German generals had advised otherwise. This decision had given Germany its greatest victory in history. Since the senior military leadership had been wrong, and he (and Manstein) right, Hitler concluded that he could rely on his "intuition." This intuition told him to downgrade the war against Britain and carry out the two desires that had obsessed him from the early 1920s—destroying the Soviet Union and the Jews of Europe.

Hitler's belief in *Lebensraum* was based on his idea that the German people needed more land to produce more food. Classical economics had long since proved that industrial states could *buy* grains and other foods for their people and did not need additional farmland. But Hitler paid no attention. Besides, the idea of more land resonated with the German people. Their parents and grandparents had sought expansion into central and eastern Europe in the early years of the century; this was one of the underlying causes for World War I, which Germany had lost. In *Mein Kampf* Hitler wrote that Germany was not a world power in 1914–1918 because it could not feed its people, and would not become a world power until it was able to do so.

Hitler's compulsion to destroy the Jews and other categories of people rested on no logical basis, only on the most malignant of prejudices. He made the Jews scapegoats for every problem that Germany faced—even the rise of the Soviet Union, whose revolution he falsely claimed had been carried out and sustained by Jews.

Hitler's political savvy warned him to avoid getting openly involved in this pogrom of hate and murder, however, and he left its operation mostly to underlings, especially Heinrich Himmler and Reinhard Heydrich of the *Schutzstaffel* or SS.

In the butchery that followed, Hitler and his willing German executioners killed 6 million Jews in what is now called the Holocaust, perhaps a million Poles and Gypsies, thousands of persons who had mental or physical disabilities or who objected to his ideas, and 7.7 million Soviet civilians. This does not count the 9.1 million Allied personnel killed in battle (7.5 million Soviets), and 5 million Soviet soldiers who died in prisoner-of-war camps or were murdered by their captors.

Aside from their horror, the killings of civilians and prisoners of war deprived Germany of the labor and mental contributions of potentially valuable workers and took immense amounts of transportation, resources, personnel, and energy badly needed for the war effort.

It is easy enough to assert that Hitler was mad. He most certainly was. His fixation on these two monstrous, irrational goals proves it. But Hitler also was in part a sensible person, possessed of great intelligence and superior political skills. His fantastic success up to mid-1940 demonstrates this.

Many of the men who served Hitler believed they might tap the sane part of Hitler's mind and deflect the mad part, and in this way lead Germany to a successful outcome of the war. The events in Hitler's headquarters from mid-1940 onward are a rolling drama of this attempt. While a number of far-sighted officers saw the way to succeed and tried to convince him, toadies catered to Hitler's prejudices. Sometimes Hitler listened to one, sometimes to the other, and sometimes to no one but himself.

✠          ✠          ✠

Until the summer of 1940, Hitler had run up a string of victories that were unprecedented in world history. He achieved most of them by the application of his remarkable political skills, and without the use of force.

Over the course of six years, beginning with his assumption of the chancellorship of Germany on January 30, 1933, Hitler got himself elected dictator of Germany less than two months later and put the state wholly under the Nazi party which he led; withdrew Germany from the League of Nations in October 1933; commenced massive secret rebuilding of German military power in 1934; introduced conscription in violation of the Versailles treaty in 1935; reoccupied the Rhineland in 1936, a German border region demilitarized under terms of the Versailles treaty; declared the treaty dead in 1937; seized the sovereign state of Austria and joined it to Germany on March 10, 1938; bullied the leaders of Britain and France into accepting his dismemberment of Czechoslovakia at the Munich conference, September 29–30, 1938, and occupied the remaining rump of the state—the Czech portions of Bohemia and Moravia—on March 15, 1939.

It was this last act of treachery that finally showed Neville Chamberlain, British prime minister, and Edouard Daladier, the French premier, that their policy of "appeasement" of Hitler was utterly misguided and that Hitler was a congenital liar. At Munich, Hitler had solemnly sworn that his final territorial aspiration in Europe was annexation of the Sudetenland, the German-speaking part of Czechoslovakia, and that he would assure the independence of the remainder of the state.

Britain and France now guaranteed the independence of Poland, the next victim on Hitler's list. It was a hopeless gesture, since neither country could help Poland. That country's fate was sealed on August 23, 1939, when the Soviet Union signed a nonaggression pact with Germany—inspired not by confidence in the peaceful intentions of Hitler but by desperation. Britain and France, who feared Communism, had refused to work with the Soviet Union to block Hitler during the early years when he could have been stopped with relative ease.

Bolstered by secret provisions of the Berlin-Moscow pact, which divided eastern Europe into German and Soviet spheres of influence, Hitler launched his armies against Poland on September 1, 1939. Poland had no chance whatsoever, being half-surrounded by German or German-held territory. The Polish army was enveloped from the first day. In addition, German General Heinz Guderian had developed a spectacular panzer arm, and German tanks cut through and rolled up Polish defenses with ease and unimagined speed in the first application of *Blitzkrieg*, or "lightning war." Within three weeks Poland was defeated—and the Poles found their land partitioned between the Germans in the west and the Soviets in the east.

Britain and France declared war on Germany on September 3, 1939. The British took some action at sea, blockading German ports and pursuing German surface raiders, but were slow to put troops on the Continent, while France did virtually nothing on the Franco-German frontier. The fall and winter of 1939–1940 became known in the British Empire and the United States as the "phony war," in France as the *drôle de guerre,* and in Germany as the *Sitzkrieg.*

Meanwhile, the Soviet Union took advantage of its pact with Germany to demand from Finland large cessions of territory as a buffer around the city of Leningrad (St. Petersburg) and elsewhere. The Finns refused and Soviet troops invaded on November 30, 1939. The Finns performed brilliantly in the "winter war," but Soviet power was too great. Russians breached the main Finnish defensive line on February 11, 1940, and Finland capitulated on March 12, ceding the land Russia wanted.

The Allies—Britain and France—saw a chance to damage the German war economy by mining the territorial waters of Norway to prevent shipment of iron ore from northern Sweden during the winter through the Norwegian port of Narvik. This ore was vital to the German war effort, but could not be moved by way of the Baltic Sea in winter because the Gulf of Bothnia froze over. At the same time Hitler coveted the deep fjords of Norway as protected places to launch German surface ships, aircraft, and submarines against British supply lines. Both sides began plans early in 1940 to occupy Norway.

Hitler struck first, seizing Denmark in a swift coup de main and occupying key ports of Norway on April 9, 1940. The Allies contested the occupation of Norway and scored some successes, especially at sea. But German efforts were more ordered and decisive, and Allied forces soon withdrew, especially as the focal point of the war shifted to the Low Countries of Belgium, Holland, and Luxembourg and to France where Hitler launched his campaign in the west on May 10, 1940.

✠        ✠        ✠

The Polish campaign should have tipped off the Allies to new uses for two elements in the German arsenal. But it did not, and they hit the Allied forces in the west like a thunderbolt. The elements were the airplane and the tank.

German generals had discovered something that the leaders of other armies had not figured out—that airplanes and tanks were not weapons but kinds of *vehicles*. Vehicles could carry armor, guns, or people, making possible an entirely new military system built around them. Armies could consist of troops carried by airplanes or dropped from them, or of self-propelled forces containing tanks, motorized artillery, and motorized infantry. Air forces could include tactical aircraft, such as dive-bombers, that functioned as aerial field artillery, or strategic aircraft with long-range and heavy bomb-carrying capacity that could bomb the enemy homeland.

Heinz Guderian had built the panzer arm on the teachings of two English experts, J. F. C. Fuller and Basil H. Liddell Hart, whose ideas of concentrating armor into large units had been largely ignored in their own country. The German high command was as hidebound as the British leadership on this point, and fought Guderian's ideas. It was the enthusiasm of Hitler for tanks that gave Guderian the opening to establish the army doctrine of putting all armor into panzer divisions, instead of dividing it into small detachments parceled out to infantry divisions, as remained the practice in the French and British armies.

In addition, Guderian won acceptance of the doctrine that panzer divisions had to be made up not only of tanks but of motorized infantry, artillery, and engineers, who could move at the speed of tanks and operate alongside armor to carry out offensive operations wherever the tanks could reach.

Erwin Rommel, who would become famous for his campaigns in North Africa, produced the best one-sentence description of blitzkrieg warfare: "The art of concentrating strength at one point, forcing a breakthrough, rolling up and securing the flanks on either side, and then penetrating like lightning deep into his rear, before the enemy has had time to react."

This was a revolutionary idea to the armies of the world. Most military leaders thought tanks should be used as they had been employed in World War I—to assist infantry in carrying out assaults *on foot* against enemy objectives. For this reason, the best Allied tanks, like the British Matilda, were heavily armored monsters that could deflect most enemy fire but could move scarcely faster than an infantryman could walk. German tanks, on the other hand, were "fast runners" with less armor, but able to travel at around 25 miles an hour and designed for quick penetration of an enemy line and fast exploitation of the breakthrough thereafter into the enemy rear.

It is astonishing that Allied (and most German) generals did not see the disarming logic of Guderian's argument. He pointed out, for example, that if one side had 2,100 tanks and dispersed them evenly across a 300-mile front to support its infantry divisions, the tank density would be seven per mile, not enough to be decisive except in local engagements. If the other side had the same number of tanks and concentrated them at a single *Schwerpunkt,* or main center of attack, the density would be as many tanks as could physically be fitted on the roads and fields in the sector. Such a concentration would be bound to break through. Defending tanks and antitank guns would be too few to destroy all the attacking armor, leaving the remainder to rush into the rear, with other motorized forces following to exploit the victory. This would inevitably destroy the equilibrium of the main line of resistance and force the entire front to disintegrate.

Nevertheless, British and French armies persisted in spreading most of their tanks among their infantry divisions. Both remained under the delusion that battles would be fought all along a continuous line, and they could move tanks and guns to block any point where a few enemy tanks achieved a breakthrough. They did not understand the effect of massing large numbers of tanks for a decisive penetration at a single point.

The radical aircraft the Germans developed was not much to look at. It was the Junker 87B Stuka, a dive-bomber with nonretractable landing gear, an 1,100-pound bombload, and a top speed of only 240 mph. It was already obsolete in 1940, but the Stuka (short for *Sturzkampfflugzeug,* or "dive battle aircraft") was designed to make pinpoint attacks on enemy battlefield positions, tanks, and troops. And, since the German Luftwaffe (air force) gained air superiority quickly with its excellent fighter the Messerschmitt 109, the Stuka had the sky over the battlefield largely to itself. The Stuka functioned as aerial artillery and was highly effective. It also was terrifying to Allied soldiers because of its accuracy and because German pilots fitted the Stuka with an ordinary whistle that emitted a high-pitched scream as it dived. The Allied air forces had not seen a need for such a plane and concentrated primarily on area bombing, which was much less effective on the battlefield.

When German panzers broke through enemy lines, they could employ both their own organic artillery and Stukas to shatter enemy positions or assist motorized infantry in attacks. It was a new way to win tactical engagements, and the Allies had nothing to match it.

# 2 THE CAMPAIGN IN THE WEST: 1940

GERMANY'S ORIGINAL PLAN FOR THE ATTACK IN THE WEST WAS ASTONISHINGLY modest. It aimed at no decision. It didn't even anticipate a victory over France.

The initial proposal, produced on Hitler's orders by the *Oberkommando des Heeres* (OKH), or army command, in October 1939, hoped merely to defeat large portions of the Allied armies and gain territory in Holland, Belgium, and northern France "for successful air and sea operations against Britain and as a broad protective zone for the Ruhr" industrial region east of Holland.

The plan resembled superficially the famous Schlieffen plan of World War I in that the main weight of the attack was to go through Belgium. Beyond that, the OKH's plan was utterly different. Count Alfred von Schlieffen had intended to defeat the entire French army. His aim was to outflank Allied forces with a wide right hook that drove down southwest of Paris, then turned back and pushed—from the *rear*—the entire enemy army up against the Franco-German frontier, compelling it to surrender.

None of this was possible in 1940. In 1914 Schlieffen had counted on strategic surprise. In 1940 the Allies anticipated the Germans would come through Belgium because a direct attack across the French frontier was impossible. In the 1930s France had constructed the Maginot Line from Switzerland to Luxembourg, a barrier of interconnected reinforced concrete fortifications and casemated cannons that could not be overcome by a direct attack.

Once the Germans tipped their hand, the Allies intended to throw forward strong forces to meet the Germans in Belgium, though it was the wrong thing to do. The sensible course would be to remain in already prepared defenses along the Belgian frontier, or withdraw to the Somme River fifty miles south, form a powerful defensive line, take advantage of the Allies' two-to-one superiority in artillery, and launch a counterstroke against the exposed southern flank of the Germans as they drove westward. The Allies might shatter the German army by such a move. Even if they didn't, they would still be dug in and ready for an attack when and where it came.

But France had suffered great devastation in World War I and did not want to fight the next war on French soil. Also, the British and French hoped to gain the help of the Belgian and Dutch armies. With them, the Allies would have as many soldiers as the Germans. They expected to use the Dyle, a north-flowing river some fifteen miles east of Brussels, as the main defensive barrier, sending their most mobile forces forty miles farther east to the Meuse (Maas) River to slow the German advance.

The Allied leaders downplayed the glaring weakness of this plan. It required their main forces to abandon already built fortifications along the frontier, move rapidly to the Dyle, and dig a new defensive line in the two or three days they were likely to have before the Germans arrived.

OKH saw the Allied disadvantages and hoped German forces could break through the two river lines with powerful frontal assaults. But the Allies, even if defeated, might still retreat behind the lower Somme, and form a continuous front with the Maginot Line. That is why Hitler and the OKH didn't expect a total victory in the west. They anticipated a stalemate, the same condition the Germans had to accept at the end of the autumn battles in 1914. The only improvement would be that the coast of northern France, Belgium, and Holland would be available to pursue a naval and air war against Britain.

When Erich von Manstein saw the plan he declared that it would be a crime to use the German army for a partial victory, leading to a long war of attrition. It would mean defeat, since the Allies, with control of the seas and access to unlimited resources from Asia, Africa, and America, had much greater capacity to win a long war than the Germans.

Manstein was chief of staff to Gerd von Rundstedt, commander of Army Group A, and he saw an opportunity that had escaped the OKH—

a way to eliminate the Allies' entire northern wing after it rushed into Belgium. This same move would open the door to a second campaign that could destroy the remainder of the French army.

With Rundstedt's approval, Manstein proposed that the main weight of the German attack be shifted to Army Group A and the Ardennes, a heavily forested region of low mountains in eastern Belgium and northern Luxembourg. He advocated that the vast bulk of Germany's ten panzer divisions be concentrated there to press through to Sedan on the Meuse River, cross it before a substantial French defense could be set up, then turn *westward* and drive through virtually undefended territory to the English Channel. This would cut off all the Allied armies in Belgium and force them to surrender.

Manstein urged that a major decoy offensive still should be launched into northern Belgium and Holland under Army Group B, commanded by Fedor von Bock. Bock's armies should make as much noise as possible to convince the Allies that the main effort was coming just where they expected it. This would induce them to commit most of their mobile forces to Belgium. The farther they advanced, the more certain would be their destruction.

"The offensive capacity of the German army was our trump card, and to fritter it away on half-measures was inadmissible," Manstein wrote.

Manstein asked Heinz Guderian whether tanks could negotiate the hills and narrow roads of the Ardennes. Guderian studied the terrain, replied yes, and became an ardent apostle of Manstein's plan.

But the OKH did not, and stonewalled for the next three months. Walther von Brauchitsch, commander of the Germany army, and Franz Halder, chief of the army staff, did not like the idea of their plan being tossed out, and they did not share Manstein and Guderian's enthusiasm for tanks. They thought like orthodox soldiers and believed crossing a major stream such as the Meuse required moving up infantry and artillery, and a carefully worked-out coordinated assault. This would take time, time the French could use as well to build a strong defensive line.

Manstein and Guderian were certain the Meuse could be breached quickly with only panzer divisions and Luftwaffe bombers, and they believed speed would guarantee that the French would not have time to bring up enough troops to stop them. Speed also would ensure that few enemy units would be in place to block the panzers as they drove right across France to the Channel.

In November 1939 Hitler directed that a new panzer corps of three divisions, the 19th under Guderian, be attached to Army Group A with Sedan as its target. Since the OKH had not told Hitler of Manstein's plan, he probably made the decision because he saw that Sedan was the easiest place to cross the Meuse. In any event, OKH ignored Manstein's bolder strategy.

At the end of November, still without changing the northern focus of the offensive, OKH did move up behind Army Group A's assembly area the 14th Corps of four motorized infantry divisions. These divisions had no tanks, but were almost as fast as the panzer divisions and could be of invaluable help in securing the flanks if the panzers were able to break out to the west.

On January 10, 1940, a staff officer of a German airborne division made a forced landing in Belgium. When captured, he was carrying orders he was only partially able to burn which gave away a large part of the German operations plan (*Fall Gelb* or "Case Yellow"). Many leaders on the Allied side concluded afterward that this was the event that caused the German high command to change its strategy. But it was not so. On January 25, at a commander-in-chief's conference with all army group and army commanders, the plan remained the same. On the Allied side, the commanders were not certain whether the captured orders were authentic or a plant. They also did not change their plans.

"Quite unconsciously," Manstein observed, "the German and Allied high commands had agreed that it was safer to attack each other head-on in northern Belgium than to become involved in a venturesome operation—on the German side by accepting the plan of Army Group A, on the Allied side by avoiding a conclusive battle in Belgium in order to deal a punishing blow to the southern flank of the German offensive."

Manstein's barrage of requests to change its strategy had become a nuisance to OKH, and on January 27, 1940, saying Manstein was due for promotion, it appointed him commander of 38th Corps, an infantry outfit with only a walk-on role in the upcoming campaign. The OKH hoped Manstein would conveniently disappear, but he used the appointment to make a decisive change in German strategy.

On February 17, Manstein was summoned to Berlin to report to Hitler for an interview and luncheon, along with other newly appointed corps commanders. Lieutenant Colonel Rudolf Schmundt, chief adjutant to Hitler, had been apprised of Manstein's proposals, and he arranged for Manstein to talk privately with Hitler after the meal.

"I found him surprisingly quick to grasp the points which our army group had been advocating for many months past, and he entirely agreed with what I had to say," Manstein wrote later.

The next day, in response to Hitler's orders, OKH issued new directives that reflected Manstein's proposals. Manstein's idea became known in the German army as the *Sichelschnitt,* or "sickle-cut plan," an apt description signifying that a strong armored thrust would cut through the weak portion of the Allied defenses like a harvester's sickle cut through soft stalks of grass or grain.

OKH set up a new "panzer group" of five armored and four motorized divisions under General Ewald von Kleist containing Guderian's 19th Corps, Hans Reinhardt's 41st Corps, and Gustav von Wietersheim's 14th Motorized Corps. These were to be *der Sturmbock* (battering ram) to breach the Meuse around Sedan. Also allocated was the 15th Corps under Hermann Hoth, whose two panzer divisions would cross the Meuse farther north at Dinant and shield Kleist's main effort on that flank. OKH allocated 2nd Army to help protect Army Group A's southern flank. OKH thus transferred the main weight to the southern wing.

At the same time Bock's Army Group B remained strong enough, with three armies, to attack into northern Belgium and Holland. Bock had the remaining three panzer divisions—two in the 16th Corps under Erich Hoepner to lead his assault, and one (the 9th under Alfred Hubicki) detailed for the Holland operation.

It was a radical and astonishing transformation and the best military decision Adolf Hitler ever made. By shifting the *Schwerpunkt* to the Ardennes Hitler set up the conditions for an overwhelming victory that could transform the world.

✠        ✠        ✠

Meanwhile the situation in the Allied camp was changing dramatically. French Premier Edouard Daladier could not summon the courage to dismiss General Maurice Gamelin, the French commander in chief, who was proving to be incompetent.

The French parliament was angry with Daladier because the Allies had done nothing to help Finland, while the Germans were massing on the frontiers of the Low Countries. On March 18, 1940, he lost a vote of confidence in the Chamber of Deputies. Paul Reynaud formed a new government, but had to accept Daladier as minister of defense, and Daladier held on to Gamelin.

This did not sit well with Reynaud, and he resigned, but the president of the republic, Albert Lebrun, induced him to run the government on a provisional basis. Thus France at the moment of its highest need found itself saddled with a weak and indecisive government.

A few weeks later in Britain, Prime Minister Neville Chamberlain could not present a convincing explanation for the Norwegian fiasco to the House of Commons, and his support, already weak because of his appeasement of Hitler, evaporated. On the evening of May 9, 1940, Labour Party leaders Arthur Greenwood and Clement Attlee refused to form a unified government with the Conservatives so long as Chamberlain remained chief of the Conservative Party. This forced his resignation.

The next day, the very day the Germans attacked in the west, Winston Churchill—the strongest and most eloquent voice in England against Hitler—seized the rudder of a unity government. Chamberlain belonged to it as Lord President (a job with little power), Lord Halifax led the Foreign Office, and Anthony Eden switched from the Colonial Office to the War Ministry. Attlee became Lord Privy Seal and deputy premier, while Greenwood became minister without portfolio. Churchill demanded for himself the newly formed Ministry of Defense. From then on, he could make agreements with the chiefs of staff over the head of the minister of war.

✠          ✠          ✠

The German forces arrayed on the frontiers of Holland, Belgium, and Luxembourg on May 10, 1940, presented a tremendously different picture from armies that had gone before. Ordinary infantry divisions were noticeably absent. These traditional orthodox mainstays that marched to battle and fought on foot had been preempted. In the campaign about to erupt, they were too slow to have decisive jobs. The real agents of victory were in part a few airborne troops attached to the northern group, but mainly the new German *Schnellentruppen,* "fast troops"—the panzer and motorized divisions.

The campaign in the west was going to be decided by only part of these fast troops—seven panzer divisions in Army Group A—a force representing only 8 percent of total German strength. The three panzer divisions of Army Group B were to play important roles. But the actual disruption of the Allied position took place in the first phase of the campaign, and the seven armored divisions in Army Group A were the instruments.

The Luftwaffe had an important task in assisting the panzers. Messerschmitt 109 Bf fighters were to destroy enemy aircraft, and the bombers, principally Stukas, were to give ground support on the battle line.

Behind the fast troops on the German right or northern flank were twenty-five infantry divisions. Stacked up behind Army Group A in the middle were thirty-eight infantry divisions. Their job was to fill out the corridor that the "panzer wedge" was to open. In the south along the Maginot Line were eighteen infantry divisions in Army Group C under Wilhelm von Leeb, with only a holding job.

The Allies had 3,370,000 men in 143 divisions—nine of them British, twenty-two Belgian, eight Dutch, the remainder French. The Germans committed 3 million men in 141 divisions. The Allies had almost 14,000 cannons, the Germans just over 7,000. However, the Allied guns were principally field artillery pieces designed to assist infantry. The Allies possessed too few guns required for the war about to be fought: antiaircraft and antitank weapons.

The Allies had more armor, about 3,400 tanks to the Germans' 2,700. But Allied armor was mostly spread out among the infantry divisions, whereas all German tanks were concentrated into the ten panzer divisions.

Only in the air was Germany clearly superior: 4,000 first-line aircraft to 3,000 Allied planes. Worse, many Allied planes were obsolete and their bombers were designed to strike area or general objectives, not targets on the battlefields as were the 400 Stukas. The French thought they could use medium bombers as "hedge hoppers" to attack enemy troops. But when they tried it they found the bombers were extremely vulnerable to ground fire.

The French had only sixty-eight Dewoitine 520 fighters, their only craft with performance approaching that of the 520 Messerschmitt 109 Bfs. The British Royal Air Force held back in England the competitive Spitfire, though a few Hurricanes were in France and could challenge the Messerschmitt on only slightly inferior terms.

✠ ✠ ✠

While the Germans were placing their faith in a new type of warfare based on fast-moving tanks supported by dive-bombers, the French (and to a large degree the British) were aiming to fight World War I all over again.

The French army was by far the strongest challenge, but its doctrine required a continuous front, strongly manned by infantry and backed up by artillery. The French expected the enemy to attack this front fruitlessly and wear down his strength. Only when the enemy was weakened and finally stopped did doctrine permit the French army to go over to the offensive. An attack was always to be a *bataille conduite,* literally "battle by guidance" but translated as "methodical battle" by the British. This system had been worked out in the late stages of World War I and refined ever since. It was slow in the extreme. French doctrine prohibited action until the commander had perfect information about his and the enemy's forces, a process requiring extensive, time-consuming reconnoitering.

When the infantry attack started it had to come behind a massive artillery barrage. The foot soldiers could advance only 1,500 meters before stopping to allow the artillery to shift its fires. After several such bounds, they had to stop until the guns could be moved forward.

All this required a great deal of time. A training exercise in 1938, for example, took eight days of preparation for an attack that was to last two days.

Guderian, who was fully aware of the enemy's battle system, was confident that the speed of the panzer advance would preclude the French from ever having time to mount a counterattack. The situation would change by the hour, and the French would never catch up. This meant to Guderian that the panzers did not have to worry about their flanks. They would reach the English Channel and victory before the French could even begin to react.

The German high commanders, who thought more like their French opposite numbers than like Guderian, were not so sure. Out of these conceptual differences much conflict would emerge.

# 3 THE DEFEAT OF FRANCE

TRUE TO THEIR PLAN, THE GERMANS DELIVERED THEIR FIRST BLOWS IN HOLLAND and northern Belgium. The strikes were so sensational and convincing that they acted like a pistol in starting the Allies' dash forward.

In the first great airborne assault in history, 4,000 paratroops of Kurt Student's 7th Airborne Division descended from the early morning sky May 10, 1940, into "Fortress Holland" around The Hague, Rotterdam, and Utrecht. The sudden appearance of this force in the heart of the Dutch defensive system staggered every Allied commander. The Dutch had expected to defend this region for a couple of weeks, long enough for the French to join them and hold it indefinitely. Immediately after Student's parachutists grabbed four airports near Rotterdam and The Hague, Theodor von Sponeck's 22nd Infantry Air-Landing Division (12,000 men) started arriving by transport aircraft.

The Germans tried to seize The Hague and the government by a coup de main, but failed, taking many casualties. They were, however, able to capture key bridges in the Dordrecht-Moerdijk-Rotterdam area and hold them until the 9th Panzer Division broke through the frontier and rushed to the bridges on May 13, 1940, eliminating all possibility of resistance.

On the same day the Germans carried out the first major aerial atrocity of World War II: their aircraft rained bombs down on the undefended center of Rotterdam, killing about a thousand civilians and terrorizing the country. Two days later, the Dutch capitulated. Their army had scarcely been engaged.

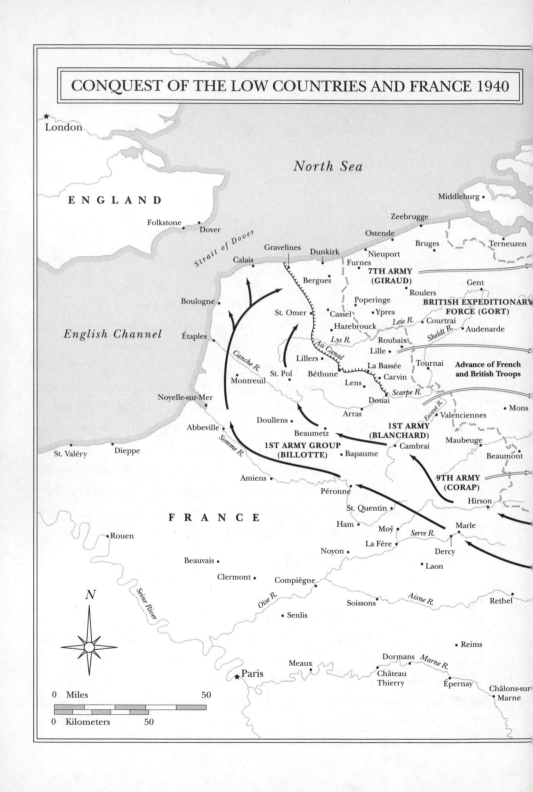

# CONQUEST OF THE LOW COUNTRIES AND FRANCE 1940

London ★

North Sea

**E N G L A N D**

Middleburg •

Folkstone •   • Dover

Zeebrugge •

*Strait of Dover*

Ostende •

Bruges •     • Terneuzen

Gravelines   Dunkirk

Calais •           • Nieuport

Furnes •

**7TH ARMY**
**(GIRAUD)**

Gent •

Bergues •

Boulogne •

Poperinge •   Roulers •

**BRITISH EXPEDITIONARY**
**FORCE (GORT)**

St. Omer •

Cassel •   • Ypres

Hazebrouck   *Leie R.*  Courtrai •

*English Channel*

Étaples •

*Lys R.*     Roubaix •   • Audenarde

*Sheldt R.*

*Canche R.*

Lillers •   *Aa Canal*

Lille •

La Bassée

Tournai •

**Advance of French**
**and British Troops**

St. Pol •   Béthune •

Lens •   • Carvin

Montreuil •

Douai •

*Scarpe R.*

Noyelle-sur-Mer •

Doullens •

Arras •

*Escaut R.*

• Mons

Valenciennes •

Abbeville •

Beaumetz •

**1ST ARMY**
**(BLANCHARD)**

Maubeuge •

*Somme R.*

**1ST ARMY GROUP**
**(BILLOTTE)**

• Bapaume

• Cambrai

• Beaumont

St. Valéry •   Dieppe •

Amiens •

**9TH ARMY**
**(CORAP)**

Péronne •

Hirson •

**F R A N C E**

St. Quentin •

Rouen •

Ham •   Moÿ •

Marle •

La Fère •   *Serre R.*

Dercy •

Noyon •

• Laon

Beauvais •

Clermont •   Compiègne •

*Oise R.*

Soissons •   *Aisne R.*

Rethel •

**N**

*Seine River*

Senlis •

Reims •

Meaux •

Dormans   *Marne R.*

★ Paris

Château
Thierry

Épernay •

Châlons-sur-
Marne •

0   Miles                    50

0   Kilometers        50

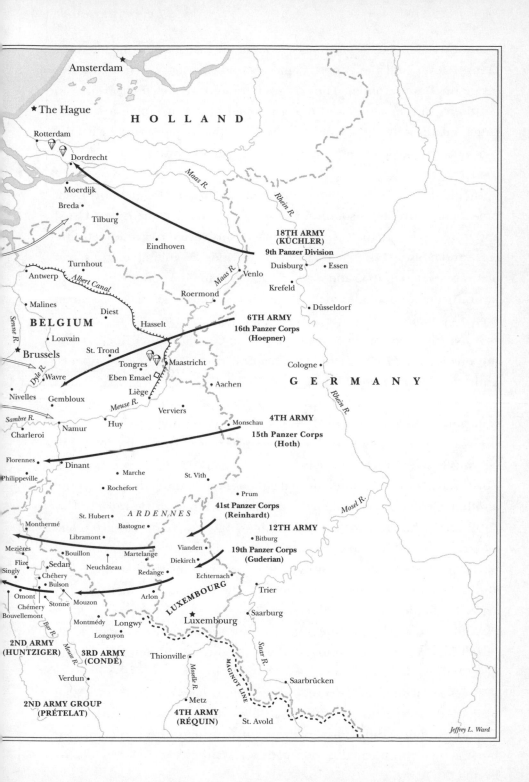

Amsterdam

★ The Hague

HOLLAND

Rotterdam

Dordrecht

Moerdijk

Breda •

Tilburg •

Eindhoven •

Maas R.

Rhein R.

**18TH ARMY
(KÜCHLER)
9th Panzer Division**

Duisburg • • Essen

Krefeld •

• Düsseldorf

Turnhout

Antwerp •

Albert Canal

Malines •

Diest •

BELGIUM

• Louvain

St. Trond •

Brussels ★

Tongres •

Wavre •

Eben Emael

Nivelles •

Gembloux •

Sambre R.

Charleroi •

Namur •

Hasselt •

Maastricht

Liège •

Verviers •

Huy •

Roermond •

Maas R.

Venlo •

**6TH ARMY
16th Panzer Corps
(Hoepner)**

Cologne •

• Aachen

GERMANY

Rhein R.

Dyle R.

Senne R.

Meuse R.

Florennes •

• Dinant

Philippeville •

Monthermé •

Mezières •

Flize •

Singly •

Sedan •

Chéhery •

Bulson •

Omont •

Chémery •

Bouvellemont •

Stonne •

Mouzon •

Montmédy •

Longuyon •

**2ND ARMY
(HUNTZIGER)**

Verdun •

**2ND ARMY GROUP
(PRÉTELAT)**

• Marche

• Rochefort

ARDENNES

St. Hubert •

Libramont •

Bouillon •

Neufchâteau •

Martelange •

Redange •

Arlon •

St. Vith •

• Prum

• Bitburg

Vianden •

Diekirch •

Echternach •

LUXEMBOURG

Bastogne •

Longwy •

Luxembourg ★

• Saarburg

Trier •

Monschau •

**4TH ARMY

15th Panzer Corps
(Hoth)**

**41st Panzer Corps
(Reinhardt)**

**12TH ARMY**

**19th Panzer Corps
(Guderian)**

Mosel R.

Bar R.

Meuse R.

**3RD ARMY
(CONDÉ)**

Thionville •

• Metz

Moselle R.

Saar R.

MAGINOT LINE

• Saarbrücken

St. Avold •

**4TH ARMY
(RÉQUIN)**

Jeffrey L. Ward

Another dramatic scenario played out at the bridges over the Maas (or Meuse) River and the Albert Canal around Maastricht—fifteen miles inside the Dutch frontier. The bridges here were vital to the Germans to get their panzers across and into the open plains of Belgium beyond. Dutch guards were certain to blow the spans the moment they heard the Germans had passed the frontier. The Germans, accordingly, decided on a surprise strike.

In addition, a way had to be found to neutralize the Belgian fort Eben Emael about five miles south of Maastricht. It guarded the Albert Canal and the Maas just to the east. Eben Emael, constructed of reinforced concrete and housing casemated 75-millimeter and 120-millimeter guns, had been completed in 1935 and was regarded as virtually impregnable. There was only one undefended part of the fort: the flat roof. This was Eben Emael's undoing.

Adolf Hitler personally selected paratroop Captain Walter Koch to lead the mission. His force included a platoon of army combat engineers, under Lieutenant Rudolf Witzig.

Early on May 10, 1940, twenty-one ten-man gliders drawn by Junker 52 transports pulled off from fields near Cologne. Over Aachen at 8,000 feet, the gliders unhooked and slowly descended over Dutch territory, ten landing beside four key bridges, and nine landing right on top of the Eben Emael roof. Lieutenant Witzig was not among them. His and another glider's ropes snapped, and his glider had to be retrieved by another Ju-52. Before Witzig arrived, his sergeant, Helmut Wenzel, had taken charge and set explosive charges in gun barrels, casemates, and exit passages. In moments the German engineers had incapacitated the fort and sealed the 650-man garrison inside. The next day German infantry arrived, and the fort surrendered.

While this attack was going on, storming parties under Captain Koch seized four Albert Canal bridges before the astonished defenders could destroy them.

But special detachments of German spies failed to grab the Maas bridges at Maastricht, and the Dutch blew them. This held up part of Erich Hoepner's 16th Corps panzers for forty-eight hours. Then they burst across, and opened a wide path for Walther von Reichenau's following 6th Army.

The Allied commander, General Maurice Gustave Gamelin, ordered the main Allied force on the left wing, the 1st Group of Armies under Gaston Harvé Billotte, to rush to the Dyle River. Included in this force were France's three "light mechanized divisions" of converted cavalry with 200 tanks apiece. On the left of this army group was the British Expeditionary Force (BEF) of eight divisions under Lord Gort. The British moved to the line Louvain-Wavre south of the Belgian army, while the French swung in below the British from Wavre southward to Namur and Dinant on the Meuse. Meanwhile Gamelin directed French cavalry—motorized forces, armored cars, and horse brigades—to penetrate into the Ardennes and hold up the Germans.

Gamelin also ordered the French 7th Army under Henri Giraud to rush to Breda, about thirty miles southeast of Rotterdam, intending to link up with the Dutch. But with Fortress Holland breached, the 7th Army withdrew to Antwerp, Belgium.

To serve as a hinge around Sedan between the Maginot Line and the armies that had swept northeastward, Gamelin relied on two French armies (the 2nd and 9th) of four cavalry divisions and twelve infantry divisions, composed mostly of older reservists. This Sedan sector was the least fortified portion of the French frontier. Cavalry would be useless against tanks, and the infantry possessed few antitank or antiaircraft guns.

Meanwhile the Luftwaffe exerted all its efforts to beat down Allied air defenses and knock out enemy aircraft on the ground. The Germans were successful in large degree because the Dutch, Belgian, and French fighters were inferior to the Messerschmitt 109s, and the British Royal Air Force held back its Spitfires in England.

German bombers attacked railways, roads, and troop assembly areas. They created fear and chaos, and made the German ground advance much easier. Planes, mainly Stukas, stayed with the German advance troops, guarding flanks, knocking out defensive positions, and stopping enemy armored movements. After a week the Luftwaffe enjoyed superiority, and by another week it had achieved air supremacy.

Behind Hoepner's panzers (3rd and 4th Divisions), the 6th Army advanced quickly, encircled the Belgian fortress of Liège, and pressed the Allies and Belgians back to Antwerp and the Dyle line. Georg Küchler's 18th Army, which had moved into Holland, turned on Antwerp as soon as the Dutch surrendered, and seized the city on May 18. The French cavalry that had advanced into the Ardennes made little impression on the German forward elements, and withdrew behind the main Allied positions.

The French First Army, with thirteen infantry divisions and 800 tanks, had been ordered to hold at all costs the "Gembloux gap," the twenty-two-mile space between Wavre on the Dyle and Namur on the Meuse. Unfortunately, the commander distributed his armor all along the line.

On May 14–15, German panzers struck around the town of Gembloux. Here about 150 French tanks were concentrated, more than the Germans brought up in the beginning. The French drove the German panzers back in a fierce, rolling battle. But more German tanks kept coming up, and the French, now outnumbered, withdrew on May 15, opening the flood gates to the German panzers.

The Belgians and the Allies fell back to the Scheldt River, fifteen to thirty miles west. It was beginning to look like a rout. But the German high command didn't want to hurry the Allies into too rapid a retreat before the net had stretched across their rear. Accordingly, it took 16th Corps away to back up the drive through the Ardennes, and also withdrew Luftwaffe support.

The German successes had stunned the world. At this moment a great voice lifted to rally the Allies, inspire democratic peoples everywhere, and defy Hitler. Winston Churchill stood before the House of Commons on May 13 and said: "I have nothing to offer but blood, toil, tears, and sweat. If you ask me, what our war aim is, I give you only one answer: Victory! Victory whatever the cost!"

☩       ☩       ☩

While the world's attention was riveted on the spectacular battles in Belgium and Holland, the actual *Schwerpunkt,* or center of gravity, of the German offensive plunged almost unnoticed through the Ardennes toward the weakest point of the French line, sixty miles away. Well behind the panzers plodded the German infantry divisions on foot, their supply wagons and artillery pieces being pulled mostly by horses.

The leading element was the 19th Panzer Corps (1st, 2nd, and 10th Divisions), commanded by the father of German armored warfare, Heinz Guderian. His tanks were targeted at Sedan on the Meuse. Just to the north was Georg Hans Reinhardt's 41st Panzer Corps with two divisions (6th and 8th), aimed at Monthermé, about fifteen miles northwest of Sedan. Each of the five panzer divisions averaged 253 tanks.

About twenty-five miles north of Reinhardt was Hermann Hoth's 15th Panzer Corps with two divisions, the 5th and 7th (under Erwin Rommel, soon to be famous), with a total of 542 tanks. This corps's job was to get across the Meuse at Dinant and keep the Allies in Belgium from interfering with Guderian and Reinhardt in their thrust westward.

Everything depended on speed. The Germans had to cross the Meuse before the Allies woke up to the danger. If they did, they still had time to assemble a formidable defensive line along the river and delay the offensive long enough to bring up reinforcements. If that happened, the Allies might counterattack through Army Group A and endanger Army Group B to the north, or they might hold the panzers along the Meuse and prevent the campaign of annihilation that Manstein had designed.

Guderian had to worry not only about the French but also about his own superiors. He met little resistance in the Ardennes, but near the frontier the French contested the advance firmly and held the Belgian town of Bouillon, eleven miles from Sedan, at nightfall on May 10.

General Charles Huntziger, commander of the French 2nd Army, asked the mayor of Bouillon whether one of the local hotels could be used for the wounded. "Of course not, General," the mayor replied. "This is a summer resort, our hotels are reserved for tourists. Do you really think there is any danger?"

The next night General von Kleist, who had never commanded armor before taking over the panzer group, got a case of jitters. The higher German commanders could not believe the French had not discovered that the main point of the offensive was aimed at Sedan, and were fearful of a French counterattack on the flank. They disbelieved Guderian, who insisted the French would take days to figure out what had happened, and more days to mount a counterstroke.

During the night of May 11–12 Kleist got reports that French cavalry were advancing from Longwy, about forty miles east of Sedan. He at once ordered the 10th Panzer Division, on the south, to change direction and drive on Longwy. This would seriously upset the German advance and, Guderian argued, was unnecessary. Many of the French cavalry were still riding horses, while their lightly armored mechanized elements were no match for German panzers. Let them come, Guderian told Kleist. They will be smashed. Kleist, after some hesitation, agreed, and the French cavalry wisely did not appear.

Guderian's 1st and 10th Panzers captured Sedan and occupied the north bank of the Meuse on the evening of May 12. Kleist ordered him to attack across the river with these formations the next day at 4 P.M.

Before the campaign started, Guderian had worked out a plan of attack by the Luftwaffe. Since few of his own artillery pieces could get to Sedan in the press of men, horses, and machines on the roads to the rear, Guderian intended to use Stukas as aerial artillery to help his infantry get across the river. He wanted a few aircraft to remain over Sedan before and during the crossing to make both actual and fake bombing and strafing runs on the French positions. Guderian was less interested in destroying the enemy than in forcing defenders to keep their heads down so his infantry could rush across the stream and find lodgment on the far side. This is what he had worked out with the Luftwaffe staff.

But when Kleist ordered an assault on the river on May 13, he insisted that the Luftwaffe mount a massive bombing attack, using large numbers of bombers and dive-bombers. This might cause considerable damage, but then the aircraft would depart, leaving Guderian's troops to face the remaining French machine guns and artillery.

When the Luftwaffe arrived, however, Guderian was astonished to see only a few squadrons of Stukas, operating under fighter cover. They used the tactics he had worked out beforehand: one group of Stukas bombed and machine-gunned trenches, pillboxes, and artillery positions (or pretended to do so), while a second group circled above, waiting to take over. Above these was a fighter shield. The air force had gone ahead with the original plan because it had no time to mount the massive bombing attack that Kleist wanted.

The effects were remarkable. When the assault force, 1st Rifle Regiment, assembled on the river just west of Sedan, enemy artillery was alert and fired at the slightest movement. But the unending strikes and faked strikes by the aircraft virtually paralyzed the French. Artillerymen abandoned their guns, and machine-gunners kept their heads down and could not fire.

As a consequence 1st Rifle Regiment crossed the river in collapsible rubber boats with little loss and seized commanding heights on the south bank. By midnight the regiment had pressed six miles south and set up a deep bridgehead, although neither artillery, armor, nor antitank guns had been able to get across the Meuse. Engineers could not finish building a bridge until daybreak on May 14.

The advance of the German infantry set off a mass retreat of French soldiers.

"Everywhere the roads were covered by artillery teams, ration and ammunition wagons, infantry weapons carriers, fatigue parties, horses, and motors," Guy Chapman wrote. "What was worse, many of the groups were headed by officers, and, worse still, their guns had been abandoned."

Meanwhile 10th Panzer Division had crossed the Meuse near Sedan and set up a small bridgehead, while Reinhardt's panzer corps got a narrow foothold across the river at Monthermé. But the terrain was extremely steep there, and Reinhardt had a hard time holding on under strong French pressure.

At the same time Rommel's 7th Panzer Division forced a large breach of the river at Dinant, about twenty-five miles north of Monthermé.

At dawn on May 14, Guderian pressed to get as many guns and tanks as possible across the one bridge that had been completed. He knew the French would try to destroy the bridgehead and were certain to be rushing reinforcements forward. At the moment, only Lieutenant Colonel Hermann Balck's 1st Rifle Regiment—with not an artillery piece nor an antitank gun to its name—was holding the vital bridgehead.

The French commanders recognized the importance of destroying the bridgehead. The 3rd Armored Division was on hand and moved up, but some of its 150 tanks had been distributed to infantry divisions.

At 7 A.M. on May 14, fifteen French light tanks with infantry attacked 1st Rifle Regiment around Bulson, about five miles south of Sedan. They were supported by some French aircraft. The Germans had nothing heavier than machine guns, but shot down several planes and slowed the tanks and infantry long enough for the first German tanks to come up a few minutes later. By 9:40 A.M. only four of the French tanks remained, and they and the infantry retreated to Mont Dieu, a couple miles south.

Meanwhile British and French airmen tried bravely to knock out the single bridge over the Meuse and other spans under construction. The Luftwaffe provided no help against them, having been called away on other missions. But Guderian's antiaircraft gunners shot down a number of Allied aircraft, and prevented any of the bridges being broken.

By midday German infantry and armor were approaching high ground near Stonne, about fifteen miles south of Sedan. This ridge dominated the country to the south, and guarded the Meuse crossings. Guderian turned over defense to General von Wietersheim, leaving the 10th Panzer Division and the independent Gross-Deutschland Infantry Regiment, now also on hand, until Wietersheim's 14th Motorized Corps could come up and take over defense of the flank.

Guderian met with the commanders of 1st and 2nd Panzer Divisions (Friedrich Kirchner and Rudolf Veiel), and, with their eager concurrence, ordered them to turn west, break entirely through the French defenses, and strike for the English Channel. By evening of May 14, elements of the 1st Panzer had seized Singly, more than twenty miles west of Sedan.

The same evening, General André Corap, commanding the French 9th Army, the only force now blocking Guderian's and Reinhardt's panzer corps along the Meuse, made a fatal mistake and ordered the entire army to abandon the Meuse and withdraw to a new line some fifteen to twenty miles to the west. He made this decision not only because of the break-through at Sedan, but because Rommel's 7th Panzer Division had crossed at Dinant. Corap was responding to wild reports of "thousands" of tanks pouring through the breach made by Rommel.

When the French arrived on the new line, Guderian's panzers were already in some of the positions the 9th Army was supposed to have occupied, while withdrawal from the Meuse removed the block holding up Reinhardt at Monthermé. His tanks now burst out and drove westward along an unobstructed path. Guderian and Reinhardt had split the 9th Army in two, blowing open a sixty-mile-wide hole through which their panzers poured like a raging torrent.

The battle of Sedan brought about a major change in battle tactics. Up to this point, panzer leaders, including Guderian, had believed rifle and armored units should be kept sharply distinct, and that tanks should be massed for a decisive thrust. Thus the 1st Rifle Regiment crossed the Meuse with only light infantry weapons. If the French had attacked with heavy weapons during the night of May 13–14, they might have destroyed the regiment.

The infantry remained in a precarious position on the morning of May 14 until the first panzers came up. It would have been safer and more effective for the Germans if individual tanks and antitank guns had been ferried across with the infantry. The lesson led to formation of *Kampfgruppen*—mixed battle groups—of armor, guns, infantry, and some-times engineers. These proved to be formidable fighting forces and dom-inated German tactical operations for the remainder of the war.

✠      ✠      ✠

Churchill arrived in Paris on May 16 to find panic setting in. Government offices were burning their papers, expecting the capital to fall at any moment. The turmoil slowly abated as word spread that an order taken from a wounded German officer showed the panzers were turning toward the west, not Paris.

Premier Reynaud reported that Gamelin had no more reserves—or ideas. He took over the defense establishment from Daladier, relieved Gamelin, appointed General Maxime Weygand, just arriving from Syria, to command the armies, and named the ambassador to Spain, Marshal Henri Philippe Pétain, as vice president of the cabinet. Weygand arrived at the front on May 21, but was unable to conceive any plan to reverse the disaster unfolding for the Allies.

✠      ✠      ✠

Kleist's panzers were rolling through territory that resembled a long cor-ridor. The region was clogged with fugitives who created chaos, while the panzers at the arrow point had to be nourished with ammunition, food, and fuel. Walls had to be formed on either side, in case the Allies were massing to counterattack. Wietersheim's 14th Motorized Corps was trying to keep up with the tanks and form blocking positions. But their numbers were too small and the distances too great. Solid lines could only be cre-ated by the infantry, most of it still far behind. Rundstedt was doing everything possible to bring them forward, but the pace was slow, gaps were impossible to close, and, to the orthodox soldiers who made up the German senior command, perils lurked at every crossroad.

The generals were as stunned as the Allies by the speed and success of the campaign. They still could only half believe it was happening. Hitler likewise had become "monstrously nervous." He hurried to see Rundstedt at Charleroi on May 15 and urged him not to drive toward "boundless shores" (*Uferlose*).

Rundstedt, also worried, ordered Kleist to stop to give the infantry time to catch up. Kleist reported none of the higher-ups' worries to Guderian, and simply ordered him to halt. But Guderian, along with the other panzer commanders, saw that a gigantic victory was within their grasp. It could be assured only if they continued to drive west at full fury and not give the distracted and increasingly desperate enemy a chance to develop countermeasures.

Guderian extracted from Kleist authority to continue the advance for another twenty-four hours, under the pretext that "sufficient space be acquired for the infantry corps that were following." With this permission to "enlarge the bridgehead," Guderian drove personally to Bouvellemont, twenty-four miles southwest of Sedan. This was the farthest projection of the 1st Panzer Division, and where the 1st Infantry Regiment had been involved in heavy fighting.

In the burning village, Guderian found the infantry exhausted. They had had no real rest since May 9 and were falling asleep in their slit trenches. Guderian explained to Colonel Balck that his regiment had to open a way for the panzers.

Balck went to his officers, who argued against continuing the attack with exhausted troops. "In that case," Balck told them, "I'll take the place on my own." As he moved off to do so, his embarrassed soldiers followed and seized Bouvellement.

This broke the last French point of resistance, and the Germans rushed out into the open plains north of the Somme with no substantial enemy forces ahead of them. By nightfall of May 16, Guderian's spearheads were at Marle and Dercy, fifty-five miles from Sedan.

Guderian assumed that this spectacular success had stilled the fears back at headquarters, and he sent a message that he intended to continue the pursuit the next day, May 17. Early in the morning, Guderian received a radio flash that Kleist would fly into his airstrip at 7 A.M. Kleist arrived promptly, didn't even bid Guderian good morning, and launched into a tirade for his disobeying orders. Guderian at once asked to be relieved of his command. Kleist, taken aback, nodded, and told him to turn over command to the next-senior officer.

Guderian radioed Rundstedt's army group what had happened, and said he was flying back to report. Within minutes, a message came to stay where he was. Colonel General Wilhelm List, 12th Army commander, was coming to clear up the matter. List arrived in a few hours and told Guderian the halt order had come from Rundstedt, and he would not resign. List was in full agreement with Guderian's desire to keep going, however, and authorized him to make "reconnaissance in force," a subterfuge that did not defy Rundstedt's command but slipped around it.

Immensely grateful, Guderian unleashed his panzers, and they surged forward. Rundstedt's army group belatedly called off its stop order. By nightfall May 17, 10th Panzer seized a bridgehead across the Oise River near Moy, seventy miles west of Sedan. The next day, 2nd Panzer reached St. Quentin, ten miles beyond Moy, while, on May 19, 1st Panzer forced a bridgehead over the Somme near Péronne, almost twenty miles west of St. Quentin.

The velocity of the panzer drive had made a powerful counterstroke almost impossible. Even so, the newly formed French 4th Armored Division under General Charles de Gaulle came forward on May 19 with a few tanks and attacked near Laon, but was severely repulsed. This failure to mass tanks was the pattern the French and British followed throughout the campaign. Even after the breakthrough, they might have stopped the advance if they had concentrated their still formidable armored strength and struck hard at a single point on the German flank.

This never happened. The French had formed four armored divisions of only 150 tanks apiece in the past winter, and had wasted them in isolated engagements like de Gaulle's attempt at Laon. Most of the 3rd Armored Division had been dispersed among the infantry along the Meuse at Sedan, while the rest had been shattered in small attacks. The 1st had run out of fuel and been overrun by Rommel's panzers, while the 2nd had been spread along a twenty-five-mile stretch of the Oise, and Guderian's leading tanks had burst through them with little effort.

In Belgium, the tanks of the ten British armored battalions had been parceled out to the infantry divisions, as had those of the three French mechanized divisions and independent French tank battalions. The few French tanks that had assembled at Gembloux, however, had performed excellently, showing what might have been achieved with concentration.

On May 20, 1st Panzer seized Amiens and pressed southward to form a bridgehead four miles deep across the Somme. During the afternoon, 2nd Panzer reached Abbéville, and that evening a battalion of the division passed through Noyelles and became the first German unit to reach the Atlantic coast. Only ten days after the start of the offensive, the Allied armies had been cut in two.

✠    ✠    ✠

The Allied forces in Belgium had formed a line along the Scheldt River, with their southern flank resting at Arras, only twenty-five miles from Péronne on the Somme. Thus the Germans had only this narrow gap through which to nourish their panzers and their offensive.

The Allies still had a chance. If they could close this gap, they could isolate the panzers, reunite the armies in Belgium with forces to the south, and bring the German offensive to a halt.

Lord Gort, commander of the British Expeditionary Force (BEF), ordered a counterattack southward from Arras on May 21. He tried to get the French to assist, but they said their forces couldn't attack until May 22. With Guderian's panzers already at the English Channel, Lord Gort decided he couldn't wait and ordered forward two infantry battalions of the 50th Division and the 1st Army Tank Brigade with 58 Mark I Matildas armed only with a single machine gun, and 16 Mark II Matildas armed with a high-velocity two-pounder (40-millimeter) gun. Matildas were slow infantry tanks, but with 75 millimeters of armor, were much more resistant to enemy fire than the lighter-skinned panzers.

The attack got little artillery and no air support.

Rommel's 7th Panzer Division had arrived south of Arras, and he swung his tanks around northwest of Arras on the morning of May 21. The division's artillery and infantry were to follow.

The British, not realizing that the German tanks had passed beyond them, formed up west of Arras in the afternoon and attacked southeast, intending to sweep to the Cojcul River, a small tributary to the Scarpe, five miles southeast of the city, and destroy any enemy in the sector.

South and southwest of Arras, the British ran into Rommel's artillery and infantry, minus their tanks, and began to inflict heavy casualties. The Germans found their 37-millimeter antitank guns were useless against the Matildas. The British tanks penetrated the German infantry front, overran the antitank guns, killed most of the crews, and many of the infantry, and were only stopped by a frantic effort—undertaken by Rommel himself—to form a "gun line" of field artillery and especially high-velocity 88-millimeter antiaircraft guns, which materialized as a devastating new weapon against Allied tanks. The artillery and the "88s" destroyed thirty-six tanks and broke the back of the British attack.

Meanwhile, the panzers turned back on radioed orders from Rommel and arrived on the rear and flank of the British armor and artillery. In a bitter clash of tank on tank, Rommel's panzer regiment destroyed seven Matildas and six antitank guns, and broke through the enemy position, but lost three Panzer IVs, six Panzer IIIs, and a number of light tanks. The British fell back into Arras and attempted no further attack.

The Allied effort had been too weak to alter the situation, but showed what could have been done if the Allied commanders had mobilized a major counterattack. Even so, the British effort had wide repercussions. Rommel's division lost 387 men, four times the number suffered until that point. The attack also stunned Rundstedt, and his anxiety fed Hitler's similar fears and led to momentous consequences in a few days.

On May 22, Guderian wheeled north from Abbéville and the sea, aiming at the channel ports and the rear of the British, French, and Belgian armies, which were still facing eastward against Bock's Army Group B. Reinhardt's panzers kept pace on the northeast. The next day, Guderian's tanks isolated Boulogne, and on May 23, Calais. This brought Guderian to Gravelines, barely ten miles from Dunkirk, the last port from which the Allies in Belgium could evacuate.

Reinhardt also arrived twenty miles from Dunkirk on the Aa (or Bassée) Canal, which ran westward past Douai, La Bassée, and St. Omer to Gravelines. The panzers were now nearer Dunkirk than most of the Allies.

While the right flank of the BEF withdrew to La Bassée on May 23 under pressure of a thrust northward by Rommel from Arras toward Lille, the bulk of the British forces moved farther north to reinforce the line in Belgium. Here Bock's forces were exerting increasing pressure, causing King Leopold to surrender the Belgian army the next day.

Despite this, Rundstedt gave Hitler a gloomy report on the morning of May 24, laying emphasis on the tanks the Germans had lost and the possibility of meeting further Allied attacks from the north and south. All this reinforced Hitler's own anxieties. He showed his paranoia by saying he feared the panzers would get bogged down in the marshes of Flanders, though every tank commander knew how to avoid wet areas.

Hitler had been extremely nervous from the start of the breakthrough. Indeed, he became *more* nervous the more success the Germans gained, worrying about the lack of resistance and fearing a devastating attack on the southern flank. He had not grasped that Manstein's strategy and Guderian's brilliant exploitation were bringing about the most overwhelming decision in modern military history. The Germans had been out of danger from the first day, but to Hitler (and to most of the senior German generals) it seemed too good to be true.

The question now arose of what to do about the British and French armies in Belgium. With virtually no enemy forces in front of them, Guderian and Reinhardt were about to seize Dunkirk and close off the last possible port from which the enemy troops could embark. This would force the capitulation of the entire BEF and the French First Group of Armies, more than 400,000 men.

At this moment, the war took a bizarre and utterly bewildering turn. Why events unrolled as they did has been disputed ever since, and no one has come close to understanding the reasons.

Hitler called in Walther von Brauchitsch, the army commander in chief, and ordered him to halt the panzers along the line of the Bassée Canal. Rundstedt protested, but received only the curt telegram: "The armored divisions are to remain at medium artillery range from Dunkirk [eight or nine miles]. Permission is only granted for reconnaissance and protective movements."

Kleist thought the order made no sense, and he pushed his tanks across the canal with the intention of cutting off the Allied retreat. But he received emphatic orders to withdraw behind the canal. There the panzers stayed for three days, while the BEF and remnants of the 1st and 7th French Armies streamed back to Dunkirk. There they built a strong defensive position, while the British hastily improvised a sea lift.

The British used every vessel they could find, 860 in all, many of them civilian yachts, ferryboats, and small coasters. The troops had to leave all their heavy equipment on shore, but between May 26 and June 4 the vessels evacuated to England 338,000 troops, including 120,000 French. Only a few thousand members of the French rear guard were captured.

Two seemingly plausible reasons have been advanced for Hitler's decision. One is that Hermann Göring, one of his closest associates and chief of the Luftwaffe, promised that he could easily prevent evacuation with his aircraft, since the panzers were needed to turn south and begin the final campaign to defeat France. The other is that Hitler wanted a settlement with Britain and deliberately prevented the destruction of the BEF to make peace easier to attain. Regardless of which motivations impelled Hitler, he made the wrong judgment. The Luftwaffe did a poor job, and the British were uplifted by the "miracle of Dunkirk," redoubling their resolve to fight on.

The Luftwaffe started late, not mounting a strong attack until May 29. Air attacks increased over the next three days, and on June 2 daylight evacuation had to be suspended. But RAF fighters valiantly tried to stop the bombing and strafing runs, and were in part successful. The beach sand absorbed much of the blast effects of bombs. The Luftwaffe did most of its damage at sea, sinking 6 British destroyers, 8 transport ships, and more than 200 small craft.

Hitler lifted the halt order on May 26, but soon thereafter army headquarters directed the panzers to move south for the attack across the Somme, leaving to Army Group B's infantry the task of occupying Dunkirk—after the Allies had gone.

On June 4, Winston Churchill rose to speak in the House of Commons. He closed his address with these words that inspired the world:

We shall go on to the end, we shall fight in France, we shall fight in the seas and oceans, we shall fight with growing confidence and growing strength in the air, we shall defend our island, whatever the cost may be, we shall fight on the beaches, we shall fight on the landing-grounds, we shall fight in the fields and in the streets, we shall fight in the hills; we shall *never* surrender, and even if, which I

do not for a moment believe, this island or a large part of it were subjugated and starving, then our empire beyond the seas, armed and
guarded by the British fleet, would carry on the struggle, until, in
God's good time, the New World, with all its power and might, steps
forth to the rescue and the liberation of the Old.

☩          ☩          ☩

The end in France came swiftly. In three weeks, the Germans had captured more than a million prisoners, while suffering 60,000 casualties.
The Belgian and Dutch armies had been eliminated, and the French had
lost thirty divisions, nearly a third of their total strength, and this the best
and most mobile part. They had also lost the assistance of eight British
divisions, now back in Britain, with most of their equipment lost. Only one
British division remained in France south of the Somme.

Weygand was left with sixty-six divisions, most of them understrength,
to hold a front along the Somme, the Aisne, and the Maginot Line that
was longer than the original. He committed forty-nine divisions to hold
the rivers, leaving seventeen to defend the Maginot Line. Most of the
mechanized divisions had been lost or badly shattered. However, the
Germans quickly brought their ten panzer divisions back to strength and
deployed 130 infantry divisions, only a few of which had been engaged.

The German high command reorganized its fast troops, combining
armored divisions and motorized divisions in a new type of panzer corps,
generally with one motorized and two armored divisions to each corps.

OKH promoted Guderian to command a new panzer group of two
panzer corps, and ordered him to drive from Rethel on the Aisne to the
Swiss frontier. Kleist kept two panzer corps to strike south from bridgeheads over the Somme at Amiens and Péronne, but these later shifted
eastward to reinforce Guderian's drive. The remaining armored corps,
under Hoth, was to advance between Amiens and the sea.

The offensive opened on June 5, and France collapsed quickly. Not all
the breakthroughs were easy, but the panzers, generally avoiding the villages and towns where defenses had been organized, were soon ranging
across the countryside almost at will, creating chaos and causing the
French soldiers to surrender by the hundreds of thousands.

An example was Erwin Rommel's 7th Panzer Division, which crossed the Somme near Hangest east of Abbéville on June 5, and moved so fast and materialized at points so unexpectedly that the French called it the "ghost division." On June 6, at Les Quesnoy, the entire division lined up on a 2,000-yard front, with the 25th Panzer Regiment in the lead, and advanced across country as if on an exercise. Two days later it reached the Seine River, eleven miles southeast of Rouen, a drive of seventy miles, then turned northwest and raced to the sea at St. Valéry, where it captured the British 51st Highland Division.

Guderian's panzers cut off northeastern France with a rapid drive to the Swiss frontier. The troops defending the Maginot Line retreated and surrendered almost without firing a shot.

With victory over France assured, Italy entered the war on June 10. The same day President Franklin D. Roosevelt was speaking at commencement at the University of Virginia in Charlottesville. Roosevelt reversed his usual emphasis on avoiding American involvement in the war and promised to extend aid "full speed ahead." But his address is most remembered for his condemnation of Italy for striking "a dagger into the back of its neighbor."

The Germans entered Paris on June 14 and reached the Rhône valley on June 16. The same night the French asked for an armistice, and on June 17 Reynaud resigned as premier and was succeeded by Marshal Philippe Pétain. While talks went on, German forces advanced beyond the Loire River. At the same time, a French light cruiser took to safety 1,754 tons of gold from the banks of France, Belgium, and Poland, while, under the direction of British Admiral William James, ships at numerous French ports carried to England nearly 192,000 men and women (144,171 Britons; 18,246 French; 24,352 Poles; 4,938 Czechs; and 162 Belgians). Many of the French joined a new Free French movement under Charles de Gaulle, who had arrived in Britain, vowing to fight on against the Germans.

On June 22 the French accepted the German terms at Compiègne, in the same railway car where the defeated Germans had signed the armistice ending World War I in 1918. On June 25 both sides ceased fire. The greatest military victory in modern times had been achieved in six weeks.

# 4 HITLER'S FIRST GREAT ERROR

THE SWIFT GERMAN VICTORY OVER FRANCE AND THE EJECTION OF THE BRITISH Expeditionary Force from the Continent without its weapons raised the immediate question of whether Britain could survive.

The obvious answer was what the world expected: German forces would sweep over the narrow seas and conquer the British isles as quickly as they had shattered France. There was only one impediment: Germany had to achieve at least temporary air and sea supremacy over and on the English Channel. Otherwise, ferries, barges, and transports carrying troops could be easily sunk by Royal Navy ships before they could land on English beaches and docks.

The crucial requirement was in the air. German navy leaders believed they could shield landing craft and ships for the short passage, but only if British warships could not run in at will among the convoys. This could be assured only if the Luftwaffe ruled the skies above the invasion fleet, and could bomb and strafe any enemy ship that showed itself.

Hitler was reluctant to invade Britain, thinking the British would come to their senses, recognize their "militarily hopeless situation," and sue for peace.

He persisted in this view in spite of a speech by Winston Churchill in the House of Commons on June 18, 1940, four days before France gave up. "The whole fury and might of the enemy must very soon be turned on us," Churchill said. "Hitler knows that he will have to break us in this island or lose the war. If we can stand up to him, all Europe may be free and the life of the world may move forward into broad, sunlit uplands. . . .

Let us therefore brace ourselves to our duties, and so bear ourselves that, if the British Empire and its Commonwealth last for a thousand years, men will say, 'This was their finest hour.' "

Shortly thereafter, Hitler got a swift lesson in British determination to continue the war.

The Germans had occupied three-fifths of France, including the whole Atlantic coast, leaving the remainder unoccupied with a government under Marshal Pétain centered in the resort town of Vichy. The big question was what would become of the French fleet. Most of it moved into the French Mediterranean harbor of Toulon, but powerful elements remained in North Africa.

Churchill's government feared a change in the balance of power if even a part of the French fleet got into German hands. The British wanted to take possession of it or eliminate it.

In surprise moves on July 3, 1940, British troops seized French ships that had taken refuge in British harbors, and a powerful British naval group including three battleships and an aircraft carrier under Admiral Sir James Somerville arrived at Oran and Mers-el-Kebir in Algeria, where the largest French flotilla outside Toulon lay at anchor.

Somerville tried to get the French to surrender, but failed, and the British opened fire on their former allies. The battleship *Bretagne* blew up, the *Dunquerque* ran aground, the battleship *Provence* beached, and the torpedo cruiser *Magador* exploded. The battleship *Strasbourg* and three heavy destroyers were able to run out to sea, break through the British ring of fire, and reach Toulon, as did seven cruisers berthed at Algiers. Almost 1,300 Frenchmen died in the Mers-el-Kebir battle. Five days later torpedo bombers from the British aircraft carrier *Hermes* seriously damaged the French battleship *Richelieu* at Dakar in Senegal.

The British attacks enraged France, but brought before the eyes of people everywhere the striking power of the Royal Navy. It helped to convince President Roosevelt and the American people that backing Britain was a good bet.

Hitler still waited until July 16 before ordering an invasion, named Operation Sea Lion. He said, however, that the undertaking had to be ready by mid-August.

Hermann Göring assured Hitler that his Luftwaffe could drive the

Royal Air Force out of the skies in short order. The invasion depended upon Göring's word.

Britain had only 675 fighter planes (60 percent Hurricanes, 40 percent Spitfires) combat-ready when the battle started. Germany had 800 Messerschmitt 109s to protect its 875 two-engined bombers and 316 Stukas. It also had 250 two-engined Messerschmitt 110 fighters, but these were 60 miles per hour slower than Spitfires, and turned out to be a great disappointment.

The Messerschmitt (or Bf) 109 had a top speed of 350 miles per hour. It was armed with three 20-millimeter cannons and two machine guns. Approximately equal was the British Supermarine Spitfire with a maximum speed of 360 mph and armed with eight machine guns. Somewhat inferior was the British Hawker Hurricane with a top speed of 310 mph, a slower rate of climb, eight machine guns, but more robust and easier to maintain. The 1940 model Hurricane could reach 330 mph and carried four 20-millimeter cannons. The Me-109 and the Spitfire both had a maximum range of about 400 miles, the Hurricane 525 miles.

Aircraft numbers were closely guarded secrets, but leaders everywhere had good estimates of the comparative strengths of the two sides, and few were betting on the British.

Göring concentrated his fighters and bombers for an all-out assault on airfields and fighters in southern England. He and other Luftwaffe leaders didn't realize that the RAF's greatest strength was not its fighter aircraft, vital as they were, but the new British-developed radar, which sent out radio signals that struck incoming aircraft and reflected them back to receiving stations. By 1940 Britain had a double line of radar stations facing the Continent. One line consisted of receivers on high towers that could detect high-flying enemy aircraft 120 miles away. The other had a shorter range but could pick up low-flying aircraft.

The radar net, combined with Observer Corps spotters on the ground who tracked aircraft once past the coast, gave the RAF advance warning of approaching bombers. The skill of RAF Fighter Command was based on shrewd use of radar. From the moment they took off from bases in western Europe, German aircraft were spotted on screens, their courses plotted. Fighter Command knew exactly where and when they could be attacked.

# BATTLE OF BRITAIN 1940

N

Group boundaries
Range of the Me-109 fighter
\* Fighter airfields
▲ High-level radar stations
△ Low-level radar stations

Aberdeen

SCOTLAND

Glasgow

Firth of Forth

FIGHTER
COMMAND
13 GROUP

North Sea

Belfast

IRELAND

Newcastle • Sunderland

Air Fleet 5 (Greiser)
from Norway
and Denmark

Recognition
range of
high-level radar
to 4,500 meters
elevation

Middlesbrough

Liverpool    Manchester

Sheffield

Nottingham

Recognition
range of
low-level radar
to 150 meters
elevation

FIGHTER
COMMAND
12 GROUP

Birmingham    Norwich
Coventry

Swansea
Cardiff

Bristol

Amsterdam

Rotterdam

HOLLAND

Bath

London

Ipswich

FIGHTER COMMAND
10 GROUP

FIGHTER
COMMAND
11 GROUP

Canterbury

BELGIUM

Exeter

Plymouth

Ventnor

Calais

Brussels

Air Fleet 2
(Kesselring)

English Channel

Cherbourg

Bruneval    Dieppe
Le Havre

Abbeville

Rouen

Brest

Paris

Air Fleet 3
(Sperrle)

FRANCE

0   Miles        100        200

0   Kilometers        200

Jeffrey L. Ward

RAF fighters could mass against each German wave, and also climb into the air just before they had to engage, thus preserving fuel. By comparison, Messerschmitts could remain protecting bombers over England only for minutes because they had to fly from the Continent and back.

In the days leading up to the start of the main campaign, Eagle Day on August 13, Stukas struck repeatedly at airfields and radar stations, and on August 12 knocked out one radar station. But the Germans didn't know how vital radar was and didn't concentrate attacks on it. The strikes showed that the Stukas were too slow and vulnerable for the long-range mission against Britain, and had to be withdrawn.

On August 13 and 14, three waves of German bombers, a total of 1,500 sorties, damaged several RAF airfields, but destroyed none. The strongest effort came on August 15 when the Germans launched 800 bombing and 1,150 fighter sorties. A hundred bombers escorted by Me-110s from Air Fleet 5 in Scandinavia, expecting to find the northeastern coast of Britain defenseless, instead were pounced on by Hurricanes and Spitfires as they approached Tyneside. Thirty aircraft went down, mostly bombers, without a British loss. Air Fleet 5 never returned to the Battle of Britain.

In southern England the Luftwaffe was more successful. In four attacks, one of which nearly penetrated to London, bombers hit four aircraft factories at Croydon, and damaged five fighter fields. But the Germans lost 75 planes, the RAF 34.

On August 15, Göring made his first major error. He called off attacks on the radar stations. But by August 24 he had learned about the second key to the RAF defense, the sector stations. These nerve centers guided fighters into battle using latest intelligence from radar, ground observers, and pilots in the air. He switched to destruction of these stations. Seven around London were crucial to protection of southern England.

From that day to September 6, the Luftwaffe sent over an average of a thousand planes a day. Numbers began to tell. They damaged five fields in southern England badly, and hit six of the seven key sector stations so severely that the communications system was on the verge of being knocked out.

The RAF began to stagger. Between August 23 and September 6, 466 fighters were destroyed or badly damaged (against 352 German losses). Although British factories produced more than 450 Spitfires and

Hurricanes in both August and September, getting them into squadrons took time. And the real problem was not machines but men. During the period 103 RAF pilots were killed and 128 seriously wounded, one-fourth of those available. A few more weeks of such losses and Britain would no longer have an organized air defense.

At this moment, Adolf Hitler changed the direction of the battle—and the war. If he had allowed the Luftwaffe to continue its blows to the sector stations, Sea Lion could have been carried out and Hitler could have ended the war with a swift and total victory. Instead, he made the first great blunder in his career, a blunder so fundamental that it changed the course of the entire conflict—and set in motion a series of other blunders that followed in its wake.

So far as can be determined from the evidence, Hitler made this devastating mistake because of anger, not calculation.

In addition to the sector stations, Göring had been attacking the British air-armaments industry, which meant that industrial cities were suffering substantial damage. Then, on the night of August 24, ten German bombers lost their way and dropped their loads on central London. RAF Bomber Command launched a reprisal raid on Berlin the next night with eighty bombers—the first time the German capital had been hit. Bomber Command followed up this raid with several more in the next few days. Hitler, enraged, announced he would "eradicate" British cities. He called off the strikes against sector stations and ordered terror bombing of British cities.

This abrupt reversal of strategy did not rest entirely on Hitler's desire for vengeance. The new campaign had a lengthy, highly touted theoretical background. It was the first extensive experiment to test the "strategic-bombing" theory espoused after World War I by an Italian, Giulio Douhet. His argument was that a nation could be forced to its knees by massive bombing attacks against its centers of population, government, and industry. Such attacks would destroy the morale of the people and war production, and achieve victory without the use of ground forces.

The Luftwaffe's original operation against British airfields, sector stations, and aircraft factories was a variation on the highly successful battles it had won in May and June, which eliminated most of the French air force and shot down or contained the few RAF aircraft on the Continent.

This was essentially a tactical campaign to gain supremacy for military forces on the ground.

The second campaign was entirely different. It aimed not at winning a battle but at destroying the morale of the enemy population. If it succeeded, as Douhet had predicted, an invasion of Britain would not even be necessary. The disheartened, defeated people of Britain would raise the white flag merely to stop the bombing.

Hitler was the first to attempt Douhet's theory, but his bombs failed to break the British people. World War II proved that human beings can endure a great deal more destruction from the skies than Douhet had thought.

On the late afternoon of September 7, 1940, 625 bombers and 648 fighters flew up the Thames River and bombed docks, central London, and the heavily populated East End, killing 300 civilians and injuring 1,300. The fires raging in the East End guided the second wave of bombers that night. Waves of bombers came in repeatedly until 5 A.M. the next day. The assault went on night after night.

On the morning of Sunday, September 15, the Germans sent in a new daylight attack. Although British fighters assailed the air armada all the way from the coast, 148 bombers got through to London. As they turned for home, sixty RAF fighters swept down from East Anglia and destroyed a number of the bombers. The Germans lost sixty aircraft, against twenty-six British fighters. Because the costs were so high, the Luftwaffe soon shifted over entirely to night attacks, concentrating on London, which it struck for fifty-seven straight nights, averaging 160 bombers a night. On September 17, Hitler called off Sea Lion indefinitely.

London took a terrible pounding. Other cities also suffered, Coventry above all. It was a grim fall and winter; 23,000 British civilians had died by the end of the year, but British morale did not collapse, nor did armament production fall. It actually rose, outproducing the Germans by 9,924 aircraft to 8,070 in 1940.

The air war thus degenerated into a vicious campaign aimed at destroying homes and people, and had no significant role in deciding the war.

✠          ✠          ✠

While the world's eyes were fastened on Britain, conditions on the Continent had worsened. On the day Paris fell Soviet Premier Joseph Stalin sent an ultimatum to the three Baltic republics of Lithuania, Latvia, and Estonia, quickly occupied them, then staged fake elections that called for their absorption into the Soviet Union. Secret police seized thousands of Baltic leaders and intelligentsia and brought them to Russia, where most died.

On June 16, 1940, the Kremlin also demanded from Romania the cession of Bessarabia and northern Bucovina, both adjoining Soviet territory. Romania capitulated at once.

Stalin's moves against his neighbors disturbed Americans greatly. A few saw them accurately as hedges against potential German aggression. But most, suspicious of Communism, took them as evidence of more brute force being let loose in the world. Stalin's aggressions, combined with shock over the fall of France and fear about Britain's survival, caused the American nation as a whole to close in on defense of the Western Hemisphere.

Before the summer was out, Roosevelt had signed a law to create by far the greatest navy on earth (doubling the fleet), began building an air force of 7,800 combat aircraft, called the National Guard into federal service, passed the first peacetime draft in American history, and swapped fifty old U.S. destroyers for long-term leases of bases on eight British colonies from Newfoundland to British Guiana (Guyana).

However, Franklin D. Roosevelt was seeking any way possible to support Britain's war against Hitler. His hand was strengthened greatly on November 5, 1940, when he became the first (and only) American president elected to a third term.

On December 17, FDR announced to reporters that he was determined to maintain Britain as the nation's first line of defense. And, since Britain could not pay for all the goods it needed, he proposed that the United States "lend" the British arms, aircraft, food, vehicles, and any other materials they required. The public responded favorably to the idea and to Roosevelt's call in a December 29 national radio "fireside chat" that the United States become "the arsenal of democracy." In his inaugural address on January 6, 1941, FDR advocated a postwar world based on the "four freedoms"—freedom of speech and worship, and freedom from want and fear.

On January 10, 1941, the "lend-lease" bill was introduced into Congress, and on March 11, 1941, it became law. Lend-lease set American factories to producing war goods at full capacity. Exploiting American economic strength was essential to success against Germany, thus lend-lease was a major step toward American entry into the war.

The likelihood became even stronger during the winter of 1940–1941 when high-level British and American military officers met in secret sessions in Washington to discuss a broad joint strategy in the event the United States entered the war. The talks (known as ABC-1 for American-British conversations) concluded on March 29, 1941, with the recommendation that the defeat of Germany, which was far more powerful than Japan, should have the highest priority. Roosevelt did not formally endorse ABC-1, but followed it.

The British and Americans couldn't agree on a policy against Japan. The British urged moving the American Pacific fleet to the Philippines and Singapore, but the Americans decided to keep it at Pearl Harbor in Hawaii and continue to negotiate with Japanese diplomats in hopes of a peaceful solution.

# 5 THE FATAL TURN TO THE EAST

HITLER HAD ALREADY SWITCHED HIS PRINCIPAL INTEREST AWAY FROM BRITAIN *before* the air war commenced. This came formally on July 31, 1940, in a conference with his senior military chiefs, when Hitler announced his "resolve to bring about the destruction of the vitality of Russia in the spring of 1941."

This statement worried a number of German senior officers. They feared leaving Britain and its potential ally the United States as threats in the west, while Germany focused its energy, thoughts, and power on destruction of the Soviet Union.

The top army generals, along with their staffs, amassed arguments to convince Hitler to neutralize Britain before turning on Russia. Perhaps they realized dimly what Winston Churchill had grasped: that Britain's best chance lay in holding out until Hitler made an irreparable slip, as Napoleon had done when he invaded Russia in 1812.

Only Erich Raeder, the German navy commander, saw the danger clearly enough to press repeatedly and with great conviction for *another* way to gain Germany's goals. He demonstrated to Hitler that the victory over France had opened a way to victory—and Hitler would not have to attack the Soviet Union to achieve it.

Major General Alfred Jodl, chief of operations for the *Oberkommando der Wehrmacht* (OKW), or armed forces supreme command, felt the same way, though less openly and less forcefully. In a June 30, 1940, memorandum Jodl wrote that if the strike across the Channel did not come off, the Mediterranean offered the best arena to defeat Britain. His recommendation was to seize Egypt and the Suez Canal. Maybe the Italians could do it alone. If not, the Germans could help.

At the time the British had only 36,000 men in Egypt, including a single incomplete armored division under the command of General Sir Archibald Wavell. Moreover, Italy's entry into the war had closed off Britain's supply line through the Mediterranean except by means of heavily guarded convoys. The main British route now had to go 12,000 miles around the Cape of Good Hope in South Africa, and up through the Red Sea.

Even if Britain devoted all its strength to building a strong army in Egypt, it would take months, perhaps a year, to do so. And Britain was *not* going to undertake such a task because it had to concentrate most of its efforts on defense of the homeland.

Italy, aided by Germany, could get superior forces to Italy's colony of Libya far more quickly. At this stage, it would be relatively easy to use Luftwaffe bombers to neutralize Malta, a British possession only sixty miles south of Sicily, where aircraft, ships, and submarines constituted a major danger to Italian supply ships and reinforcements moving between Italy and Tripoli in Libya.

Hitler in his July 31 meeting did not wholly exclude a "peripheral strategy" in the Mediterranean, and Generals Walther von Brauchitsch, commander in chief of the army, and Franz Halder, chief of staff in the army high command, *Oberkommando des Heeres* (OKH), proposed sending panzer forces (an "expeditionary corps") and aircraft to Libya to help the Italians, who were planning an offensive into Egypt.

But Hitler hadn't responded to Jodl's memorandum and wouldn't commit himself to a panzer corps and combat planes in Africa. The only thing in the Mediterranean that excited Hitler was the possibility of capturing the British base of Gibraltar, and thereby closing the western end of the Mediterranean to the Royal Navy. Britain had won this strategic rock from Spain in 1704 and had held it resolutely ever since.

Hitler could think of no way to grab Gibraltar except by direct assault. This meant German forces would have to approach through Spain. The Spanish dictator, Francisco Franco, would have to cooperate. Seeing that Hitler was deeply taken with the idea, the senior generals sent Admiral

Wilhelm Canaris, chief of the *Abwehr*—the military counterintelligence service—to Madrid July 20–23 to get Franco's reaction. Cagily, Franco didn't reject Spanish help out of hand, but refused to commit.

The Gibraltar plan—the only idea ever considered was a headlong attack on the heavily fortified rock—now became a leitmotiv that ran through most of the discussions that followed. It was an absurd idea, and shows how unrealistic Hitler was.

The plan required Spanish entry into the war, an extremely dangerous move that would benefit Spain little, yet cause dire and immediate consequences. The British would cut off food imports from Argentina and other American countries Spain depended on, and would seize the Spanish Canary Islands off the northwestern coast of Africa. Franco wanted nothing to do with the plan, yet with the Wehrmacht on his border, he didn't dare say so.

Aside from Gibraltar, Hitler also came up with other nonsensical ideas that demonstrated a profound lack of appreciation of the strategic possibilities that had opened to him. He waxed hugely enthusiastic about seizing two groups of Portuguese islands, the Azores, in the Atlantic 1,200 miles west of Lisbon, and the Cape Verde Islands, in the south Atlantic 150 miles west of Dakar off the coast of Africa. He also studied capture of the Canaries prior to a Gibraltar attack—with the idea of beating the British to the punch.

In theory, all three island groups would be useful as air and sea bases to break up British convoys that moved regularly through the Atlantic. Hitler's excitement about the Azores, however, rested mainly on hopes of building long-range bombers that could reach the United States. If he could get these aircraft built and stationed on the Azores, he said, the threat would force the United States to concentrate on its own defense, and help Britain less.

The Atlantic islands idea was more absurd than the Gibraltar plan. Only Admiral Raeder dared to tell Hitler so, and even he couched his objections in discreet terms. The German navy could actually seize the islands in surprise moves, Raeder assured Hitler, but it could *not* protect the sea lanes to them thereafter. The Royal Navy would erect an iron blockade in days. German garrisons would be cut off from supplies, except driblets that might be flown in. Few attacks on British convoys—much less air attacks on the United States—could be mounted, because the Germans could get little fuel to the islands.

Raeder's logic was overwhelming and should have ended the matter right there. But it didn't. Hitler continued to agitate for capture of the Atlantic islands on into the fall and beyond.

Since the army generals had been unable to sway the Fuehrer to carry out a Mediterranean strategy, Admiral Raeder weighed in on September 6 and September 26, 1940. At the second conference Raeder cornered Hitler alone and showed him step by step how Germany could defeat Britain elsewhere than over the English Channel. Doing so would put Germany in a commanding position against the Soviet Union.

Raeder, bowing to Hitler's passions, said the Germans should take Gibraltar and secure the Canary Islands. But his main concern in that part of the world was the great northwestern bulge of Africa, largely controlled by France.

An imponderable regarding Hitler's thinking is why, when he was negotiating France's surrender, he did not demand admission of German troops into French North Africa—Algeria, Tunisia, and Morocco. If the French refused, he could have threatened to occupy all of France and deny the French a government at Vichy. Besides, the French had so few troops in North Africa they couldn't have prevented a German occupation.

The importance of the region was forced upon him only three days before the September 26 conference: a joint operation of British and Free French forces under Charles de Gaulle had tried to seize Dakar, but had been beaten off by Vichy French guns. This reinforced Raeder's conviction that the British, supported by the United States, would try to get a foothold in northwest Africa in order to move against the Axis. He urged Germany to team up with Vichy France to secure the region.

But Raeder's main argument was that the Axis should capture the Suez Canal. After Suez, German panzers could advance quickly through Palestine and Syria as far as Turkey.

"If we reach that point, Turkey will be in our power," Raeder emphasized. "The Russian problem will then appear in a different light. It is doubtful whether an advance against Russia from the north [that is, Poland and Romania] will be necessary."

No one realized this truth better than Winston Churchill. In a message to President Roosevelt a few months later, he asserted that if Egypt and the Middle East were lost, continuation of the war "would be a hard, long, and bleak proposition," even if the United States entered.

But Adolf Hitler had a much more difficult time seeing what was clear to Churchill. According to Raeder, Hitler agreed with his "general trend of thought" but had to talk things over with Mussolini, Franco, and Pétain. This shows Hitler was seeking limited tactical gains in the Mediterranean. Although a drive through Suez would call for an agreement with Mussolini, it would not require concurrence of Franco or Pétain. This indicates Hitler did not grasp that the victory over France had transformed the entire strategic outlook for Germany.

Raeder felt the senior army generals had a "purely continental outlook," did not understand the war-winning opportunities that had opened up on the south shore of the Mediterranean, and would never counsel Hitler correctly. Although the OKH, the army high command, and the OKW, the armed forces high command, did advise Hitler to send troops to North Africa, their proposals lacked Raeder's urgency. Never did Brauchitsch, Halder, Jodl, or Field Marshal Wilhelm Keitel, chief of staff of the OKW, express the conviction that the war could be won in the Mediterranean, although Keitel told Benito Mussolini that capture of Cairo was more important than capture of London. Part of their hesitancy lay in the knowledge that Hitler had been fixed for a long time on destroying the Soviet Union and gaining *Lebensraum* in the east. Their careers depended upon not rocking that boat. However, they never stressed to Hitler, as did Raeder, that victory in the Mediterranean would make it easier to achieve victory over the Soviet Union.

Once Axis forces overran Egypt and the Suez Canal, they would close the eastern Mediterranean to the Royal Navy. The British fleet would immediately retreat into the Red Sea, because it could not be adequately supplied by convoys through the western Mediterranean. Whether or not the Germans seized Gibraltar, Britain would be strategically paralyzed.

The Axis would be able to move at will into the Middle East, for the British had no substantial forces there. This region produced much of the world's oil, and its capture would provide ample amounts of Germany's single most-needed strategic material.

An advance on the southern frontier of Turkey would put the Turks in an impossible position. Hitler was already gaining Hungary, Romania, and Bulgaria as allies. Therefore, Turkey could be approached both by way of Bulgaria at Istanbul and from northern Iraq and Syria. Turkey would be forced to join the Axis or grant passage for Axis forces and supplies. A defiant stance would result in the swift defeat of the Turkish army and disaster.

Passage through Turkey would reduce the importance of Malta and Gibraltar. This way, both could be eliminated without the active support of Franco and without direct assault.

German forces could occupy French North Africa with or without Vichy France's cooperation. From French Morocco, they could approach from the *south* the small strip of Morocco along the Strait of Gibraltar ruled by Spain. Spain would be forced to grant transit rights, or stand aside if German forces occupied the strip without permission. Spain could not resist for fear of a German attack into the heart of Spain from France. Consequently, German airfields and batteries could be set up along the south shore of the strait. This would close it to Britain—without an expensive military assault on the rock of Gibraltar.

Sealing the Strait of Gibraltar would force the British to abandon Malta, because they could not supply it.

With the Royal Navy out of the Mediterranean, it would become an Axis lake. This would permit German forces to occupy all of western Africa, including the French base at Dakar in Senegal. Aircraft, ships, and submarines from Dakar could close down much of Britain's convoy traffic through the South Atlantic, even without seizure of the Cape Verde islands.

In the Middle East the strategic payoff would be much greater. German forces in Iran would block that country as a route for supplies to the Soviet Union from Britain and the United States. Russia would be left with only the ports of Murmansk on the Barents Sea and Archangel on the White Sea through which goods from the west could be funneled. This would require dangerous passages in atrocious weather, with constant danger of attacks by German ships and aircraft stationed in Norway.

Even more important, the Soviet Union's major oil fields were in the Caucasus and along the western shore of the Caspian Sea, just north of

Iran. Germany could threaten not only an attack directly from Poland and Romania in the west but also from the south through the Caucasus to the Soviet oil fields. This danger of envelopment and quick loss of oil would immobilize Stalin, and obligate him to provide Germany with whatever grain and raw materials it might need. In other words, Germany—without loss of a single soldier—would have the benefits of the Soviet Union's vast materials storehouse, as well as delivery of tin, rubber, and other goods from Southeast Asia by way of the Trans-Siberian Railway.

A German position in Iran would also pose a huge threat to British control of India, which was agitating for independence under Mohandas K. Gandhi and other leaders. From Iran Germany could reach India through the Khyber and other passes, invasion routes used long before and long after Alexander the Great made the passage in 326 B.C. Germany would not actually have to do a thing. The threat alone would force Britain to commit every possible soldier to defend its crown jewel. Germany, again without the expenditure of a single man, could immobilize Britain.

In possession of the Middle East, all of North and West Africa, and Europe west of Russia, its armed forces virtually intact, its economy able to exploit the resources of three continents, Germany would be virtually invincible. Britain's defiance on the periphery of Europe would become increasingly irrelevant. Germany would not have to inaugurate an all-out U-boat war against its shipping. Britain's remaining strength would have to be expended in protecting its empire and the convoys to and from the home islands.

The United States would have no hope of launching an invasion of mainland Europe against an undefeated and waiting German army until it had spent years building a vast navy, army, and air force, not to speak of the transports, landing craft, vehicles, and weapons necessary for such a giant undertaking. It is possible that the United States would take on this task, but the chances for its success would be extremely small. Far more likely, the American people would turn first to counter the expansion of Japan in the Pacific.

Meanwhile Germany could consolidate its empire, bring subject nations into an economic union, and grow more powerful economically, militarily, and politically every day. Before long, the world would become accustomed to the new German Empire and insist on a return to normal international trade.

This at last would give Hitler the opportunity he had dreamed of since the 1920s—seizure of all the Soviet Union west of the Urals. Once a de facto cease-fire had been achieved, Hitler could strike at European Russia from south and west, drive Stalin and the surviving Soviets into Siberia, and get the *Lebensraum* he coveted.

✠    ✠    ✠

In the weeks that followed Raeder's proposal Hitler appeared to be less firmly fixed on war in the east, at least in regard to timing, and looked on the navy commander's proposals favorably. Senior German officers began to hope for a change in Hitler's resolve.

Hitler's ambivalence was based on faith that the Italian offensive into Egypt would have quick success. It had commenced on September 13, 1940, under the command of Marshal Rodolfo Graziani. The Italian army of six divisions was about three times the size of defending British forces. But German fears (and British optimism) began to rise almost at once, as Graziani advanced along the coast with extreme caution against little British resistance. Fifty miles inside Egypt, he stopped at Sidi Barrani, less than halfway to the British position at Mersa Matruh.

Here Graziani established a chain of fortified camps that were too far apart to support one another. Week after week passed with the Italians doing nothing. Meanwhile Wavell received reinforcements, including three armored regiments rushed out on Churchill's orders from England in three fast merchant ships.

German military leaders had long harbored doubts about the ability of the Italian army to achieve much, and Graziani's performance fanned these fears. Italian forces had shown only limited interest in war, and had poor or obsolete equipment and few mechanized forces of any kind. However, the German General Staff felt the principal deficiency was not poor weapons, but poor leadership. The Italian officer corps was ill-trained, lived separate from the men, and even had special food. There was little of the easy camaraderie between officers and men that marked the German army, and the high standards and special skills demanded of German officers were little stressed in the Italian military. On the other hand, German generals had great respect for the British army, especially its tenacity.

Consequently, senior German officers offered the panzer corps and air-craft, but Mussolini didn't respond. He kept hoping Graziani would show some drive, push the British back, and give him and Italy some glory. But it didn't happen. Even so Mussolini was reluctant to call in the Germans because it would look like an admission of failure. On the other hand, he didn't want to lose Libya.

With the Italian army sitting at Sidi Barrani in October 1940, the German high command sent a panzer expert, Major General Wilhelm von Thoma, to North Africa to find out whether German forces should help the Italians—and also, unofficially, to look over the Italian army in action (or rather inaction).

Thoma reported back that four German armored divisions could be maintained in Africa and these would be all the force necessary to drive the British out of Egypt and the Suez and open the Middle East to conquest. At the time Germany possessed twenty panzer divisions, none being used.

Hitler called Thoma in to discuss the matter. He told Thoma he could spare only one panzer division, whereupon Thoma replied that it would be better to give up the whole idea. Thoma's comment angered Hitler. He said his concept of sending German forces to Africa was narrowly political, designed to keep Mussolini from changing sides.

Hitler's comments to Thoma reveal he didn't see the road to victory through Suez that Raeder had pointed out to him. If he had, he would have insisted on committing German troops.

Hitler's interest was focused on keeping Mussolini happy and on wild schemes like assaulting Gibraltar. He had not absorbed Raeder's strategic insight. His mind remained fixed on Russia. He was hoarding his tanks to use there. That's why he couldn't spare more than a single panzer divi-sion for Africa.

✠          ✠          ✠

The denouement in North Africa came swiftly. On December 7, Lieutenant General Sir Richard O'Connor assembled 30,000 British troops with 275 tanks in the Western Desert Force and moved out from Matruh against Sidi Barrani.

Graziani had 80,000 men at the front but only 120 tanks. The Italian infantry had little motor transport and were vulnerable to being surrounded by mobile British columns in the open desert country, where military formations could find little or no cover. Also, the Italian tanks were fourteen-ton M13 models with moderate armor and a low-power 47-millimeter gun. They were not wholly inadequate for the period but they had a bad reputation. Soldiers on both sides referred to them as "self-propelled coffins." The British on the other hand had fifty heavily armored Matildas impervious to most Italian guns. These played a decisive role in the battles that followed.

O'Connor decided to approach the Italian camps from the rear, since the Italians had mined the spaces in front. On the night of December 8, the British passed through a gap in the enemy's chain of camps, and early on December 9 stormed Nibeiwa camp from behind, with Matildas leading the way. The garrison, surprised, ran off, leaving 4,000 prisoners. Early in the afternoon the Matildas stormed two other camps to the north, Tummar West and Tummar East, sending these garrisons flying as well. Meanwhile the 7th Armored Division, soon to gain fame as the "Desert Rats," drove westward, reached the coast road, and got astride the Italians' line of retreat.

The next day the 4th Indian Division, aided by two tank regiments sent back by 7th Armored, moved north, converged on both sides of camps clustered around Sidi Barrani, and overran the position, taking thousands of prisoners.

On the third day, the reserve brigade of 7th Armored bounded westward twenty-five miles to the coast beyond Buq-Buq, where it intercepted a large column of retreating Italians, and captured 14,000. Within three days, half the Italians in Egypt had surrendered.

The remainder of the Italian army took refuge in the coast fortress of Bardia, just inside the Libyan frontier. The 7th Armored swiftly isolated Bardia by sweeping around to the west. It took until January 3, 1941, to bring up infantry to assault Bardia with twenty-two Matildas leading the way. The whole Italian garrison gave up: 45,000 men and 129 tanks.

The 7th Armored Division immediately rushed west to isolate Tobruk. When Australian infantry attacked on January 21 behind the sixteen

Matildas still working, 30,000 Italians surrendered with eighty-seven tanks.

The Italians were offering practically no resistance, and at the rate they were going the British could have continued on to Tripoli. Unfortunately, Churchill decided to hold back British reserves to take advantage of another blunder that Benito Mussolini had made—on October 28 he had invaded Greece from Albania, which he had occupied in 1939. It was an act of strategic lunacy, for it involved Italy in a two-front war when it was having almost insuperable difficulties maintaining a one-front operation in North Africa. Il Duce (the leader), as Mussolini was called, hoped to carve out an Italian empire, but the Greeks resisted fiercely, drove the Italians back into Albania, and were threatening to rout the whole Italian army.

Hitler only learned about the attack after meeting with Mussolini in Florence the day it started. He was furious, because it disrupted all his plans, even his hesitant thinking about sending troops to North Africa.

Hitler had just come from meetings with the Spanish dictator Franco on the French border at Hendaye on October 23, and Pétain the next day at Montoire.

The talks at Hendaye went on for nine hours with no commitment on Franco's part to enter the war and allow German troops to assault Gibraltar. Hitler departed frustrated and angry, calling Franco a "Jesuit swine." The meeting with Pétain went better. Pétain agreed to collaborate with Germany to bring Britain to its knees. In return, France would get a high place in the "New Europe" and compensation in Africa for whatever territory France was forced to cede to others.

Churchill pushed the Greeks to accept a British force of tanks and artillery, but General Ioannis Metaxas, head of the Greek government, declined, saying the British would provoke German intervention but would be too weak to stop it. Even so, Churchill held forces in Egypt and ordered Wavell not to give O'Connor any reinforcements.

O'Connor meanwhile pushed on westward. His 7th Armored Division had shrunk to only fifty cruiser tanks. On February 3 he learned from air reconnaissance that the Italians were about to abandon the entire Benghazi corner of northwestern Cyrenaica. O'Connor at once ordered the 7th Armored to move through the desert interior to reach the coast road, Via Balbia, well to the south of Benghazi. Rough going through heavy sand slowed the tanks, and on February 4, Major General Sir Michael Creagh, commanding the division, organized an entirely wheeled force of infantry and artillery and sent it ahead with a group of armored cars. By the afternoon of February 5, this force had set up a barrage or barrier across the enemy's line of retreat south of Beda Fomm. That evening the division's twenty-nine still-serviceable cruiser tanks arrived and took up concealed positions.

When the main Italian force came up, it was accompanied by a hundred new cruiser M13 tanks that, combined, could have blasted the British out of the way and opened a clear path to Tripoli. But they approached in packets, not massed. The British tanks overpowered each group as it arrived. By nightfall February 6, sixty Italian tanks had been crippled and forty abandoned. With no armor to protect them, the Italian infantry surrendered—20,000 men. The total British force was only 3,000 men. It was one of the most overwhelming victories in the war, and raised British morale immensely.

There were few Italian troops left in Libya, and O'Connor confidently expected to rush on to Tripoli, where Italian officers were packing their bags for a hasty departure.

✠      ✠      ✠

On February 6, 1941, the day the last Italian elements were being wiped out at Beda Fomm, Adolf Hitler summoned Erwin Rommel, forty-nine years old, to take command of a German mechanized corps that he had finally decided to send to rescue the Italians. The force was *not* the four panzer divisions General von Thoma had calculated was needed to seize Suez and conquer the Middle East. Rather it consisted of the single panzer division Hitler said he could spare (the 15th), plus a small tank-equipped motorized division (5th Light).

He had selected Rommel because, next to Heinz Guderian, he was the most famous panzer leader in Germany. Rommel's 7th Panzer Division had moved so fast and mysteriously in May and June that the French called it the "ghost division." Rommel's high visibility made him the ideal choice for Africa, since Hitler was seeking primarily a public relations gesture to support Mussolini, not so much to reach a decision in Africa.

The first elements of Rommel's new *Deutsches Afrika Korps* (DAK), or German Africa Corps, began arriving in mid-February 1941, though the whole 5th Light Division couldn't get to Libya until mid-April, and the 15th Panzer Division would not get there till the end of May. There was still plenty of time, therefore, for the British to push on against minuscule opposition to Tripoli, and evict Italy from North Africa.

Just at that moment Prime Minister Churchill pulled up the reins on Wavell and O'Connor. He directed Wavell to prepare the largest possible force for Greece. This ended the advance on Tripoli. The radical change had occurred after General Metaxas died unexpectedly on January 29, and the new Greek prime minister succumbed to Churchill's urgings to invite the British in.

Churchill foolishly hoped he could build a coalition of Balkan nations against Germany. The Greeks had thrown back the ill-equipped and unenthusiastic Italians, but the primitive Balkan armies were no match for German panzers. And, with the commitment of British forces to the Continent only months before he planned to attack the Soviet Union, Hitler saw his entire position threatened, particularly since British aircraft in Greece could strike at the Romanian oil fields at Ploesti. Hitler depended upon these for his war machine.

He ordered the army to prepare for an invasion of Greece through Bulgaria. By the third week of February 1941 the Germans had massed 680,000 troops in Romania. Bulgarian leaders, excited by Hitler's promise to give them Greek territory and access to the Aegean Sea, allowed passage of German troops through the country. On February 28, German units crossed the Danube and took up positions to assault Greece.

The first of 53,000 British troops, mostly motorized forces from Australia and New Zealand, landed in Greece on March 7 and moved forward to help their new Greek allies. Off Cape Matapan south of Greece on March 28, the British fleet destroyed three Italian cruisers in a night battle, thereby ensuring that Mussolini's battle fleet never dared challenge the Royal Navy again.

The Yugoslavs meanwhile had been under intense pressure to join the Axis. But the Yugoslav people, especially the Serbs, were violently opposed. The Yugoslav premier and foreign minister slipped out of Belgrade by night to avoid hostile demonstrations and signed the Tripartite Pact in the

# CONQUEST OF YUGOSLAVIA AND GREECE 1941

GERMANY

2ND ARMY
(WEICHS)

HUNGARY

TRANSYLVANIA

ITALY

Ljubljana

Trieste

Fiume

Zagreb

Karlovac

Save R.

Mitrovica

Belgrade

ROMANIA

Ploesti

Bucharest

Zadar

Sarajevo

Nis

Danube R.

YUGOSLAVIA

Panzer Group 1
(Kleist)

BULGARIA

Adriatic Sea

Kotor

Sofia

12TH ARMY
(LIST)

ITALY

Skopje

ALBANIA

Durazzo

Tirana

9th and 11th
Italian Armies
(October 28, 1940)

Lake
Dojran

Bitola

METAXAS LINE

Alexandroúpolis

Florina

Valona

Saloníki

Samothrace

Lemnos

TURKEY

GREECE

Larissa

Greek attack
(November 10–
December 8, 1940)

Ioánnina

Árta

Lamia

Mytilene

Chios

Ionian Sea

N

Patras

Athens

Aegean Sea

Sicily

Peloponnisos

Kalamáta

Monemvasia

Malta

German air landing
(May 20, 1941)

Cape Matapan

Crete

0   Miles   100        200        300

0   Kilometers   200        300

Mediterranean Sea

air landings

German advance April 6–20, 1941

Jeffrey L. Ward

presence of Hitler and Foreign Minister Joachim von Ribbentrop in Vienna on March 25.

The next night in Belgrade, a popular uprising led by air force officers under General Dusan Simovic overthrew the government and the regent, Prince Paul, who had agreed to join the Axis. They packed Prince Paul off to Greece. Prince Paul had intended to kidnap Prince Peter, the eighteen-year-old heir to the throne, but Peter escaped down a drainpipe, and the rebels at once declared him king.

The coup threw Hitler into a wild rage. He ordered an immediate attack on Yugoslavia from all quarters.

At dawn on April 6, 1941, German armies of overwhelming strength fell on Yugoslavia and Greece. Maximilian von Weichs's 2nd Army in Austria and Hungary rushed into Yugoslavia from the north and east.

Wilhelm List's 12th Army in Bulgaria had the crucial task. While its 30th Corps pressed to the Aegean against no opposition near European Turkey, parts of the 18th Mountain Corps smashed against the Metaxas Line, but bounded back in repulse. This was Greece's main defense in the northeast, held by six divisions.

Meanwhile the motorized 40th Corps under Georg Stumme and Panzer Group 1, five divisions under Ewald von Kleist, drove westward into southern Yugoslavia and split the Yugoslavs from the Greeks. Kleist's panzers turned north, captured Nish, and raced down the Morava River valley toward Belgrade, meeting Georg Hans Reinhardt's 41st Panzer Corps pressing on the capital from Romania.

The Yugoslav army in theory had thirty-five divisions. But it was poorly armed, and Yugoslavia was about to rip apart into its separate ethnic groups. Only about half the reservists, mostly Serbs, had answered the call to mobilize. The remainder, largely Croats and Slovenians, had remained at home.

The army command tried to concentrate its scattered Serbian troops around Sarajevo, but the German 41st Panzer Corps cut through Bosnia and forced about 300,000 men to surrender. Simovic and young King Peter flew out, first to Greece, later to Palestine.

Meanwhile, the German 40th Corps pressed into the Vardar River valley, seized Skopje in southern Yugoslavia, then turned through the Monastir Gap into Greece, about seventy-five miles west of Saloniki.

At the same time, parts of the 18th Mountain Corps slipped around Lake Dojran, twelve miles west of the point where the Greek, Yugoslav, and Bulgarian borders joined. Thereby flanking the Metaxas Line, they drove down the Vardar (Axios) valley to the Aegean and seized Saloniki. This isolated the Greeks on the Metaxas Line, and forced them to surrender.

The British expected the Germans to advance directly southward from Saloniki past Mount Olympus and along the Aegean. This is where they placed most of their troops. Instead, the Germans thrust southwestward from the Monastir Gap toward the west coast of Greece, cut off the Greeks in Albania, and turned the western flank of the British. This produced the quick collapse of resistance.

General Wavell, with agreement of London, ordered the expeditionary corps to evacuate. British warships and transports ran into harbors around Athens and the Peloponnisos, to which the British and some Greeks were hurrying, and began taking out troops, leaving most of their weapons behind. The Royal Navy evacuated 51,000 men by the end of April. Around 13,000 British were killed or forced to surrender.

As King George II of Greece, his family, and high officials flew out on British flying boats, German panzers rolled into Athens on April 27 and hoisted the swastika over the Acropolis. Most of the Greek army capitulated.

It had taken the Germans only three weeks to overrun Yugoslavia and Greece and drive the British once more off the Continent. Field Marshal List's 12th Army alone had captured, in addition to the British, 90,000 Yugoslavs and 270,000 Greeks, at a cost of barely 5,000 killed and wounded.

# 6 ATTACKING THE WRONG ISLAND

ADOLF HITLER NOW MADE A DECISION THAT FLEW IN THE FACE OF LOGIC, DIS-regarded the actual military situation in the Mediterranean, and revealed his inability to see a different way to pursue the war than by attacking the Soviet Union.

He decided to use his highly trained parachute and glider troops to seize the relatively unimportant island of Crete in the eastern Mediterranean, but he refused to capture Malta, which lay directly on the seaway between Italy and Libya.

This absurd choice—made over the objections of Admiral Raeder, the navy high command, and elements in the OKW—marked Hitler's final rejection of a Mediterranean strategy that could have brought him victory. If a campaign to conquer North Africa was going to be waged by the Axis, it was imperative to secure Malta. If, on the other hand, Hitler was sending troops to Libya merely to mollify Mussolini, with no large strategic aim, then German brains, men, and equipment were being wasted in a foolish and reckless manner.

Crete, home of the ancient Minoan civilization, is a large Greek island (3,200 square miles) 180 miles south of Athens, and some 250 miles north of Egypt and eastern Libya, or Cyrenaica. It is 152 miles long, but only 8 to 35 miles wide.

Once the Balkans had been seized by the Germans, Crete strategically fell into a twilight zone. For the British, long-range bombers based on Crete could reach the Ploesti oil fields in Romania, 675 miles north, but RAF bases on the island could be blasted by German aircraft a hundred miles away in southern Greece. For the Germans, occupation made no more sense, because aircraft based there would be farther from Cairo and Alexandria than planes in eastern Cyrenaica.

The situation was entirely different in regard to Malta. This small British-ruled island group (122 square miles), only 60 miles south of Sicily and 200 miles north of Tripoli, was a dagger sticking into Italian and German backs in North Africa. Here the British had based airplanes, submarines, and warships with the explicit purpose of interdicting traffic to Libya.

The danger of Malta was emphasized to everyone when the British sank a transport meant for Rommel's Africa Corps on the night of April 15–16, 1941. British threats from Malta soon made nearly every passage to Libya a throw of the dice. Sometimes the ship got through, sometimes it didn't. Sunken Italian and German cargo vessels began to litter the seabed of the Sicilian Narrows between the two continents.

Hitler didn't consider the question of Crete seriously until the RAF landed air and army units on the island on November 1, 1940. Soon thereafter Hitler's attention focused on Malta. After Marshal Graziani's humiliating defeat, Hitler decided to send German forces to Libya. Mussolini, fearing loss of his possession, now wanted help.

Officers examined the possibility of neutralizing Crete and Malta solely by air raids. But any successful bombing campaign lasts only as long as it is continued. The only certain way to eliminate a threat is to seize the ground with troops, and Admiral Raeder and the navy high command agitated for an assault on Malta. Capture of this island, they asserted, was "an essential precondition for a successful war against Britain in the Mediterranean."

Raeder and his senior officers were trying to reverse a preliminary decision of February 22, 1941, when the OKW informed them that Hitler planned to delay the conquest of Malta until the autumn of 1941 "after the conclusion of the war in the east." Thus Hitler was expecting to dispose of the Russians in a swift summer campaign, then turn back at his leisure and deal with the small problem of Malta!

Several OKW staff officers—awake to the danger of Malta after the ship bound for Rommel went down—also pleaded with Jodl and Keitel to urge Hitler to tackle the island at once.

It was no wonder that they, Raeder, and his officers were wrought up. The decision ignored Rommel's urgent needs and subordinated everything to a war against the Soviet Union—whose dimensions, duration, and outcome could not possibly be foreseen. Furthermore, the defending garrison at Malta was small, because convoys to the island had to run a gauntlet of attacks from Italian air and sea forces. Yet the British controlled the eastern Mediterranean and could put as large a force as they desired onto Crete.

Hitler's final decision came on April 21, 1941, as the campaign in the Balkans was winding down. He decided to attack Crete, which was given the code name Operation Mercury. Malta would have to wait. Crete, Hitler declared, was more important. He wanted to eliminate all danger of British sea and air forces from southeastern Europe. British forces on Malta would be dealt with by the Luftwaffe. Furthermore, Barbarossa, the attack on Russia, was set for June 1941, and Mercury *had* to be completed before then.

With this decision Adolf Hitler lost the war. The assault on Crete guaranteed two catastrophes for Germany: it limited the Mediterranean campaign to peripheral or public relations goals, and it turned German strength against the Soviet Union while Britain remained defiant, with the United States in the wings.

✠    ✠    ✠

Hitler was not the only leader fooled into thinking Crete was important. General Halder, chief of the army staff, showed how little he knew about supplying troops on an island in a sea dominated by an enemy fleet. Halder concluded that capture of the island was "the best means to support the advance of Rommel toward the Suez Canal."

Winston Churchill also fell into the trap. He wanted to strengthen British forces on Crete, in the face of strong opposition from General Wavell, the Middle East commander, and the war ministry in London. The ministry feared heavy losses on Crete, since airstrips on mainland Greece were close and the Luftwaffe could bomb British bases with ease.

Churchill insisted, however, and beginning in February 1941 more British army troops moved to the island as construction crews built three RAF landing strips there.

Meanwhile, British intelligence picked up word that parts of 11th Air Corps—Kurt Student's elite parachute and glider force that had overcome Holland in days—were arriving at Bulgarian airfields. But the British intelligence network was not clear whether the target was Crete, Syria, or Cyprus, a British island in the eastern Mediterranean.

Churchill on April 17 ordered some of the troops being evacuated from Greece to be disembarked on the island. General Wavell informed London that he only had sufficient troops to hold Libya and that he thought Crete should be abandoned, as did the Admiralty in London.

However, Churchill decided to defend Crete. He saw a chance of inflicting damage on German airborne troops, and believed a strong defense would have good effects on Turkey and other Middle Eastern states.

On April 30, Lieutenant General Bernard Cyril Freyberg took command of 28,600 British, New Zealand, and Australian troops, and 7,000 Greek army forces on Crete. Most of the men had been evacuated from Greece and had only light weapons. Freyberg sent frantic calls to Egypt for heavy weapons, but only a few arrived.

It was clear that the German attack had to hit the north shore. Here were all the main landing places and principal towns. Most roads ran east-west. Only a few rough tracks led south over the steep mountains that fell directly into the Libyan Sea.

Intelligence had figured the attack would come in the western part of Crete, and Freyberg posted the 2nd New Zealand Division around the village of Maleme and the airfield located near the seashore. He put about 14,000 British and Australians at Khania and Suda Bay, a few miles east to defend against a sea assault. At Rethimnon, thirty miles east of Khania, Freyberg posted the 19th Australian Brigade, and at Iraklion, forty miles farther east, he placed the 14th British Brigade. At all these points, Freyberg also positioned Greek forces as backup.

Mercury commander General Alexander Löhr divided his airborne forces into three groups: West, Middle, and East. In the first wave in the early morning of May 20, 1941, Group West was to land at two locations: Maleme, and around Khania and Suda Bay. In the second wave in the afternoon, Group Middle would drop just east of Rithymnon, and Group

East on both sides of Iraklion. Once Maleme airfield had been secured, the 5th Mountain Division would come in by transport planes. General Wolfram von Richthofen's 8th Air Corps had 280 bombers, 150 Stukas, 180 fighters, and 40 reconnaissance aircraft to cover the attack.

Richthofen's aircraft began hitting the 40 British aircraft on Crete so hard early in May that the RAF removed all planes to Egypt. This gave the Germans complete air supremacy. They used it to pound every British position they could find, but British camouflage was so good the soldiers suffered few losses.

German air reconnaissance discovered a few days before the attack that strong elements of the Royal Navy had moved south and west of Crete. This showed that the British were determined to defend the island.

Thus on May 20 the Germans held command of the air and the British command of the sea. But the Royal Navy, with no air shield, was operating at high risk.

✠        ✠        ✠

Preceded by early morning air attacks that knocked out some British communications and antiaircraft guns, the first wave of Germans came in on gliders at Maleme and south of Khania. Immediately afterward, paratroops dropped around the airport, the town of Khania, and docks at Suda Bay. All told, 6,000 Germans landed or fell out of the sky in this first wave. The British, New Zealanders, and Australians were waiting.

It was nearly a total disaster for the Germans.

Some gliders crashed before reaching their targets. Others landed but the troops were slaughtered as they emerged from the planes. Many of the paratroops jumped directly on defensive positions and were shot as they came down. One of the reasons this happened was the prevailing wind, which blew from the interior toward the sea. For fear of dropping the troops in the sea, the pilots tended to drop them too far inland—some of them actually in British lines.

The Germans came down with only light weapons. Because of intense fire, many could not reach the containers holding heavier weapons that had been dropped, but fell wide of the troops.

Germans who dropped south of Khania could not take the town or

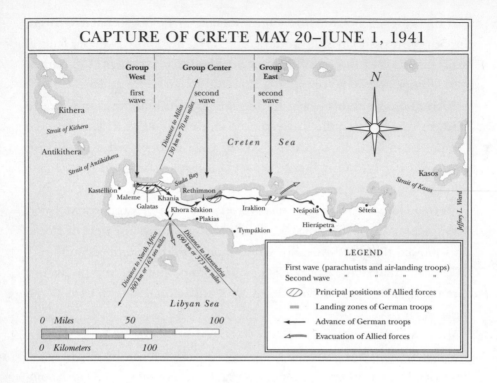

## CAPTURE OF CRETE MAY 20–JUNE 1, 1941

Suda Bay and had to go over to the defensive that night. Only in the narrow Tavronitis River valley just west of Maleme were units able to assemble and attack the dominating heights south of the Maleme airport. The New Zealanders emplaced on these heights held off the Germans and kept them from grabbing the airport.

During the night, however, the local New Zealand commander got the false impression that his men were so weakened they couldn't hold off the enemy. With approval of his brigade commander, he pulled them east a mile or so. This permitted the Germans to move forward and seize a piece of the airfield, plus the heights south of Maleme. This opened part of the field to German aircraft, though it remained within range of British artillery and infantry weapons.

The troops of Group West lost radio contact with headquarters in Greece for a time. Air crews returning to pick up troops for the second wave had not seen what had happened, and thought things had gone well.

Consequently, when the bad news began to come in sometime later, it was too late to change plans. Also, delays in refueling aircraft and the poor condition of Greek runways slowed departure of the second wave, while Richthofen's bombers and fighters had gone ahead to bomb and strafe Rethimnon and Iraklion. By the time the second-wave transports arrived, they were often without protection.

Consequently, the losses at Rethimnon and Iraklion were even higher than in the morning attack. About half the paratroopers were killed as they descended or in the first fights on the ground. The Germans could capture neither town nor local airfields, and survivors, in small isolated detachments, had to go over to the defensive.

Generals Löhr and Student decided the only thing to do was to reinforce the little success they had achieved, at Maleme airfield. On the morning of May 21, some transports landed at a strip of the airport in German hands and delivered urgently needed weapons and munitions. That afternoon several companies of paratroops jumped into this area as well.

With the newly arrived paratroops and their own men, Group West finally cleared the airfield. In the late afternoon, the first 5th Mountain Division troops landed in transports. Even so, they suffered losses, because British guns continued to fire onto the field. By that evening (May 21) eighty destroyed or severely damaged aircraft lay on the airfield.

The Germans around the airport tried to move east in hopes of joining their other units. But the 5th New Zealand Brigade stopped them at Pirgos, a few hundred yards away.

General Freyberg had made a grave tactical error in the first two days. He thought the main German attack was going to come by sea, and refused to move his forces out of their coastal positions at Khania and Suda Bay to shift over and wipe out the Germans around Maleme.

The Germans had in fact planned to send in heavy weapons, equipment, and a few 5th Mountain Division soldiers on May 21 in twenty-five Greek caiques, or small motorized sailing vessels, escorted by an Italian destroyer. But British warships caught the flotilla north of Crete, sank most of the caiques with nearly all the weapons and equipment, along with 300 mountain troops, and sent the remaining vessels flying for the island of Milos to the north.

An even larger group of caiques tried to reach the island on May 22, but Royal Navy ships met them twenty miles south of Milos. This flotilla escaped the fate of the other because an Italian warship bravely shielded the vessels, while Richthofen's aircraft attacked so hard that the British ships had to turn southwest into the Kithera Strait.

Now commenced the first great air-sea battle of the Second World War. Richthofen's Stukas were the major killers, giving the first strong lesson in the effectiveness of dive-bombers against naval vessels. In the battles around Crete, the British lost three cruisers and six destroyers, while thirteen other ships were badly damaged, including two battleships and the only aircraft carrier then in the Mediterranean fleet.

The fleet commander, Admiral Sir Andrew Cunningham, pulled most of his ships back to Alexandria on May 23, and began sending fast supply ships to Crete at night to avoid Luftwaffe attacks.

General Freyberg meanwhile had realized his error, and ordered the 5th New Zealand Brigade to win back the Maleme airfield. The attack got under way early on May 22. The New Zealanders almost reached the Tavronitis River on the south, advancing to the eastern edge of the airfield along the coast. At daylight, however, the Luftwaffe moved in to attack and forced them back east of Pirgos. A day later, threatened by a German encircling movement, the New Zealanders withdrew to Galatas. This permitted General Julius Ringel, new commander of Group West, to join forces with isolated parachutists southwest of Khania. Now the Maleme airfield no longer was in range of British artillery. The remainder of the 5th Mountain Division troops arrived, while supply craft came in steadily, transforming the tactical situation.

General Löhr directed Ringel to capture Suda Bay and break the British line of supply, and after that to relieve the parachute units still isolated and pinned down at Rethimnon and Iraklion. Ringel ordered his airborne troops to drive straight eastward on the main road, where they ran up against a solid New Zealand defense at Galatas. It took unrelenting Luftwaffe attacks to break the line and permit the Germans to reach Khania on May 27.

Freyberg informed Wavell that his troops had reached the end of their endurance. On May 27, Churchill and Wavell gave permission and he

began to withdraw his force southward twenty-three miles to Khora Sfakion on the south coast and evacuate from there.

On May 28 the Germans broke through bitterly defended rear-guard positions east of Khania and occupied Suda Bay. Meanwhile Freyberg's main body was moving over a poor track to the south coast. It entirely escaped General Ringel that most of the enemy were heading south, and he sent only a small regiment down the Khora Sfakion road. He directed his main body eastward, which relieved the decimated German units holding out around Rethimnon on May 29 and forced the surrender of an Australian battalion east of the town the next day. The Aussies had not received orders to evacuate until too late. However, entirely unnoticed by the Germans, the British brigade and some Greeks, about 3,500 men, got out on British warships at Iraklion on the night of May 28–29.

The Royal Navy rescued 13,000 soldiers at Khora Sfakion over four nights. The evacuation was a hard, difficult, and dangerous job for the sailors, under constant attack by Luftwaffe aircraft. One of Admiral Cunningham's staff officers pointed out that the navy had already suffered heavily and wondered whether it should risk more losses.

Cunningham replied: "It takes the navy three years to build a ship, but three hundred years to build a tradition; we must not let the army down."

General Wavell ended the evacuation on June 1 when he learned that the remaining soldiers no longer had the strength to hold off the German mountain troops who were pressing hard against the port. The 9,000 British soldiers and 1,000 Greeks left behind surrendered.

☩          ☩          ☩

Looked at objectively, the Cretan operation was a disaster all around. The British lost about 12,000 soldiers on Crete, while navy dead exceeded 2,000. Material losses were enormous. Only about 2,000 Greeks got off the island, and many of the survivors who remained died in guerrilla operations, massacred wherever found, along with numbers of Cretan civilians.

More than half the Germans who landed on Crete died or were wounded. Altogether 11th Air Corps lost 6,000 men, two-thirds dead, the rest wounded. The highest losses were in the most battle-tested, best-trained outfits. Student said after the war that "the Fuehrer was very upset by the heavy losses suffered by the parachute units, and came to the conclusion that their surprise value had passed. After that he often said to me, 'The day of parachute troops is over.' "

General Halder's glib hope that the capture of Crete would lead to easier supply for North Africa remained the mirage it had always been. The main Axis supply line ran as before past Malta.

# 7 ROMMEL'S UNAPPRECIATED GIFT

ON THE MORNING OF FEBRUARY 11, 1941, GENERAL ERWIN ROMMEL, commander of the as yet nonexistent Africa Corps, along with Adolf Hitler's adjutant, Lieutenant Colonel Rudolf Schmundt, flew in a Heinkel 111 bomber from Catania, Sicily, to Tripoli. Rommel wanted to check out the situation in Libya before the leading elements of his corps arrived.

At Catania he had asked the commander of the German 10th Air Corps, General Hans Geisler, to bomb Benghazi and British columns reported nearby. Geisler protested that he couldn't do that, because many Italian officers and officials owned homes at Benghazi and Italian authorities didn't want the place hit. Exasperated, Rommel queried Hitler's headquarters and got quick approval for the Luftwaffe to strike.

At Tripoli, the Italian officers were packing their bags for imminent departure, and saw little hope of holding Sirte, some 230 miles east of Tripoli, where Rommel wanted to set up a defensive line. Rommel decided to take command himself at the front, and that afternoon flew off with Schmundt in the Heinkel to Sirte.

Rommel's first view of Africa was sobering. The terrain alternated between sandy wastes and featureless hills. Through it all, he wrote, the only paved road in Libya, "the Via Balbia, stretched away like a black thread through the desolate landscape, in which neither tree nor bush could be seen as far as the eye could reach."

At Sirte only a single Italian regiment was on guard. The closest British troops were at El Agheila, 180 miles farther east. They were stopped there, not by the Italians, but because they were at the end of an extremely long supply line (630 miles back to Mersa Matruh and the British railhead), and because the Middle East command was transferring many British troops to Greece.

The remaining Italian troops in Libya were 200 miles west of Sirte around Tripoli. At Rommel's insistence, leading elements of three Italian divisions there began moving toward Sirte on February 14.

On the same day the first German troops—the 3rd Reconnaissance Battalion and the antitank battalion of 5th Light Division—arrived at Tripoli on a transport. Rommel insisted, despite danger of air attack, on unloading the ship by searchlight throughout the night. The next morning the two German outfits, in their new tropical uniforms, paraded through Tripoli, then moved off to Sirte, arriving twenty-six hours later.

Rommel had already grasped the essence of the war in Libya and Egypt: everything depended upon mobility.

"In the North African desert," he wrote, "nonmotorized troops are of practically no value against a motorized enemy, since the enemy has the chance, in almost every position, of making the action fluid by a turning movement around the south."

This was why the Italians had been beaten almost without a fight—they had moved largely on foot; the British were in vehicles. Nonmotorized forces could be used only in defensive positions, Rommel saw. Yet such positions were of little consequence, because enemy motorized units could surround them and force them to surrender, or bypass them. In other words, foot soldiers in the desert had no impact beyond the reach of their guns.

Rommel discerned that desert warfare was strangely similar to war at sea. Motorized equipment could move at will over it and usually in any direction, much as ships could move over oceans. Rommel described the similarity thus: "Whoever has the weapons with the greatest range has the longest arm, exactly as at sea. Whoever has the greater mobility . . . can by swift action compel his opponent to act according to his wishes."

The Italians were discouraged, and little interested in challenging the British, while Rommel had only two battalions of 5th Light Division. The whole division couldn't get there until mid-April, and Rommel's main striking force, 15th Panzer Division, would take till the end of May to assemble.

Rommel knew that Hitler's interest in North Africa was limited to helping the Italians hold Libya. Otherwise, he would have provided more adequate forces. However, Rommel, who had won Germany's highest decoration for valor in World War I (the Pour le Mérite, or "Blue Max"), was a resourceful and determined officer, not deterred by obstacles. No one knew it at the moment, but Erwin Rommel was one of the greatest generals of modern times. Moreover, he possessed a burning ambition to succeed.

✠          ✠          ✠

Rommel decided to use the modest tools on hand to strike a surprise blow at the British, who were somewhat complacently sitting between El Agheila and Agedabia, sixty miles farther northeast. General O'Connor had gone back to Egypt, succeeded by Lieutenant General Sir Philip Neame, who had little experience in desert warfare. General Wavell had replaced the experienced 7th Armored Division (the "Desert Rats") with half of the raw 2nd Armored Division, just arrived from England, while the other half had been sent to Greece. He had also replaced the seasoned 6th Australian Division with the 9th Australian Division, but, because of supply difficulties, part of the division had been retained at Tobruk, 280 air miles northeast.

Wavell thought the few Italians still in Tripolitania could be disregarded. And though he'd received intelligence reports that the Germans were sending "one armored brigade," Wavell concluded, on March 2, 1941, "I do not think that with this force the enemy will attempt to recover Benghazi."

That was a reasonable conclusion. No ordinary general would attack with such a small force. But Rommel was not an ordinary general.

Since none of his tanks had arrived, Rommel got a workshop near Tripoli to produce large numbers of dummy tanks, which he mounted on Volkswagens. These small vehicles served as the jeeps of the German army. They looked deceptively like tanks—at least to RAF reconnaissance pilots—and gave the British command pause.

Meantime Rommel moved up the two German battalions and his dummy tanks to Mugtaa, twenty miles west of El Agheila. Elements of two Italian divisions, the Brescia and Pavia, followed, along with the Ariete,

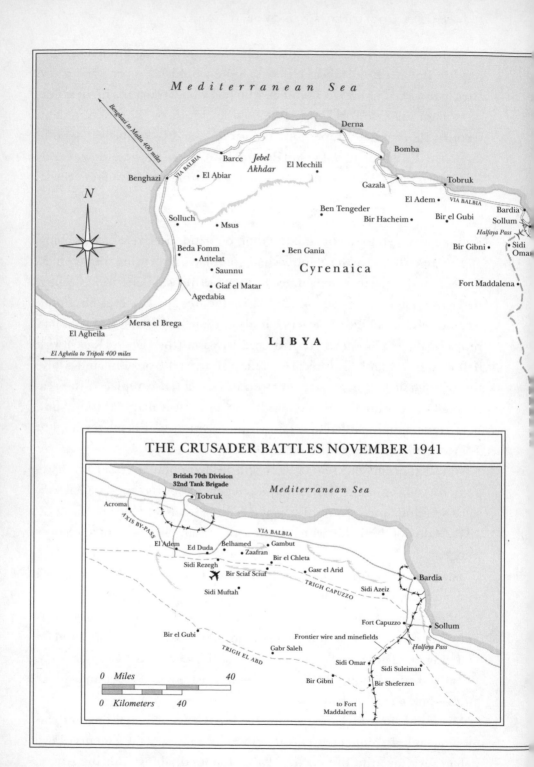

**Mediterranean Sea**

Benghazi to Malta 400 miles

Derna

Bomba

Barce · *Jebel Akhdar*

El Mechili

El Abiar ·

Benghazi ·

VIA BALBIA

Gazala

Tobruk

El Adem · VIA BALBIA

Bardia

Solluch ·

Ben Tengeder ·

Bir Hacheim ·

Bir el Gubi ·

Sollum

Msus ·

*Halfaya Pass*

Beda Fomm ·

Bir Gibni ·

Sidi Omar

· Antelat

· Ben Gania

**N**

· Saunnu

**Cyrenaica**

· Giaf el Matar

Fort Maddalena ·

Agedabia

· Mersa el Brega

**LIBYA**

El Agheila

El Agheila to Tripoli 400 miles

## THE CRUSADER BATTLES NOVEMBER 1941

British 70th Division
32nd Tank Brigade

*Mediterranean Sea*

Acroma ·

· Tobruk

AXIS BY-PASS

VIA BALBIA

El Adem ·

Ed Duda ·

Belhamed · Gambut

Bardia

Sidi Rezegh ·

· Zaafran

Bir el Chleta

· Gasr el Arid

Bir Sciaf Sciuf

TRIGH CAPUZZO

Sidi Azeiz

Sidi Muftah ·

Fort Capuzzo

Sollum

Bir el Gubi ·

Frontier wire and minefields

*Halfaya Pass*

TRIGH EL ABD

Gabr Saleh ·

Sidi Omar

Sidi Suleiman

Bir Gibni ·

· Bir Sheferzen

| 0 | Miles | 40 |

| 0 | Kilometers | 40 |

to Fort
Maddalena

# WAR IN THE DESERT 1941–42

0  Miles  100

0  Kilometers  100

Sidi Barrani

Buq Buq

Habata

Mersa Matruh

Fuka

El Daba

El Alamein

Alexandria

Nile Delta

Libyan Plateau

Qattara
Depression

Alam Halfa
Ridge

Cairo

Nile River

E G Y P T

Jeffrey L. Ward

# THE GAZALA BATTLES MAY–JUNE 1942

Mediterranean Sea

Minefields

Bir Temrad

Gazala

Alem Hamza

1st S. African Div

VIA BALBIA

209

Acroma

Kings
Cross

Tobruk

VIA BALBIA

32nd
Tank Brig

50th Div

Eluet et
Tamar

1st
Tank Brig

151st Brig

69th Brig

Sidra Ridge

Rigel Ridge

CALDRON

Raml Ridge

Batrina Ridge

Bir Lefa

El Adem

Ed Duda

8th Army
Hqs

TRIGH
ENVER BEI

Mteifel
Rotonda

Got el Ualeb

Sidi Murtah

Aslagh Ridge

Bir el
Tamar

Knightsbridge

Naduret et
Ghesceuasc

Belhamed

Zaafran

Gambut

Sidi Rezegh

178

175

Bir el Chleta

TRIGH CAPUZZO

150th Brig

Minefields

Bir el
Harmat

175

TRIGH EL ABD

Free French Brig

Bir Hacheim

Bir el Gubi

0  Miles  40

0  Kilometers  40

Italy's only armored division in Africa, which had just eighty tanks, most of them obsolete light models.

General Neame, suspicious of the buildup at Mugtaa, modest as it was, moved the main British body back to Agedabia, seventy miles northeast, leaving only a small holding force at El Agheila.

On March 11, the 5th Panzer Regiment of 5th Light Division—the "armored brigade" Wavell had heard about—arrived at Tripoli. This regiment, the only armored force that Africa Corps was to get until the 15th Panzer Division arrived, had 120 tanks, half of them medium Mark IIIs and IVs, the rest light tanks with only a limited combat role. Although 5th Light was not a panzer division, it had the normal complement of tanks of a panzer division in 1941. This total, however, was only a little more than half the number Rommel had commanded in his 7th Panzer Division in the 1940 campaign. After the French campaign, Hitler doubled the number of panzer divisions, but gave each division fewer tanks.

On March 19, Rommel flew to Hitler's headquarters to get fresh instructions. Walther von Brauchitsch, commander in chief of the army, and Franz Halder, chief of staff, told Rommel there was no intention of striking a decisive blow in Africa, and he could expect no reinforcements.

Rommel tried to convince them that the weakness of the British in North Africa should be exploited. But his pleas fell on deaf ears. Brauchitsch and Halder were preoccupied with preparations for Barbarossa and distracted by the campaign against Greece about to commence. To them, Libya was a sideshow to a sideshow.

Rommel wanted two additional panzer divisions to complete conquest of Egypt. It was obvious that transporting them to Tripoli was the key problem, and to solve it Malta had to be neutralized by severe bombing attacks or seized in an air-sea operation. But Halder chose to ignore this unmistakable fact and asked Rommel how two additional divisions could be maintained and supplied. Rommel, exasperated, replied: "I don't give a damn. That's your affair!"

Back in Africa, Rommel sent his reconnaissance battalion to seize El Agheila on March 24. The small British force put up little fight, and withdrew to Mersa el Brega, twenty miles east. This was a potentially formidable position. Mersa el Brega was on a commanding height near the sea, while to the south was the Bir es Suera salt marsh, and south of the marsh was the extensive, sandy Wadi Faregh. Both were almost impassable for vehicles.

Rommel could wait for the rest of his troops to arrive at the end of May, or attack with the small force he had in place. For him the decision was easy: attack. If he waited, the British would have time to build a powerful defensive line.

When elements of 5th Light Division struck on March 31, the British hurled them back. In the afternoon Rommel found a way around the British between the Via Balbia and the sea. That night 8th Machine Gun Battalion's vehicles crashed through the gap in a headlong rolling attack, flanked the British, and caused them to beat a hasty retreat, leaving behind fifty Bren gun-carriers and thirty lorries.

Luftwaffe reports showed that the British were pulling back from Agedabia. It was an opportunity Rommel couldn't resist. He at once ordered his forces to advance on Agedabia, gaining it on April 2.

Neame, with Wavell's permission, decided to evacuate Benghazi and retreat eastward. The abrupt withdrawal was a bonanza for Rommel, and he rushed to exploit it.

"I decided to stay on the heels of the retreating enemy, and make a bid to seize the whole of Cyrenaica at one stroke," Rommel wrote.

Now commenced one of the most dramatic running battles in world history, in which an inferior force attacked and completely routed a superior enemy. Rommel ordered the reconnaissance battalion to drive straight toward Benghazi on the Via Balbia behind the retreating British, while Ariete Division's reconnaissance battalion was to rush across the chord of the Cyrenaican bulge to get to the sea and cut off retreat before the British arrived.

Rommel made the decision to cut through the Cyrenaican interior despite warnings from Italian generals that the route was a death trap. Rommel examined the country by air, found it good for driving, and the Italians' fears baseless.

Rommel learned that the British had already abandoned Benghazi, and at once ordered the 3rd Reconnaissance Battalion to drive into the town. It arrived on the night of April 3.

On the morning of April 4, Rommel directed the main body of 5th Light Division to move through Ben Gania and on to the sea at Derna, while

Ariete Division following the same route turned north to seize El Mechili, south of Jebel el Akdar, the mountain range along the coast. Speed was now everything. Rommel wanted to bring at least part of the British army to battle before it withdrew from Cyrenaica and escaped danger.

During the night, Rommel learned that British forces were still holding Msus, about seventy miles southeast of Benghazi and fifty miles northwest of Ben Gania. He also learned that the best route for his supply trucks was through Msus.

On the morning of April 5, Rommel ordered most of his armor—5th Panzer Regiment and forty Italian tanks—to head straight for Msus, destroy the enemy there, and press on to Mechili. Though held up by sandstorms, the tanks took Msus on the evening of April 6, but got lost on the way to Mechili, moved far to the north, and were only discovered by Rommel flying in his light Storch reconnaissance plane on the evening of April 7.

Meanwhile, a newly arrived British motorized brigade had occupied Mechili. While Rommel sent a small force to the sea at Derna to close the Via Balbia in both directions, he sent his main force from east and west against the British brigade at Mechili on April 8, forcing its surrender. He then rushed tanks on to Derna, where German forces captured many more prisoners, including General Neame and General O'Connor, who had come back from Egypt to assist Neame. Their unescorted car had run into Germans on the Via Balbia.

By April 11, 1941, the British had been swept entirely out of Cyrenaica and over the frontier into Egypt, except for two divisions that shut themselves up in the port of Tobruk, which the Italians had built into a fortress before the war, and which the Royal Navy could supply by sea.

Rommel had won by deceiving the British into believing his forces were much stronger than they were, and he moved with great speed, bewildering the British and causing their forces to disintegrate.

Rommel had too little power to undertake a heavy assault against Tobruk, yet he insisted on mounting several attacks, all of which failed against the resolute Australian and British garrison.

✠          ✠          ✠

The date of Rommel's eviction of the British from Libya, except Tobruk, is significant. The campaign against Yugoslavia and Greece had been launched on April 6, and German forces were already scoring decisive successes, indicating that the campaign would soon be completed.

Rommel had handed Hitler an entirely unexpected victory that left the Africa Corps poised within striking distance of the Suez Canal. All that would now be required to win Egypt would be the swift transfer, as soon as the Greek campaign ended, of two panzer divisions to reinforce Rommel. The British were reeling from defeats in Greece and Libya, and could not have withstood a concerted attack.

The garrison at Tobruk could have been blocked by Italian divisions, braced by a few German tanks. With an offensive launched against the Egyptian delta, the British could not have mounted an offensive from that fortress.

Admiral Raeder and the naval staff recognized what Rommel had achieved, and proposed to Hitler "a decisive Egypt-Suez offensive." If Rommel had been reinforced, he almost surely would have occupied Egypt long before the end of 1941.

Unfortunately for the Germans, none of this happened. Hitler didn't recognize the gift that Rommel had handed him and turned his gaze once more on the Soviet Union.

☩          ☩          ☩

In his appraisal of his first campaign, Rommel came to virtually the same conclusions that Admiral Raeder had reached half a year previously.

"It is my view," he wrote, "that it would have been better if we had kept our hands off Greece altogether, and rather created a concentration of strength in North Africa to drive the British right out of the Mediterranean area."

The air forces employed in Greece should have been used to protect convoys to Africa, he added. Malta should have been taken instead of Crete. Powerful German motorized forces in North Africa could then have seized the whole of the British-occupied Mediterranean coastline, as well as the Middle East as sources for oil and bases for attack on Russia.

"This would have isolated southeastern Europe. Greece, Yugoslavia, and Crete would have had no choice but to submit, for supplies and support from the British Empire would have been impossible."

Rommel blamed his superiors in the army high command. He was right in noting the reluctance of the senior generals to endorse a full-scale operation in Libya. But at the time Rommel didn't know it was Hitler who had rejected a Mediterranean strategy, and Brauchitsch and Halder had adjusted their viewpoint to conform. The silence of Brauchitsch, Halder, Jodl, and Keitel in the presence of Rommel's incredible gift speaks volumes, either about their lack of vision or about their fear of Hitler.

# 8  BARBAROSSA

THE PURPOSE OF MILITARY STRATEGY IS TO DIMINISH THE POSSIBILITY OF RESIS-
tance. It should be the aim of every leader to discover the weaknesses of
the enemy and to pierce his Achilles' heel. This is how battles and wars
are best won.

Such advice goes back at least to Sun Tzu in the fifth century B.C., but
it is extraordinarily difficult for human beings to follow. The attack
against the Soviet Union on June 22, 1941, is the most powerful example
in the twentieth century of how a leader and a nation—in this case Adolf
Hitler and Germany—can ignore clear, eternal rules of successful warfare, and pursue a course that leads straight to destruction.

Attacking Russia head-on was wrong to begin with, because it guaranteed the greatest resistance, not the least. A direct attack also forces an
enemy back on his reserves and supplies, while it constantly lengthens the
supply and reinforcement lines of the attacker. The better strategy is to
separate the enemy from his supplies and reserves. That is why an attack
on the flank is more likely to be successful.

Nevertheless Hitler could still have won if he had struck at the Soviet
Union's weakness, instead of its strength.

His most disastrous error was to go into the Soviet Union as a conqueror
instead of a liberator. The Soviet people had suffered enormously at the
hands of the Communist autocracy for two decades. Millions died when
the Reds forced people off their land to create collective farms. Millions
more were obliged to move great distances and work long hours under ter-

rible conditions in factories and construction projects. The secret police punished any resistance with death or transportation to horrible prison gulags in Siberia. In the gruesome purges of the 1930s, Joseph Stalin had systematically killed all leaders and all military officers who, in his paranoid mind, posed the slightest threat to his dictatorship. Life for the ordinary Russian was drab, full of exhausting work, and dangerous. At the same time, the Soviet Union was an empire ruling over a collection of subjugated peoples who were violently opposed to rule from the Kremlin.

Vast numbers of these people would have risen in rebellion if Hitler's legions had entered with the promise of freedom and elimination of Soviet oppression. Had Hitler done this, the Soviet Union would have collapsed.

Such a policy would not have given Hitler his *Lebensraum* immediately. But once the Soviet Union had been shattered, he could have put into effect anything he wanted to with the pieces that remained.

Hitler followed precisely the opposite course of action. His "commissar order" called for the instant shooting down of Communist party agents in the army. He sent *Einsatzgruppen*—or extermination detachments—to come behind the army and rout out and murder Jews. He resolved to deport or allow millions of Slavs to starve in order to empty the land for future German settlers.

Two days before the Germans struck, Alfred Rosenberg, Hitler's commissioner for the regions to be conquered, told his closest collaborators: "The job of feeding the German people stands at the top of the list of Germany's claims in the east. . . . We see absolutely no reason for any obligation on our part to feed also the Russian people."

The genuine welcome that German soldiers received as they entered Soviet towns and villages in the first days of the campaign was quickly replaced by fear, hatred, and a bitter guerrilla war behind the lines that slowed supplies to the front, killed thousands of Germans, and increasingly hobbled the German army.

As wrong as this policy was, Hitler's actual military plans were so false strategically that they could only succeed if the Red Army collapsed from internal stress. That, in fact, is what Hitler counted on. He did not expect to win by a superior method or concept, but by relying on the Russian army to disintegrate after a series of initial battles.

Great generals don't win wars in this fashion. They don't depend upon their enemies to make mistakes or give up. A great general relies upon his *own* ideas, initiative, skill, and maneuvers to put the enemy in a position where he must do the general's bidding. A great general wins his battles *before* he fights them. He obligates the enemy to take positions he cannot defend or from which he cannot extricate himself.

Hitler's greatest strategic mistake was his refusal to concentrate on a single, decisive goal. He sought to gain—all at the same time—three widely distant objectives: Leningrad, because it was the birthplace of Russian Communism; Ukraine and the Caucasus beyond, for its abundant foodstuffs, 60 percent of Soviet industry, and the bulk of the Soviet Union's oil; and Moscow, because it was the capital of the Soviet Union and its nerve center.

Hitler wanted *all* of them. Indeed, he expected to reach the line Archangel–Caspian Sea in 1941. That is 300 miles *east* of Moscow, and only about 450 miles from the Ural Mountains. But Germany did not have the strength to achieve all these goals in a single year's campaign. At best, it had the strength to achieve one.

Hitler scorned such a limitation, and ordered Army Group North to go for Leningrad, Army Group Center for Moscow, and Army Group South for Ukraine. These objectives, spread over the entire western face of the Soviet Union, could not possibly be coordinated. Leningrad is 940 airline miles from Odessa on the Black Sea. Each army group would be required to conduct a separate campaign. Because resources were to be divided in three directions, no single effort would have the strength to achieve a war-winning decision.

The task Hitler set for Germany was almost inconceivable. He hoped to seize a million square miles of the Soviet Union in 1941, a region the size of the United States east of the Mississippi. The campaign in the west, on the other hand, had been fought out in an area of 50,000 square miles, roughly the size of North Carolina or New York State. Therefore, the ratio of space to men was twenty times greater in the east than in the west.

Field Marshal Brauchitsch, commander of the army, and General Halder, chief of staff, wanted the primary objective to be Moscow, with forces concentrated in the center. They contended that conquest of Leningrad, Ukraine, and the Caucasus depended on defeating the Red

Army. The main body of this army, or an essential part of it, would be met on the road to Moscow.

Stalin would be compelled to fight for Moscow. It was the hub of railroads, mecca of world Communism, headquarters of the highly centralized government, and a great industrial center employing more than a million workers.

Moreover, an attack into the center of the Soviet Union would turn the nation's vastness—generally thought of as its greatest asset—into a liability. Once the Germans possessed Moscow's communications node, Red Army forces on either side could not coordinate their efforts. One would be cut off from aid and succor to the other, and the Germans in the central position between the two could have defeated each separately.

The German army and economy could support a drive on Moscow. Though 560 miles east of the frontier, it was connected by a paved highway and railroads.

This would have still been a direct, frontal assault against the strength of the Red Army, but the ratio of force to space was so low in Russia that German mechanized forces could always find openings for indirect local advances into the Soviet rear. At the same time the widely spaced cities at which roads and railways converged offered the Germans alternative targets. While threatening one city north and another city south, they could actually strike at a third in between. But the Russians, not knowing which objective the Germans had chosen, would have to defend all three.

Hitler understood that he could not defeat the entire Red Army all at once. But he hoped to solve the problem by committing two of his four panzer groups, under Heinz Guderian and Hermann Hoth, to Army Group Center, commanded by Fedor von Bock, with the aim of destroying Red Army forces in front of Moscow in a series of giant encirclements— *Kesselschlachten,* or caldron battles. The Russians, to his thinking, could be eliminated in place.

Army Group Center was to attack just north of the Pripet Marshes, a huge swampy region 220 miles wide and 120 miles deep beginning some 170 miles east of Warsaw that effectively divided the front in half. Bock's armies, led by the panzers, were to advance from East Prussia and the German-Russian frontier along the Bug River to Smolensk.

Army Group North under Wilhelm von Leeb, with one panzer group

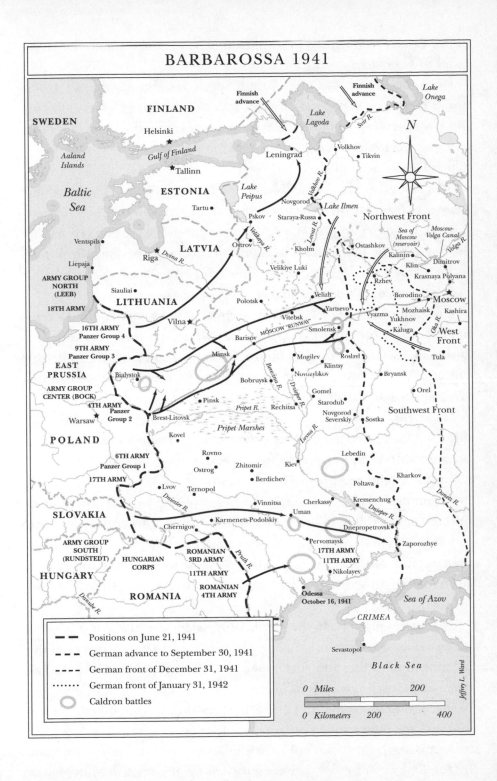

# BARBAROSSA 1941

**SWEDEN**

**FINLAND**

Helsinki •

*Aaland
Islands*

*Gulf of Finland*

★ Tallinn

*Baltic
Sea*

**ESTONIA**

Tartu •

Finnish
advance

*Lake Lagoda*

Finnish
advance

*Suir R.*

*Lake
Onega*

Volkhov •

Leningrad

• Tikvin

Novgorod

*Lake Ilmen*

*N*

Ventspils •

Liepaja •

**ARMY GROUP
NORTH
(LEEB)**

**18TH ARMY**

Riga ★

*Dvina R.*

Siauliai •

**LITHUANIA**

Vilna ★

*Lake
Peipus*

Pskov •

Ostrov •

*Velikaya R.*

Staraya-Russa •

Kholm •

Velikiye Luki •

Polotsk •

*Lovat R.*

Ostashkov •

Velizh •

Yartsevo •

Vitebsk •

Smolensk •

*Sea of
Moscow
(reservoir)*

*Moscow-
Volga Canal*

*Volga R.*

Kalinin •

Klin •

Dimitrov •

Krasnaya Polyana •

Rzhev •

Borodino •

Vyazma •

**Northwest Front**

Mozhaisk •

**Moscow**

Kashira •

*Oka R.*

Yukhnov •

Kaluga •

**West
Front**

**16TH ARMY
Panzer Group 4**

**9TH ARMY
Panzer Group 3**

**EAST
PRUSSIA**

**ARMY GROUP
CENTER (BOCK)**

**4TH ARMY
Panzer
Group 2**

Warsaw ★

**POLAND**

Bialystok •

Brest-Litovsk •

Barisov •

Minsk •

MOSCOW "RUNWAY"

Mogilev •

*Berezina R.*

*Dnieper R.*

Bobruysk •

Novozybkov •

Klintsy •

Roslavl •

Gomel •

Tula •

Bryansk •

Orel •

Pinsk •

*Pripet R.*

Rechitsa •

Starodub •

Novgorod
Severskiy •

Sostka •

**Southwest Front**

Kovel •

*Pripet Marshes*

*Desna R.*

**6TH ARMY
Panzer Group 1**

**17TH ARMY**

Lvov •

Ternopol •

Rovno •

Ostrog •

Zhitomir •

Berdichev •

Kiev •

Lebedin •

Kharkov •

*Dniester R.*

Vinnitsa •

Cherkassy •

Poltava •

Kremenchug •

*Donets R.*

**SLOVAKIA**

Chernigov •

Karmenets-Podolskiy •

Uman •

*Dnieper R.*

Dnepropetrovsk •

Zaporozhye •

**ARMY GROUP
SOUTH
(RUNDSTEDT)**

**HUNGARY**

**HUNGARIAN
CORPS**

**ROMANIAN
3RD ARMY**

**11TH ARMY**

**ROMANIAN
4TH ARMY**

*Pruth R.*

**ROMANIA**

*Danube R.*

Pervomaysk •

**17TH ARMY**

**11TH ARMY**

Nikolayev •

**Odessa
October 16, 1941**

*Sea of Azov*

*CRIMEA*

Sevastopol •

*Black Sea*

— — —  Positions on June 21, 1941

– – –  German advance to September 30, 1941

- - -  German front of December 31, 1941

· · · · ·  German front of January 31, 1942

◯  Caldron battles

0   Miles                    200

0   Kilometers    200         400

*Jeffrey L. Ward*

under Erich Hoepner, was to drive from East Prussia through the Baltic states to Leningrad.

Gerd von Rundstedt's Army Group South, with the last panzer group under Ewald von Kleist, was to thrust south of the Pripet Marshes toward the Ukrainian capital of Kiev, 300 airline miles from the jump-off points along and below the Bug, then drive to the industrial Donetz river basin, 430 miles southeast of Kiev.

The first great encirclement was to be in Army Group Center around Bialystok, fewer than sixty miles east of the German-Soviet boundary in Poland, the other around Minsk, 180 miles farther east. The two panzer groups were then to press on to Smolensk, 200 miles beyond Minsk, and bring about a third *Kesselschlacht*. After that, Hitler planned to shift the two panzer groups north to help capture Leningrad.

Only after Leningrad was seized, according to his directive of December 18, 1940, ordering Barbarossa, the German attack on the Soviet Union in 1941, "are further offensive operations to be initiated with the objective of occupying the important center of communications and of armaments manufacture, Moscow."

Hitler, however, showed his intention of gaining all three objectives by directing that, when the caldron battles were completed (and Leningrad presumably taken), pursuit was to proceed not only toward Moscow but also into Ukraine to seize the Donetz basin.

In summary, Hitler's original directive required massive strikes deep into the Soviet Union in three directions by three army groups, followed by a shift of half the army's armor 400 miles north to capture Leningrad, then a return of this armor to press on Moscow, while Army Group South continued to drive into Ukraine, over 700 miles from the German-Soviet frontier.

This was impossible. In the event, Hitler made the task worse because he seized an opportunistic chance to destroy a number of armies in the Ukraine around Kiev and abandoned his original strategy. Once the caldron battles were completed in Army Group Center, he sent only one panzer group north toward Leningrad, and ordered the other south to help seal the enemy into a pocket east of Kiev.

Army Group North did not have enough strength to seize Leningrad. By the time the diverted panzers got back on the road to Moscow, the rainy season had set in, then the Russian winter. As a consequence the strike for Moscow failed as well. With insufficient armor remaining in the south, the effort to seize all of Ukraine and open a path to the oil of the Caucasus also collapsed.

Hitler, by trying for too much, and then altering his priorities by sending a panzer group from the center into the Ukraine, failed everywhere. These failures meant Germany had lost the war. By December 1941, there was no hope of anything better than a negotiated peace. This Hitler refused to consider.

✠     ✠     ✠

Hitler's plan rested on two false assumptions. The first was that he would have time enough (even without the shift of panzers to the Ukraine) to switch armor to the north then back to the center in time to win a decisive victory before the rains and snows of autumn. Distances were simply too great, Russian roads and climate too poor, and Red Army resistance too intense for such a plan to have had any hope of success. As Guderian summarized the campaign to his wife on December 10, 1941, "The enemy, the size of the country, and the foulness of the weather were all grossly underestimated."

The second great mistaken assumption was that after destroying the Red Army in caldron battles, Stalin would be unable to create any more armies. That is, once the *Kesselschlachten* were over, the Soviet Union would collapse, and the Germans could occupy the rest of the country at their leisure and without resistance. But Hitler did not count on the resilience of Soviet leadership and the willingness of the Russian people to defend their homeland. Moreover, Hitler's ally Japan refused to attack Siberia, allowing Stalin to release a quarter of a million soldiers to rush west to fight the Germans at a crucial moment.

Although Moscow was the only target the Germans might have gained in 1941, neither Brauchitsch nor Halder was willing to confront Hitler on the point. They hoped, when the time came, they could convince him to keep the panzers in the middle, change his ideas about shifting them, and continue the drive on Moscow. They were wrong.

✠     ✠     ✠

The concept of caldron battles appears on the surface to be a highly dangerous strategy—to rely on the enemy conveniently allowing German forces to wrap themselves around great concentrations of his troops, and forcing them to surrender. However, Stalin made this a feasible strategy because he lined up the vast majority of his forces along the frontier. Consequently, German breakthroughs at a few points would permit German forces to sweep past and behind large segments of the Red Army, blocking their retreat and creating a caldron.

Such encirclements were a part of German doctrine, advocated by German theorists as far back as Karl Clausewitz in the early nineteenth century. They modeled their ideas on Hannibal's classic destruction of a Roman army at Cannae by encirclement in 216 B.C. The greatest German victory up to the 1940 campaign in the west had been another—the encirclement of a Russian army at Tannenburg in East Prussia in August 1914.

The Russian campaign was not to be a repetition of the blitzkrieg of 1940 in the west. Rather it was to be a series of classic encirclements, accelerated only by using the panzers to swing around the enemy flanks to create caldrons.

✠        ✠        ✠

In most wars, the inherent strength of the belligerents becomes more and more important once past the initial or opening campaign or phase. If a power is unable to achieve a decision with its original force, then long-term factors generally decide the war. Superior power exerted over time to wear down an opponent is called attrition. This is the single greatest danger that a weaker belligerent encounters.

This is what Adolf Hitler faced. The Soviet Union's resources were immense compared to Germany's. Its great size forced an enormous dispersal of German military strength. Its population was more than twice Germany's. It had unlimited quantities of oil, minerals, and power. Soviet war production over time would outstrip German production. In addition, the Soviet Union could tap the resources of the rest of the world, especially the United States, because the Allies controlled the seas and could deliver goods by way of Iran.

Hitler had to gain a quick victory or be forced into a war of attrition that he could not win. Hitler refused to see this, and it was the cause of his destruction.

✠          ✠          ✠

For immediate use in the attack, Hitler assembled 107 infantry divisions, 19 panzer divisions, 18 motorized divisions, and one cavalry division, a total of three million men, with supporting troops. This represented the bulk of the total German strength of 205 divisions. The Barbarossa forces included 3,350 tanks, 7,200 artillery pieces, and 2,770 aircraft.

The great weakness of the panzer divisions was the condition of the roads. In the vast Soviet Union there were only 40,000 miles of paved highways. Most routes were dirt and turned into muddy morasses in wet weather. In a panzer division fewer than 300 vehicles were fully tracked, while nearly 3,000 were wheeled and largely restricted to roads. In the west this had been little problem, because of the abundance of all-weather roads. In Russia their relative absence meant that panzer mobility would end with the first mud.

The Red Army was not prepared for the German onslaught, in part because of the condition of its forces, in part because too many troops were positioned right against the frontier, but also in part because Joseph Stalin had guessed wrong where the main German onslaught would come and put a preponderance of his forces south of the Pripet marshes.

The Russians assembled 171 divisions in five army groups or "fronts" along the frontier. Behind the five forward fronts, separate groups of five field armies were being formed as a second strategic echelon. This Reserve Front was assembling on the line of the Dnieper and Dvina rivers, some 180 miles east and 100 miles northeast of the frontier. Before hostilities these forming reserves were virtually invisible to German intelligence.

Soviet authorities had ample warning of the attack, but Stalin hoped the Soviet Union could escape Hitler's wrath, at least for a time, and ignored plain evidence.

On March 20, 1941, Sumner Welles, United States undersecretary of state, informed the Soviet ambassador of the attack, picked up by the American commercial attaché in Berlin. Winston Churchill alerted Stalin in a personal note delivered on April 19, 1941, based on Ultra intelligence intercepts (which he didn't reveal to Stalin). American Ambassador Laurence Steinhardt informed Molotov of reports to U.S. legations pinpointing the attack almost to the day. High-altitude Luftwaffe reconnaissance aircraft made more than 300 overflights of Soviet territory in the weeks leading up to D-Day, June 22, 1941. On June 16, the German embassy evacuated all but essential personnel. There were many more warnings.

Up to the last day, the Soviet Union continued to supply Germany with raw materials, including 4,000 tons of rubber, plus manganese and other minerals shipped from the Far East over the Trans-Siberian Railway.

But Stalin had actually been preparing for war. On May 6, he took over personally as chairman of the Council of People's Commissars, or prime minister, replacing Molotov, who remained foreign minister. It was the first time Stalin had taken a government office.

In April Stalin implemented readiness measures, including partial mobilization. He transferred forces from Siberia to the west, sent twenty-eight rifle divisions and four armies to the border, and began assembling a fifth army near Moscow. In late May he called up 800,000 reservists.

Nevertheless, the Soviet Union was not ready. Its forces were poorly arrayed, trained, and equipped. Soviet political leadership had been paralyzed by its fixation on maintaining peace. Hope clouded reality.

For example, when Mikhail P. Kirponos, commander of the Kiev military district, deployed some troops to the frontier in early June, the Kremlin countermanded the order, and told Kirponos flatly: "There will be no war."

The purges had left a severe shortage of trained commanders and staff officers, unlike the German army with its long emphasis on officer quality, its experience in war so far, and its supreme confidence. Red Army officers had learned to keep a low profile. Any independent judgment might lead to a firing squad or a trip to a Siberian gulag.

Few troops were concentrated where most needed. Aside from more troops being stationed below the Pripet Marshes, they were spread evenly across the front, and not many were held back for counterattack. These dispositions played directly into German tactics of punching a few holes with overwhelming force, then sending powerful motorized forces rushing through the gaps into the rear.

The Soviets had about 110 infantry (or "rifle") divisions along the western frontier. In theory they were about the same size (15,000 men) as German divisions, but in June 1941 they averaged only about 8,000 men.

The greatest fault of the Red Army was its organization of armored and motorized forces. It possessed fifty tank divisions and twenty-five mechanized (motorized) divisions, far more than the Germans, but Stalin had not accepted the German doctrine of concentration of armor. The largest armored formation was a mechanized corps of one motorized and two tank divisions. These corps were widely dispersed across the front, not massed as were German panzer formations. Furthermore, each corps's divisions were often a hundred kilometers apart. Some corps had the job of supporting local counterattacks. Others were held in reserve to take part in counterthrusts under front (army group) control. Soviet armor, spread out in small packets, thereby repeated the error that the British and French had made in the 1940 campaign.

# 9 FALLING BETWEEN TWO STOOLS

As Hitler left Berlin by train for his new headquarters *Wolfsschanze* (wolf's lair or entrenchment) near Rastenburg in East Prussia, Luftwaffe aircraft rose from airstrips at 3 A.M. Sunday, June 22, 1941, and bombed and strafed Soviet airfields, catching hundreds of planes on the ground and attacking any that rose into the air. Before the day was up, the Luftwaffe had destroyed 1,200 Red aircraft. Within days the Germans had driven most Soviet planes from the sky and achieved air supremacy.

German panzers massed at key crossing points broke across the frontier and drove deep into the interior. Everywhere they achieved almost total surprise and were successful, except in the south. Here the German infantry struck strong defenses west of Lvov (Lemberg) and on the Styr River.

Stalin's belief that Hitler would make his main effort into Ukraine had resulted in the Southwestern Front being especially strong in armor—six mechanized corps, with a larger proportion of new T-34s than elsewhere. The T-34 was a great shock to the Germans. It had good armor, good speed, a high-velocity 76-millimeter gun, and was superior to any German tank. Mikhail Kirponos, Southwest commander, mounted armor attacks on both flanks of the panzer thrusts of Kleist's Panzer Group 1. The 5th Army operating out of the Pripet swamps had a firm base for the assault. The 6th Army on the open steppe to the south did not. The fight was tough, but the two arms of the Russian pincers never met, and Kleist drove on to seize Lvov on June 30. From there the panzers swept past Rovno and Ostrog through the "Zhitomir corridor" toward Kiev.

In the extreme south, the 11th Army of Romanians and Germans attacked across the Pruth River into Bessarabia, winning it in a week, then moving on, with all-Romanian formations, to besiege Odessa along the Black Sea.

Army Group North pushed out of East Prussia, led by Panzer Group 4 (Hoepner), and pressed through the Baltic states toward Leningrad.

In Army Group Center, Guderian's Panzer Group 2 plunged across the Bug River at Brest-Litovsk, and Hoth's Panzer Group 3 drove out of East Prussia with Minsk, 215 miles northeast of Brest, as their initial objective. The Russian garrison defended the fortress at Brest, but it was hopeless because German infantry surrounded it and pounded it into submission in a week.

Since the Russians were surprised, Guderian's panzers got across the Bug easily, some of his tanks fording thirteen feet of water using water-proofing developed for Operation Sea Lion.

Two days later, while meeting with a group of panzer commanders at Slonim, a hundred miles northeast of Brest, two Russian tanks appeared out of the smoke, pursued by two German Mark IVs. The Russians spotted the officers.

"We were immediately subjected to a rain of shells, which, fired at such extremely close range, both deafened and blinded us for a few moments," Guderian wrote.

Most of the officers were old soldiers who hit the ground, and were uninjured. But a rear-echelon colonel visiting from Germany didn't react fast enough and was badly wounded. The Russian tanks forced their way into the town, firing away, but were finally put out of action.

As the panzers moved eastward and enveloped both sides of the Russian forces around Bialystok, Field Marshal Bock ordered his infantry 4th and 9th Armies to encircle these bypassed Russians (twelve divisions) east of Bialystok. The first great *Kesselschlacht* began to develop.

By June 28, Guderian's panzers had reached Bobruysk on the Beresina River, 170 miles northeast of Brest-Litovsk, while Hoth's tanks had seized Minsk, eighty miles northwest of Bobruysk, thereby nearly closing off fifteen Russian divisions in another caldron west of Minsk.

The Germans learned that they could outmaneuver the Russians with their *Schnellentruppen*, or fast troops, but could not outfight them. Everywhere the Russians resisted stoutly. They were slow to panic and surrender when closed into caldrons. One German general described the first days of the campaign: "Nature was hard, and in her midst were human beings just as hard and insensitive—indifferent to weather, hunger, and thirst. The Russian civilian was tough, and the Russian soldier still tougher. He seemed to have an illimitable capacity for obedience and endurance."

In both *Kesselschlachten* the Russians took advantage of the fact that the panzers had moved on, and German infantry had to close the circles. Many escaped, though in small groups. Those who remained fought doggedly, but made only limited efforts to break out. Part of the reason was the strong rings the Germans finally threw around the surrounded troops. Another was that Soviet commanders feared they would be shot if they ordered withdrawal—something that shortly did happen. Another was that the Russians had few vehicles and little means to escape. The Russians also were more willing to surrender in the first weeks of the war because they did not know the murderous treatment they would receive in captivity. These factors explain the stupendous numbers of Russians who passed into German POW cages during the summer of 1941.

It did not take the Russian people many weeks to realize they were facing an implacable, bloodthirsty foe, however. The anti-Bolshevik indoctrination of the German army had led to a feeling of intolerance of and superiority over Russian *"Untermenschen."* Hitler directed that soldiers guilty of breaking international law were to be excused. This no-court-martial order released barbaric tendencies in many soldiers, and the "commissar order" caused some to feel any Red—commissar, or ordinary soldier—might be shot on the spot.

Only a few days after the start of the campaign, General Joachim Lemelsen, commander of Guderian's 47th Panzer Corps, complained that shootings of Russian POWs and deserters were not being done properly. He explained the correct method:

"The Fuehrer's instruction calls for ruthless action against Bolshevism (political commissars), and any kind of partisans [guerrillas]. People who have been clearly identified as such should be taken aside and shot only by an order of an officer."

Since the Germans could label anybody a commissar or a partisan, Russians soon stopped surrendering and often fought to the death in desperate situations.

This was not true in the caldron battles around Bialystok and Minsk, and up to July 9 the Germans took 233,000 prisoners, including numerous generals, 1,800 cannons, and destroyed 3,300 tanks, but very few T-34s, which appeared only a few times and in small numbers. Even so, about as many Russians escaped from the German pincers as were caught within them.

Meanwhile Hoth's and Guderian's panzer groups, now formed into the 4th Panzer Army under Günther von Kluge, were already rushing 200 miles beyond Minsk for the third great series of encirclements near Smolensk. Since Army Group Center's infantry divisions were still miles behind the panzers, Kluge wrapped his tanks, half-tracks, and motorized divisions around three caldrons, two smaller ones east of Mogilev and west of Nevel, a greater one between Orscha and Smolensk.

After grim resistance the Germans shattered three Soviet armies, and by August 6 had taken 310,000 POWs, destroyed 3,200 tanks, and captured 3,100 guns. Nevertheless, about 200,000 Russians escaped to fall back and continue to block the road to Moscow.

In the other two army groups advances had been spectacular as well.

In Army Group South, Kleist's Panzer Group 1, with the help of 17th Army and a Hungarian corps, encircled two Russian groups around Uman, 120 miles south of Kiev, capturing 103,000 Russians.

Army Group North occupied Latvia. Panzer Group 4 (Hoepner) pressed through Ostrov, about two hundred miles southwest of Leningrad, while 18th Army (Küchler) penetrated into Estonia. The Finns, who had joined the Germans, moved down the Karelian isthmus but did not threaten Leningrad.

✠     ✠     ✠

Because Stalin had made the colossal error of pushing most of his forces to the frontier, where they were largely overrun or captured in encirclements, the Germans, despite the widely diffused nature of their offensive, were within sight of victory. Indeed, both Hitler and Halder thought they *had* won. However, instead of taking advantage of Stalin's potentially fatal mistake, Hitler commenced a series of disastrous delays and vacillations that canceled out his victories.

The success in Army Group Center had been astonishing. There were few Soviet troops still guarding the Moscow road. A stunning opportunity had materialized. Guderian's and Hoth's tanks had advanced 440 miles in six weeks, and were only 220 miles from Moscow. The dry weather was certain to continue until autumn. Although tank strength had fallen to half that at the start, there was every reason to believe the remaining armor could reach the capital and drive a dagger into the heart of the Soviet Union.

The successes of the caldron battles had reinvigorated Brauchitsch and Halder in thinking that everything possible should be committed to the central front and capture of Moscow. Yet at this moment Hitler turned the campaign in a completely different direction—and thereby lost the one chance that the caldron battles had given him to seize Moscow. Ignoring the virtually open road to the capital, he issued a directive on July 19 ordering Hoth's panzer group to turn north to assist Leeb's advance on Leningrad, and Guderian's panzer group to swing south and help Rundstedt's army group seize Kiev.

Guderian went to a conference at Army Group Headquarters at Novi Borisov on July 27 to be informed of the new orders. Here he learned he'd been promoted to army commander and his group renamed Panzer Army Guderian, and he was outraged by instructions to halt the advance on Moscow.

Bock agreed with Guderian, but, like Brauchitsch and Halder, did not have the stomach to challenge Hitler. He and army headquarters (OKH) were willing to let the impetuous Guderian challenge Hitler alone and tacitly went along with a delaying operation Guderian set in motion to frustrate Hitler's orders.

The effort hinged on seizing the town of Roslavl, seventy miles southeast of Smolensk, at the junction of roads to Moscow, Kiev, and Leningrad. Roslavl was important as a jumping-off point for Moscow. But Guderian's principal aim was to entangle his forces so deeply in this operation that orders to assist Rundstedt would be canceled and he could resume his drive to Moscow.

The Russians inadvertently took part in the conspiracy. Stalin rushed reserves to Roslavl—raw units in training and militia outfits called into service, Stalin's only source of fresh troops. Hitler postponed the diversion of Hoth and Guderian on July 30 and agreed to visit Army Group Center on August 4 to see the situation for himself.

At this conference, Bock, Hoth, and Guderian separately told Hitler that continuing the offensive against Moscow was vital. Hitler then assembled the officers and demonstrated how little he could be moved by logic and military considerations. He announced that Leningrad was his primary objective, and he was inclined to select the Ukraine next because its raw materials and food were needed, Rundstedt seemed on the verge of victory, and the Crimea had to be occupied to prevent Russian planes there bombing the Ploesti oil fields.

"While flying back," Guderian wrote, "I decided in any case to make the necessary preparations for an attack toward Moscow."

He planned to concentrate his panzers on the Roslavl-Moscow highway, roll up the Russians along that road through Spas Demensk to Vyazma, about 90 miles east of Smolensk, and thereby ease the path of Hoth's panzers also heading toward Moscow on the north.

Meanwhile, on August 7, Jodl and Halder persuaded Hitler to renew the advance on Moscow. Three days later resistance at Leningrad caused him to change his mind again and order Hoth's tanks to help Leeb. Hitler now saw that OKW, Bock, and Guderian were prevaricating, lost his patience, reinstated the order that Guderian assist Rundstedt, and sent a wounding letter to Brauchitsch accusing him of a lack of "the necessary grip." Brauchitsch suffered a mild heart attack. Halder urged him to resign, and did so himself, but Hitler refused it.

Everything came to a head on August 22, when Guderian got an alert to move his group south to help destroy Russian armies around Kiev. The next day at a commanders' conference at army group headquarters Halder announced that Hitler now had decided that neither the Leningrad nor Moscow operations would be carried out, and efforts were to be focused on capturing Ukraine and Crimea.

Everyone present knew this meant a winter campaign, for which the German army was not prepared, and the conflict would turn into a war of attrition.

Bock and Halder arranged a personal interview of Guderian with Hitler to try to get him to change his mind. Guderian flew back to Rastenburg with Halder. Hitler heard him out, but then launched into a verbal offensive.

His commanders "know nothing about the economic aspects of war," he said. He insisted that the economic zone from Kiev to Kharkov had to be seized, and the Crimea captured to prevent Soviet aircraft bombing Ploesti. Since the other officers in Hitler's circle were in full support or were afraid to oppose him, Guderian realized it was pointless to argue.

✠       ✠       ✠

Hitler's irresolution had consumed a month of dry summer when his panzers could have rolled to Moscow. Now he delayed even longer in order to seize Ukraine. On August 25 Guderian turned south on the new mission that would take another month to finish. By the time he could get back on the Moscow road the autumn rainy season would arrive, a period of mud called *Rasputitsa* (literally "time without roads"), which would slow or stop vehicles and the advance. After that would come the Russian winter.

The disputes in July and August demonstrated that Adolf Hitler did not possess a fundamental prerequisite of great commanders. Successful generals from Alexander the Great on have thought out their objectives in advance and adhered doggedly to them in the stress and chaos of battle, ignoring peripheral targets, however attractive, and passing up partial victories in order to achieve total success at the end.

Hitler could conceive of no great strategic plan. And once embroiled in a campaign, he was ready to toss aside even his general goal to seize an opportunity that appeared. He had shown this irresolution in a negative way in the 1940 campaign, wanting to halt the panzers out of fear just as they were about to break out into undefended space, and actually stopping the tanks before Dunkirk.

The attack on Kiev is one of the greatest examples in history of how a leader can be seduced by the vision of a short-term gain into abandoning a course of action that would have given him victory. At Kiev Germany won a great local victory, but surrendered its last chance to win the war.

Kiev did offer a tempting target. Army Group South had not taken Kiev, but had seized Dnepropetrovsk on the bend of the Dnieper River, 250 miles southeast of Kiev. Stalin had ordered the defense of the Kiev region at all costs, and Soviet supreme headquarters (Stavka) sent three additional armies to reinforce the Southwestern Front under General Mikhail Kirponos and Marshal Seymon Budenny.

The situation was now set for a giant envelopment, for Guderian's Panzer Army at Starodub was far to the east and north of Kiev. If Kleist's

Panzer Group 1 at the Dnieper bend advanced north, while Guderian drove south, they could close off the region around Kiev. This was the opportunity that Hitler had seen, and this prospect is what drew him away from the attack on Moscow.

The campaign got under way on August 25. While 2nd Army pressed south from Gomel, Guderian's panzers struck from Starodub, seventy-five miles to the east, and seized a bridge over the Desna River, sixty miles south, before the Russians could destroy it. Heavy Soviet resistance required a week of bitter fighting for Guderian to break out and continue south.

Meanwhile Kleist's Panzer Group 1 moved from Dnepropetrovsk to the more westerly crossing of the Dnieper at Kremenchug, and launched his arm of the pincers on September 12.

By this time, the Soviets were beginning to realize their danger, but could do little to stop Guderian. Budenny sent a general to Moscow asking permission to retreat. But Stalin replied: "Hold at any price." He also replaced Budenny with Semen Timoshenko as Southwestern Front commander. The Soviet army group was left in a hopeless position. On September 14–15 the points of the German armored columns met at Lokhvitsa, 125 miles east of Kiev. The caldron was closed.

When Timoshenko arrived, he recognized the incredible danger, and on September 16 ordered withdrawal on his own, despite the example of Western Front commander Dimitri G. Pavlov, whom Stalin had ordered shot on July 1 over the disaster at Minsk. Kirponos dared not carry out the order, however, and wasted two days in a futile effort to get permission from Stalin. By then it was too late. The Germans had formed an iron ring around the caldron and tore the Russian armies apart as they tried to break out. Kirponos died in the fighting. By September 19, when the Germans seized the city of Kiev itself, Russian resistance had virtually ended.

The Germans captured 665,000 men in the Kiev caldron, the largest single military success in history and the largest haul of prisoners ever attained in one battle.

# 10 FAILURE BEFORE MOSCOW

DURING THE FRANTIC FIRST DAYS OF THE CAMPAIGN, SOVIET OFFICIALS TRANS-ferred 1,500 factories and as much machinery as possible, along with workers, by rail to the Urals and western Siberia. This exhausting, chaotic undertaking resulted in enormous drops in production and terrible living conditions for workers, but ensured that Soviet industry would ultimately recover and produce weapons and war goods in great quantities. In the interim, much depended on the willingness of the west to support the Soviet Union.

In the United States and Britain there was doubt that Russia could last out the summer. Americans in general were gleeful that the world's two worst dictatorships were tearing at each other's vitals and hoped they would fight to mutual exhaustion. President Roosevelt and Prime Minister Churchill, however, were terrified that Hitler would win and the democracies would be faced with the combined resources of Europe and the Soviet Union.

Roosevelt's first reaction to Soviet pleas for help was caution, and he dodged questions from the press about extending lend-lease to Russia. But he quickly decided that aiding the Red Army might be worth the gamble, and in mid-July sent his closest confidant, Harry Hopkins, to London to discuss the matter with Churchill.

Churchill endorsed American help to Russia, but he didn't like the idea of supplies destined for Britain being diverted to the Reds. Hopkins decided to go to Moscow himself to assess the situation. The trip was long

and hard, but in Moscow Hopkins found confidence, high morale, and "unbounded determination to win." Stalin vowed he'd fight beyond the Ural Mountains even if Moscow fell.

✠      ✠      ✠

At the moment the United States was as preoccupied with Japan as it was with Hitler's advances into the Soviet Union. On July 2, at a secret imperial conference in Tokyo, Japanese leaders decided not to join the war against Russia, unless the Red Army collapsed. Instead they elected to continue their drive south to seize most or all of Southeast Asia, overrunning the colonies of the Netherlands, France, and Britain. Shortly after France's defeat in 1940, the Japanese demanded and got permission to occupy northern French Indochina (Vietnam, Laos, and Cambodia).

The Kremlin knew the results of the July 2 conference from its spy in Tokyo, Richard Sorge. But Stalin took no chances. Though he desperately needed the thirty divisions, many tanks, and 2,800 warplanes he had in the Far East, he kept most in place, and actually strengthened defenses around Manchuria, where the Japanese army was massed.

This sealed Japan's decision to move south, and on July 14 the government demanded of the Vichy French agreement to occupy eight air bases in southern Indochina and to use France's naval base at Camranh Bay. The French quickly capitulated.

FDR and Cordell Hull, secretary of state, didn't know of the imperial conference, but were aware of much that was going on in Tokyo. American army and navy cryptanalysts by August 1940 had discovered the secrets of the Japanese encoding machine known as "Purple," which diplomats used in radio messages to and from Tokyo. American intercepts of these messages in the decoding program named "Magic" picked up indications of Japanese intentions in Southeast Asia.

This galvanized Roosevelt into taking a step on July 25, 1941, which he had shrunk from for over a year: he froze Japanese assets, instantly ending all trade with Japan. Britain, its dominions, and the Dutch East Indies followed quickly.

Roosevelt and Churchill hoped this action would slow the Japanese drive toward war, but it actually accelerated it. Without oil imports from the United States or the East Indies, Japan's military operations would collapse within months. The army and navy started preparing for armed confrontation.

✠          ✠          ✠

Hopkins got back to London from Moscow just in time to climb aboard the British battleship *Prince of Wales* taking Churchill and his staff to meet Roosevelt at Placentia Bay, Newfoundland—the Atlantic Conference on August 9–12, 1941, and the first meeting of the two leaders. Hopkins told FDR that all-out aid to Russia was a good bet. At the worst it would delay Hitler long enough for the United States to prepare for war. He recommended that the Soviets be declared eligible for lend-lease.

Roosevelt sent Stalin a message promising strong aid after three months. FDR's decision was influenced by the fear that Stalin might conclude a peace with Hitler, something hardly less bad than a German victory.

As Churchill turned back toward Britain, a de facto anti-Hitler coalition had been sealed. On the last day of the conference, August 12, 1941, the House of Representatives extended the draft by a single vote, 203–202. Narrow as the vote was, it demonstrated American determination to rearm and defend itself. Freezing trade with Japan was one sign of this resolve, and Roosevelt did more: he extended U.S. Navy protection of British convoys to Iceland and prepared deliveries to the Soviet Union along this route.

On August 25, Britain and the Soviet Union occupied Iran and ensured an all-weather, unopposed supply line to Russia. Soviet forces from the north and British from the south took over the country, required Shah Reza Pahlevi to abdicate in favor of his son, and mobilized forced labor to build a highway between Shatt al Arab and the Caspian Sea to expedite American exports.

✠          ✠          ✠

When Guderian's panzer group moved south to assist in the Kiev caldron battle, Hitler sent Hermann Hoth's panzer group to join Army Group North's efforts to seize Leningrad. But the Finns refused to press down from the north beyond their old prewar boundary. Half a million of the city's three million people helped to build fortifications around the city—620 miles of earthworks, 400 miles of antitank ditches, thousands of concrete pillboxes.

German panzers were able to seal off the southeastern approaches to the city, the only land bridge to the rest of Russia. This put the city under siege, but left open a water route east of the city across Lake Ladoga. The situation for the people was grim, but there was no thought of surrender. In mid-September Georgy K. Zhukov, dismissed as chief of staff because he had advised Stalin to abandon Kiev, arrived with orders to hold the city.

Zhukov brought up every gun and mortar available to blast the Germans and prevent penetration of the city's defense line. Leeb informed Hitler on September 24 that his attacks had failed. The Leningrad front slowly subsided into a gruesome siege that lasted until the spring of 1944, killed or starved millions, but had no major effect on the war.

Meanwhile, far to the south, Rundstedt's army group overran the Donetz basin and, on November 21, seized Rostov on the Don, at the entrance to the Caucasus. But without Guderian's tanks, he could not drive on the oil fields. The Russians soon pushed his exhausted troops out of the city.

Rundstedt wanted to pull back to a good defensive line along the Mius River, about forty miles west of Rostov, but Hitler forbade the withdrawal. Rundstedt responded that he could not comply with such an order. Contrary to his custom, Hitler came to Rundstedt's headquarters at Poltava with Brauchitsch and Halder.

Hitler tried to blame Rundstedt for losing Rostov. Rundstedt answered that responsibility must lie with those who devised the campaign. "Hitler looked for a moment as though he were about to hurl himself against Rundstedt, and tear the Knight's Cross from his uniform," Walter Goerlitz wrote. Brauchitsch promptly had another heart attack.

Rundstedt persisted in his demands for freedom. When Hitler refused, he asked to be relieved of command. Hitler agreed, but at a final meeting told Rundstedt that in the future he would not consider any request by generals for retirement.

Meanwhile, Erich von Manstein, who had been given command of 11th Army with orders to seize the Crimea, reached the neck of the peninsula on September 29, and by November 18 had driven most of the surviving

Russians into Sevastopol. Attacks against the fortress failed, and Manstein finally called off the effort on December 30, 1941. Meanwhile, Russians landed on the Kerch peninsula in the eastern part on December 26 and tried to reconquer the Crimea. With great difficulty Manstein sealed off the peninsula, but anticipated that the Red Army would make another attempt in the spring of 1942.

✠      ✠      ✠

With the conclusion of the Kiev encirclement, Hitler at last was ready to attack Moscow. He ordered it, code-named Operation Typhoon, to commence on September 30. The principal aim was the destruction of Soviet forces blocking the road to the Soviet capital "in the limited time which remains available before the onset of the winter weather."

He transferred back Hoth's and Guderian's panzer groups, and sent along all but one corps (Rudolf Schmidt's 29th) of Hoepner's group from Army Group North. In theory Army Group Center's commander, Field Marshal Fedor von Bock, had a formidable force in the panzer formations, plus 4th Army (Kluge), and 9th Army (Strauss), a maneuver mass of seventy divisions.

But the German army as a whole had lost half a million men since June 22. Almost no units were at full strength. Many of the 600,000 horses the Germans had brought into Russia to carry supplies were dead, and there were no replacements. Ammunition had to be left on the sides of the roads. The simplest necessities disappeared—razor blades, soap, toothpaste, shoe-repair kits, needles and thread. The sick could not be left in the rear, because the forests behind were infested with partisan guerrillas. Rain began in September with cold northeast winds. Shelter everywhere was inadequate or nonexistent. Boots were falling apart, clothing turning into rags.

The infantry divisions were 2,000 to 4,000 men below strength. The three panzer groups (thirteen panzer and seven motorized divisions) possessed only about a thousand tanks altogether. Still they were superior to the 480 tanks (only forty-five new T-34s and KV-1s, both with high-velocity 76-millimeter guns) that Ivan S. Konev's Western Front had to oppose them.

The Russians had had two months to build field fortifications across the approaches to Moscow, and about 800,000 men were facing them. But they were mostly raw replacements with little training and poor leadership.

German panzers broke the Russian front in five places. Guderian drove northeast from Sostka to Orel, eighty miles south of Moscow. His advance was so rapid that the electric streetcars were still running in the city, and evacuations of factories were under way as his tanks rolled in. Workers had to abandon machinery and tools on the streets.

Guderian then turned west on Bryansk. With the help of 2nd Army to the west and Hoepner's Panzer Group 4 to the north, he trapped thousands of Russians south and west of Bryansk. Meanwhile 4th and 9th armies and Hoth's Panzer Group 3 formed another caldron west of Vyazma (only 135 miles from Moscow).

The battles were turbulent. Frequently German troops were cut off and had to fight their way free. Russian aircraft bombed frequently, but flew so high their aim was inaccurate. Counter strokes by T-34 and KV-1 tanks led to critical battle situations.

Guderian commented on a collision of 4th Panzer Division northeast of Orel on October 11: "Numerous Russian T-34s went into action and inflicted heavy losses on the German tanks. Up to this time we had enjoyed tank superiority, but from now on the situation was reversed."

German tankers found that the short-barreled 75-millimeter gun on the Mark IV could knock out a T-34 only if it could hit the grating above the engine in the rear, a shot rarely possible. The 480-mile-wide battlefield was covered with fallen soldiers, dead horses, shot-up tanks, and the first American jeeps.

Stalin had rushed many militiamen with virtually no training into ranks, and large numbers of them gave up without a fight. Once more, linear Russian dispositions had allowed the Germans to break through at selected points and surround great bodies of troops. On October 13, resistance in the Vyazma caldron ceased. A week later the last Russians surrendered in the Bryansk pocket. The Germans counted 650,000 prisoners altogether, almost as many as were taken in the Kiev caldron.

There were now very few Soviet soldiers between the Germans and Moscow. The entire Soviet army in European Russia was down to 800,000 men and 770 tanks. But the situation had changed radically since August. The first snow fell on October 7. It melted quickly, but was followed by heavy rains.

"The roads rapidly became nothing but canals of bottomless mud,"

Guderian wrote, "along which our vehicles could only advance at a snail's pace and with great wear to the engines."

In the crisis, Stalin brought Georgy Zhukov back from Leningrad on October 10 to direct the defense of Moscow. Panic was setting in among the people. Rumors of advancing Germans spread widely. People began to flee from the city.

Zhukov stilled the panic by mobilizing every person he could find to build antitank ditches outside the city. A quarter of a million people, three-quarters of them women, did the work by hand with shovels, spades, and buckets. Using whatever troops he could find, Zhukov manned the Mozhaisk line, the Russians' last defensive position, running from the "Sea of Moscow," a reservoir on the Volga River seventy miles north of the city, in a semicircle around to the Oka River, fifty-five miles south of Moscow.

Stalin ordered the Soviet government along with all top officials, the diplomatic corps, and many specialists to evacuate 420 miles east to Kuybyshev, north of the Caspian Sea.

But Stalin did not leave and did not lose his nerve. He lived in a small villa far outside the Kremlin, and worked mostly in the nearby subway station Kirovskaya, where the Stavka high command also operated. On October 5 he had received a radio message from his spy Richard Sorge in Tokyo that the Japanese would go to war with the United States in the next few months. This meant that the huge army he was maintaining in the Far East no longer was needed, and he ordered twelve divisions with 1,700 tanks and 1,500 aircraft (altogether 250,000 men) in eastern Siberia and Outer Mongolia to come to the defense of Moscow. Until their appearance weeks would go by. Whether the Soviets would get that much leeway depended principally upon the weather.

*Rasputitsa,* the period of mud, reached its high point. Vehicles sank to the hubcaps. The entire German supply system was hobbled.

But on November 2, 1941, the weather began to improve. A light frost permitted the troops to become mobile. Artillery pieces were dragged out of the mud. Trucks could roll once more. Train lines reopened.

Bock ordered a final great exertion to reach Moscow by means of a double-sided encirclement. In the center 4th Army (Kluge) was to hold the enemy by a frontal attack. On the north Panzer Groups 3 and 4 were to fight to the Moscow-Volga canal running up to the Sea of Moscow. On the south Guderian was to advance past Tula to Kolomna, on the Oka River about sixty miles southeast of Moscow.

This final offensive went down in the annals of the German army as *"die Flucht nach vorn,"* or "the flight to the front"—a desperate attempt to get into the shelters of Moscow before the onset of winter.

The attempt began on November 15 in clear frosty weather. The panzer units of the northern wing gained a bridgehead across the canal at Dimitrov, and one division came within eighteen miles of Moscow at Krasnaya Polyana. Guderian went around toughly defended Tula and approached Kashira, only thirty-two miles from Kolomna.

Perhaps members of a most-forward German patrol saw the towers of the Kremlin, as legend has it, perhaps not. In any case a glimpse is all they got. The German offensive stopped. The reasons were the onset of cruel winter and the decision of Zhukov to move to the offensive, when a part of the reinforcements from the Far East arrived.

Temperatures sank to minus 20 degrees Celsius, then fell further. The German army was not able to cope with such cold. Soldiers lacked winter clothing (fur caps, parkas, felt boots, snow hoods). The number of frost-bite cases rose to 228,000. Tanks, machine weapons, and radios failed. Boilers of locomotives burst.

An attempt by 4th Army to renew its attack broke down. Over the next fourteen days the offensive north and south also collapsed. Between the weather and Soviet spoiling attacks, only local advances occurred. T-34 tanks struck Guderian's right flank east of Tula, catching the 112th Infantry Division with no weapons that could stop them, and sending most of the division in panicked retreat. But Soviet commanders ordered the 44th Mongolian Cavalry Division in an attack near Klin, fifty-five miles northwest of Moscow, across an open, snow-covered field. German defenders with machine guns and artillery killed 2,000 men and horses with no loss to themselves.

Stalemate was setting in. Bock doubted the value of pushing on, and asked OKH on December 1 to suspend the operation. But Brauchitsch, desperately fearful of Hitler's anger, insisted the attacks must continue.

The soldiers at the front pressed a few miles forward. But at that moment, December 5, Zhukov launched a counteroffensive. He threw in not only the reinforcements from the Far East, but three new armies that had been forming deep in the Russian hinterland east of the Volga. Some of the new divisions were equipped with Katyusha rocket launchers ("Stalin organs"), a terrifying but inaccurate new battlefield weapon that could throw sixteen fin-stabilized 132-millimeter rockets from rails on the back of a truck. For the first time as well, strong Soviet fighters appeared in the skies.

The counterblow hit the worn-out German divisions at the moment of their greatest weakness. Guderian, attacked by what he called "Siberians," had to give up the positions he had won around Tula. On December 6 a Soviet penetration of four armies spread in the direction of Klin, forcing the Germans back from their closest approach to the capital. South of Moscow, other Soviet forces threatened to cut off Guderian's advanced forces around Kashira, and he withdrew to the line of the upper Don River, sixty miles to the south.

Russian forces were too weak to encircle the German units before they escaped, but the initiative had been wrested from the Germans. The Germans doggedly held on, however, and stopped the Red Army attacks on both sides of Moscow.

In the midst of this crisis, Japan attacked the American Pacific Fleet at Pearl Harbor, Hawaii, on Sunday, December 7, 1941. Four days later, Hitler declared war on the United States, dragging Mussolini along with him. It was another of Hitler's foolish decisions, because—with American attention and anger focused on the "sneak attack" of the Japanese—it would have been difficult for President Roosevelt to get Congress unilaterally to declare war on Germany.

Six months before Hitler faced only Britain. Now, by deliberate choice, he had arrayed against him the three greatest industrial powers in the world, with a great preponderance of manpower.

German senior officers paid little notice to their new foe, because they were frantically trying to stave off Russian attacks. Halder did not even note in his diary on December 11 that Germany had declared war. Brauchitsch proposed that the army move back to a shortened "winter line" east of Yukhnov-Rzhev, a withdrawal of about a hundred miles. Hitler refused.

He accepted the resignation of Brauchitsch. Though ostensibly based on a severe heart attack Brauchitsch had suffered, it actually resulted from his and Hitler's long-disturbed relationship. Hitler made himself commander in chief of the army, and ordered "fanatical resistance." He authorized withdrawals only with his personal approval. Despite his orders, German forces fell back in numerous places to avoid being surrounded and destroyed.

Barbarossa had failed. Hitler never saw that he made any mistake. He blamed the defeat on the "unexpectedly early onset of severe winter." Losses rose to 775,000 dead, wounded, and missing—almost one-fourth of the entire strength of the field armies.

A leadership crisis followed. Hitler had relieved Rundstedt because he wanted to withdraw to the Mius River. He now removed both other army group commanders—Bock, ostensibly for sickness, Leeb because Hitler rejected his proposal to withdraw from exposed positions around Leningrad. Three army commanders also departed—Maximilian von Weichs (2nd), Adolf Strauss (9th), and Karl Heinrich von Stülpnagel (17th)—along with thirty other general officers, including Hoepner, whom Hitler expelled from the army for an unauthorized retreat. Most significantly, he ousted Guderian. The best panzer leader in the German army went into the army officers reserve pool.

By January 1, 1942, Soviet forces had retaken Kalinin, a hundred miles northwest of Moscow, and Kaluga, a hundred miles southwest, and were besieging German strongholds that had been bypassed and surrounded. The threat to Moscow had ended.

At this point Hitler issued an order for all troops to stand fast. On January 7, Stalin launched a counteroffensive along the whole front, something the Red Army was too weak to accomplish. The Russians failed to eliminate the surrounded Germans, and made only limited advances elsewhere. The German army survived the winter of 1941–1942 because Stalin attempted too much. But Hitler thought the reason was his stand-fast order. For the rest of the war this encouraged him in his insistence to defend every inch of ground.

It was a pity for Germany that Adolf Hitler never heeded the advice of the Swiss military analyst Antoine-Henri Jomini, commenting on Napoleon's 1812 invasion: "Russia is a country which is easy to get into, but very difficult to get out of."

# 11 To and Fro in the Desert

WITH THE FAILURE OF ROMMEL'S ATTACKS AGAINST TOBRUK AND THE REFUSAL of Hitler to reinforce Africa Corps, a stalemate descended over North Africa in the spring of 1941. Rommel didn't have enough forces to advance beyond the Egyptian frontier, and the British didn't have enough power to relieve Tobruk.

However, Winston Churchill, unlike the German high command, recognized the importance of the Suez Canal, and ran great risks to hold it. To improve the strength of the Middle East commander, General Sir Archibald Wavell, he directed that a five-ship convoy with 295 tanks and forty-three Hurricane fighter planes be run directly through the Mediterranean, instead of around the Cape of Good Hope. He wrote the British Chiefs of Staff on April 20, 1941, that the war in the Middle East and saving the Suez Canal "all may turn on a few hundred armored vehicles. They must if possible be carried there at all costs." Aided by misty weather, the convoy got through to Alexandria on May 12 without Axis attacks, but lost one ship with fifty-seven tanks to a mine in the Sicilian Narrows.

Wavell didn't wait for the tanks to get to the front. He launched his first effort to relieve Tobruk, Operation Brevity, on May 15, sending twenty-six Matilda tanks in support of the 22nd Guards Brigade in a direct assault against enemy forces guarding Sollum and Halfaya Pass along the coast. Sollum and Halfaya were the only places along the Libya-Egypt frontier where troops could cross the 600-foot escarpment that stretches from Sollum southeastward into Egypt. Meanwhile, twenty-nine cruiser tanks with a Support Group of motorized infantry and artillery moved around the desert flank to the south and tried to get on the Axis rear.

The British seized Halfaya Pass, losing seven Matildas in the process. However, threats of German counterattacks on the flank caused the British to withdraw, leaving a small garrison at the pass. Rommel launched a sudden converging attack on May 27 and recaptured the pass. He dug in four high-velocity 88-millimeter antiaircraft guns, which had emerged as Germany's best tank-killers. The guns, their barrels horizontal with little visible above ground, were to be of great importance in the next British effort, Operation Battleaxe.

Wavell planned Battleaxe as two separate operations. In the first, an infantry force, supported by half the British armor, a brigade of Matildas, was to seize Halfaya, Sollum, and Fort Capuzzo, eight miles to the west. In the second, the remaining armor was to cover the desert flank to the south to guard against the panzer regiment Rommel had posted there. Rommel's other panzer regiment was near Tobruk and could move as needed.

Wavell's plan betrayed the ambivalence about armor that bedeviled the British in North Africa. He split his armor into two separate forces, neither of which could support the other. Yet Rommel could send his second panzer regiment quickly to reinforce his first.

Another mistake of the British was their misunderstanding of the role of the 88s at Halfaya. British doctrine was largely fixed on the idea of tank versus tank battles, whereas Rommel used antitank guns to the maximum degree possible, holding his tanks back for decisive strikes or movements.

When the Matildas attacked Halfaya—dubbed by British soldiers as "Hellfire Pass"—on June 15, 1941, the commander radioed back his last message: "They are tearing my tanks to bits." Only one of thirteen Matildas survived the trap of the four 88s. The attack collapsed.

The Germans also mounted four 88s and 50-millimeter antitank guns on Hafid Ridge, a few miles southwest of Capuzzo. When the British cruiser tanks coming around the southern flank reached Hafid, the German gun trap stopped them cold. By now most of Rommel's forward panzer regiment had arrived, and had threatened an attack on the flank of the armored brigade, inducing Wavell to pull it back into Egypt.

By nightfall, the British had lost more than half their tanks, mostly to fire from the 88s and antitank guns, while Rommel's tank strength had been little affected.

✠        ✠        ✠

Rommel had learned something the British had not grasped about desert warfare: that attrition or wearing down of an enemy force and destruction of the enemy's organic cohesion had to be the tactical aims. In other environments where few units were mechanized, like Poland in 1939 and western Europe in 1940, the greatest danger a force could face was being surrounded. When encircled, and subjected to fire from all sides, a force tended to disintegrate, and could be destroyed or forced to surrender.

In the desert, surrounded motorized forces nearly always could mass at a single point and break out, thereby nullifying what elsewhere would be a devastating trap.

Rommel accordingly concentrated on winning battles of attrition and shattering the enemy's organization. He came up with a five-point method of doing this. A commander, he wrote, must (1) concentrate his forces, while trying to split the enemy forces and destroy them at different times; (2) protect his supply lines, while cutting the enemy's; (3) attack enemy armor with antitank guns, reserving his own tanks for the final blow; (4) operate near the front so as to make immediate decisions when tactical conditions change; (5) achieve surprise, maintain great speed of movement, and overrun disorganized enemy formations without delay. Speed is everything, Rommel wrote. And, after dislocating the enemy, he must be pursued at once and never be allowed to reorganize.

Rommel had only one "secret" weapon, the 88-millimeter antiaircraft (AA) gun that he and other German generals discovered in the 1940 campaign could blast through 83 millimeters of armor at 2,000 yards. This made the 88 the most formidable antitank weapon on either side. The British had a comparable high-velocity AA gun of about the same caliber (3.7 inches), which could have been as effective, but they did not use it against tanks.

Rommel also had the 50-millimeter antitank (AT) gun, which slowly replaced the poor 37-millimeter gun developed before the war. The 50-millimeter gun could penetrate 50 millimeters of armor at 1,000 yards. Although the Matilda with its heavy frontal armor was largely invulnerable to this gun, the more lightly armored cruisers could often be stopped, especially at close range. Both the 88 and the 50-millimeter AT gun could fire solid shot, to cut through armor, or high explosive, which could destroy or neutralize British AT weapons or crews.

By comparison, the British two-pounder (40-millimeter) AT gun was ineffective. It fired only solid shot, requiring a direct hit to destroy enemy AT weapons, and could penetrate merely the thinner side plates of armor at ranges below 200 yards. The British 25-pounder (87-millimeter) gun-howitzer, a superb field artillery piece, had to be pressed into service as an antitank weapon, though often at the expense of protecting infantry. Only in the spring of 1942 did the British begin to receive the six-pounder (57-millimeter) AT gun, which fired high-explosive as well as solid shot and had 30 percent greater penetration than the German 50-millimeter gun.

The British took a long time recognizing that Rommel was sending antitank guns against their tanks. In offensive or attack situations, Rommel leapfrogged the comparatively nimble 50-millimeter AT guns from one shielded vantage point to another, while keeping his tanks stationary and below the horizon. Once the AT guns were established, they protected the tanks as they swept forward.

In defensive situations, Rommel tried to bait or lure the British. He sent light tanks forward to contact the enemy, then retire. The typical British response was to mount a "cavalry" charge. But since visibility was obscured by stirred up dust and sand, British tankers usually did not see the 50-millimeter AT guns waiting in ambush in hollows and draws, nor the "gun line" of 88s drawn up at the rear. The 50s picked off British tanks that got within range, while the 88s took on the advancing enemy armor at distances far beyond the capacity of the tanks' two-pounder (40-millimeter) guns to respond. The British added to the success of Rommel's tactics by usually committing their armor piecemeal, mostly single units, instead of full brigades, and never massed brigades.

In addition to halving their armor by dividing their tanks between cruisers and infantry or "I" tanks, the British made two additional mistakes: they persisted in forming "support groups" and they dispersed their armor widely.

A support group of combined infantry and artillery units had successfully blocked the retreat of the Italians at Beda Fomm in February 1941.

Its success led to repetition. The British saw no need to include tanks, as the Germans did with their *Kampfgruppen* or battle groups, which could take on any enemy force. As a result support groups had to depend upon a few 25-pounder howitzers and two-pounder AT guns, which were not always sufficient against strong German or German-backed Italian forces.

The British dispersed their tanks because it was impossible to conceal armor in the desert from the air. Rommel tried to practice the opposite policy, drawing together every possible tank and gun to work against a single objective—which, because of British dispersion, was often a fragment of total British armored strength.

Finally, the British failed to copy the Stuka dive-bomber, which was in effect mobile artillery that could deliver fire on the point a forward force wished to destroy, or through which it wished to advance. The dive-bomber offered the vanguard of an attacking force a way to eliminate an enemy strongpoint shortly after its discovery without having to bring up more weapons. If tanks could not knock out such a point, the only other way to break it was to advance field artillery, a time-consuming job that often gave the enemy the chance to strengthen his position or move.

Since the start of World War II and the unveiling of blitzkrieg with tanks and dive-bombers, the offensive had dominated the defensive. This period was now coming to a close. The inherent superiority of the defense over the offense was being reasserted. It had marked World War I and had been brought on by the great power of defensive weapons like field fortifications, artillery, and the machine gun.

The enormous offensive battles that burst upon the world in Russia in the summer and fall of 1941 obscured this point for a time. But the Tobruk battles and Operation Brevity foreshadowed what Battleaxe now demonstrated: when resolute troops held strong defensive positions, and possessed weapons that could immobilize tanks, they could prevail. This lesson, learned in the trenches of the western front 1914–1918, was going to be relearned on the battlefields of the Second World War.

☦       ☦       ☦

As the giant caldron battles of Barbarossa slowly played out in the Soviet Union in the fall of 1941, the British prepared for their first major offensive against Rommel in North Africa.

Adolf Hitler *(left)* confers with Field Marshal Wilhelm Keitel and General Alfred Jodl. Keitel was chief of staff of the *Oberkommando der Wehrmacht* (OKW), or armed forces supreme command, while Jodl was OKW chief of operations. Keitel was a toady to Hitler, but Jodl gave Hitler limited advice, though he never dared clash with the Fuehrer. *(Topham/ The Image Works)*

Field Marshal Sir Alan Brooke *(center)*, chief of the British Imperial General Staff, with Lieutenant Generals Laurence Carr *(left)* and Sir G. le Q. Martel. *(Topham/The Image Works)*

Italian dictator Benito Mussolini *(left)* and Adolf Hitler in a motorcade in Berlin. *(Topham/ The Image Works)*

Hermann Göring, chief of the German Luftwaffe, or air force, and a crony of Hitler. *(Topham/The Image Works)*

British General Sir Harold Alexander, Allied commander in Tunisia and Italy *(in front seat)*, with American Lieutenant General Mark Clark, 5th Army commander *(in back seat, left)*, and Major General John Coulter. *(Topham/The Image Works)*

*(Top left):* General Franz Halder, chief of staff of the German army since 1938, persisted in pointing out the dangers of dividing German forces between Stalingrad and the Caucasus. Hitler paid no attention and removed him on September 15, 1942. *(AP/Wide World Photo)*

*(Bottom left):* Grand Admiral Erich Raeder *(left),* chief of the German navy, leaves a vessel after an inspection in December 1939. Raeder tried repeatedly to convince Hitler to commit enough German forces to seize Egypt, the Suez Canal, and the Middle East, but Hitler refused and continued with his fixation on destroying the Soviet Union by a direct attack. Hitler removed Raeder early in 1943. *(AP/Wide World Photo)*

*(Top right):* Field Marshal Erich von Manstein conceived the plan that defeated France in six weeks in 1940 and carried out withdrawals that saved the southern wing of the German army in Russia early in 1943 after Hitler's disastrous decision to sacrifice the 6th Army at Stalingrad. *(AP/Wide World Photo)*

British soldiers form a human chain to wade through the surf during the evacuation of Dunkirk, France, in June 1940. The British mobilized every vessel they could find, from private yachts to warships, to rescue 338,000 beleaguered British and French troops, cut off by the German thrust through the Ardennes to the English Channel. *(AP/Wide World Photo)*

General Heinz Guderian in his command vehicle. Guderian was father of the German panzer, or armored, divisions; he led the breakout through the Ardennes to the English Channel in May 1940 and directed the main panzer thrust at Moscow in the fall of 1941. *(Topham/The Image Works)*

The major German commanders in Africa in 1941 *(from left):* Field Marshal Albert Kesselring, German chief in the Mediterranean; Major General Stefan Froehlich, Luftwaffe commander in Africa; Lieutenant General Alfred Gause, Rommel's chief of staff; General Erwin Rommel, field commander; and Lieutenant General Ludwig Cruewell, chief of Africa Corps. *(Topham/ The Image Works)*

German soldiers crouch behind a bullet-pocked wall during fighting in the Crimea in November 1941. *(AP/Wide World Photo)*

German panzers roll through Libya toward the battlefront on the Egyptian frontier in April 1941. The German commander, Erwin Rommel, was preparing for a British offensive there around Sollum and Halfaya Pass. *(AP/Wide World Photo)*

German troops rush through a burning Russian village in the early stages of the invasion in June 1941. *(Topham/The Image Works)*

Soviet T-34 tanks advancing into action. The T-34, with good speed, sloping thick armor that could deflect many shells, wide tracks that could move well in mud or snow, and a high-velocity 76-millimeter cannon, was the most successful tank in World War II. Panzer leader Heinz Guderian attributed the collapse of the German attack on Moscow in December 1941 to the T-34. Later the Soviets mounted an even more powerful 85-millimeter gun on the tank. *(Topham/The Image Works)*

A German antitank gun crew in action in Russia in the summer of 1942. German armored forces could generally outmaneuver Soviet defenders because German organization and leadership were normally superior. This allowed German panzers to make astonishing advances despite heavy opposition. Adolf Hitler forfeited this great advantage of maneuverability by requiring German forces to fight a close-in, street-by-street battle in Stalingrad and by demanding that Germans defend every inch of the territory they occupied. *(Topham/The Image Works)*

General Hans-Jürgen von Arnim, commanding the German 5th Panzer Army in Tunisia, was envious of Erwin Rommel's fame and withheld forces Rommel might have used to sweep behind the Allied armies and force their surrender or retreat in the battle of Kasserine Pass in February 1943. *(Topham/The Image Works)*

Friedrich Paulus *(foreground)*, commander of the German 6th Army at Stalingrad, shortly after he surrendered on January 31, 1943. Hitler promoted Paulus to field marshal on the assumption that he would shoot himself to avoid capture. He did not. *(Topham/The Image Works)*

The major Allied leaders at the Teheran conference in late November 1943. Seated *(from left):* Soviet dictator Joseph Stalin; American president Franklin D. Roosevelt; and British prime minister Winston Churchill. *(Topham/The Image Works)*

German SS General Sepp Dietrich, commander of the 6th Panzer Army in the Battle of the Bulge, December 1944. *(Topham/The Image Works)*

General Charles de Gaulle inspects French soldiers who escaped from German prison camps and joined the Free French movement, which de Gaulle led. De Gaulle received wild acclaim when he arrived in Paris with liberating forces on August 25, 1944. *(Topham/ The Image Works)*

*(Above left):* SS Lieutenant Colonel Joachim Peiper, whose battle group massacred eighty-six captured and unarmed Americans and a number of Belgians at Malmédy during the Battle of the Bulge in December 1944. *(Topham/The Image Works)*

*(Above right):* Brigadier General Anthony C. McAuliffe, who said "Nuts!" to a German demand that he surrender the American 101st Airborne Division he commanded at Bastogne during the Battle of the Bulge in December 1944. *(Topham/The Image Works)*

*(Right):* General George S. Patton Jr., the most aggressive and imaginative Allied commander in the west, who led the American 7th Army into Sicily and the 3rd Army through France after the breakout from Normandy in late July 1944. *(Topham/The Image Works)*

Leaders of Overlord, the invasion of Normandy in June 1944. Seated *(from left):* RAF Air Chief Marshal Sir Arthur Tedder, deputy commander; General Dwight D. Eisenhower, supreme commander; British field marshal Sir Bernard L. Montgomery, ground forces commander. Standing *(from left):* General Omar Bradley, American ground commander; Royal Navy Admiral Sir Bertram H. Ramsey, naval commander; RAF Air Chief Marshal Sir Trafford Leigh-Mallory, air support commander; and Lieutenant General Walter Bedell Smith, Eisenhower's chief of staff. *(Topham/The Image Works)*

Field Marshal Gerd von Rundstedt awards Iron Cross decorations to German soldiers who distinguished themselves in combat. Rundstedt commanded Army Group A, which struck through the Ardennes in May 1940 and led quickly to the defeat of France and the eviction of the British from the Continent. Rundstedt commanded an army group in Russia and was commander in chief in the west when the Allies invaded Normandy in June 1944. *(Topham/ The Image Works)*

The senior Allied commanders in Normandy in June 1944 *(from left):* Field Marshal Bernard L. Montgomery, chief of all ground forces; General Miles C. Dempsey, commander of the British 2nd Army; and General Omar Bradley, commander of the American 1st Army. *(Topham/The Image Works)*

General George C. Marshall, chief of staff of the U.S. Army and President Roosevelt's principal military adviser. Marshall was slated to become commander of the invasion of Normandy in 1944, but Roosevelt decided that he could not dispense with his advice and gave the command to Dwight D. Eisenhower. *(Topham/The Image Works)*

General Hasso von Manteuffel *(second from right)* discusses defense plans in France just prior to the Allied invasion on June 6, 1944. Manteuffel conducted a brilliant defense in Tunisia in 1943 against Allied forces and commanded the 5th Panzer Army in the Battle of the Bulge in December 1944. *(AP/Wide World Photo)*

*(Right):* Marshal Georgy K. Zhukov, who led the Soviet drive into Germany in 1945, makes a toast at Frankfurt shortly after the German surrender. With him is American General Dwight D. Eisenhower, western Allied supreme commander. *(Topham/The Image Works)*

*(Below):* Albert Speer *(left)*, Nazi armaments chief; Grand Admiral Karl Dönitz *(center)*, German U-boat chief and last chancellor of the German Reich; and General Alfred Jodl, operations chief of the high command, at their arrest at Flensburg, Germany, on May 24, 1945. *(Topham/The Image Works)*

Winston Churchill had been agitating for such an attack for months, and poured as many troops and as much equipment as he could find into Egypt. Four days after the end of Battleaxe, he relieved General Wavell and replaced him with General Sir Claude Auchinleck, commander in India, and immediately began pressing him to mount a major effort to wrest Libya from the Axis.

The campaign that opened on November 18, 1941, code-named Operation Crusader, developed into the most spectacular tank battle in history, a battle fought at extreme speed over a desert that allowed almost complete freedom of movement.

However, Crusader is notable because Auchinleck started with a false concept—he sought to destroy the enemy's forces—and also dispersed his armor so widely that he never achieved decisive strength at any point. The result was that Rommel, though vastly outnumbered in tanks and other weapons, was able to block the British and turn what appeared to be certain defeat into almost a victory.

Armored forces are so fluid they are unsuited to be an objective. They usually can be destroyed only by indirect means. The British could have done this by throwing a strategic barrage or barrier across the Axis line of supply, requiring Rommel to commit his panzers to reopen the line under conditions favorable to the British.

Such a choke point existed: Acroma, on the Axis supply route twenty miles west of Tobruk. A concentrated attack on Acroma would have relieved the siege of Tobruk without a fight and forced Rommel to attack the barrier frontally or retreat for lack of fuel and supplies. Yet the British never aimed at Acroma or any other strategic point astride the Axis supply line. Instead, they crashed against Rommel's gun-lined traps in direct, costly assaults that, moreover, were delivered by numerous individual units, and never by massed armor.

Consequently Rommel repeatedly caught British armor dispersed. As he remarked to a captured British officer after the battle: "What difference does it make if you have two tanks to my one, when you spread them out and let me smash them in detail?"

The British desert force had been renamed 8th Army, placed under the command of Lieutenant General Sir Alan Cunningham, and divided into two corps: the 13th under Lieutenant General A. R. Godwin-Austen with the 2nd New Zealand and 4th Indian Divisions and a force of infantry or "I" tanks; and the 30th under Lieutenant General C. W. M. Norrie with the "Desert Rats" of the 7th Armored Division (7th and 22nd Armored Brigades, plus an infantry and artillery Support Group), 4th Armored Brigade, 22nd Guards Brigade, and 1st South African Division. In reserve was the 2nd South African Division.

The British plan was for 13th Corps to pin down Axis troops holding the frontier from Sollum and Halfaya Pass to Sidi Omar, twenty-five miles inland, while the 30th Corps swept around south of Sidi Omar, destroyed Rommel's armor, then linked up with the Tobruk garrison, seventy miles beyond the frontier.

British perversity in splitting armor is shown in the fact that the three armored brigades of 30th Corps aimed from the outset at divergent objectives—although Auchinleck and Cunningham had identified the Sidi Rezegh airfield, atop an escarpment only twelve miles southeast of the Tobruk defensive perimeter, as their principal target. If the airfield could be seized, tanks there and tanks from Tobruk could open a link, relieve the siege, and endanger the Axis position.

On the night of November 18, 1941, 30th Corps swept around Rommel's desert flank, without encountering any resistance. The next day Cunningham sent two of three regiments of the 7th Armored Brigade to capture Sidi Rezegh airfield. The third regiment and the division's Support Group did not come up until the following morning, November 20. By then Rommel had rushed up part of 90th Light Division and a large number of antitank guns to block the advance.

Meanwhile, the other two British armored brigades drove off to widely separated places, and promptly ran into trouble. The 22nd, newly arrived from England, encountered the dug-in guns of Trieste Armored Division at Bir el Gubi, twenty-two miles south of Sidi Rezegh. Without waiting to call for assistance, the brigade launched a "charge of the Light Brigade" against the Italian guns, losing forty of 160 tanks within minutes, and completely bogging down.

The 4th Armored Brigade stopped at Gabr Selah, thirty miles southeast of Sidi Rezegh. The reason was to keep in touch with the left or southern flank of 13th Corps, although this could have been done by radio. One of the brigade's three regiments rushed off twenty-five miles in pursuit of a

German reconnaissance unit and was lost for the day. Rommel sent 21st Panzer Division's tank regiment, plus twelve field guns and four 88s, against the two remaining regiments of 4th Brigade, and destroyed twenty-three Stuart tanks against a loss of three German tanks.

The Germans, too, made a serious error. General Ludwig Cruewell, commanding Africa Corps, led all of his armor on a wild-goose chase toward Fort Capuzzo on the morning of November 20, after receiving a false report that a British advance was coming from that direction.

Although General Cunningham was informed of Africa Corps's departure—which opened up a giant hole in the Axis position—he took no advantage of the bonanza. He should have concentrated his armor, driven straight for the Sidi Rezegh airfield, and relieved Tobruk. This would have fatally compromised the entire Axis position. Instead he did nothing, giving the Germans a chance to retrieve Cruewell's blunder.

Although 21st Panzer Division ran out of gasoline near Sidi Omar, and didn't get refueled until after nightfall, 15th Panzer Division swept back southwest, and, in the afternoon, struck 4th Brigade, still sitting at Gabr Saleh, and inflicted more heavy damage on it. Cunningham ordered the 22nd Armored Brigade to assist, but it didn't complete the twenty-eight-mile trek from Bir el Gubi until after the battle had ended. However, the "I" tank brigade of 13th Corps was only seven miles to the east of 4th Brigade, and eager to advance. But, because it had "infantry" tanks, Cunningham did not call on it.

Rommel was exasperated by Cruewell's rush off to Fort Capuzzo, but, since 8th Army was not advancing into the void, he saw that 7th Armored Brigade and Support Group at Sidi Rezegh airfield were in a dangerous position. They were stopped from advancing on the Tobruk defenses by 90th Light, while Cunningham had done nothing to protect their rear. Accordingly, Rommel ordered Africa Corps to advance on the tail of the force the next morning, November 21, in hopes of destroying it.

General Norrie, commander of 30th Corps, had his eyes focused on Tobruk, not on his backside. He was planning to advance toward Tobruk on the morning of November 21 with 7th Tank Brigade and Support Group, in conjunction with a tank-led sortie coming out of Tobruk.

However, at 8 A.M. Norrie saw German panzers approaching Sidi Rezegh from the south and east. Instead of turning his whole armored force to meet this threat, Norrie left the 6th Royal Tanks to continue the attack toward Tobruk, and diverted his other two regiments, the 7th Hussars and the 2nd Royal Tanks, to challenge Cruewell. The result was disaster. The 6th Royal Tanks charged 90th Light's well dug-in guns and were shattered, while Rommel himself directed 88-millimeter fire on a tank sortie that tried to break out of Tobruk, knocked out several "I" tanks, and halted the advance.

Meanwhile, to the southeast of Sidi Rezegh, 15th Panzer Division drove a wedge several miles wide between the 7th Hussars and the 2nd Royal Tanks. This allowed 21st Panzer Division to overrun and almost wipe out the now-isolated 7th Hussars. After refueling, Africa Corps came back in the afternoon and attacked 2nd Royal Tanks, advancing antitank guns ahead of the tanks and around the flanks of the British armor. The AT guns took such a toll that the regiment was saved from annihilation only by the belated arrival of 22nd Armored Brigade from Gabr Saleh. The 4th Brigade didn't come up until the next day.

Artillery of Support Group stopped an attempt by Africa Corps to overrun Sidi Rezegh airfield, but the panzer corps was now in what Napoleon called "the central position" between two enemy forces, each inferior to the central force. That is, Africa Corps was between Support Group and remains of 7th Tank Brigade on one side, and 22nd and 4th Armored Brigades approaching from the south on the other. Rommel saw that Africa Corps could destroy each in turn, and ordered Cruewell to carry out the assaults the next day.

But Cruewell had not recognized the incredibly favorable position Africa Corps had gained. Instead, he once more made a foolish error. He had planned to take Africa Corps eastward during the night, in order to achieve "complete freedom of maneuver." Getting Rommel's order, he made a third mistake. Instead of turning the whole corps back to the central position, he sent 15th Panzer toward Gambut, twenty miles northeast of Sidi Rezegh, and directed 21st Panzer to reassemble between Belhamed and Zaafran, some seven miles north of the airfield.

Cruewell thus separated the two panzer divisions by eighteen miles, abandoned the central position, and permitted 30th Corps to concentrate its remaining 180 tanks.

Rommel arrived around midday November 22 at 21st Panzer and discovered that his armor had been split. He determined nevertheless to oust Support Group from the airfield. While 21st Panzer's infantry and artillery attacked Sidi Rezegh from the north, locking Support Group in place, he wheeled the panzer regiment, along with a number of 88s and 50-millimeter AT guns, to the southwest, struck the western flank of the British position, overran the airfield, and shattered part of Support Group.

Once more the British did not use their tanks in mass: 22nd Armored Brigade came up to help, but 4th Brigade inexplicably held back. German 88s and AT guns destroyed half of the 22nd's tanks before the brigade withdrew. When 4th Brigade at last came into the fight at dusk, it was unable to retrieve the situation.

The British now decided that the airfield was untenable and withdrew south to await 1st South African Division, which had been ordered northward, although only its 5th Brigade was coming up by the morning of November 23.

Meanwhile, Cruewell returned with the 15th Panzer and struck the 4th Armored Brigade from the east after it had drawn into a defensive "hedgehog" perimeter. The Germans seized the brigade headquarters and a large number of men and tanks, mutilating the brigade to such a degree that it was unable to reassemble the next day.

Africa Corps had gained command of the battlefield. The 15th Panzer was at Bir Sciaf Sciuf, fifteen miles east of Sidi Rezegh; 21st Panzer was holding the Sidi Rezegh area; and the Italian Ariete and Trieste Divisions were assembling around Bir el Gubi, twenty-two miles to the south.

Rommel had received reports that 7th Armored Division's remnants had withdrawn from the airfield, and assumed that the division had moved about twelve miles south of Sidi Rezegh. He saw that 7th Armored and 5th South African Brigade might be destroyed on November 23 by a concentric attack, with the Italians moving northeast, and Africa Corps enveloping them by driving south and west.

However, Cruewell had put in motion his own plan by the time Rommel's order arrived, thereby showing that even the best concepts of a commander can be upset by a subordinate who does not comprehend what the commander is doing.

Meanwhile, 2nd New Zealand Division of 13th Corps had advanced directly from the east, seized Fort Capuzzo, and sent its 6th Brigade westward along an Arab desert trail, the Trigh Capuzzo. Soon after daylight on November 23, after Cruewell had departed, the brigade bumped into Africa Corps headquarters at Gasr el Arid, twenty-five miles east of Sidi Rezegh, and seized it after a bitter fight. Loss of the corps staff and its radio links seriously handicapped Rommel in the days to follow.

Cruewell's plan to destroy 7th Armored Division and 5th South African was foolish. He ordered 21st Panzer's infantry and artillery to hold the escarpment and airfield south of Sidi Rezegh, while the division's panzer regiment joined 15th Panzer for a wide sweep around the rear of 7th Armored Division and the South African brigade, and join up with the Ariete and Trieste Divisions moving up from Bir el Gubi. Cruewell's idea was *not* a concentric assault on the enemy from all sides, as Rommel intended, but an assault by all the assembled Axis strength head-on against the British and South Africans.

However, when Cruewell's forces rumbled southwestward through early morning mist on November 23, they ran smack into the *center* of 7th Armored's position.

General Norrie had not moved the division twelve miles south to link up with the South Africans, as Rommel thought, but a few miles southeast. The British were as surprised as the Germans, and the arrival of the panzers set off a wild stampede in all directions by British tanks and other vehicles trying to get away. The scattering of the division offered Cruewell a golden opportunity to destroy the whole force in detail. But Cruewell, intent on linking up with the Italians, called off pursuit, and, swinging on an even wider outflanking movement, continued to the southwest. Thus Cruewell missed one of the great chances in the war.

Cruewell didn't reach the Italians until midafternoon. And it took a while to line up his forces for attack on the South Africans, now to the north. In the long delay Cruewell had given them, the South Africans moved most of their guns to the exposed flank and formed a powerful defensive barrier.

Cruewell now committed one further error. Instead of following German tactical doctrine and advancing antitank guns forward and around the flanks to engage enemy armor and neutralize enemy artillery and tanks before committing his panzers, Cruewell formed up his tanks in long lines, and, ordering his infantry to follow in trucks, launched a headlong charge. They met a curtain of fire. Tank after tank was shattered, truck after truck full of infantry destroyed. The Germans had to commit all of their artillery to silence the South African guns, while British and German tanks and antitank guns fought tremendous duels. By late afternoon the panzers finally punched a few holes in the front and the tank attack moved forward, destroyed the 5th South African Brigade, and killed or captured 3,000 soldiers. As darkness fell, hundreds of burning vehicles, tanks, and guns lit up the horizon.

Cruewell's attack had succeeded, but at enormous cost. Hundreds of German infantry had been killed, and Africa Corps lost seventy of its remaining 160 tanks. Although 30th Corps had only seventy tanks fit for action, and these widely dispersed, out of 500 at the start, the British had large tank reserves, the Germans almost none.

The tank losses in this one mad attack largely offset the gains of Rommel's superb maneuvers over the past several days.

Rommel's offensive power had been crippled. But he was not ready to back off, and he conceived a brilliant riposte: to strike deep into the British rear, with the aim of cutting enemy supply lines, and restoring the situation on the Sollum–Halfaya Pass front. Rommel hoped Cunningham would be so unnerved by this unexpected move he would give up the fight.

In light of Axis weakness and British strength, this was the boldest decision Rommel ever made. A more conventional commander would have finished off the remnants of 30th Corps scattered all over the battlefield, or crushed 2nd New Zealand Division, still advancing westward toward Tobruk. But Rommel knew direct assaults on either of these forces would consume what little strength he had remaining. Besides, British cruiser tanks were faster than his own, and could avoid destruction by escaping.

Rommel saw that the only hope for victory was a vigorous strike into the heart of enemy resistance. This might shake enemy morale, and it especially might play on the fears of the British commanders.

Rommel scraped together a weak force from various formations to keep up the Tobruk siege. Then, at midday on November 24, he struck eastward with 21st Panzer, ordering 15th Panzer, Ariete, and Trieste divisions to follow.

The unexpected advance scattered the 7th Armored and 1st South African divisions in front of him, and, in five hours, he reached the frontier sixty miles away at Bir Sheferzen, twenty miles south of Halfaya Pass. Rommel at once sent a battle group through a gap in the frontier wire and belt of mines to Halfaya to dominate 8th Army's route of retreat and supply along the coast road.

The move threw 30th Corps into chaos, and caused Cunningham to do precisely what Rommel hoped he'd do: call for immediate withdrawal of 8th Army back into Egypt. But General Auchinleck arrived at 30th Corps headquarters and ordered continuation of the campaign. It was a brave decision. Auchinleck's commanders had panicked at Rommel's surprise move, and could think only of flight. But Auchinleck knew that Rommel's strength was practically exhausted, while 8th Army still had great untapped resources, including many tanks in rear depots. He had the moral courage to stand when many another commander would have run. The decision ensured Rommel's defeat.

It was obvious to Auchinleck that Cunningham had to be replaced, and on November 26 he named Lieutenant General Sir Neil Ritchie, his deputy chief of staff, to command 8th Army. This guaranteed that, whatever the risks, the battle would continue.

Rommel's own vehicle got stranded on the opposite side of the frontier fence because of engine trouble. But Cruewell's command vehicle, a covered van captured from the British, came past, and picked him up. When night fell, the German commanders could not find their way through the frontier minefields, so they and their staffs spent the night with Indian dispatch riders going back and forth and British tanks and trucks moving past. At daybreak they slipped away unchallenged, and crossed back into Libya.

On his return Rommel found that 15th Panzer had still not reached the frontier, while Ariete and Trieste Divisions had halted well to the west upon encountering a brigade of 1st South African Division. Also, supply columns bringing fuel and ammunition had failed to arrive. Rommel now could not carry out his plan to send a battle group to seize Habata, the new British railhead thirty-five miles southeast of Halfaya Pass, or to block the British supply and escape route along the escarpment running southeast into Egypt from Halfaya. His bid to force the British to retreat had failed. Even so, Rommel stubbornly held on, hoping for an opportunity to strike a killing blow.

Meanwhile, 13th Corps, led by 2nd New Zealand Division and ninety "I" tanks, pushed on westward toward Tobruk. The scratch force that was left to defend the Sidi Rezegh area was soon under great pressure. On November 25, the New Zealanders seized Belhamed, only nine miles southeast of the Tobruk perimeter. The next night, the Tobruk garrison crashed through Axis besiegers and gained the top of the escarpment at Ed Duda, only a couple of miles from the New Zealanders.

Panzer Group headquarters sent frantic radio signals asking for return of the panzers, but Rommel was not willing to give up so readily. He ordered Cruewell to drive north and clear the Sollum front by thrusts of 15th Panzer on the west and 21st Panzer, already at Halfaya, on the east. However, 15th Panzer had gone back to Bardia, fifteen miles north of Sollum, to refuel. At the same time 21st Panzer also headed toward Bardia because of a misinterpreted order.

Rommel realized his hopes were gone and ordered 21st Panzer back to defend Tobruk, but kept 15th Panzer south of Bardia. Early on November 27 the division's tanks overran headquarters of 5th New Zealand Brigade at Sidi Azeis, ten miles southwest of Bardia, and captured the commander, 800 men, and several guns. With this success, Rommel ordered 15th Panzer to move back toward Tobruk as well.

On the frontier, Africa Corps had gained nothing decisive. Now it was down to only a fraction of its original strength, while the British, left in possession of the Sidi Rezegh battlefield, had been able to repair many tanks and receive replacements from Egypt. British tank strength was now 130 to 40 German, but Rommel continued to use his armor in concert, while the British kept theirs scattered.

Rommel hoped to keep the Tobruk garrison isolated, and to destroy the two New Zealand brigades (2nd and 4th) in the Belhamed area. On November 29, 15th Panzer detoured to the south and west around Sidi Rezegh and, in a bitter engagement, seized Ed Duda in an advance from the southwest. Ariete Division and 21st Panzer were to attack the New Zealanders from the east and south, but made little headway against British armor that drove against them on their southern flank.

The men of Panzer Group were exhausted, the weather was cold, the country without water, and the Axis supply line in tatters. Although the New Zealanders were nearly encircled, strong British armor threatened to push aside the light forces covering the Axis southern flank, and the 1st South African Division was coming forward to help.

But Rommel was still determined, and so were his men. On the morning of November 30, 15th Panzer with the help of battle groups from 90th Light attacked southward from the escarpment north of Sidi Rezegh. By evening they had gained some New Zealand positions, 600 prisoners, and twelve guns. During the same period, 21st Panzer and Ariete stopped a relieving attack by British armor from the south.

During the night most of the New Zealanders broke out, although the Germans captured more than 1,000 men and twenty-six guns. British armor and infantry moved south and east to regroup. Tobruk once more had been isolated.

Rommel appeared to have won. But the price had been too high. He had no offensive power left, while British tank strength was growing daily with shipments from the rear. If his army were to survive to fight another day, Rommel had to extricate it.

With the same boldness he had employed in the attack, Rommel pulled back his forces swiftly in a masterful series of engagements, preventing the British in every case from surrounding Axis units and forcing their surrender.

On January 6, 1942, Rommel reached Mersa el Brega, on the border of Tripolitania. Once more all of Cyrenaica had been evacuated. The Axis garrison marooned at Bardia surrendered on January 2, 1942, but a starving force at Halfaya Pass didn't give up until January 17. This so delayed British movements, especially of supplies, that the British could maintain only the 1st Armored Division, fresh from England, and the 201st Guards Brigade at Agedabia.

Meanwhile Rommel's supply situation had improved vastly because Hitler had transferred a Luftwaffe air corps to Sicily and Italy, and it beat down British air and sea domination over the sea route to Libya. On January 5, 1942, an Italian convoy reached Tripoli with fifty-five tanks and a number of antitank guns. Counting repaired armor, Rommel now had 111 German and 89 Italian tanks on January 20. The British 1st Armored Division had 150, all manned by inexperienced crews.

At once Rommel resolved on a counteroffensive. To preserve secrecy, he kept his plans from both the German and Italian high commands. He lulled the British into complacency by forbidding all air reconnaissance, camouflaging his tanks to look like trucks, and massing his forces by short night marches.

When he struck, therefore, on the night of January 20–21, 1942, he achieved absolute surprise. Rommel sent a battle group of 90th Light and some tanks northward along the Via Balbia, while Africa Corps advanced about forty miles inland, along the Wadi el Faregh. Rommel hoped to block the retreat of the British. But the going was so hard through the sand dunes that the enemy had time to escape, concentrating east of Agedabia. Africa Corps ran out of fuel, but Rommel took personal command of the 90th Light battle group and rushed into Agedabia, seized the town on January 22, and continued on northward on the Via Balbia, throwing British supply columns into confusion.

Rommel now tried to block the retreat of 1st Armored Division, but the bulk of it escaped, although Africa Corps was able to surround and destroy one combat group with seventy tanks near Saunnu, forty miles northeast of Agedabia. The remaining British tanks broke for Msus, forty miles north. In one of the most extraordinary chases of the war, the panzers pursued the British armor, and wrecked more than half of the remaining tanks.

Rommel now feinted with Africa Corps toward El Mechili, eighty miles northeast of Msus across the chord of the Cyrenaican bulge. Since Rommel had used this route in his first offensive in April 1941, Ritchie took the bait and concentrated all his armor to meet it. Instead, Rommel rushed 90th Light along the coast to Benghazi, where it captured mountains of supplies and 1,000 men from the 4th Indian Division. The victory brought promotion to colonel general from Hitler, but no additional troops.

The men of the Panzer Group were at the end of their strength. When Ritchie withdrew to Gazala, only forty miles west of Tobruk, and began building a new defensive line, all the Germans and Italians could do was to come up on the line on February 6, 1942.

Once more, Rommel had gained much with little. At Gazala, he was positioned to resume the attack as soon as he could rebuild his army.

# 12 No Change in Strategy

WITH THE ENTRY OF THE UNITED STATES INTO THE WAR, A WHOLLY NEW STRATE-gic challenge faced Germany. The potential power of America was immense. But its application lay in the future. Hitler had to decide between two alternatives: Should he continue the attack on the Soviet Union, or should he go on the defensive there and concentrate on keeping American and British forces away from the continent of Europe?

For Admiral Erich Raeder, the choice was easy. On February 13, 1942, he proposed that Germany's primary military tasks should be for Rommel to drive through Egypt to the Middle East, while the army in Russia did only two things: capture Murmansk and close that ice-free port to Allied convoys, and drive into the Caucasus to seize Soviet oil wells. After that the way would be clear to cross into Iran, close off that supply line to Russia, and join up with Rommel. Meanwhile, German war production should be shifted over predominately to the navy and air force to build more submarines and other vessels and aircraft to interdict the flow of supplies from America.

Two days later, an airplane brought Rommel to Hitler's headquarters at Rastenburg in East Prussia. Rommel pressed hard for more forces, three more divisions, to double the German troops he possessed in North Africa. With these, he said, he could smash the British, capture Egypt, drive the Royal Navy out of the Mediterranean, and press to the oil fields of Iraq and Iran.

Rommel's proposals strengthened Raeder's argument for a sea change in German strategy—away from Russia and, at long last, aimed at the

British and their new American allies. Despite the terrible losses suffered in the Russian campaign—more than a million men had been killed, wounded, or captured in eight months of fighting, one-third of the entire German army in the Soviet Union—Raeder's and Rommel's proposals still could have saved the war for Germany.

Much would be gained if North Africa and the Middle East were finally captured, the remaining strength of the German army largely preserved, and an all-out campaign undertaken to stop the flow of supplies across the Atlantic. Because of Japan's advances, it would be a year, at least, before the United States could exert any substantial strength beyond the Pacific, and more time would go by before it could build enough ships, landing craft, air fleets, and armies to invade western Europe. When the time came, Germany might be much stronger and much more able to resist.

But at this moment Adolf Hitler made the final decision that closed off any hope of reaching a negotiated settlement. He refused to consider Raeder's and Rommel's proposals. He made it clear that he wanted first to destroy the Red Army and eliminate its sources of strength. After that, other courses might be followed. But for now, the *Ostheer*—or army in the east—was to receive priority, and the German economy was to be directed at rearming this army, not at building a great U-boat fleet and air force, and not at reinforcing Rommel.

Consequently, as the year 1942 opened, Hitler continued to avert his strategic gaze from the west and maintained his fixation on destroying the Soviet Union. The British and the Americans didn't know it yet, but they had been granted a long reprieve and a great opportunity to build their power.

The defeat at Pearl Harbor had so shocked and angered the American people, however, that it was an open question whether they would turn on Germany before they had smashed the Land of the Rising Sun. Prime Minister Churchill, fearful they might choose Japan over Germany as the major enemy, traveled to Washington only days after the Japanese attack.

With Churchill on the battleship *Duke of York* was a large entourage to work out a joint strategy with the United States. These talks, code-named Arcadia, led to reaffirmation of the "Germany first" policy established in the British-American ABC-1 meetings in the winter past and to the formation of the Combined Chiefs of Staff Committee (CCSC), a joint authority to direct the war made up of the heads of the armed services of both countries.

But agreement on a broad plan to defeat Germany before turning full American power on Japan did not mean that the British and the American leaders saw eye to eye. It quickly became clear that the Americans—led by General George C. Marshall, U.S. Army chief of staff and principal military adviser to the president—wanted to strike directly at German power by crossing the English Channel, challenging the Germans in a stand-up fight on the beaches, then driving them back into Germany and destroying their army. The British, with far fewer men and much leaner resources, preferred an indirect approach through the Mediterranean, which Churchill characterized as "the soft underbelly of the Axis."

There were arguments either way. A straight shot across the Channel would be a shorter route to the vitals of Germany. But the British believed that the long way around might be the shortest way home. Not only would a direct attack, being the most obvious, be the most heavily contested, and therefore the most expensive in men and materials, but it would also drive the Germans back on their reserves and supplies rather than cutting them off from their means to resist.

A Mediterranean strategy had the advantage of striking where the Germans were weak. No one had much concern for the Italians, whose weapons were so poor and desire for war so uncertain that they were likely to surrender at the first opportunity. On the other hand, a campaign up the boot of Italy would be extremely difficult, given the mountainous nature of the terrain, while an invasion of the Balkans would be far from the vitals of Germany, in a region laced with mountains and cursed with poor roads and insufficient rail lines.

The dispute over where to concentrate the blow was to consume a vast amount of time and cause much rancor between the British and the Americans.

At Arcadia, the British were able to get tentative agreement on an invasion of French North Africa (Operation Gymnast). This sort of diversion was precisely what General Marshall opposed. He and Henry L. Stimson, secretary of war, got Gymnast postponed in March 1942, but the victory was only temporary.

At the moment the Americans and British were most concerned with a new phase in the Battle of the Atlantic. German U-boats operating off the coast of the United States and in the St. Lawrence estuary in Canada sank 79 ships with 429,000 tons in March 1942, and two months later 123 ships and 569,000 tons.

For the first half of 1942 the threat of German submarines frightened American and British leaders badly. But it was only a passing phase. The Allies had two major assets of their own, and one given them by Hitler. Their assets were, first, the enormous productive capacity of the Allied, principally American, shipyards where seven million tons of shipping were being built, and, second, the slow but steady introduction of destroyers, destroyer escorts, corvettes, and escort carriers to shepherd Allied convoys and apply weapons like sonar and radar which located German U-boats in darkness and the worst of weather.

The gift of Hitler was to suppress the construction of U-boats. To counteract the launching of ships by the Allies, the Germans had to sink 600,000 tons of shipping a month. This required nineteen to twenty new U-boats a month to replace those lost. But Hitler's decision to concentrate on the army eliminated any hope of U-boat construction reaching the necessary level. Consequently, Allied sailors slowly gained the upper hand, and, by mid-1943, had won the Battle of the Atlantic.

✠          ✠          ✠

For Adolf Hitler, the early months of 1942 closed off the last chance he possessed to change strategic direction. Even at this late date, he might have reversed the course of the war if he had gone over to the defensive in Russia, following the strategy the Germans adopted in World War I, and concentrated most of Germany's resources on the Battle of the Atlantic and on helping Rommel capture Suez and the Middle East.

Franz Halder, the army chief of staff, wanted to revert to the defensive in Russia, and even opposed Admiral Raeder's limited objectives for 1942—seizure of the Caucasus oil fields and Murmansk. But Halder and the Fuehrer's remaining close military advisers never could see the opportunities still beckoning to them from the southern shore of the Mediterranean.

As Erwin Rommel wrote with great vexation:

It was obvious that the high command's opinion had not changed from that which they had expressed in 1941, namely, that Africa was a "lost cause," and any large-scale investment of material and troops in that theater would pay no dividends. A sadly shortsighted and mis-guided view! For, in fact, the supply difficulties which they were so anxious to describe as "insuperable" were far from being so. All that was wanted was a real personality in Rome, someone with the author-ity and drive to tackle and clear away the problems involved.

But no one could alter Hitler's fixation on destroying the Soviet Union. Admiral Raeder was not going to get his submarines. And General Rommel, Germany's unrecognized military genius, had to be satisfied with the three German and the three Italian armored or motorized divi-sions allotted to him if he was going to alter the course of history. In the campaign about to unroll, he very nearly did.

# 13 THE DRIVE TO EL ALAMEIN

FOR NEARLY TWO YEARS, THE AXIS POWERS HAD SQUANDERED A SPLENDID strategic advantage in the Mediterranean. While British ships had to take a 12,000-mile journey around the Cape of Good Hope, the Italians and Germans had only a 300-mile passage across the Sicilian Narrows between Sicily and Tripoli.

Yet the British had built up a seven-division army in eastern Libya, all motorized, with twice as many tanks as the Axis, and were about to embark on a major offensive with the intention of driving the Axis out of Africa.

The Italians and Germans had not even eliminated the British base of Malta, which lay smack in the middle of the Axis sea lanes between Italy and Tripoli, and from which British planes, ships, and submarines constantly sank Axis supply vessels.

It's no wonder that Erwin Rommel was so exasperated by the failure to seize Malta that he offered "to have this pleasant task entrusted to my own army." But he was turned down.

Rommel was also exasperated by the refusal of Adolf Hitler to give him more than three divisions. Mussolini sent only one motorized and two armored divisions, and Italian tanks were so inferior they could not stand up in tank-to-tank battles. All the rest of the Italian forces in Libya were footbound infantry who were more a liability in desert warfare than an asset.

Thus, for the want of resolve, not strength, the Axis position in the Mediterranean was on the threshold of being ripped away.

Yet the seemingly inevitable British victory did not come about in the spring and summer of 1942 because of the intervention of a single mind:

Erwin Rommel's. This officer took the poor hand dealt him and played it with such skill that he nearly won a total victory.

The world can be thankful that Adolf Hitler was so preoccupied with his obsessions and hates that he did not see what Rommel was achieving, and did not give him the modest additional forces he needed. If he had, Hitler could have ridden Erwin Rommel's military genius to a negotiated peace, even in the summer and fall of 1942, when Germany's position in the Soviet Union was collapsing.

✠          ✠          ✠

Hitler's principal concern in the Mediterranean was to keep Mussolini in the war. He sensed that the Italian people were hunting for any excuse to withdraw, and, late in 1941, sent into the Mediterranean 2nd Air Corps from Russia and twenty-three U-boats from the Atlantic. Although his aim was to help Mussolini, they eased Rommel's supply situation dramatically.

U-81 sank the British aircraft carrier *Ark Royal* and U-311 the British battleship *Barham.* Also the Italian submarine *Scirè* grounded the last two battleships in the Mediterranean Fleet, the *Queen Elizabeth* and the *Valiant.*

The 2nd Air Corps and some Italian aircraft commenced heavy bombardment of Malta. Supplies of food, water, and munitions declined. German bombers destroyed aircraft flown in from carriers. The 10th Submarine Flotilla was forced to depart the island. Rommel began to receive adequate supplies.

The Italian supreme commander, General Ugo Cavallero, started planning an air-sea assault on Malta (Operation Hercules). But the Italians were relying on German assistance, and though Hitler approved the idea at first, he soon backed out, suspecting the Italian navy and air force would leave German parachute troops in the lurch if they landed on the island. He moved 2nd Air Corps back to Russia.

✠          ✠          ✠

By the spring of 1942, the British concentration of seven motorized divisions at Gazala, two of them armored, with about 900 tanks, and more in reserve, added up to a striking force about twice that of Rommel's Panzer

Army. Rommel had 560 tanks, but 50 were Mark IIs and 240 Italian models that could not stand up to British tanks.

Moreover, the British deployed 170 decidedly superior tanks, American Grants, carrying a side-mounted high-velocity 75-millimeter and a turret-mounted 37-millimeter gun and 57 millimeters of armor. The British had 230 more Grants in reserve. The Grant's disabilities were a high silhouette and a limited traverse of the 75-millimeter gun. The closest German competitors were nineteen new Mark III Specials mounting a long-barreled, high-velocity 50-millimeter gun and 50 millimeters of armor. Older Mark IIIs, armed with a short-barreled 50-millimeter gun, and Mark IVs, mounting a short-barreled 75-millimeter gun, made up the bulk of Rommel's strength. They could be shattered by the Grant's gun at ranges beyond either tank's capacity to penetrate the Grant's armor.

The British also armed their motorized infantry with the new six-pounder (57-millimeter) antitank gun, possessing 30 percent more penetration than the German 50-millimeter AT gun. The German 88-millimeter AA gun remained the most formidable tank killer on either side, but Rommel had only forty-eight of them.

The Germans assembled 542 aircraft, the RAF assembled 604. But, with improved Me-109 fighters that outclassed the British Hurricanes and American-built P-40E Kittyhawks, the Luftwaffe was dominant in the early stages of the campaign.

The British position rested on a heavily mined fifty-mile-long defensive line of 13th Corps, now commanded by Lieutenant General W.H.E. "Strafer" Gott. It ran from Gazala on the Mediterranean to Bir Hacheim, where the 1st Free French Brigade of 4,000 men, plus a small Jewish Brigade, held a strongly fortified "box," or defensive "hedgehog" perimeter.

For ten miles on the north the 1st South African Division manned a firm sector. Below it, however, the three brigades of the British 50th Division occupied widely separated defensive boxes, flanked only by minefields. Two boxes were most exposed: the division's 150th Brigade at Got el Ualeb, half a dozen miles south of the east-west Arab caravan route Trigh Capuzzo, and, sixteen miles farther south, the Free French box at Bir Hacheim.

Some thirty miles southeast of Gazala and twelve miles east of the 150th Brigade box was Knightsbridge box, held by the 201st Guards Brigade, at the junction of the Trigh Capuzzo and a north-south Arab trail. About twenty miles east of Knightsbridge and seventeen miles south of Tobruk was the El Adem box, garrisoned by parts of 5th Indian Division.

The Gazala line evoked memories of powerful defensive positions along the western front in World War I. It was a product of the close association of British generals with infantry, not mobile, warfare. But a static defensive line was bound to lead to disaster in desert warfare. As Rommel pointed out, any position in North Africa had an open desert flank on the south and could always be turned. To be successful, defense in the desert had to be conducted offensively.

The boxes also might be bypassed or surrounded and forced to surrender. An added problem was that the new British forward railhead and supply base was only forty-five miles east of the Gazala line at Belhamed. The vast supplies there made British commanders hesitant to maneuver armor in any way that might uncover Belhamed.

Behind the Gazala line the British had a mobile reserve: the 1st and 7th Armored Divisions in 30th Corps, still under Lieutenant General C. W. M. Norrie, with three brigades of cruiser tanks (including the Grants). However, the British continued to divide their armor, leaving two brigades of "I" (infantry) tanks (mostly Matildas) posted in support of the 1st South African and 50th Divisions.

German intelligence had clear signs that the British were building up for an offensive. Since the southern flank lay wide open, a bold British armored strike around it into the rear against the Axis supply line could force Rommel's army to abandon the field. Retreat would be fraught with difficulties, because most of the Italian divisions were nonmotorized.

"But the British were not to have the chance of exploiting their opportunities," Rommel wrote, "for I had decided to strike first."

Generals Auchinleck and Sir Neil Ritchie, commanding 8th Army, were not ready to commence their offensive, and posted their armor defensively in case Rommel did attack. Oddly, Auchinleck thought Rommel was not likely to strike around the undefended southern flank, but would drive into the center along the Trigh Capuzzo. He advised Ritchie to concentrate his two armored divisions along this trail, so that he could move against a thrust along it or meet a turning move around the flank if it did come.

Ritchie, instead, kept 1st Armored (with the 2nd and 22nd Armored Brigades) around the Trigh Capuzzo, and sent 7th Armored, with its single 4th Armored Brigade, southward to support the French at Bir Hacheim and the 3rd Indian Motorized Brigade holding a guarding position a few miles east. Thus, as the battle opened, British armor was split into three segments: two "I" brigades (the 1st and 32nd) in the north, 1st Armored in the center, and 7th Armored in the south.

Rommel had planned all along to swing around the southern flank. But to disguise this move, he ordered trucks and tanks driven in circles behind the Gazala line to deceive the British into thinking he was assembling armor. In daylight just before the attack, he sent all motorized forces toward the Italian infantry divisions detailed to demonstrate along the Gazala line, then brought them to their assembly points after nightfall.

Rommel's striking force consisted of Africa Corps (15th and 21st Panzer Divisions), the 20th Italian Motorized Corps (Ariete Armored and Trieste Motorized Divisions), and 90th Light Division. The whole force was to circle around Bir Hacheim. The Italians were to storm and take Bir Hacheim in a coup de main, thus opening a shorter supply corridor, while Africa Corps was to strike directly for Acroma and the coast, cutting off and destroying the armor and troops along the Gazala line. At the same time 90th Light, with trucks mounting aircraft engines to simulate dust clouds raised by advancing tanks, was to push into the El Adem–Belhamed area, about fifteen miles southeast of Tobruk, and cut off the British from their supplies and reinforcements.

On the night of May 26, 1942, after Italian infantry under German General Ludwig Cruewell made a diversionary frontal assault against the Gazala line, Rommel's mobile forces in 10,000 vehicles struck out in moonlight through swirling dust and sand. Luftwaffe planes dropped flares on Bir Hacheim to show the drivers the limit of the British lines. By daybreak, having encountered no opposition, the force was east of Bir Hacheim and the Germans set out at full speed for the British rear. The Italians turned back to storm Bir Hacheim, but were stopped by mines and French antitank fire.

By 10 A.M. on May 27, 90th Light seized El Adem and numerous supply dumps, but stirred up a furious battle with British forces in the area.

At the same time, Africa Corps, now under General Walter Nehring, collided with 4th Armored Brigade fifteen miles northeast of Bir Hacheim near Bir el Harmat. In violation of Rommel's orders, Nehring's panzers attacked without artillery support. They were stunned by the long-range penetrating power of the 75-millimeter Grant gun. Tank after tank burst into flames or was disabled. Only after they had brought up antitank guns and 88s were the Germans able to make headway. Tanks now worked around the enemy flanks, finally shattering the British brigade, whose remnants fell back toward El Adem.

As 4th Armored Brigade drew away, 21st Panzer drove northward, overwhelmed 3rd Indian Motorized Brigade in a forty-minute fight, and shattered 7th Motorized Brigade trying to hold a position a few miles on.

In the late morning the British 22nd Armored Brigade arrived from the north. An officer with an advance element wrote: "On topping a rise we could see on the eastern skyline a solid mass of vehicles stretching southward into the haze as far as the eye could see." This was Africa Corps moving toward the Trigh Capuzzo.

The 22nd Brigade, caught isolated, was mauled in a concentric attack by both panzer divisions and also forced to withdraw. Africa Corps advanced to the Trigh Capuzzo and met the third British armored brigade, the 2nd, which attacked from the west but didn't coordinate with the 1st Army Tank Brigade that charged recklessly from the east.

There was a period of panic when sixty Matildas and Grants smashed into the midst of the German forces, and overran a motorized infantry battalion. Nehring threw in his headquarters defense unit, a battery of 88s, a few tanks, and a company of light antiaircraft guns. Joined by sixteen additional 88s, the defenders formed a solid gun line, destroyed twelve enemy tanks, and forced the remainder to withdraw. The assaults cut off supply columns trying to bring up fuel and ammunition, and forced Africa Corps to close into a hedgehog perimeter for the night about three miles north of the Trigh Capuzzo.

The Axis forces had been forced to halt in a highly dangerous position with British forces blocking their movement north. Moreover, the only way the Germans and Italians could be supplied was by way of a wide detour around Bir Hacheim.

If the British had not wasted their strength in uncoordinated isolated fights by individual brigades, they might have converged on Rommel's

armor and ended the campaign in North Africa then and there. Rommel
was especially astonished at the sacrifice of 7th Armored Brigade south of
Bir el Harmat. "It was all the same to the British whether my armor was
engaged there or on the Trigh Capuzzo," he wrote. "The full motoriza-
tion of their units would have enabled them to cross the battlefield at
great speed to wherever danger threatened."

Despite the failure on May 27, General Ritchie possessed another great
opportunity to destroy Africa Corps on May 28 by a concentric attack,
using the armor he already had in place, and bringing up the 32nd Tank
Brigade, which had not been committed. But Ritchie took no such action,
and Rommel had time to reorganize.

On May 28, Rommel intended for 90th Light to withdraw from the El
Adem area and join Africa Corps for a concerted attack northward. But
the division could not extricate itself from an attack by 4th Armored
Brigade. As a result, Ariete Division and Africa Corps fought a confused
series of engagements with British armor, which once more came in
piecemeal. By the end of the day, Africa Corps had 150 tanks left fit for
action, the Italians 90, while the British still had 420.

The 90th Light was able to withdraw during the night to Bir el Harmat,
and early on May 29 Rommel himself led a supply column to replenish
Axis forces with fuel and ammunition. On this day the British again
launched one uncoordinated attack after another. The Germans were little affected and remained in a strong position.

But Rommel realized he could not continue northward until his supply line was secure, since trucks coming around south of Bir Hacheim
were being attacked by British motorized forces.

He then made a bold decision that saved the campaign. While the rest
of his forces went over to the defensive, Rommel ordered 90th Light to
drive west while Italian infantry advanced east along the Trigh Capuzzo.
In this way, he broke a supply line directly through the Gazala line minefields.

The 150th Brigade box at Got el Ualeb and the Free French box at Bir
Hacheim were now isolated, and Rommel decided to destroy both. Their
capture would eliminate all danger to the south and give him freedom of
action.

Nevertheless, the plan posed enormous danger. Axis armor was still stymied deep in the British rear and could do nothing until an avenue of advance opened. Yet Ritchie had a clear path to victory. He could use his infantry and artillery to break a hole through the weak Italian divisions manning the Gazala line on the coast and drive west to sever the Axis supply line. Rommel had little to stop him. Such a move would leave Rommel's panzers without fuel and endanger his whole position in Africa.

Rommel saw the peril clearly. But he had judged his opponents accurately. He knew the British generals would not think so much of opportunity as of danger. If they drove west along the northern coast road with part of their armor, they feared Rommel would rush north and cut their supply line. Yet the British had 400 tanks, plus AT guns, and—with the rest of their tanks—could have blocked Rommel's remaining 130 German and 130 Italian tanks until their fuel ran out. Rommel was confident that the British would fix their attention on the Axis armor and "continue to run their heads against our well-organized defensive front and use up their strength."

This is what happened. On May 30 British armor made sporadic, uncoordinated attacks broken up by German 88s and AT guns. By the end of the day, Axis forces had shattered fifty-seven tanks and established a firm front on the east-west Sidra Ridge, a mile north of the Trigh Capuzzo, and on Aslagh Ridge, about five miles south, enclosing an area the British named the Caldron.

Rommel thus had the time to assault the Allied boxes. On May 31 he personally led 90th Light, Trieste, and elements of Africa Corps against the 150th Brigade box. Aided by a regiment of Matildas, the British resisted stubbornly, but their situation was hopeless, and the next day, after a heavy attack by Stuka dive-bombers, out of ammunition and water, they gave up 3,000 men.

On June 2, 90th Light and Trieste assaulted the Bir Hacheim box. The fight turned into one of the fiercest in the war, lasting ten days. The French and Jewish defenders fought skillfully from field positions, machine-gun and AT nests, and slit trenches. They endured intense dive-bombing: 1,300 Stuka sorties in nine days. The Luftwaffe suffered, for RAF fighters shot down forty Stukas on a single day.

On June 5, the British tried once more to destroy Axis armor in the Caldron, but they still made direct, obvious, piecemeal attacks.

To the north, slow, heavy Matilda and Valentine infantry tanks lumbered forward in daylight, unsupported by artillery fire, and provided perfect targets for AT guns of 21st Panzer on Sidra Ridge. The British armor ended in a minefield and were shot to pieces, losing fifty of seventy tanks engaged.

To the southeast the 10th Indian Brigade drove Ariete Division off Aslagh Ridge. The 22nd Armored Brigade then passed into the Caldron, followed by the 9th Infantry Brigade. The British tanks received tremendous fire from German AT guns and artillery, and withdrew to Bir el Tamar, between Aslagh and Sidra Ridges. At midday, Rommel launched one of his most brilliant counterstrokes. While 21st Panzer thrust southeast toward Bir el Tamar, 15th Panzer emerged from a gap in the minefields south of Aslagh Ridge and struck the flank and rear of the Indian troops holding the ridge. By nightfall the Axis had shattered 9th Infantry Brigade and formed a ring around 10th Indian Brigade on Aslagh, as well as the armored division's Support Group and four field artillery regiments to the north.

Rommel predicted that the British generals would draw no forces from the Gazala line or from the Tobruk garrison to exert pressure against the Germans ringing the British in the Caldron. They did not, though this was the only way to rescue the trapped soldiers.

"In a moment so decisive, they should have thrown in all the strength they could muster," Rommel wrote. "What is the use of having overall superiority if one allows one's formations to be smashed piece by piece by an enemy who, in each separate action, is able to concentrate superior strength at the decisive point?"

By the end of the day on June 6, Africa Corps had destroyed a hundred tanks, wiped out 10th Brigade, and captured 3,100 men, ninety-six cannons, and thirty-seven antitank guns. Total British tank strength had fallen to 170.

This defensive fight broke the British barrier at the Caldron and opened the way for rapid movement. But Rommel decided first to eliminate Bir Hacheim before bursting forward.

On June 8, elements of 15th Panzer joined other Axis forces in a coordinated attack of extreme violence from all directions against the Free French brigade, under the inspired leadership of Pierre Koenig. A German *Kampfgruppe* finally cracked the main position on June 10, but the greater part of the garrison broke out during the night and was picked up by the 7th British Motor Brigade. This demonstrated how difficult it is to contain a determined force. Only 500 soldiers fell into German hands, most of them wounded.

✠        ✠        ✠

The way was now open for Rommel to drive into the British vitals, though Ritchie had brought up reinforcements and now had 330 tanks, twice the remaining strength of Africa Corps. But the Germans were smelling victory, while the British had been badly shaken.

On June 11, 1942, 15th Panzer turned northeast toward El Adem, with 90th Light, now down to 1,000 men, on its right, and Trieste Division on the left. By nightfall the force was south and west of El Adem, facing the 2nd and 4th Armored Brigades.

Rommel ordered 21st Panzer to swing around to the northeast the next day and attack the enemy armor in the rear. The British tank units, not realizing they could not remain stationary while the whole Axis army was on the move, was trapped. German AT guns moved forward and began a systematic execution. When 22nd Armored Brigade came down from the north to help, it was too late, caught by 21st Panzer and Trieste, and suffered heavy losses.

The two cornered brigades tried to flee, the 2nd withdrawing in some order with 22nd Brigade toward Knightsbridge box, a few miles north, but the 4th's retreat turned into a rout, and it lost most of its force, 120 tanks.

The next day Rommel turned north, aiming at the Knightsbridge box. But the British had finally realized that defensive boxes in the open desert were prisons not bastions, and they withdrew, with the panzers harrying the fleeing armor. By nightfall Ritchie had barely 100 tanks left, and Rommel enjoyed tank superiority for the first time. He also was in possession of the battlefield and recovered many tanks.

With the Germans overflowing the rear, the British along the Gazala line were in danger of being cut off and, on Ritchie's orders, withdrew on the morning of June 14. The same morning Rommel sent Africa Corps past Acroma with urgent orders to seal off the Via Balbia during the night and intercept the fleeing enemy.

But the German tank crews were so exhausted they dropped down short of the highway at the end of the day. During the night most of the South Africans escaped, moving back fast to the Egyptian frontier. The survivors of the British 50th Division broke out *west* through the Italian front, and moved in a long circuit south, then back east to the frontier.

The shattered British armored brigades were now no match for the panzers, and they withdrew into Egypt. Africa Corps swept around the Tobruk perimeter, garrisoned by 2nd South African Division and other forces, and seized airfields at Gambut, thirty-five miles east of Tobruk. This forced British aircraft to withdraw farther east, beyond easy range of Tobruk. The panzers then turned back on Tobruk.

This fortress was a symbol of British resistance, and Rommel was determined to have it. The British, seeing the panzers go past, did not expect an attack, but Rommel mounted one quickly, cracked a hole in the southeast perimeter on June 20 with artillery and dive-bombers, and widened the gap with infantry. Panzers now poured through, drove straight into the heart of the town and overcame the dazed defenders. Tobruk surrendered the next day, giving up 35,000 prisoners. The loss was second only to the capture of Singapore by the Japanese as the greatest British disaster of the war. Hitler was so impressed he promoted Rommel to field marshal. But Rommel wrote his wife: "I would rather he had given me one more division."

The unexpected loss of Tobruk shocked General Ritchie to such a degree that he gave up potentially strong positions at Sollum and Halfaya Gap on the frontier. This shows how the actions of a commander can affect the will of the general opposing him. Ritchie had three times as many tanks as Rommel in reserve, and three almost intact infantry divisions there, with a fourth on the way up.

But Ritchie decided to make his stand at Mersa Matruh, 130 miles farther to the east. Auchinleck, who saw Ritchie no longer had the confidence to lead the 8th Army, took over direct command on June 25 and decided to withdraw all the way to El Alamein, 110 miles farther east, and only 60 miles from Alexandria, the Royal Navy's vital Mediterranean base.

El Alamein was literally the last-ditch defense line for Egypt and the Middle East. If Rommel threatened Alexandria, the British fleet would have to abandon the Mediterranean, severing the main supply line to Malta, assuring its abandonment, and turning the sea into an Axis lake. Rommel then could get ample supplies with which to seize the Egyptian Delta, Palestine, and Syria.

Auchinleck's decision raised a fearful storm in London, but his choice was shrewd and strategically brilliant. Auchinleck knew Rommel was at the end of his strength. He had only a few dozen tanks, and his infantry force was only a shadow of its original size. El Alamein could counter Rommel's only remaining advantage, his ability to maneuver. This was because the immense Qattara Depression was only thirty-five miles to the south and its salt marshes and soft sand formed an impassable barrier for tanks. With British armor, infantry, and artillery deployed along the short El Alamein front in emplaced fortifications, Auchinleck could stop Rommel's few remaining tanks and force him to fight the static, set-piece battle of attrition in which the British excelled.

If Rommel could once be stopped, the Axis position would rapidly become hopeless. The British were close to their supply sources, and had many more tanks, airplanes, guns, and troops to draw on in any case. Rommel was at the tag end of an immensely long supply line, and the guns, tanks, and troops he needed would not arrive. The Italians would not dare send in convoys to Mersa Matruh for fear of challenging the Royal Navy. The only ports the Italians would use were Benghazi and Tripoli, requiring road transport of 750 or 1,400 miles to El Alamein.

In other words, Rommel had to seize El Alamein at once, or he had lost the campaign.

Rommel recognized the merciless equation as well as Auchinleck and pushed his men and vehicles forward in hopes of getting past El Alamein before the British could organize a defense. But now he had only forty tanks and 2,500 motorized German infantry, while his 6,000 remaining Italian infantry were much less mobile and slower coming forward.

Despite Auchinleck's decision, British forces tried to defend Mersa Matruh. Rommel knew that everything now depended on audacity, speed, and the moral effect of his aura of victory. He parlayed this psychological advantage into a bold attack with his three extremely weak German divisions on June 26.

While 90th Light reached the coast road east of Matruh on the evening of June 27, blocking the direct line of retreat, 21st Panzer made a deep penetration south of Matruh, threatening the line of retreat of 13th Corps's mobile forces posted in the Matruh area. The corps commander, General Gott, ordered withdrawal, but failed to inform the two divisions holding Mersa Matruh perimeter until the next morning. Nearly two-thirds of the garrison escaped the following night in small groups, but 6,000 fell prisoner, a number larger than Rommel's entire striking force.

Rommel now sent the panzers all out for Alamein. They reached it on June 30. Auchinleck had established four boxes along the thirty-five miles from the sea to the Qattara Depression. But the intervals between them were covered only by small mobile columns. Rommel, however, believed Auchinleck had concentrated his tanks north of the depression, not realizing they were still in the desert to the southwest, trying desperately to get to Alamein.

Fearing the tanks, Rommel paused briefly to work out an attack. It was a fatal delay. It gave the British armor just enough time to get behind Alamein and form a defensive force. Rommel had had just one chance to break through at Alamein. If he had struck at once, he could have rushed on to Alexandria and the Delta. He did not. This was the moment Rommel lost the war in Africa.

Rommel attacked the next day, Wednesday, July 1, 1942. His reputation was so awesome that the news terrified the British. The fleet withdrew through Suez into the Red Sea. In Cairo, headquarters hastily burned files. Commanders frantically planned to evacuate Cairo and the Delta.

Africa Corps's assault went in about twelve miles south of the sea at Deir el Shein and hit a box Rommel didn't know was there. Defended by the 18th Indian Brigade, the box held till evening, when the Germans smashed it and captured most of the defenders. British armor arrived too late to save the brigade, but in time to check Rommel's efforts during the night to penetrate to the rear.

From this point on, Axis presence in Africa was doomed. Rommel renewed the attack the next day, but he had fewer than forty tanks now and was forced to halt when he saw British tanks blocking their way, as well as others moving around their flank. Rommel tried again on July 3. By now he had only twenty-six tanks, yet he advanced nine miles before British fire halted them. During the day a New Zealand battalion captured nearly all of Ariete Division's artillery in a flank attack, while the remaining Italians took to their heels. It was clear evidence of exhaustion and overstrain.

Rommel, at last recognizing reality, broke off the attack. Auchinleck had at last gained the initiative. He counterattacked on July 4. The Axis troops held, and both sides soon stopped out of exhaustion. Now the two opponents slowly built their strength. In the following weeks they exchanged savage attempts to crack the other's line. The tactical situation altered little. But the strategic situation had been transformed. The Axis had no hope of matching the huge buildup that had begun apace on the British side.

Churchill flew out to Cairo on August 4 and changed commanders when he found Auchinleck strongly resisting his insistence on renewing the offensive. Auchinleck wanted to wait until September so newly arrived troops could learn desert warfare. Churchill handed over the Middle East command to General Sir Harold Alexander and brought out General Sir Bernard Montgomery from England to run the 8th Army. Montgomery turned out to be more insistent than any officer in the army in meticulously tidying up his forces before doing anything. He took even longer than Auchinleck, but Churchill couldn't admit he'd been wrong, and gave way.

Rommel launched one more desperate offensive on August 30. It had to go in on a less-fortified stretch to the south, but 8th Army had mined the region, and German mobility was limited by shortage of fuel. Rommel at last had to pull back, defeated. From this point on, the Axis forces simply hung on, waiting for the British blow to fall.

# 14 STALINGRAD

THE STALINGRAD CAMPAIGN IN RUSSIA IN 1942 IS ONE OF THE MOST POIGNANT examples ever recorded of a ruler engineering his own destruction.

When the army chief of staff, Franz Halder, protested the self-defeating operations, Hitler removed him. Only in the late stages when the German 6th Army had been isolated and a quarter of a million men were about to be lost was Erich von Manstein able to induce Hitler to grant just enough leeway to keep the entire southern wing of the German army from being destroyed as well.

After Stalingrad, Germany surrendered the initiative in Russia. Hitler never could summon enough strength thereafter to alter the balance of power against him. Despite heroic efforts by his soldiers, he had doomed himself to the slow, inevitable destruction of his army and his regime.

Two elements of the 1942 campaign stand out. First, Hitler committed the oldest and most obvious mistake in warfare: he neglected the principle of concentration and split his efforts between capturing Stalingrad on the Volga River and seizing the oil fields of the Caucasus. Either task would have been enough for his gravely weakened army. It was madness to attempt both, since the two thrusts diverged in different directions over hundreds of miles, leaving insufficient strength in either arena. The Red Army seized the opportunity, stopped both offensives, and concentrated against the closest danger, Stalingrad.

This brought on the second element of the campaign: Hitler, instead of being satisfied with an advance to the Volga and interdicting traffic on the river, which had been his stated aim, insisted on 6th Army capturing the city itself. This forced it to concentrate in the built-up area at the end of an extremely deep salient, offering the Russians an invitation to lock 6th Army in place by launching a street-by-street urban battle. As this titanic hand-to-hand clash went on, the Soviets assembled armies on the long, weakly held defensive lines on either flank, unleashed a powerful counteroffensive, and surrounded 6th Army.

Russian preparations for this counteroffensive were unmistakable. Yet Hitler refused to allow 6th Army to withdraw, and—because he had committed his other forces to the Caucasus—had insufficient troops to strengthen either flank of the salient.

Well before the Russians actually launched their counterstrike on November 19, 1942, the battle for the city had been lost. After 6th Army was encircled, Hitler refused to marshal strength from less-threatened theaters to break through the Russian ring and free the trapped army. The forces made available to Manstein, who was saddled with the job, were too few and arrived too late.

In the end, Manstein could not save 6th Army, and had to expend his skill and troops to keep an even greater Stalingrad from being created by a thrust of the Red Army to Rostov, where it could cut off Manstein's army group and the army group in the Caucasus.

At every stage Hitler made disastrous decisions—dividing his army in the first place, insisting on seizure of Stalingrad, refusing to allow 6th Army to retreat, failing to go all out to save the army once it had been surrounded, and refusing to heed evidence that the Russians were about to isolate the two army groups in the far south.

By 1943 the incapacity of Adolf Hitler as a commander was revealed for all to see. This showed Red Army generals not only that he could be beaten, but *how* he could be beaten. And it proved to senior German officers that, since Hitler would not listen to them, there was little chance of a stalemate, and the Allies would almost surely insist on total subjugation of Germany.

✠          ✠          ✠

The German army in the east (*Ostheer*) came out of the winter of 1941–1942 with 2.4 million men on the front, counting replacements, more than 600,000 fewer than had started the campaign in June 1941.

The situation was worst among infantrymen, whose numbers had fallen 50 percent in the south and 65 percent in the center and north. This weaker army had to defend a line that, since Hitler prohibited straightening out loops and protuberances, wove in and out for 2,800 miles from the Baltic to the Black Sea.

The quantity of German weapons was declining as well. Tank production was below 600 units a month. When Halder told Hitler Soviet tank manufacture was more than three times as great, Hitler slammed the table and said it was impossible. "He would not believe what he did not want to believe," Halder wrote in his diary.

At least the Mark IV tanks had been rearmed with long-barreled high-velocity 75-millimeter guns and could meet the Soviet T-34s on better terms. But nearly a third of the artillery pieces were old French cannons, the number of combat-ready aircraft had fallen to half what it had been in June 1941, while shortages of fuel and ammunition were great and growing.

In the early spring, special operations removed dangerous Soviet penetrations and freed a number of German forces that had been surrounded. Manstein launched a surprise thrust in the Kerch peninsula of the Crimea, May 8–18, which shattered three Russian armies and yielded 169,000 prisoners. This induced the Russians, under Semen K. Timoshenko, to make a premature diversionary attack in the Kharkov region to the north, giving the Germans an opportunity to thrust into their flank in the Donetz region. These battles, May 17–22, used up a great part of the Soviet forces from the Volga to the Don. The Germans captured 239,000 men, and destroyed more than a thousand tanks and two thousand cannons.

Manstein opened a third offensive against the Crimean fortress of Sevastopol on June 7, a gruesome confrontation that lasted three weeks. After storming Soviet positions, Germans captured 97,000 enemy soldiers, but 100,000 got away on ships of the Soviet Black Sea fleet.

Soviet morale declined from these defeats, and Stalin commenced a new drive to get the western Allies to establish a second front to draw off German forces. Foreign Minister Vyacheslav Molotov signed an alliance with Britain on May 26, but this brought no guarantees and not many supplies.

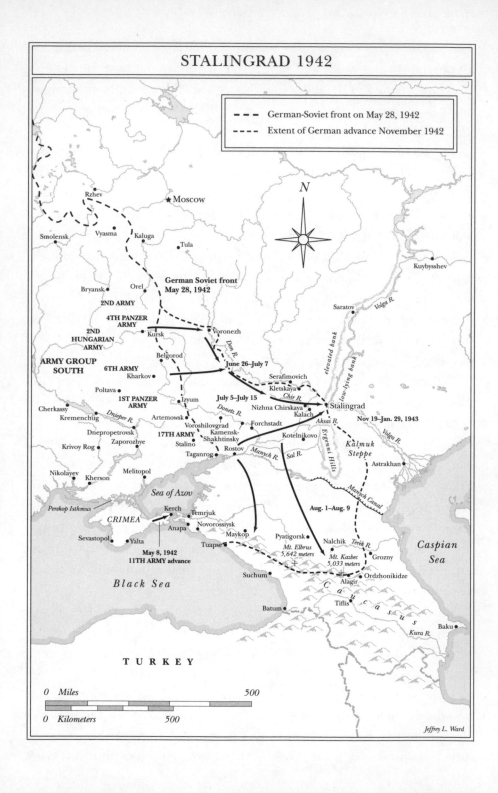

# STALINGRAD 1942

- – – – – German-Soviet front on May 28, 1942
- – – – Extent of German advance November 1942

N

Moscow

Rzhev

Smolensk  Vyasma  Kaluga

Tula

Kuybysshev

Bryansk  Orel  **German Soviet front May 28, 1942**

**2ND ARMY**

**4TH PANZER ARMY**

**2ND HUNGARIAN ARMY**  Kursk  Voronezh

Saratov  Volga R.

Belgorod

**ARMY GROUP SOUTH**  **6TH ARMY**

Kharkov

Poltava

Don R.

June 26–July 7

Serafimovich

Kletskaya

elevated bank

low-lying bank

**1ST PANZER ARMY**  Izyum

July 5–July 15

Chir R.

Nizhna Chirskaya  Stalingrad

Cherkassy

Kremenchug  Dnieper R.  Artemowsk  Donetz R.  Forchstadt  Kalach

Nov 19–Jan. 29, 1943

Dnepropetrovsk  Voroshilovgrad

Aksai R.

Zaporozhye  **17TH ARMY**  Kamensk-Shakhtinsky  Kotelnikovo

Volga R.

Krivoy Rog

Stalino  Ergeni Hills  **Kalmuk Steppe**

Nikolayev  Melitopol  Taganrog  Rostov  Manych R.  Sal R.

Kherson

Astrakhan

*Sea of Azov*

Manych Canal

Perekop Isthmus  Kerch  Temrjuk

Aug. 1–Aug. 9

**CRIMEA**  Anapa  Novorossiysk

Sevastopol  Yalta  Maykop  Pyatigorsk  Nalchik  Terek R.

**May 8, 1942 11TH ARMY advance**  Tuapse  Mt. Elbrus 5,642 meters  Mt. Kazbec 5,033 meters  Grozny

*Caspian Sea*

*Black Sea*  Suchum  Alagir  Ordzhonikidze

Batum  Tiflis  Caucasus

Baku

Kura R.

**T U R K E Y**

0  Miles  500

0  Kilometers  500

*Jeffrey L. Ward*

✠          ✠          ✠

Although army chief of staff Franz Halder tried to get Hitler to remain on the defensive in 1942, Hitler insisted on a summer offensive in the south (Operation Blue). Hitler called for Army Group South under Fedor von Bock to advance in two directions—eastward across the Don to Stalingrad on the Volga with one army, and southward to the oil fields of the Caucasus with four.

The campaign opened on June 28, 1942. Hermann Hoth's 4th Panzer Army with two armored corps (800 tanks and self-propelled assault guns) achieved complete surprise, broke through the Russian lines, and seized Voronezh in a few days. The army then swung southeast down the west bank of the Don through ideal tank country—open rolling plains, dry and hard from summer drought, broken occasionally by deep valleys in which villages were tucked away. Infantry divisions attacked simultaneously and secured the flanks and rear of the armor. Hoth hoped to trap many Russians in the great bend of the river.

While Hoth's fast troops rolled down the Don, 17th Army (Richard Ruoff) and 1st Panzer Army (Ewald von Kleist) seized Rostov on July 23.

Nevertheless, Russian commanders were able to withdraw numerous divisions across the Don south of Rostov and at Kalach, forty-five miles west of Stalingrad. Hitler blamed Bock and removed him from command.

Hitler now made an irretrievable error. He had concluded, because of the initial success of the offensive, that Soviet strength had been broken, and diverted Hoth's 4th Panzer Army south to help Kleist's 1st Panzer Army cross the lower Don to open a path to the Caucasus.

"It could have taken Stalingrad without a fight at the end of July," Kleist said after the war. "I did not need its aid, and it merely congested the roads I was using. When it turned north again, a fortnight later, the Russians had gathered sufficient forces at Stalingrad to check it."

Panzer leader Friedrich-Wilhelm von Mellenthin voiced the opinion of nearly all senior officers in this campaign. When Stalingrad was not taken in the first rush, it should have been shielded with defensive troops and not attacked directly.

"By concentrating his offensive on a great city and resorting to siege warfare," Mellenthin wrote, "Hitler was playing into the hands of the Russian command. In street warfare the Germans forfeited all their advantages in mobile tactics, while the inadequately trained but supremely dogged Russian infantry were able to exact a heavy toll."

On the day Rostov fell, Hitler set up two new army groups, with new goals. Army Group A (17th and 1st Panzer Armies) under Wilhelm List was to seize the mountain passes and oil fields of the Caucasus, while Army Group B (2nd, 6th, and 4th Panzer Armies) under Maximilian von Weichs was to build a defense along the Don, drive to Stalingrad, block off the land bridge between the Don and the Volga, and interdict traffic on the Volga.

In his original plan, Hitler intended four armies to press into the Caucasus, while one went toward Stalingrad. Now three armies marched on Stalingrad—an objective of infinitely less importance than the oil fields—while two armies drove into the Caucasus.

This was lunacy to every professional soldier, and Halder protested to Hitler. But the Fuehrer paid no attention, and also ignored evidence of powerful Soviet formations to the east of the Volga and in the Caucasus. Hitler transferred his headquarters to Vinnitsa in Ukraine, and took over direct command of the southern part of the front.

Army Group A swept over the lower Don into the Caucasus. The 17th Army seized Krasnodar, crossed the Kuban River, and penetrated the thickly wooded west Caucasus Mountains to Novorossiysk on the Black Sea. Elsewhere, mountain troops could not drive the Russians out of the high passes. Kleist's 1st Panzer Army, slowed by fuel shortages, captured the oil field of Maykop, 200 miles south of Rostov, though not before the Russians had destroyed it. But Kleist did not have the strength to drive to Batum, Tiflis, and Baku, which would have secured the Caucasus.

In Army Group B, 2nd Army fought around Voronezh, while the huge 6th Army with twenty divisions under Friedrich Paulus pressed toward Stalingrad. The ever-lengthening north flank of 6th Army along the Don was covered by the Hungarian 2nd Army, the Italian 8th Army, and the Romanian 3rd Army, while the Romanian 4th Army held a thin line in the Kalmuk steppe south of Stalingrad. The flanks thus were guarded by extremely weak forces, since none of the allies had good equipment or adequate training.

Hoth's 4th Panzer Army had now turned northeast and was pressing through Elista across the steppe toward Stalingrad. About fifty miles south of the city, Hoth's attack broke down against fierce resistance by the Soviet 57th and 64th Armies.

✠          ✠          ✠

Originally the Soviet high command, Stavka, did not plan to hold Stalingrad. It intended to withdraw Red forces east of the stream, so the Germans would be forced to overwinter on the unprotected steppe. But the unexpected splitting of the German offensive called for new decisions. Stalin removed Timoshenko from command in the south and ordered Andrei I. Eremenko to take over and keep the city.

Stalingrad was no fortress. The old city of Tsaritsyn (Stalin had named it after himself in 1925) was surrounded by a jumble of old wooden structures, barrack-like apartments, industrial installations, and railroad switchyards sprawling fifteen miles along the west bank of the river, and two to four miles back from it. Above the apartments and factories reared water towers and grain silos. Numerous balkas (dry ravines or gullies with steep banks) and railway embankments eased the defense, as did the high western bank of the Volga and, west of the city, a twenty-nine-mile arc of woods, a mile wide at its thickest, protecting against dust and snowstorms. In August 1942 Stalingrad held about 600,000 people, including refugees.

Eremenko had five armies, some hard-hit. But Stalin issued a *"Ni shagu nazad!"* ("Not a step back!") order on July 28, and reinforcements began to arrive. Eremenko got eleven divisions and nine Guards brigades, supplied from dumps on the steppe east of the river. He mobilized 50,000 civilian volunteers into a "people's guard," assigned 75,000 inhabitants to the 62nd Army, organized factory workers into rifle companies and tank units (using T-34s driven right off the floor of the tractor plant Dzherhezinsky where they were made), assigned 3,000 young women as nurses and radio operators, and sent 7,000 boys aged thirteen to sixteen to army formations. But Eremenko did order the evacuation of those too old or young to fight—200,000 crossed over to the east bank in a three-week period.

Paulus's mobile spearhead reached the Don near Kalach on July 28, but because of fierce Soviet resistance it was August 23 before 6th Army forced passage of the Don. Massive Stuka bombing attacks on the city during the day and night of August 24 killed many civilians, turned office blocks into rubble, and set fire to wooden structures in older neighborhoods.

Meanwhile, 16th Panzer Division under one-armed General Hans Hube swept aside Russian infantry west of the city and women workers crewing antiaircraft guns at the Barricade gun factory, and reached the Volga near Rynok, ten miles north of Stalingrad, at 6:30 P.M., August 24, 1942. The original purpose had thus been attained: German artillery at Rynok could seal off traffic on the Volga.

On August 27, Stalin appointed General Georgy K. Zhukov as deputy supreme commander of the Red Army, and sent him to direct the defense of Stalingrad.

In oppressive heat (it had not rained for two months), German forces backed by tanks crashed against barricades that blocked nearly every street. Russians fought back from machine-gun nests, within buildings, and amid the rubble. Mortars hidden in holes and crevices dropped shells on the advancing Germans. The Russians defended fortresslike complexes—the steelworks Red October, the artillery factory Barricade, the warehouse complex Univermag, and the tractor plant Dzherhezinsky. The Germans were soon exhausted. Supplies were slow arriving and insufficient; ammunition was in short supply. Progress was slow, counterattacks frequent, and losses high. The name Stalingrad began to have a hypnotic effect on Russians and Germans alike, especially Hitler, who insisted on capture of the entire city.

At Rynok 14th Motorized Corps came under almost unrelenting attack as the Russians tried to sweep around this northern anchor and roll up the German positions. Day after day more than a hundred tanks along with massed Russian infantry hurled themselves against the corps behind a curtain of artillery fire. The Russian commanders ignored high casualties. The only thing that saved the corps was its artillery, the guns sometimes shooting up assembly areas before the Russians could launch their attacks. The Germans learned not to occupy inclines facing the enemy (forward slopes), as they could not be protected from Russian armor.

Instead they held the reverse slopes, massing tanks in hollows just behind the main line of resistance, and knocking out enemy armor as it reached the crests above.

General Gustav von Wietersheim, commanding 14th Motorized Corps, watched his strength decline. He recommended that 6th Army be withdrawn to the west bank of the Don, forty-five miles away. The only result was that Hitler removed him because he was "too pessimistic."

As the German offensives stumbled to a halt, radical changes in leadership came about. On September 10 Hitler relieved List, because his army group had not captured the whole Caucasus. He did not name a successor, and commanded the army group himself in his spare time from supreme headquarters.

Hitler's long conflict with Halder came to a head. Hitler reproached Halder and the army general staff, calling them cowards and lacking drive. When Halder presented proof of new Soviet formations totaling 1.5 million men north of Stalingrad and half a million in the southern Caucasus, Hitler advanced on him, foaming at the mouth, crying out that he forbade such "idiotic chatter" in his presence.

Halder, who looked and acted like a prim schoolmaster, persisted in explaining what would happen when the new Russian reserve armies attacked the overextended flanks that ran out from the Stalingrad salient. On September 24, Hitler dismissed him.

Hitler said arguments with Halder had cost him half his nervous energy. The army, he said, no longer required technical proficiency. What was needed was the "glow of National Socialist conviction." He couldn't expect that from officers of the old German army.

The new chief of staff was Lieutenant General Kurt Zeitzler, a tank expert and man of action. Zeitzler soon took note of the cliques and intrigue in Hitler's headquarters, became excessively cautious, and did nothing to challenge Hitler's decision to keep 6th Army at Stalingrad.

Yet, as Field Marshal Manstein wrote: "A far-sighted leader would have realized from the start that to mass the whole of the German assault forces in and around Stalingrad without adequate flank protection placed them in mortal danger of being enveloped as soon as the enemy broke through the adjacent fronts."

Hitler held stubbornly to the idea that had become fixed in his mind:

the enemy was shattered, and would not rise again. He accepted no evidence to the contrary, and he was ready to sack any officer who did not obtain objectives, however unrealistic, or who wanted to pull back to more defensible positions.

Stalingrad had virtually been destroyed. The Germans had gained eight-tenths of the rubble but couldn't oust the Russians from the rest.

The principal problem, of course, was the flanks. General Hoth had at his disposal on the south two widely spaced corps of the Romanian 4th Army. Beyond the Romanians a 120-mile hole had opened in the Kalmuk steppe, only meagerly veiled by a German motorized division. To the west, the Romanian 3rd Army, Italian 8th Army, and Hungarian 2nd Army held a 400-mile front along the Don. None possessed antitank guns that could stop Russian T-34s.

✠          ✠          ✠

The Russians had assembled a million men with 13,500 cannons, 900 tanks, and 1,100 aircraft in three army groups or fronts on either side of Stalingrad.

In thick fog on November 19, 1942, Southwest Front commander N. F. Vatutin launched the first arm of a giant pincers movement (Operation Uranus) some eighty miles west of Stalingrad at Kletskaya and Kremensk on the Don. The target was the Romanian 3rd Army. Soviet artillery had previously registered targets, and guns laid down a curtain of shells on the unsuspecting Romanians. Soviet tanks used compasses to guide them. The Romanians stood up to the assault only briefly before they ran away. A giant hole twenty miles wide opened in the German front. Soviet tanks streamed south toward Kalach.

The next day Stalingrad Front commander Eremenko smashed a broad fissure in the Romanian 4th Army south of Stalingrad. This army disintegrated as well. With virtually no opposition, the Russian attack wedge swung to the northwest to link up with the Soviet advance from the Don.

If 6th Army had been given freedom of movement at once it might have broken out of the trap with its men and equipment intact. But Hitler had no intention of allowing the army to retreat, and, when Paulus asked permission to do so, Hitler refused.

On November 22 the Soviet 26th and 4th Tank Corps closed the back of the pincers around Kalach. With this, 250,000 men in twenty German and two Romanian divisions were closed within a pocket at Stalingrad measuring thirty miles east and west, and twenty-five miles north and south.

General Paulus asked for freedom of action, but Hitler refused. The army, Hitler commanded, had to curl up in a ball like a hedgehog. Hermann Göring, chief of the Luftwaffe, promised grandiloquently that the army would be supplied by air until a new battle group could be formed to break the caldron.

Senior Luftwaffe officers said it couldn't be done, but Hitler listened to Göring, not the air generals.

As the Luftwaffe tried to organize an airlift, the Russians forged a double-ring around 6th Army to hinder a breakthrough from either inside or out. They posted 395 antiaircraft guns along the Luftwaffe line of flight and sent in 490 fighters to shoot down the transports.

The daily needs of 6th Army totaled 700 tons. Colonel Fritz Morzik, Luftwaffe air transport chief, said that in the best of circumstances he could fly in 350 tons. The entire Luftwaffe, he pointed out, possessed only 750 Ju-52 cargo aircraft, and there was enormous demand for them elsewhere. Though the air officers pulled additional air freight assets together, along with airplanes from flight schools, they could assemble only about 500 machines, of which on average only a third were ready for operations on any given day. Weather was atrocious, and this reduced deliveries. Göring had ordered at least 300 tons to be flown in every day. But from November 25 to 29 6th Army received 269 tons total, and from November 30 to December 11 only 1,267 tons.

Ammunition supplies dropped, fuel became scarce, and the men of 6th Army began to starve.

Meanwhile the Soviet army group Voronezh Front under F. I. Golikov on the north opposite the Italian 8th Army prepared for another—even more dangerous—enveloping movement. Hitler, ignoring the threat, handed Manstein the task of relieving 6th Army.

# 15 MANSTEIN SAVES THE ARMY

WITH STALINGRAD SURROUNDED, AND TWO ROMANIAN ARMIES VIRTUALLY EX-tinguished, it was apparent to senior officers on both sides that a war-winning victory lay within reach of the Russians.

Only 150 miles separated Rostov and a flimsy new defensive line Manstein formed along the Chir River, a hundred miles west of Stalin-grad. Yet the left wing of Army Group A lay deep in the Caucasus 375 miles from Rostov, while 4th Panzer Army, south of Stalingrad, was 250 miles from Rostov.

If the Russians could crash through to Rostov, they could cut off the remainder of Army Group B, the scratch forces Manstein was throwing together in his new Army Group Don, and the two armies of Army Group A in the Caucasus—in other words, *all* German forces on the southern wing.

If the southern German flank were eliminated, the remaining German forces in the east would be too weak to fend off the Red Army, and Germany would lose the war in months, if not weeks.

The Red Army was planning to unleash this strategic thunderbolt and had selected a vulnerable point of attack: the Italian 8th Army on the Don just northwest of the Chir.

Manstein formed an emergency defense line with communications zone troops in Hoth's 4th Panzer Army around Kotelnikovo, eighty miles southwest of Stalingrad, closing a void where the Romanian 4th Army had vanished.

Although worried about a Russian strike for Rostov, Manstein's foremost task was to liberate 6th Army. Unless this army was freed, there was no hope of restoring the situation on the southern wing. If the army remained at Stalingrad, it would die. Any relief operation had to break open a path for 6th Army to come out, not to reestablish a supply line to it. Surely, Manstein told himself, Hitler would see the light when the time came and allow the army to withdraw.

There were two possible escape routes. The closest was straight west to Kalach. Here, however, the Russians were massed and would contest every inch. There was a slightly better chance to break through around Kotelnikovo and drive northeast toward Stalingrad.

Once a relief operation started from Kotelnikovo, pressure on 6th Army would ease, because the Red Army would have to challenge the relief forces. When this happened, Manstein reasoned, German elements on the Chir could strike toward Kalach, smash into the rear of the Soviet siege ring there, and facilitate 6th Army's breakout.

But time was of the essence. Army chief of staff Zeitzler agreed to send 57th Panzer Corps under Friedrich Kirchner (23rd and 6th Panzer Divisions, and 15th Luftwaffe Field Division) to 4th Panzer Army to spearhead the relief drive from Kotelnikovo, and eight divisions in a new Army Detachment Hollidt (General Karl Adolf Hollidt) to advance from the upper Chir. These forces were to arrive in the first days of December.

They might be enough, if they came in time, to cut a corridor to 6th Army, replenish it with fuel, ammunition, and food, restore its freedom of movement, and get it out. Manstein so informed the Fuehrer on November 28.

"I told Hitler," Manstein wrote later, "it was strategically impossible to go on tying down our forces in an excessively small area while the enemy enjoyed a free hand along hundreds of miles of front."

It was December 3 before Hitler even replied, and he refused to allow 6th Army to switch troops from its northern flank to the southwest to prepare for the relief force. Manstein did not realize that Hitler had not the slightest intention of evacuating 6th Army from Stalingrad.

Most of the reinforcements did not arrive on time. Of the eight divisions for Army Group Hollidt, three didn't appear at all, one of the panzer divisions was so shot up as to be useless, and one Luftwaffe Field Division arrived too late. All that came in time for Hollidt was the 48th Panzer

Corps under Otto von Knobelsdorff with the 11th Panzer and the 336th Infantry Division, and a Luftwaffe Field Division. For Hoth, only the 57th Panzer Corps arrived.

With so few troops, Manstein gave up the idea of relieving 6th Army from two directions. Everything now depended upon a direct strike (code-named Winter Tempest) by 4th Panzer Army from Kotelnikovo.

Because of delays in the arrival of 57th Panzer Corps, Manstein had to postpone the strike to December 12. Meantime, a dangerous threat appeared on the Chir front. On December 7, the Russian 1st Armored Corps forced its way over the river near Surovikino, twenty miles upstream (northwest) from the Chir's junction with the Don at Nizhna Chirskaya. The Russians swept toward State Farm 79 fifteen miles in the rear. General Knobelsdorff had lined his 336th Infantry Division along the river on the right or east, and the Luftwaffe Field Division on the left.

The situation was grim. A Soviet breakthrough on the Chir would unhinge the drive toward Stalingrad, clear the way to the Morosovsky and Tatsinskaya airfields only twenty-five and fifty miles away, from which supplies were being flown to Stalingrad, and open a path to crossings of the Donetz River and Rostov.

Hermann Balck's 11th Panzer Division checked the Russian advance at the state farm. While his antiaircraft guns and his engineers formed up below the farm to prevent the Russians moving south, one panzer grenadier (motorized infantry) regiment delivered an attack on the farm from the southwest at dawn on December 8. Once the Russians were locked in this engagement, Balck's panzer regiment and his second panzer grenadier regiment thrust into the rear of the Russians from a low ridge northwest of the farm.

This rear attack caught the Russians just as they were about to advance northward against the rear of 336th Division. Truck after truck loaded with infantry went up in flames as the panzers charged through the column. The tanks destroyed this force, then turned into the rear of the Russian armor at the state farm, knocking out fifty-three tanks and sending the remainder fleeing.

Over the next four days, Balck's panzer division, using the 336th Division as a pivot, turned back two simultaneous assaults by the Russian

5th Tank Army, one half a dozen miles northwest of Nizhna Chirskaya, the other fifteen miles upstream. On December 17 and 18 two new violent attacks broke across the Chir. The 11th Panzer drove one back to a narrow foothold, then turned on the other. The division had only twenty-five tanks left, but got on the rear of the advancing Russian armor and destroyed sixty-five enemy tanks before the Russians woke up to what was happening. The remaining Russians fled. Over the next few days, new Russian attacks convulsed the Chir front, but 11th Panzer, acting like a fire brigade, broke the back of one breakthrough after another, and by December 22 the Soviets had given up.

Part of the reason for the German success was the expertise and discipline of the panzer troops. Part was due to the Russian tank crews, who had scarcely any training. Likewise, the Russian commander sent in tank corps (groups of brigades about the size of divisions) without coordinating times of attacks, permitting Balck's panzers to deal with one crisis at a time.

While these fights were going on, Manstein launched Operation Winter Tempest, using only 57th Panzer Corps. His attack surprised the enemy, and made good progress, although the Russians brought up troops from around Stalingrad and counterattacked again and again.

The real threat now came in a massive way and from a new direction. On December 16, 1942, the Russian 1st Guards Army overran the Italian 8th Army on the upper Chir, and knocked a sixty-mile hole in the line to the left or northwest of Army Detachment Hollidt. It was obvious the objective was Rostov and a far greater "Stalingrad." Manstein ordered Army Detachment Hollidt to pull back on a shorter front to guard the Donetz crossings of Forchstadt and Kamensk-Shakhtinsky, only eighty-five miles northeast of Rostov.

But Manstein held doggedly to his advance on Stalingrad, calling on the army high command (OKH) to order 6th Army to break out toward 4th Panzer Army.

There was still hope. The strike against the Italians had drawn off most Soviet mobile formations, leaving a narrow window of opportunity at Stalingrad. If 6th Army and 4th Panzer Army attacked toward each other, they could crack through the defensive shell and meet. However, they had to use every ounce of their collective strength.

But Hitler refused to sanction a breakout. Incredibly, he ruled that 4th Panzer Army was to continue to attack toward the city, but 6th Army was to remain in place. Hitler wanted to hang on to Stalingrad and supply it by a land corridor.

In desperation, Manstein flew his intelligence officer into the caldron on December 18 to get General Paulus to defy Hitler and save the army. Manstein promised to put the onus entirely on his own shoulders, relieving Paulus of responsibility. Paulus replied that he couldn't do anything because the surrender of Stalingrad was forbidden "by order of the Fuehrer."

Manstein hoped he would change his mind. The critical moment came on December 19. The 57th Panzer Corps crossed the Aksai River, against bitter Russian resistance, and reached the narrow Miskova River, just thirty miles from the siege front. Behind the front Manstein had assembled transport columns with 3,000 tons of supplies, plus tractors to mobilize part of 6th Army's artillery. All were to be rushed through as soon as tanks cleared a way. Manstein sent an urgent appeal to Paulus and Hitler: 6th Army must disengage and drive southwest to join 4th Panzer Army.

Hitler took hours to reply: 6th Army *could* break out, he said, but it *still* had to hold existing fronts north, east, and west of the city. This was manifestly impossible. Paulus now showed his moral cowardice. He informed Manstein that his one hundred tanks had enough fuel to go only twenty miles. Before he could move, air deliveries had to bring in 4,000 tons of fuel. There was no possibility of this, and Paulus knew it.

Drawn between Hitler demanding he stay and Manstein demanding he move, Paulus clutched at the straw of fuel to do nothing. Not even to save his army was Paulus going to buck his Fuehrer. Yet he and Manstein knew that the fuel could have been allocated to half his tanks, giving them mobility for forty miles—enough to break through.

In the week that followed, the fate of 6th Army was decided. For six days Army Group Don had run every conceivable risk to keep the door open. But Manstein could leave 4th Panzer Army in its exposed position no longer.

The panzer corps was having to fend off stronger and stronger attacks, and a greater danger was growing to the west where most of the Italian army had disappeared and Army Detachment Hollidt's left flank was being threatened. Russian spearheads were driving toward the Donetz River and were not more than 120 miles from Rostov.

On December 22, Manstein was forced to release 48th Corps from the Chir to restore Army Detachment Hollidt's left wing, and he had to send 6th Panzer Division from Hoth's army to help. Manstein knew there was now no chance of 6th Army breaking out. On December 27, two Soviet armies and four mechanized corps launched a major assault against the weakened 57th Panzer Corps, now down to only a couple dozen tanks, threatened to envelop both flanks, and compelled it to withdraw to Kotelnikovo. The attempt to relieve Stalingrad had failed.

☦        ☦        ☦

It was now plain that 6th Army was going to die. Adolf Hitler had caused it. But while the senior German generals grieved the fate of the army, most were frantically trying to figure how to block the Soviet thrust toward Rostov.

At this nadir of German fortune, Erich von Manstein saw opportunity where the rest of the senior German officers saw disaster.

Manstein conceived a spectacular plan to transform defeat into victory. He proposed that the German army surrender the territory it had won in the summer, which it couldn't hold anyway, and that all forces on the southern front, except 6th Army, of course, withdraw in stages to the lower Dnieper, some 220 miles west of Rostov.

Manstein was certain when withdrawal commenced that the Russians would launch an offensive aimed at cutting the Germans off from the vital Dnieper crossings at Dnepropetrovsk and Zaporozhye where all supplies came through. This would create a vastly extended Russian front stretching across lower Ukraine.

Manstein proposed that a powerful German force be concentrated near Kharkov, 250 miles northwest of Rostov and 125 miles northeast of Dnepropetrovsk. When the Soviets extended themselves westward toward the Dnieper crossings, the German forces around Kharkov would drive into their northern flank. As Manstein told Hitler and the OKH, this would "convert a large-scale withdrawal into an envelopment operation" that would push the Russians against the Sea of Azov and destroy them.

Manstein's idea would have thrown the enemy on the defensive and transformed the situation in the south. But Hitler refused. He didn't want to give up his summer conquests, ephemeral as they were. He wanted to keep his troops not only at Stalingrad but in the Caucasus.

Manstein came to have wide personal experience with Hitler's thinking about war and concluded that he "actually recoiled from risks in the military field." Hitler refused to allow temporary surrender of territory. He could not see that, in the wide reaches of Russia, the enemy could always mass forces at one point and break through. Only in mobile operations could the superiority of German staffs and fighting troops be exploited. The brilliant holding action of the 48th Panzer Corps along the Chir River demonstrated how superior German leadership and flexible responses, if applied by the whole German army, almost certainly could have stopped Soviet advances and brought about a stalemate. But such a policy was beyond Hitler's grasp.

Manstein also found that Hitler feared to denude secondary fronts to gain superiority at the point where a decision had to fall. For example, the failure to assemble a large army to relieve Stalingrad had proved disastrous. Hitler could not make rapid decisions. In most cases he finally released too few troops, and sent them too late.

"Obstinate defense of every foot of ground gradually became the be all and end all" of Hitler's leadership, Manstein wrote. "Hitler thought the arcanum of success lay in clinging at all costs to what he already possessed." He could never be brought to renounce this notion.

✠         ✠         ✠

When Hitler refused to approve withdrawal of German forces to the Dnieper and a campaign to transform defeat into victory, Manstein turned to the now-urgent job of saving the southern armies from being cut off and destroyed.

While Manstein's thin forces sought desperately to build a defensive wall in front of the Donetz, 6th Army's death struggle began. Air supplies dwindled in the face of atrocious weather, long flights, and fierce Russian air defenses. On December 26, only seventy tons of supplies were flown in. Bread began to run out, fats virtually vanished, soldiers went on an iron ration of one meal a day. As the new year began, numbing cold, hunger, and steady Russian attacks weakened the army day by day.

On January 9, 1943, a Russian delegation called on 6th Army to give up. On Hitler's orders Paulus rejected the demand. Manstein supported the Fuehrer's decision. Although the army was perishing, it still had a strategic role to play—tying down the maximum number of Soviet troops to permit the rest of the German army to get away.

The Soviets were fully aware of 6th Army's continued service and unleashed a violent attack on January 11, breaking through at several points. They ousted the Germans from most remaining shelters, especially in the westernmost part of the pocket. The Germans now huddled in the ruins closer to the Volga.

Weather and Soviet fighters reduced air deliveries to a trickle. Soviet attacks seized Pitomnik, the best airfield. Supplies totaled only 90 tons from January 17 to 23, 1943. Russian forays broke up the caldron into separate blocks. After January 28, the wounded and sick no longer were given bread. The Germans lost their last airfield at Gumrak. Efforts by Luftwaffe crews to throw out packages from the air helped little. Soviet regiments climbed out of their covers and overran one position after another. On February 2, the last resistance ceased.

The Luftwaffe had evacuated 25,000 wounded and specialists, but about 160,000 men died and 91,000 were captured. Most of the prisoners soon succumbed to exposure or typhus. Only 6,000 saw their homeland again, some after twelve years of captivity. Paulus, promoted by Hitler to field marshal on the assumption that he would shoot himself, did not, and surrendered to the Russians.

✠          ✠          ✠

Manstein got little help from Hitler in saving the remainder of the German forces on the southern front. In a series of massive retreats, Germans abandoned Kursk and fell all the way beyond Kharkov, 430 miles west of Stalingrad.

But Manstein prevented a rout, overcame Hitler's inability to see the danger facing the army, and held Rostov open long enough for the Germans to withdraw from the Caucasus. Even so, Hitler insisted on keep-

ing the 17th Army in the Kuban region of the northern Caucasus opposite the Crimea, where it served no purpose. Manstein formed a new line
along the Mius River, some forty miles west of Rostov, and stopped the
Soviet advance.

Manstein was even able to get Hitler's permission to authorize an envelopment of the overextended Russian forces at Kharkov, which Manstein
recaptured on March 14, 1943. It was the last great success of German
arms on the eastern front.

# 16 THE WESTERN ALLIES STRIKE

IN JULY 1942, WITH ROMMEL STOPPED JUST SIXTY MILES FROM ALEXANDRIA AND the Germans advancing toward Stalingrad and the Caucasus, there were two major issues dividing the Allies: what the Americans and British were going to do to help defeat Hitler and whether Stalin would seek a separate peace.

American and British leaders were well aware that they could not overcome Germany without the Soviet Union. However, Joseph Stalin, complaining bitterly that they were leaving virtually all the fighting to the Red Army, was putting out peace feelers in Stockholm.

Western leaders didn't think these feelers would amount to much if they attacked the Germans directly and took pressure off the Soviet Union, as Stalin had been demanding for months. But the British and Americans were virtually immobilized by an acrimonious dispute about *what* they should do. The Americans, led by George C. Marshall, army chief of staff, wanted a direct advance by a five-division amphibious landing around Cherbourg in Normandy in 1942 (Operation Sledgehammer). But the British pressed for an indirect or peripheral strategy, a combination of massive air attacks on German cities and smaller, less-dangerous invasions in the Mediterranean.

President Franklin D. Roosevelt saw more clearly than anyone that the western Allies must show Stalin that Russia was not being left to face Hitler alone. He decided that the Americans had to fight the Germans *somewhere* in 1942. Since an invasion of France was out, given British opposition,

FDR cut the Gordian knot and ruled that the American strike had to be in North Africa.

Roosevelt left it to Marshall to decide where Americans would go in Africa—as reinforcements to the British 8th Army building strength to challenge Rommel at El Alamein or landings in French North Africa (Morocco, Algeria, Tunisia), controlled by Vichy France. Marshall, knowing that 8th Army would remain under British General Sir Bernard Montgomery, chose French North Africa (code-named Gymnast), and was able to name his protégé, Lieutenant General Dwight D. Eisenhower, as commander.

Gymnast was an old British plan that called for a descent on Algeria if 8th Army won decisively in Libya and pushed for the Tunisian border. As Montgomery was now girding at El Alamein, the aim of Gymnast (its name changed to Torch because it sounded grander) was to seize Tunisia before the Germans got there and force Panzer Army Africa and the Italians to surrender.

Torch at once gained the advantage Roosevelt was hoping for: when Stalin heard about it, he stopped complaining about a second front. But the decision to turn to the Mediterranean aroused dark suspicions among American planners that Churchill was maneuvering the United States into the "soft underbelly" strategy. They feared this would lead to the invasion of Italy, and perhaps Greece, and fatally undermine the plan to collide with the Germans on the beaches of France.

President Roosevelt was less worried, because he hoped "an air war plus the Russians" could defeat Hitler, and a cross-Channel assault might not be necessary.

Western Allied military strength was not being concentrated in ground forces, as was the case for Russia and Germany. The United States and Britain put great emphasis on air and naval power, and Roosevelt set a limit of 90 army divisions for Europe *and* the Pacific, while the British mobilized 27. Many U.S. divisions had not even been formed, and only 70 ever got to Europe, yet Germany had 260 divisions actually in the field, and the Russians many more.

The Allies decided to invade French North Africa, but not when or where. Because of supply and troop transport problems, the American chiefs of staff set the date at November 8 and announced they planned to confine the landings to the west or Atlantic coast of Morocco, primarily around Casablanca. The British were shocked. The invasion, they said, should be made inside the Mediterranean on the Algerian coast, so troops could advance quickly to Tunisia.

The Americans chose Casablanca—1,100 miles from Tunis and Bizerte, the main Tunisian ports—because they feared the French would resist strongly in Algeria, while the Germans might rush through Spain, seize Gibraltar, block the Strait of Gibraltar, and prevent supplies from reaching the troops.

The British were dismayed at such extreme caution and argued that the American plan would allow the Germans to seize Tunisia, frustrating the entire purpose of the operation. Eisenhower came around to the British point of view, and proposed eliminating the Casablanca landings.

But Marshall would not take the chance of supplies being cut off at Gibraltar and FDR ruled the Americans had to land at Casablanca, to guarantee an Atlantic supply base, but could also land at Oran, 250 miles west of Algiers. He suggested that the British land a few days later at Algiers and points eastward. Roosevelt also wanted the British to keep a low profile, reasoning that the French were angry with them for attacking their ships after France surrendered in 1940 and for invading the French colony of Madagascar in May 1942. The 135,000 men in the French forces would probably resist the British, but perhaps not the Americans.

Churchill was willing to play down British participation, but said Algiers—the biggest city and nerve center of French North Africa—should be occupied the same time as Oran and Casablanca. FDR and Churchill finally agreed to joint American-British landings at Algiers simultaneous with the others.

But in the exchanges, the idea of landings farther east was dropped—killing any chance for a quick Allied victory in North Africa and prolonging the diversion of Allied effort in the Mediterranean.

In the final plan, the Western Task Force, guarded by U.S. Navy ships with 24,500 Americans under Major General George S. Patton Jr., was to land at Casablanca. The 102 ships (29 transports) sailed directly from Hampton Roads, Virginia. Center Task Force, protected by the Royal Navy with 18,500 American troops under Major General Lloyd R. Fredenall, was to capture Oran. It sailed from the Firth of Clyde in Scotland. Eastern

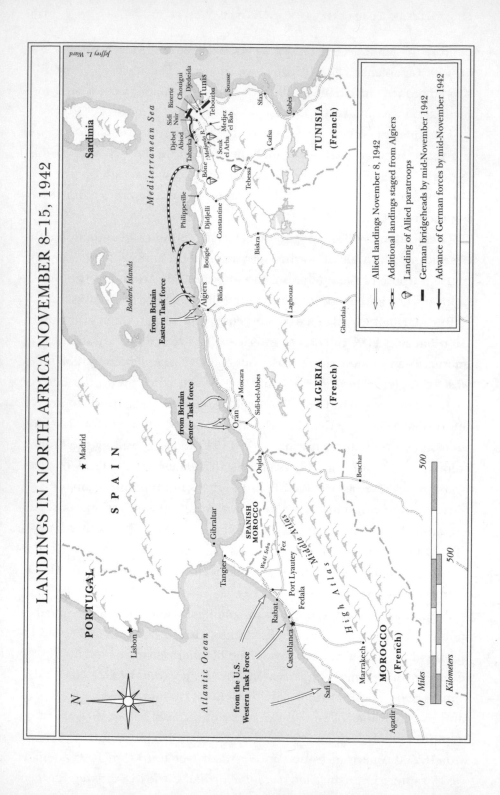

# LANDINGS IN NORTH AFRICA NOVEMBER 8–15, 1942

Jeffrey L. Ward

Task Force, also sailing from the Clyde and guarded by the Royal Navy with 9,000 British and 9,000 American troops, plus 2,000 British Commandos under American Major General Charles W. (Doc) Ryder, was to land at Algiers. Once ashore all Allied forces at Algiers were to come under a newly created British First Army commanded by Lieutenant General Kenneth A. Anderson and drive toward Tunisia.

✠　　　✠　　　✠

Americans and Britons landed in North Africa on November 8, a couple weeks after General Montgomery's 8th Army finally attacked Rommel's weak and poorly supplied army at El Alamein. Resistance by the French army was symbolic in most cases, though not all, and the French air force was nowhere to be seen. But the French navy defended itself strongly.

The solely American landings of George Patton's Western Task Force took place in three points on the Moroccan Atlantic coast: a main effort at Fedala, fifteen miles north of Casablanca; and subsidiary ones at Mehdia, fifty-five miles farther north; and at Safi, 140 miles south of Casablanca. Fedala was the nearest landing beach to Casablanca, the only large and well-equipped harbor in this part of Africa. Mehdia was the closest beach to Port Lyautey, whose airfield had the sole concrete runway in Morocco. Safi served to guard against intervention by a large French garrison at inland Marrakech, and also had a port where medium tanks could be unloaded. The new LSTs (Landing Ships Tanks) now being produced were not ready for Torch.

French army resistance was insignificant at Fedala and Safi, and by the afternoon of November 8, the Americans had attained their goals. Only at Mehdia did French troops resist strongly. Fighting ceased on November 11 after the senior French officer in North Africa, Admiral François Darlan, signed a cease-fire.

However, a sea fight broke out north of Casablanca at 7:04 A.M., November 8, between the American battleship *Massachusetts* and two French heavy cruisers, coastal batteries, and the battleship *Jean Bart,* which lay immobile in Casablanca harbor. American gunfire destroyed the main artillery batteries of the battleship. Other American warships warded off an attempted attack on troop transports by a French light cruiser and eight destroyers. Only one French ship returned undamaged, but the French made heavy hits on American warships.

The landings of the Center Task Force at Oran and the Eastern Task Force at Algiers took place with little resistance.

Eisenhower's principal goal was to assemble his troops, build a supply line, and advance on Tunis, in hopes of getting there before the Germans. But the Atlas Mountains of eastern Algeria proved difficult, and bringing forward supplies a great problem. Now the extreme caution of the Americans in refusing to land closer to Tunisia began to exact its toll.

✠      ✠      ✠

The German navy had held since 1940 that Tunisia was the key position in the Mediterranean—because it dominated Axis traffic routes to Africa and was an ideal base from which to invade Sicily and mainland Italy. The navy believed the Allies would try to seize Tunisia at the first opportunity.

The Axis had ample warning. The German foreign office was flooded with news, much of it dead on target. A report from the Vatican, for example, pinpointed the landings and said they would take place between mid-October and mid-November. A failed British-Canadian raid on Dieppe, France, on August 19 gave an even more certain sign. It showed that no landing would be made on the Continent in 1942, and this turned the arrow on French North Africa.

Adolf Hitler did nothing to prepare for the expected invasion. But, once it came, he moved fast, though not in great force, to hold a bridgehead in Tunisia. On the morning of November 9 he gave Albert Kesselring, German commander in the Mediterranean, a free hand, and the same day Kesselring sent in one fighter and two Stuka groups, and parts of the 5th Parachute Regiment, to occupy the Tunis airport, and, on the night of November 12, the city of Tunis.

Hitler also marched into unoccupied France and seized the French island of Corsica. The move (Operation Anton) began on November 11 and was finished in three days. The shock this gave did much to swing French officers in North Africa to the Allied side. The Germans did not immediately advance into the harbor of Toulon, where the vast bulk of the remaining French fleet lay at anchor. They hoped they could keep the fleet for Axis use, while Admiral Darlan was trying, without success, to get it to move to North Africa. On November 27, after having mined the harbor exits, German troops pressed into the base with the aim of seizing the ships. The French crews scuttled the entire fleet, including the battleship *Strasbourg*, before the eyes of the Germans.

General Walther Nehring, former commander of Africa Corps, took charge in Tunisia on November 15 as commander of 90th Corps, though he had only about 3,000 troops. Without waiting to concentrate, he thrust westward. The French division in Tunisia, under General George Barré, though much stronger, pulled back toward Algeria, hoping to join the Allies before clashing with the Germans.

General Anderson sent a British force to capture the port of Bougie, 110 miles east of Algiers, on November 11, and the next day seized the harbor and airfield of Bône, sixty miles from the Tunisian border. Coastal convoys began running in supplies and troops to both ports.

Anderson sent the British 78th and 6th Armored Divisions to take Tunisia. One part reached Djebel Abiod, fifty miles west of Bizerte, on November 17, where it collided with a small German parachute engineer battalion under Major Rudolf Witzig, the same officer who had seized Belgium's fort Eben Emael in 1940. Another British force seized Tabarka, a few miles west. The day previously a British paratroop battalion took Souk el Arba, south of Tabarka and eighty miles from Tunis. Meanwhile the American 509th Parachute Battalion landed near Tébessa, close to the Tunisian border, to cover the southern flank and secure an airfield there. Two days later it made an eighty-mile bound southeast and seized Gafsa, only seventy miles from the Gulf of Gabès.

General Anderson delayed his advance to consolidate his forces, giving the Germans a chance to expand the bridgehead. On November 17, a German parachute battalion of 300 men under Captain Walter Koch pushed westward, against a French force under General Barré that withdrew to the road center of Medjez el Bab, thirty-five miles west of Tunis, with an important bridge over the Medjerda River. There the French were reinforced by a British parachute battalion and an American artillery battalion.

General Barré received an ultimatum to withdraw to the Algerian border. It was quite a bluff by Captain Koch, for he had only one-tenth the troops of the Allies. When Barré tried to play for time, the Germans opened fire. Soon afterward Stukas bombed the Allied positions, shaking up the defenders and adding weight to the deception. The German paratroopers made two small but noisy ground attacks, which gave an exaggerated idea of strength, then small parties swam the river and simulated an even bigger attack. It was too much for the Allies. They left the bridge undamaged and fled eight miles to the rear.

Meanwhile other fast-moving German units took Sousse and Sfax, while two Italian battalions from Libya came up the coast to Gabès on November 20, just in time to foil a move on the town by the American 509th Parachute Battalion. On November 22, a small German armored column evicted the French from the road junction of Sbeitla, a hundred miles into the Tunisian interior, turning it over to an Italian detachment—which in turn was expelled by a detachment of the 509th Parachute Battalion.

On November 25 Anderson finally began his offensive on Tunis in three columns, reinforced by tanks and motorized infantry of the U.S. 1st Armored Division, which had rushed 700 miles from Oran. By this time German forces had trebled, though they remained far weaker than the Allies. Major Witzig's parachute engineers held up the northern column, finally stopping its advance by an ambush on November 30. The center column, with a hundred tanks, thrust to the Chouigui pass, a few miles north of Tebourba. Next morning, however, ten German tanks, supported by two infantry companies, pushed south against the Allied flank and led the command to break off the attack.

Meanwhile, the third column attacked Medjez el Bab, partially encircled Koch's battle group there, and drove on toward Djedeida, only twelve miles from Tunis. In the afternoon seventeen American tanks reached the airfield at Djedeida and destroyed twenty aircraft.

German antiaircraft guns disabled three of the tanks, and the remainder fell back, but the unexpected strike unnerved Nehring, and he ordered his forces to pull back to a small bridgehead around Tunis, giving up Bizerte, everything west of Djedeida, and all the coast from just south of Tunis. This would cut off the connection with Libya and Rommel. A fuming Kesselring arrived on November 28 and ordered the decision reversed.

Nehring now sent all armored and reconnaissance vehicles into an attack westward toward Tebourba. Since parts of 10th Panzer Division had arrived, Nehring had 64 tanks, including five 56-ton Tigers with high-velocity 88-millimeter guns and 100 millimeters of armor—Hitler's new "secret weapon," the most formidable tank to come out of World War II, which he sent to Tunisia to test in combat.

The attack was aimed as a flanking move from the north toward Chouigui pass, with the intention of swinging onto the British rear around Tebourba. The Germans, in two converging columns, overran British forces guarding the flank and pushed on toward Tebourba, but were checked by artillery fire and bombing before they could get astride their objective, the Tebourba–Medjez el Bab road. But the threat caused Anderson to pull back his spearhead to Tebourba. Next day Nehring increased pressure, cutting off the road and forcing the Allies to evacuate Tebourba by a dirt track along the Medjerda River, leaving more than a thousand prisoners.

The Germans erected a new defensive line eight miles east of Medjez el Bab, running north to the sea and south to Libya. Nehring had built a solid line of resistance, but Hitler replaced him with Colonel General Hans-Jürgen von Arnim and renamed the forces in Tunisia 5th Panzer Army, though Arnim had fewer than 25,000 fighting men. The Allies deployed 40,000 in the line, and held many more in the rear.

By now the winter rainy season had begun, and General Eisenhower decided to give up the offensive till the weather improved. This gave Adolf Hitler and Benito Mussolini time to make a stupendous military error. They commenced shipping in more and more troops, altogether about 150,000 men. Yet the Allies had assembled overwhelming sea and air forces—many times more than had ever threatened Rommel—and could throttle the German-Italian army by cutting off its supplies. Sooner or later its fuel, ammunition, and food would be exhausted and it would have to surrender, leaving few Axis troops to defend Sicily and Italy.

Erwin Rommel noted dryly afterward that, if Hitler had sent him in the spring of 1942 only a fraction of the troops he poured into Tunisia, he could have conquered Egypt, the Suez, and the Middle East, and virtually ruled out an Allied invasion of northwest Africa.

✠      ✠      ✠

After Rommel's last offensive failed at El Alamein around the first of September 1942, it was obvious from Ultra intercepts of German messages that supplies and men were not getting to Rommel in any quantity. Therefore, the British 8th Army possessed overwhelming superiority and could push the Axis out of Egypt and Libya at any time.

But Bernard Law Montgomery, the new commander of 8th Army, was not only a difficult, eccentric man concerned with his own glory, he was also excessively methodical. For the next seven weeks Montgomery worked out details of a set-piece counteroffensive, assembling even more tanks, artillery, and men.

The attack was supposed to commence well before the Operation Torch landings, but Montgomery would not be hurried, and finally set the date at October 23.

By this time 8th Army's fighting strength totaled 230,000 men, while Rommel had fewer than 80,000, of whom only 27,000 were German. The British committed 1,440 tanks, while Rommel had 210 German tanks and 280 obsolete Italian tanks. The RAF could send in 1,200 combat aircraft; the Luftwaffe and Italians could send in only 350.

Because of poor food, many Axis troops had become sick. Rommel was one of the casualties, and in September he went back to Europe for treatment and rest. He was replaced by General Georg Stumme, while General Wilhelm von Thoma took over Africa Corps. Both were from the Russian front and were unused to desert conditions. On the first day of the attack, Stumme drove to the front, ran into heavy fire, and died from a heart attack. Rommel, convalescing in Austria, flew back on October 25 and resumed command of a front already heaving from British attacks.

Montgomery took no advantage of his overwhelming strength by sweeping around the Axis positions. Instead, he launched a frontal attack near the coast, which led to a bloody, protracted struggle. British armor pushed a narrow six-mile wedge into the Axis line. The 15th Panzer Division lost three-fourths of its tanks resisting the advance, but also inflicted huge losses on the British. By October 26 the British armored wedge was stuck in a deep German antitank field. Stymied, Montgomery brought another armored division, the 7th, north to launch a secondary attack toward the coast from within the wedge on October 28. But this attack also hung up in a minefield. Rommel moved his 21st Panzer and Ariete Divisions to meet the new attack, and though his tanks achieved a knockout ratio of four to one, the British still ended up with eleven times as many tanks—800 to 90 German.

Montgomery reverted to his original line of thrust, but it took till November 2 to shift the armor. Minefields again caused delay. While the tanks were immobilized, Rommel launched a counterstrike with the last of his armor. He destroyed 200 British tanks, but lost three-quarters of his own. Rommel was now at the end of his resources. Africa Corps, which started with 9,000 men, was down to 2,000 and thirty tanks. The British still had 600.

Rommel decided to fall back to Fuka, 55 miles west, but Hitler issued his familiar call to hold existing positions at all costs. Rommel recalled the columns already on the way—a decision he regretted bitterly, writing that if he had evaded Hitler's "victory or death" order he could have saved the army.

Two British infantry divisions opened a breach on the southwest, and on the morning of November 4 three armored divisions passed through it with orders to swing north and block retreat along the coast road.

It was now possible to cut off Rommel's entire army, especially as General Thoma was captured during the morning and an order to retreat that Rommel now issued—in defiance of Hitler—was not sent out till the afternoon.

But as soon as they heard the order, Rommel's men moved fast, piled into any vehicles remaining, and escaped to the west, since the British were advancing slowly and hesitantly. Nevertheless, the delay imposed by Hitler caused Rommel to lose most of his remaining armor and a large number of the nonmotorized Italian infantry (about 20,000), who could not escape the British mobile columns.

Over the next few days, British attempts to cut off the retreating Axis troops failed because the turning movements were too narrow and too slow. The final blow to British hopes came on November 6, when heavy rain stopped pursuit. From this point on, 8th Army could not catch Rommel, and he slowly withdrew toward Tripolitania.

The British lost 13,500 men, but captured 7,900 Germans and 20,000 Italians, and killed about 2,000. Most of the remainder got away, though only 5,000 Germans and fewer Italians were able to keep their weapons.

Rommel proposed the correct strategic solution to his superiors—withdraw at once all the way to Wadi Akarit, 225 miles west of Tripoli near Gabès, Tunisia, and 45 miles beyond the Mareth line, a fortified barrier built by the French in 1939–1940. Wadi Akarit was much more defensible than the Mareth line, having only a fourteen-mile frontage between the sea and a salt marsh inland. But Mussolini and Hitler rejected the recommendation and insisted on holding one defensive line after another—Mersa el Brega, Buerat, and Tarhuna-Homs. Yet the work of fortifying these lines was useless, because the British could swing around the flank of all of them.

"If only the Italian infantry had gone straight back to the Gabès line and begun immediately with its construction, if only all those useless mines we laid in Libya had been put down at Gabès, all this work and material could ultimately have been of very great value," Rommel wrote.

In hopes of getting the Fuehrer to face reality, Rommel flew to his headquarters at Rastenburg on November 28, 1942. He got a chilly reception, and when he suggested that the wisest course would be to evacuate North Africa, in order to save the soldiers to fight again, "the mere broaching of this strategic question had the effect of a spark in a powder keg." Hitler flew into a rage, accusing members of the panzer army of throwing away their weapons.

"I protested strongly, and said in straight terms that it was impossible to judge the weight of the battle from here in Europe," Rommel wrote afterward. "Our weapons had simply been battered to pieces by the British bombers, tanks, and artillery, and it was nothing short of a miracle that we had been able to escape with all the German motorized forces, especially in view of the desperate fuel shortage."

But Hitler would listen to no further argument.

"I began to realize that Adolf Hitler simply did not want to see the situation as it was," Rommel wrote in his journal.

Hitler finally said he would do everything possible to get supplies to Rommel, and Reichsmarschall Hermann Göring would accompany him to Italy to work things out. Rommel rode with Göring in his private train to Rome.

"The situation did not seem to trouble him in the slightest," Rommel wrote. "He plumed himself, beaming broadly at the primitive flattery heaped on him by imbeciles from his own court, and talked of nothing but jewelry and pictures." Göring had stolen hundreds of masterpieces from art museums all over occupied Europe.

As Rommel suspected, Göring did nothing to induce the Italians to make greater efforts to supply the army in Africa. But Rommel, by the time he turned back to Africa on December 2, had gained permission from Mussolini to withdraw his forces to Buerat, 240 miles west of Mersa and 180 miles east of Tripoli. This improved the supply situation and saved the army for the moment, but Mussolini and Hitler resolved that Buerat "must be held under all circumstances and with all means."

This was unrealistic because Buerat could be flanked on the south. Rommel, after much pressure, secured from Marshal Ettore Bastico, the Axis supreme commander in Africa, authorization to retreat to Tarhuna-Homs, sixty miles east of Tripoli, when the British attack finally came on January 15, 1943.

Rommel told everybody in authority that the Axis should abandon Libya and retreat to the Mareth line, since Hitler and Mussolini would not consider the better Wadi Akarit position. There Rommel could link up with Axis forces in Tunisia, and, because of the mountains, would be secure from encirclement. On the new line the army could revive itself and, should the occasion arise, go over to the offensive—"be it to the west or the east." But once again he got no response.

The British overran the Buerat position in two days, but were stopped at Tarhuna-Homs on January 19 by Axis artillery fire. When the British swung around to the south to encircle the position, Rommel sent his motorized forces to shield the flank and ordered all his infantry out of Tarhuna-Homs. Within hours the foot soldiers were gone.

The British continued on westward, aiming to encircle Tripoli from the west and to close the entire German-Italian Panzer Army Africa into a caldron.

Seeing this, Rommel on January 23 ordered all forces to withdraw west of Tripoli, to take all war material possible, and to destroy the rest. Rommel's attention now focused on getting the 30,000 men in the non-motorized Italian infantry divisions and his supplies to the Mareth line. He didn't wait for approval from Mussolini or Hitler.

Rommel's desperate bid succeeded, primarily because Montgomery stopped at Tripoli to bring up new supplies. The Germans and Italians had time to withdraw the last of their armor and motorized forces into the Mareth line.

On January 26, Rommel received a signal from the Italian high command relieving him of duty at such time as he himself was to determine. The reason cited was Rommel's physical condition—he was suffering violent headaches and "nervous exhaustion"—but the real reason was payback for his defiance of Hitler and Mussolini, and for telling them the truth about the situation in Africa. Italian General Giovanni Messe was to take command.

But Rommel had one more trick up his sleeve. And before he left Africa, he was going to show it.

☦          ☦          ☦

With the Tunisian campaign stalled in winter mud, Roosevelt and Churchill decided on a meeting to plot future operations.

When Stalin said he could not come to a conference, Churchill pushed for a meeting at Marrakech, a favorite haunt of his in the Atlas Mountains in southern Morocco. But Roosevelt insisted on Casablanca, close to American troops. The conference began on January 14, 1943.

At the conference, Britain and the United States agreed on a strategic bombing campaign against German industry and cities, which fitted in with British ideas of a war of attrition. Top RAF and U.S. air commanders saw strategic bombing as possibly decisive, leading to German surrender and fewer battlefield losses. There was no disguising that the campaign was aimed at civilian targets to undermine the morale of the German people.

While the British continued to concentrate on heavy nighttime area raids that laid down massive loads, especially of incendiaries, burning huge portions of German cities, the Americans put much faith in precision bombing of specific targets with their four-engine B-17 Flying

Fortresses, which air enthusiasts claimed could fend off German fighters with their .50-caliber machine guns, and could bomb far into the depths of Germany in daylight.

But as the raids extended into Germany beyond the range of fighter protection, the bomber fanatics were found to be wrong: the B-17s were highly vulnerable to German fighters, and losses became prohibitive. In time the Americans hit upon a solution: the P-51 Mustang fighter with extra fuel tanks on the wings, which could be dropped off in flight. The Mustang was the best fighter to come out of the war, and it made long-range daylight bombing feasible. The campaign commenced in 1943, but did not reach its zenith until autumn 1944, when increasing aircraft production allowed full implementation of the theory.

Actually, strategic bombing did not have a decisive effect on the war. German production was not crippled. Though German morale declined, the bombs did not bring about a demand for surrender. In sum, Germany was devastated by the bombing, but the war was decided by the Allied armies, not the air forces.

The Allies were also concerned about German U-boat attacks on Atlantic convoys, and they intensified efforts to defeat the submarine menace.

Three other events took place at Casablanca with wide implications for the future. On December 2, 1942, scientists at the University of Chicago induced a nuclear chain reaction, which proved that the atomic bomb was possible. The Allies decided at Casablanca to go all out to produce the bomb.

On the final day of the conference, January 24, 1943, Roosevelt announced that the Allies would demand unconditional surrender from the Axis powers. Although there was much argument later that this lengthened the war by strengthening the enemies' will to resist, there is no evidence this was true. Unconditional surrender was an assurance to Stalin that he would not be left alone to fight the Germans.

Finally, the Allies agreed to invade Sicily. This would lead to an assault on Italy. There was going to be a Mediterranean strategy, after all.

# 17 KASSERINE AND THE END IN AFRICA

THE BATTLE OF KASSERINE PASS OCCUPIES A SPECIAL PLACE IN THE MYTHOLOGY of American wars. It was the most staggering and unequivocal defeat in American history, with the exception of the Union debacle at Chancellorsville in the Civil War. But at Chancellorsville Americans were fighting themselves. Analysts of that battle focused on the incompetence of Union General Joe Hooker compared to the brilliance of Confederate Generals Robert E. Lee and Stonewall Jackson. They didn't raise questions about the quality of the American fighting man. After Kasserine, however, a crisis of confidence shook the Allied military. American morale plummeted, and doubts arose about the quality of American soldiers, especially among the British.

Actually the failure at Kasserine could be traced, as at Chancellorsville, to the quality of leadership they received. Leadership explains the differences in the performance of nearly all armies at all times. At Kasserine a Hooker-level incompetent named Lloyd R. Fredendall had the misfortune to come up against Erwin Rommel, the one true military genius to emerge in World War II.

Chancellorsville and Kasserine demonstrate that the outcome of battles depends upon leadership. But laying full responsibility on the commander is difficult for human beings to accept. Most people assume that groups arrive at decisions by the interaction of their members. This leads many to attribute a defeat (or victory) to the alleged inherent nature of the soldiers or their nation, not the leaders.

After Kasserine British officers and men condemned Americans as "our Italians," implying Americans were inferior soldiers, as they felt the Italians were. The Italians did perform poorly, but the British forgot that the failures were not due to the soldiers but to their leaders, who sent Italian armies into battle with grossly inferior equipment and under incredibly poor commanders. In the few cases where Italians had good leadership they performed well, sometimes in spite of their atrocious weapons.

Kasserine taught a lesson all wars teach: a military organization *must* make life-and-death choices. It does not arrive at these choices by consensus. Seeking consensus leads first to debate, then to disintegration, since some will accept hard choices, while others will not. Military forces work *only* when decisions are made by commanders. If commanders are wrong, the units will likely fail. If they are right, they may succeed.

Kasserine taught another lesson: envious or blind officers on one's own side can nullify the insight of a great general and prevent him from achieving a decisive victory.

When Erwin Rommel pulled his beaten panzer army into Tunisia in late January 1943, he spotted an opportunity to transform the military situation in North Africa by a single, great stroke. If it succeeded, it could throw the Allies on the defensive and possibly lead to stalemate.

Montgomery was moving toward the Mareth line with his usual agonizing slowness. His army could be ignored for a couple weeks. The Allies in Tunisia had been stopped by the rains of Mediterranean winter and were arrayed on a north-south line with the British in the north, the newly organized French 19th Corps in the center, and the U.S. 2nd Corps under Fredendall in the south.

Rommel, in the Mareth line, recognized he had landed in Napoleon's "central position" between two enemy armies, and could strike out and defeat one before having to turn back and confront the other.

Rommel saw something else: the Americans and the French were advanced far eastward into central Tunisia holding the Eastern Dorsal passes at Fondouk, Faid, and Gafsa, and shielding the passes in the Western Dorsal Mountains sixty to seventy miles to the west.

If Axis forces could seize Faid and Gafsa, and drive on to the Western

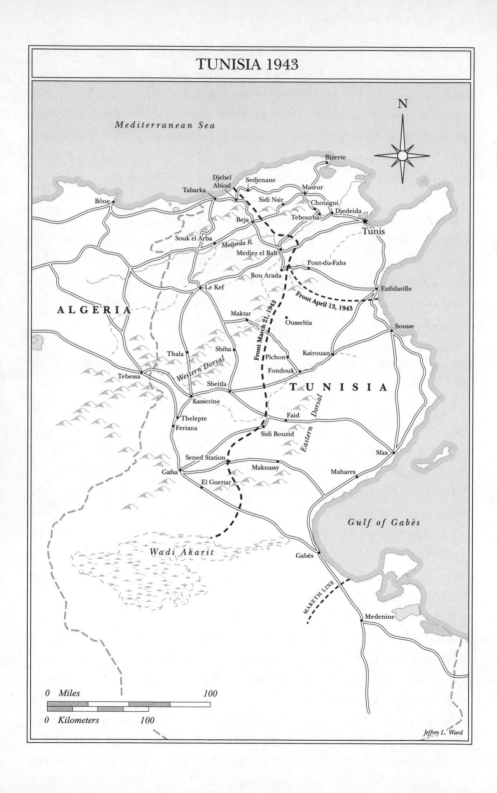

# TUNISIA 1943

N

*Mediterranean Sea*

Bizerte

Djebel
Abiod · Sedjenane · Mateur

Tabarka · Sidi Nsir · Chouigui · Djedeida

Bône · Beja · Tebourba · **Tunis**

Souk el Arba · *Medjerda R.*

Medjez el Bab · Pont-du-Fahs

**ALGERIA** · Bou Arada

Le Kef · Enfidaville

*Front April 13, 1943*

Maktar · Ousseltia · Sousse

*Front March 21, 1943*

Thala · Sbiba · Pichon · Kairouan

Tebessa · *Western Dorsal* · Fondouk · **TUNISIA**

Sbeitla

Kasserine · Faid

Thelepte · *Eastern Dorsal*

Feriana · Sidi Bouzid

Sened Station · Sfax

Gafsa · Maknassy · Mahares

El Guettar

*Wadi Akarit* · *Gulf of Gabès*

Gabès

MARETH LINE

Medenine

0  Miles                    100

0  Kilometers            100

*Jeffrey L. Ward*

Dorsal passes beyond Feriana and Kasserine, they would arrive at the huge American supply base and headquarters of Tebessa. At Tebessa Axis forces would be well *west* of the Allied line in Tunisia and deep into the Allies' communication zone. If Axis armor then struck *north* to the sea a hundred miles away, it might cut off the entire Allied army in Tunisia, or force it to withdraw into Algeria.

Then Rommel could turn back on Montgomery, with his own forces and Arnim's 5th Panzer Army, and either destroy 8th Army or drive it into precipitate retreat.

General Fredendall had played into Rommel's hand. Although Eisenhower had instructed him to set up a mobile reserve behind a screen of reconnaissance forces and light delaying elements, Fredendall had lumped his infantry on isolated djebels, or hills, along the line and scattered his reserves in bits and pieces.

On February 1, 1943, 21st Panzer Division, now under 5th Panzer Army and mounting 91 tanks (half authorized strength), overwhelmed a poorly armed French garrison at Faid pass. This caused Allied commanders to conclude the Axis were planning an offensive, but they figured it would come at Fondouk, thirty miles north of Faid. General Anderson, commanding the whole front, held back in reserve behind Fondouk Combat Command B of the U.S. 1st Armored Division, with 180 tanks and 18 tank-destroyers, half the strength of the division.

Rommel's intention in seizing Faid was to gain a starting point to thrust on to Sidi Bouzid and Sbeitla, 15 and 35 miles west. At Sbeitla two roads led through passes in the Western Dorsals, one due north twenty miles to Sbiba, the other by way of Kasserine, twenty miles west, toward Tebessa. To assist 21st Panzer, Rommel asked Arnim to send down 10th Panzer Division, with 110 tanks, plus a dozen Tiger tanks. But Arnim envied Rommel's fame and did not want to help him gain more. He provided only one tank battalion and four Tigers, and withdrew these shortly afterward for an attack he was planning farther north.

Meanwhile around Gabès, Rommel assembled a combat group with 26 tanks and two small infantry battalions from Africa Corps under Major General F. K. von Liebenstein. These, with the 23 obsolete tanks remaining to the Italian Centauro Division, were to seize Gafsa.

The attack from Faid opened on February 14, under the command of Lieutenant General Heinz Ziegler, Arnim's deputy. One group from 21st Panzer made a wide sweep from the north around U.S. 1st Armored Division's Combat Command A near Sidi Bouzid and struck the Americans in the flank, while another went around the other flank and attacked from the rear. Meanwhile, two groups from 10th Panzer swept straight through Faid pass and pinned down the Americans frontally. The Americans fled the field, leaving 40 tanks, 60 half-tracks, and the guns of five artillery battalions behind. Next morning Combat Command C counterattacked across thirteen miles of an open plain directly on Sidi Bouzid, to be met by a storm of shells when it came within range of German guns. The shellfire halted the charge, and pincer attacks on each flank routed the whole command. It lost another 54 tanks, 57 half-tracks, and 29 guns.

As the Germans swarmed through the gaps around Faid, they quickly isolated, encircled, and forced the surrender of the Americans on adjoining djebels, ending any chance to block the advance. Anderson ordered withdrawal to the Western Dorsals.

The panzers attacked the Americans in front of Sbeitla on the morning of February 17. The Americans fought stubbornly until nightfall, then fell back. In three days, the Americans had lost 150 tanks and nearly 3,000 men captured, while German losses had been minuscule.

Meanwhile the battle group under General Liebenstein occupied Gafsa, which the Americans had abandoned, and rushed on to capture Feriana, twenty miles southwest of Kasserine, on February 17, destroying a number of American armored personnel carriers (APCs) and guns, then seized the airfield at Thelepte, where the Americans destroyed thirty aircraft on the ground to prevent capture.

As the crisis unfolded, General Fredendall acted in panic, pulling American forces back to Tebessa and setting fire to some of the supply dumps there. British General Sir Harold Alexander, who took over command of the whole Tunisian front on February 19, reported that "in the confusion of the retreat American, French, and British troops had become inextricably mingled; there was no coordinated plan of defense, and definite uncertainty of command."

Rommel now resolved to drive through Tebessa and then turn north. This would force the Allies to pull their army out of Tunisia, or face its destruction. But the strike had to be made at once. Otherwise the Allies could assemble large forces to block the way.

Furthermore, Rommel told Arnim, "the thrust northward had to be made far enough behind [that is, *west* of] the enemy front to ensure that they would not be able to rush their reserves to the [Western Dorsal] passes and hold up our advance."

But General Arnim either could not see the possibilities of the strike or, as Rommel believed, "wanted to keep the 10th Panzer Division in his sector for a small private show of his own."

Rommel appealed to the Italian *Comando Supremo.* The Italian supreme command agreed to an attack, but prohibited a thrust by way of Tebessa. Instead it had to go by way of Thala to Le Kef; that is, through Kasserine and Sbiba passes and northward just behind the Western Dorsals.

To Rommel this was "an appalling and unbelievable piece of short-sightedness," for it meant the thrust was "far too close to the front and was bound to bring us up against the strong enemy reserves."

But it was no time for argument. Rommel put his Africa Corps on the road at once for Kasserine pass, while 21st Panzer got orders to strike northward from Sbeitla to Sbiba, twenty-five miles east of Thala. Rommel ordered 10th Panzer Division to Sbeitla, where it could support the Africa Corps or 21st Panzer, whichever needed help. But Arnim delayed sending 10th Panzer, so none of it was on hand when the attacks opened.

The blow toward Thala came where Alexander was expecting it, and he ordered Anderson to concentrate his armor for the defense of the town. Anderson sent the British 6th Armored Division to Thala, and the 1st Guards Brigade to Sbiba.

At Kasserine, German motorized infantry, used to desert warfare, tried to rush the pass. They ignored the 5,000-foot mountains on either side, which the Americans held and from which forward observers called down heavy mortar and artillery fire on the Germans. This stopped the attack in its tracks.

Meanwhile 21st Panzer Division came to a halt in front of Sbiba, held up by water-soaked roads, a dense minefield, and the guards brigade. This division, too, made the mistake of attacking frontally in the valley instead of striking off across the hills.

Just as Rommel had predicted, the strike to Sbiba and toward Le Kef

was so close to the Allied lines that reserves could get into blocking positions quickly. Some took positions in the hills that were difficult to assault,
gaining time to bring up more reinforcements.

Rommel concluded the Allies were weaker at Kasserine, and he
focused his attack there, ordering up 10th Panzer Division. When
Rommel arrived on the morning of February 20, General Friedrich von
Broich, 10th Panzer commander, told him he'd brought only half his
force—General von Arnim had held back the rest, including the Tigers,
which Rommel was counting on.

Panzer grenadiers and Italian mountain troops now made flanking
attacks on both sides of the pass, while, for the first time in Africa,
Rommel unleashed *Nebelwerfer*—rocket launchers—modeled after the
Russian Katyusha launcher. *Nebelwerfer* could throw 80-pound rockets four
miles. They shook the Americans badly, and by 5 P.M. that day the pass was
in German hands. Rommel reported that the Americans fought extremely
well, and that German losses were considerable.

During the night Rommel moved his armor toward Thala to the north
and Tébessa to the northwest. His aim was to confuse the Allies as to the
direction of his next thrust and to force them to divide their reserves. The
Allies fell for the bait. Fredendall brought Combat Command B of 1st
Armored Division to guard the road from Kasserine to Tébessa, while the
British 26th Armored Brigade Group moved south from Thala and took
up a position ten miles north of Kasserine pass.

On February 21, a battle group of 10th Panzer (30 tanks, 20 self-
propelled guns, two panzer grenadier battalions) pressed north against
26th Brigade, repeatedly flanking its positions, and destroying 40 tanks
while losing a dozen of its own. The British withdrew to Thala, but a string
of German tanks, led by a captured Valentine, a British infantry tank, followed on the 26th's tail, got into the position, overran some infantry, shot
up many vehicles, and captured 700 prisoners.

Next day Rommel learned from aerial reconnaissance that Allied reinforcements were approaching, reducing chances of driving through
Thala. Meanwhile, Africa Corps on the Tébessa road had been checked
by heavy American artillery fire.

On the afternoon of February 22, Rommel and Kesselring, realizing
their weakness, concluded nothing more could be accomplished and

ordered withdrawal. Fredendall, not seeing what was happening, did not organize an effective counterstrike, and the Germans retreated with little loss through Kasserine pass.

Rommel's whole operation killed or wounded 3,000 Americans and netted more than 4,000 prisoners and 200 destroyed Allied tanks, against fewer than a thousand Axis casualties and far lower tank losses. But, if Arnim had cooperated and the *Comando Supremo* had shown any vision, the Axis gains could have been immensely greater.

Meanwhile Arnim, using the armor he had withheld from Rommel, launched his operation in the north on February 26. They were largely direct attacks at eight points along a seventy-mile stretch. The main objective was Beja, sixty miles west of Tunis.

Rommel described the plan as "completely unrealistic." The main attack became trapped in a narrow, marshy defile ten miles short of Beja, and British artillery knocked out all but six tanks. Although the attacks netted 2,500 British prisoners, the Germans lost 71 tanks, the British fewer than 20.

The attack also delayed a strike Rommel was planning against Montgomery's 8th Army at Medenine, facing the Mareth line, giving Montgomery time to quadruple his strength and to stop Rommel's attack when it came on March 6. After losing 40 tanks, Rommel called off the effort. This ended any chance of defeating Montgomery before his army linked up with the other Allied army in Tunisia.

Rommel, elevated February 23 to command all forces in Africa, but facing an enemy twice as strong in men and nine times as strong in armor, concluded it was "plain suicide" for the Axis to remain. He took his long-deferred sick leave to Europe on March 9, hoping to convince Mussolini and Hitler to evacuate while there was still time. Mussolini, Rommel wrote, "seemed to lack any sense of reality," while Hitler, impervious to Rommel's arguments, concluded he had "become a pessimist," and barred his return to Africa.

✠      ✠      ✠

The issue in Africa was no longer in doubt. With command of the sea and growing command of the air, with vastly larger combat forces, the Allies were certain to win. Hitler's only hope to save the approximately 180,000 Germans and Italians in Tunisia was to abandon guns and tanks, and institute a swift evacuation of the men by air and sea. But this Hitler would not countenance. As he had proclaimed for Stalingrad, the Axis forces in Africa had to stand or die. Mussolini, overwhelmed by the fate bearing down on him, asserted no independent judgment, merely approving everything Hitler ordained.

General Alexander had two strategic choices. He could drive a wedge between Arnim's forces in the north around Tunis and Bizerte, and General Giovanni Messe's 1st Italian Army, the new name for Rommel's old Panzer Army Africa, on the Mareth line, encircling and destroying the two forces separately. Or he could squeeze the Axis armies together into an increasingly small bridgehead around Tunis and Bizerte until they lost their airfields and room to maneuver and were forced to surrender.

Alexander chose the second method, which required Montgomery's 8th Army to advance northward along the coast, driving the Axis forces into a Tunis-Bizerte pocket, while the remaining Allied forces pressed against the line in Tunisia to hurry the Axis retreat along.

The first choice was the better one, by far, and Alexander knew it. Montgomery would plod forward with maddening slowness, adding to Allied and Axis casualties, and prolonging the Tunisian campaign far into the spring. But Alexander rejected the idea of splitting the two Axis armies because the agent would have to be U.S. 2nd Corps, and, as General Omar Bradley wrote, Alexander had a "complete lack of faith in the American soldier"—the product of the defeat at Kasserine. Instead, 2nd Corps was to "demonstrate" and "make noise" with limited feinting attacks eastward, out of the mountains.

But Eisenhower had replaced Fredendall with an entirely different sort of general, George S. Patton Jr. He was an overwhelmingly aggressive commander and was galled by Alexander's instructions, especially as Eisenhower had raised 2nd Corps to four divisions and 88,000 men, four times the troops the Axis could find to oppose it.

Patton arrived at 2nd Corps headquarters on March 7, 1943, leading a long procession of armored scout cars, sirens shrieking, his "command car" sporting two metal flags with two huge white stars of a major general on a field of red, and Patton himself standing in the car like a charioteer. Patton immediately instituted his "cure" for the alleged problems of 2nd Corps: every soldier had to wear a tie, even on the battlefront, and everybody, including nurses tending patients in rear hospitals, had to wear a heavy metal combat helmet.

Patton was heir to a California fortune, and had married a rich Boston heiress, yet he never had any doubts about his destiny to be a great soldier. His grandfather, a Virginian, commanded a Confederate regiment and died of battle wounds. Patton graduated from West Point in 1909, won the Distinguished Service Cross in battle in France in 1918, and showed great promise as a tank commander in maneuvers in 1940. Patton was dyslexic, and the difficulty he had reading and writing gave him an enduring sense of insecurity. To cover his insecurity, an innate shyness, and a high, squeaky voice, Patton developed a public demeanor of bravado and bombast. This led him to become a publicity hound and to be extremely hard on his men. Eisenhower summed up Patton as a shrewd soldier who believed in showmanship, talked too much, and was not always a good example to subordinates. But Eisenhower believed he would turn into a superb field commander.

Montgomery proceeded with slow, exasperating preparations for an attack on the Mareth line, planned for March 20, two weeks after the Medenine battle. The attack by 2nd Corps was to be launched three days earlier but was to be limited to drawing off Axis reserves, regaining the forward airfield at Thelepte to assist Montgomery's advance, and setting up a forward base at Gafsa to help reprovision 8th Army as it moved northward.

On March 17, 1943, the U.S. 1st Infantry Division under Terry Allen occupied Gafsa without a fight, the Italians withdrawing twenty miles down the road to a defile east of El Guettar, blocking the road to Gabès. Meanwhile the U.S. 1st Armored Division under Orlando Ward, with elements of the U.S. 9th Infantry Division, drove eastward from Kasserine, occupied the railway station at Sened, and moved toward Maknassy and the pass there through the Eastern Dorsals.

But Ward's tanks and trucks got bogged down in mud from heavy rains, and, though Ward launched successive attacks on March 23, he was stymied by an eighty-man German detachment (Rommel's former bodyguard) under Colonel Rudolf Lang on a dominating hill (322). Ward renewed the attack the next day with three infantry battalions, supported by artillery and tanks—and again failed.

Patton, livid with anger, ordered Ward to lead another attack himself. Ward did so, but it failed as well. Alexander suggested that Ward be relieved. Patton agreed privately but resented Alexander's proposal as another criticism of Americans. In the end, he sent Omar Bradley, deputy commander of 2nd Corps, to do the deed, replacing Ward with Ernest N. Harmon.

At El Guettar, Terry Allen's infantry broke into the Italian position on March 21, but on March 23 was hit by a counterattack of the 10th Panzer Division, rushed up from the Mareth line. The panzers overran the American forward positions, but were stopped by a minefield, then hit by American artillery and tank destroyers, which knocked out 40 German tanks. Although the Americans made few gains, their strikes at El Guettar and Maknassy drew off much of the enemy's scanty tank strength. This helped Montgomery when he launched his attack on the Mareth line.

Montgomery had assembled 160,000 men to Messe's 80,000, and deployed 610 tanks and 1,400 guns, while Messe had only 150 tanks (including the 10th Panzer's already withdrawn) and half as many guns. As at El Alamein, however, Montgomery made his main effort straight into the heart of the Axis line, a frontal assault of three infantry divisions, hoping to break open a gap through which his armor could rush. Meanwhile, a New Zealand corps made a wide outflanking march 25 miles inland from Gabès to menace the enemy's rear. This effort started well but 21st Panzer and 164th Light Divisions stopped it.

The frontal attack bogged down after making only a shallow dent in the Axis line. A counterattack by 15th Panzer Division, with only 30 tanks and two infantry battalions, overran the forward British infantry, stopping the entire British effort.

On March 23 Montgomery shifted his forces to the inland flank. Since Montgomery's frontal attack had failed, the Axis commanders had already shifted 15th Panzer Division to this flank two days before.

It might have been another defeat for Montgomery, except that Arnim, now commander of the whole front with the departure of Rommel, decided to withdraw Messe's army back to the fourteen-mile-wide Wadi Akarit bottleneck, 43 miles to the rear. At Wadi Akarit Montgomery went through his laborious preparations all over again.

Meanwhile Patton renewed his efforts at El Guettar and Maknassy. By March 27 Montgomery had reached Gabès on the way to Wadi Akarit, and Alexander launched Patton's tanks toward the coast without waiting for infantry to clear a path. However, a chain of antitank guns stopped the tanks. Patton called on his infantry to crack the barrier, but they failed as well.

However, Arnim had transferred 21st Panzer to help 10th Panzer, reducing strength at Akarit, and making it easier for Montgomery to crack the line, which his infantry did April 5. Once more Montgomery was slow to exploit success, and by morning the Axis troops were moving up the coast, heading for Enfidaville, only 50 miles south of Tunis. Here was a narrow coastal plain with a hill barrier on the west.

Alexander tried to intercept the enemy's retreat, using a new corps (the 9th) under British General John Crocker to strike on the night of April 7–8 through Fondouk pass, with the aim of driving through Kairouan to Sousse, twenty-five miles south of Enfidaville. Crocker commanded the British 6th Armored Division, a brigade of the British 46th Division, and the U.S. 34th Infantry Division, which had 350 tanks. But the 34th troops were three hours late starting, soon stopped, and took cover. This permitted the enemy to shift fire northward to stop 46th Division. Crocker threw in his 6th Armored tanks to force a passage on April 9. But they took till afternoon to break through fifteen antitank guns and lost 34 tanks. By the time Crocker's tanks got to Kairouan on April 10, Messe's army had already passed through. It was a remarkable feat by a few Axis defenders and a sorry show by the Allies, especially 34th Division.

Messe's army got to Enfidaville by April 11, and linked up with Arnim's 5th Panzer Army in a hundred-mile arc around Tunis and Bizerte. Even so, the Axis position was hopeless, because German and Italian strength and supplies were declining, while Allied strength was rising.

Just as the Allies poised for a knockout blow, a great dispute threatened to tear the Allies apart. Since 8th Army was coming up the coast from the south, and the British 1st Army was already positioned opposite Tunis and Bizerte on the north, Alexander selected them to smash into the bridgehead and force the Axis surrender. The U.S. 2nd Corps, despite now having 95,000 men, had been neatly pinched off, with no role to play in the victory march. This didn't sit well with Patton or Bradley, and they complained loudly to Eisenhower, who demanded that 2nd Corps be shifted to the north and strike out on its own for Bizerte.

The 2nd Corps, now under Bradley since Patton was planning for the invasion of Sicily, moved north, 2,400 vehicles a day, driving behind British lines.

The attack opened on April 19, with 8th Army striking northward through Enfidaville toward Tunis, while the British 1st Army made the main effort by attacking April 22 near Medjez el Bab against a 15-mile sector held by only two regiments of the German 334th Division. On the north, Bradley's 2nd Corps struck on April 23 against Hasso von Manteuffel's scratch division of 8,000 men.

Allied combat strength was now approaching 300,000 men and 1,400 tanks, while the nine German divisions, backbone of the defense, counted only 60,000 men, and had fewer than 100 tanks.

Thus the Allied attack should have been a walkover. But it wasn't. Italians and Germans at Enfidaville stopped Montgomery cold. The advance by 1st Army made slow progress against tenacious defense by the two German regiments, then was pushed back by an improvised brigade comprising all the remaining tanks of Army Group Africa. In the north the U.S. 2nd Corps made slow progress through rough country, then found Manteuffel had slipped back to a new line a few miles in the rear. The Allied offensive came to a halt.

But the Axis, because their supply lines had been virtually choked off, were down to only enough fuel to run their vehicles for twenty-five kilometers, while ammunition was sufficient for only three days, and food was getting desperately short.

On April 21, Montgomery suspended his attacks at Enfidaville because of losses, permitting Arnim to shift his armor northward to stop the British from breaking through east of Medjez el Bab.

Meanwhile Bradley's 2nd Corps resumed its attacks on April 26, but was held up by obstinate resistance. Manteuffel's men were virtually out of ammunition, however, and withdrew to a new line east of Mateur, only fifteen miles from Bizerte. There was now little maneuver room in the Axis position, and any breakthrough would be fatal. The Germans had also lost their air cover, because the Allies had seized the main fields, and aircraft had been withdrawn to Sicily.

The Allied breakthrough on May 6 came on a narrow front, less than two miles wide, in the Medjez el Bab sector, by four British divisions, two infantry, two armored, with 470 tanks. Although the lead tanks poured through the gap, the commander halted after six miles—although there was nothing between him and Tunis, since the Germans were immobilized by lack of fuel. His aim was to keep all his brigades together.

The advance resumed early on May 7, but the British, again showing excessive caution, only reached Tunis in the afternoon, though there was no resistance.

Meanwhile, 2nd Corps discovered the road ahead empty on May 7, and drove into Bizerte in the afternoon.

Mass surrenders began. Hitler had called for resistance to the death, but the Axis soldiers gave up everywhere. The bulk of the battle-tested German and Italian troops in the Mediterranean, about 160,000 men, were marched off to prisoner-of-war cages. If they had been evacuated to Sicily and Italy, an attack on either would have been an expensive, possibly prohibitive exercise. Rommel had been right. The army would die if it remained in Africa.

# 18 THE INVASION OF SICILY

ALLIED OPERATIONS IN THE MEDITERRANEAN AFTER THE CAPTURE OF TUNISIA presented a case study of how Germany might have achieved a deadlock if Hitler had moved over to defensive warfare. Hitler's senior generals had been pleading with him to follow this strategy ever since the failure to capture Moscow in December 1941.

The disaster of Stalingrad should have convinced Hitler that there was no hope for a decision in the east. At the same time, western Allied commanders were proving to be so cautious that they were offering him a chance to reverse by defense many of the strategic errors he had committed by offense.

Victory, of course, no longer was possible. But Germany might have achieved a standstill in the west if Hitler had transferred much of his army and air force to challenge landings by the western Allies. By husbanding his forces in the east, and above all by avoiding an offensive that might consume his little remaining striking power, he also might have held back the Soviet Union until everyone was weary of war.

But such a reversal would have required Hitler to see that he had made mistakes—and this Hitler could not do. On the contrary, he began in the spring of 1943 to concentrate every man, gun, and tank possible for a final confrontation with the Red Army in the Kursk salient northwest of Kharkov. This campaign, Operation Citadel, was to be a make-or-break effort to regain the initiative. In this continued quest to destroy Russia and Communism, he neglected the Mediterranean and the northern coast of France. It was his ultimate failure as a field commander.

German generals in the Mediterranean were seeing that the principal Allied commanders were hesitant, slow-moving, and insistent upon overwhelming superiority before they undertook operations. Allied obsession with security played directly into the strengths of the German army. Compared to Allied commanders, German generals were, on balance, bolder, more flexible, more inventive, more willing to take chances, and more confident of their ability to overmaster opponents.

A couple of decisions illustrate the attitude of Eisenhower, Alexander, Montgomery, and other senior commanders. First, though no one expected much opposition, they earmarked ten divisions for the invasion of Sicily (Operation Husky), more than they were later able to get on the beaches of Normandy. Second, they insisted on attacking the Italian boot at Salerno because it was within the 200-mile range of Spitfires operating from northeast Sicily. Since the Germans knew about the Allied fixation on air cover, they spotted Salerno as the target and prepared a gruesome reception there.

☩          ☩          ☩

After Tunisia, the Americans had committed themselves only to an inva-. sion of Sicily. In mid-May 1943 Winston Churchill made his third visit to Washington, hoping to get an agreement to assault the boot of Italy. This, he argued, would lead to a quick Italian surrender. Churchill avoided mention of his real purpose: to turn the Americans away from a cross-Channel invasion.

But General Marshall insisted that Operation Bolero, the buildup in Britain for a cross-Channel attack (Operation Roundup), take precedence over anything else. This did not rule out an invasion of Italy, but Marshall hoped to prevent any shift toward the Mediterranean.

He was partly successful. The conference, code-named Trident, established early March 1944 as the date for the invasion of France, an operation that soon received the new code name Overlord. Nothing was said about Italy.

Churchill didn't accept the silence at Washington as final and called a meeting at Eisenhower's headquarters in Algiers for May 29, 1943, to push for an Italian invasion, and, by inference, abandonment of Overlord. General Marshall attended, but Churchill stacked the deck with Alan

Brooke, chief of the imperial staff, and all British commanders in the Mediterranean.

Eisenhower was interested in gaining the airfields around Foggia in southern Italy to attack the Ploesti oil fields and targets in southern Germany, but he was not enthusiastic about a campaign up the rugged mountainous boot of Italy, especially since rain, mud, and immobility would be coming with winter.

Churchill was cagey enough not to propose more than seizure of southern Italy, but Brooke confessed privately to Eisenhower that he wanted to avoid any wider land front than the Allies could sustain in Italy, and preferred applying Allied air and naval power to blockade Germany and destroy its industry.

Eisenhower knew Marshall would never accept abandonment of Overlord, but he found himself agreeing to seize Naples and the Foggia airfields. Churchill and Brooke were satisfied. An Allied army was unlikely to stop with Naples and Foggia. Once the camel's nose got under the tent, the whole animal was likely to follow. Churchill might still get his Mediterranean strategy.

✠      ✠      ✠

The key to Sicily was the narrow Strait of Messina (in Greek mythology guarded by Scylla and Charybdis), less than three miles wide, which divides the northeastern tip of the island from the toe of Italy (Calabria). Any supplies to and evacuation from Sicily had to pass this bottleneck.

Since the Allies held command of the sea, the way to assure the capitulation of the enemy on Sicily without firing a shot was to invade the toe of Italy. There were virtually no Axis troops in Calabria. Its occupation would have separated Sicily from the mainland and prevented the evacuation of troops from the island—except those few who might have been flown out.

This idea never received serious consideration. Part of the reason was the hesitation by the Americans to commit to an invasion of mainland Italy. But the principal reason was Eisenhower's unwillingness to undertake any operation that was not conservative, sure, and direct. The American naval historian Samuel Eliot Morison wrote: "The entire Husky plan was wrong. . . . We should have attacked the Messina bottleneck first."

General Heinrich-Gottfried Vietinghoff-Scheel, who commanded the

German 10th Army in Italy, wrote that the Allies could have seized the Strait of Messina "without any special difficulty." If this had happened, Albert Kesselring, German commander in chief south, said it "would have turned the landing in Sicily into an overwhelming victory."

Instead, Eisenhower approved a completely frontal attack. General Montgomery's 8th Army was to land at the southeastern corner of Sicily, while George Patton's U.S. 7th Army was to come ashore immediately to the west.

This was where the Italians and Germans expected the invasion, and where the Axis commander, Italian General Alfredo Guzzoni, had posted his 275,000 men in eight coastal divisions (static forces made up mostly of Sicilian conscripts), and four mobile Italian divisions, with two German divisions (the 15th Panzergrenadier and the Hermann Göring Panzer) divided into five mobile reserve groups.

Hitler had not sent more troops to Sicily because he suspected Mussolini might be overthrown and the Italians sue for peace. He also was not sure the Allies would land in Sicily. To him Sardinia was a more logical target. Possession of this island would provide an easy jump to Corsica just to the north, and from Corsica the Allies could strike at southern France or northern Italy. He also thought the Allies might land in Greece and push northward through the Balkans.

British intelligence officers abetted Hitler's misconceptions. They planted papers on the body of a "British officer" washed ashore on the Spanish coast. In addition to identity papers and personal letters, the documents included a private letter written by Sir Archibald Nye, vice chief of the Imperial General Staff, to General Alexander saying the Allies intended to land in Sardinia and Greece while aiming to convince the Axis that Sicily was the target.

Nazi agents in Spain were convinced the letter was authentic. Though it didn't sway Kesselring or the Italian chiefs, it made a strong impression on Hitler. He sent 1st Panzer Division from France to Greece, the 90th Panzergrenadier Division to Sardinia, and Kurt Student's 11th Air Corps of two parachute divisions to the south of France to intervene when the Allies invaded Sardinia.

It took Eisenhower and his senior generals until May 13 to finish their plans. Yet, since only one of the divisions intended for Husky was being

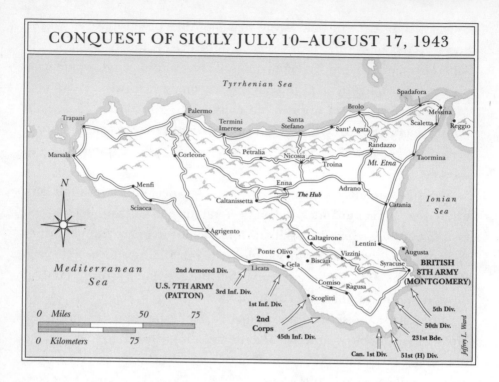

## CONQUEST OF SICILY JULY 10–AUGUST 17, 1943

used in the last stages of the Tunisian campaign, the invasion could have followed directly on the heels of the Axis surrender. If this had happened, the attackers would have found the island virtually bereft of defenders and could have seized it almost without casualties.

Because of extreme caution, therefore, the Allied invasion of Sicily was delayed to July 10, 1943. The only surprise was that a storm unexpectedly blew up, and the members of the Italian coastal divisions, who were not much interested in fighting anyway, went to sleep thinking the Allies would wait for good weather.

Four British divisions landed on a forty-mile stretch on the southeastern corner of Sicily around Syracuse and Cape Passero, while four American divisions landed to the west on a forty-mile front across the beaches around Scoglitti, Gela, and Licata. A total of 150,000 troops came ashore on the first three days; ultimately there were 478,000: 250,000 British, 228,000 American.

The American landing was made possible by use of new LST (Landing Ships Tank) and DUKW amphibious trucks.

Italian naval response was weak. Only four ships and two LSTs were lost—to submarine attack. Meanwhile Allied aerial superiority was so great (4,000 aircraft against 1,500 German and Italian) that enemy bombers had withdrawn to central Italy.

The worst Allied losses were in airborne troops. Parts of the British 1st and the American 82nd Airborne Divisions were to land inland and seize key points. But high winds scattered the Americans over a fifty-mile radius and caused 47 of 134 British gliders to fall into the sea.

On none of the landing sites did the Italians offer any resistance. General Sir Harold Alexander, in command of land forces, wrote: "The Italian coastal divisions, whose value had never been rated very high, disintegrated almost without firing a shot, and the field divisions, when they were met, were also driven like chaff before the wind. Mass surrenders were frequent."

From the first day of the invasion, the whole burden of the defense fell on the Germans. Only one major counterattack occurred. The Hermann Göring Division had a force of 56-ton Tiger tanks around Caltagirone, twenty miles inland from the Gela plain. On the morning of July 11, the Tigers overran outposts of the U.S. 1st Infantry Division and those of the 45th Infantry Division, reaching the sand dunes bordering the beaches. It was scary, but well-directed naval gunfire broke up the attacks.

With Italian forces surrendering to any Allied troops that appeared, the Germans withdrew to the northeast corner of Sicily to cover the routes to Messina. They formed a powerful defensive line around the Mount Etna massif with the help of two additional divisions, all under a new head-quarters (14th Panzer Corps) commanded by Valentin Hube.

As Montgomery attacked northward up the east coast, Patton's 7th Army swung around to the west and central portions of the island, captured Palermo, all with little or no opposition, and drove along the north coast toward Messina.

As Sicily was being overrun, the Italians ousted Mussolini on July 25 and turned the government over to the king, Victor Emanuel, and Marshal Pietro Badoglio. The new leaders arrested Mussolini, but to deceive their German allies attested their determination to continue the war, all the while establishing secret contacts in Lisbon with the Allies.

President Roosevelt and Winston Churchill were holding their Quebec conference (code-named Quadrant, August 14–24, 1943), and they superintended the negotiations. Churchill was hoping Mussolini's ouster would turn the Americans away from Overlord and lead to a move through northern Italy into southern France or toward Vienna. He also sought to wrest Greece and the Balkans from the Germans. He especially wanted landing craft to attack the Italian-ruled island of Rhodes in the Dodecanese Islands in the eastern Mediterranean. On this, Churchill ran up against adamant opposition from General Marshall.

"Forgive me," Marshall told the prime minister, "but no American soldier is going to die on that goddamn beach."

At Quadrant the western Allies agreed to opportunistic moves in the Mediterranean, but Overlord was to receive absolute priority.

Hitler recognized that the Italians were going to quit and, equally in secret, set in motion Operation Axis to take over Italy. Marshal Rommel rushed eight divisions into northern Italy—ostensibly to allow the Italian troops there to move south to confront the Allies—and secured the passes through the Alps as well as all key locations in the region. Hitler directed Hube's troops in Sicily to delay but to evacuate as quickly as possible through Messina. He also ordered SS Captain Otto Skorzeny to spy out the place Il Duce was being held and free him.

General Hube conducted highly effective delaying actions, causing heavy Allied casualties, while, over six days and seven nights, Fregattenkapitän Gustav von Liebenstein, under the cover of German fighter aircraft and strong antiaircraft artillery, evacuated 40,000 German and 60,000 Italian soldiers. Although the Italians left nearly all their equipment, the Germans took off 10,000 vehicles, forty-seven tanks, ninety-four guns, and 17,000 tons of supplies.

On August 17, the Americans and the British arrived in a Messina empty of enemy forces.

Since only about 60,000 Germans had moved into Sicily while 13,500 wounded were evacuated by air and 5,500 were captured, relatively few Germans were killed. Total British casualties were almost 13,000, American 10,000—about 5,500 killed all told.

Marshal Badoglio was getting frightened that the Germans might seize him and the king, and demanded a major landing of Allied paratroops on Rome as a condition of Italian surrender. This was far too dangerous for Eisenhower, since Hitler had moved Kurt Student with his 2nd Parachute Division and the 3rd Panzergrenadier Division close to Rome. Student had instructions to disarm all Italian forces around the capital as soon as Badoglio announced surrender.

It is a comment on Allied and German attitudes that although Badoglio had five Italian divisions at Rome, the Allies had no confidence they could protect a landing site, while Student was sure his much smaller force could eliminate them.

Eisenhower demanded an immediate cease-fire. Badoglio gave in. On September 3, 1943, near Syracuse, Eisenhower's chief of staff, Walter Bedell Smith, signed the capitulation document with Giuseppe Castellano, who had conducted the Lisbon negotiations. At the same moment, Victor Emanuel and Badoglio received the German ambassador to assure him that Italy would remain true to its Axis partner. On the same day British divisions crossed the Strait of Messina and formed a bridgehead on the Italian mainland. The Allies announced the cease-fire over Radio Algiers on September 8, 1943. Shortly thereafter the main invasion of Italy (Operation Avalanche) began.

Kesselring declared all of Italy to be a war theater. Rommel disarmed Italian troops in the north. Parachutists overpowered Rome. In general the Italian soldiers either took off their uniforms and faded into the population or allowed themselves to be carted off as prisoners of war. Only in the Balkans did a very few Italian units put up some resistance, none effective. It was a pathetic end to Mussolini's dreams of a new Roman empire. Victor Emanuel, the queen, Crown Prince Umberto, Badoglio, and other members of his government fled to Brindisi on the Adriatic coast.

Most of the Italian fleet surrendered at Malta, but a newly designed German radio-guided gliding bomb sank the Italian flagship, *Roma*, on the way.

Meanwhile Skorzeny had tracked down the place where Mussolini was being held—on the 2,900-meter Gran Sasso in the Abruzzi Mountains seventy miles northeast of Rome. At 2 P.M. on September 12, 1943, eight gliders landed on the grounds of the Campo Imperiale Hotel. In moments seventy parachutists and Waffen-SS commandos spread out, intimidated the Italian guards, and rescued Mussolini. Shortly afterward a light Fieseler Storch landed on the grounds, picked up Mussolini and

Skorzeny, and flew them to a nearby airport, where a transport carried Il Duce to Hitler at Rastenburg in East Prussia. The entire raid took less than twenty minutes.

Mussolini, a broken man, formed a "republican-socialistic government," with Salò on Lake Garda as his "capital." But he was a puppet of Hitler, with no power.

☩     ☩     ☩

Two incidents in Sicily in August cast severe doubt on the capacity of George Patton as a senior commander. Visiting an evacuation hospital August 3, Patton came upon an enlisted man who had no wounds. Patton asked him where he was hurt.

"I guess I can't take it," the soldier replied.

Patton burst into a rage, cursed the man, slapped his face with his gloves, and stormed from the tent. The soldier had been diagnosed with dysentery and malaria. That evening Patton issued a memo to commanders berating cowards who went into hospitals "on the pretext that they are nervously incapable of combat."

On August 10 at another hospital Patton was walking down a line of cots with a medical officer. Coming to a man shivering in bed, Patton asked what the trouble was.

"It's my nerves," the soldier said, and started to cry.

"Your nerves, hell," Patton shouted. "You are just a goddamned coward, you yellow son of a bitch. You're a disgrace to the army, and you are going back to the front to fight, although that's too good for you. You ought to be lined up against a wall and be shot. In fact, I ought to shoot you myself right now, goddamn you."

Patton pulled his pistol from the holster and waved it, then struck the man across the face with the gloves he held in his other hand. He ordered the medical officer to move the man out at once. "I won't have these other brave boys seeing such a bastard babied." He started to leave the tent, turned, and hit the weeping soldier again.

The doctor placed himself between Patton and the patient, and Patton departed. The medical authorities sent a report to Omar Bradley, commander of 2nd Corps in Patton's army. Bradley locked the paper in his safe and said nothing. The doctors, however, also forwarded their report to Eisenhower. He sent Patton a letter that questioned his judgment and self-discipline, ordered him to explain his actions, and told him to apologize to those who witnessed the events.

When some newspaper correspondents got wind of the incident, Eisenhower asked them to withhold publication because it would require him to fire Patton. The journalists agreed. Meanwhile Patton wrote a humble letter to Eisenhower; summoned doctors, nurses, and medical personnel of the two hospitals to Palermo and expressed his regret; and called the two soldiers into his office, apologized, and shook hands.

Eisenhower hoped the matter had ended. In November, however, Drew Pearson, an American newspaper columnist, revealed the slapping incidents on a national radio broadcast. In the public furor that followed, many citizens demanded Patton's dismissal. The storm slowly subsided. But when Eisenhower named the army group commander to direct American ground troops going into Normandy, he selected Bradley. Patton stayed for months in Sicily without a job, but on January 22, 1944, Eisenhower ordered him to Britain to take command of the U.S. 3rd Army—and delivered him from disgrace.

# 19 THE CITADEL DISASTER

THE CAMPAIGNS OF 1941 AND 1942 HAD PROVED THAT GERMAN PANZERS WERE virtually invincible when they maneuvered freely across the great open spaces of Russia and Ukraine. The proper decision for Germany in 1943, therefore, was to make strategic withdrawals to create fluid conditions so panzers could carry out wide movements and surprise attacks. This would have given maximum effect to the still superior quality of German command staffs and fighting troops.

Instead, as General Friedrich-Wilhelm von Mellenthin, one of the most experienced panzer leaders on the eastern front, wrote, "The German supreme command could think of nothing better than to fling our magnificent panzer divisions against Kursk, which had now become the strongest fortress in the world."

Head-to-head confrontation was becoming increasingly unrealistic as the disparity of strength between Germany and the Allies grew. By mid-1943, even after urgent recruiting of non-Germans, Hitler's field forces amounted to 4.4 million men. The Red Army alone had 6.1 million, while Britain and the United States were mobilizing millions more. In war production the Allies were far outproducing Germany in every weapon and every vital commodity.

Erich von Manstein offered Hitler the best strategic plan still open to him shortly after the recapture of Kharkov in late winter. The German front projected dangerously as a "balcony" southeastward from Kharkov more than two hundred miles down the Donetz and Mius rivers to Taganrog, on the Sea of Azov. The 17th Army also was still in the Kuban peninsula of the Caucasus.

"The bulge in the German front," Manstein wrote, "was just begging to be sliced off."

The Russians might break through east of Kharkov and drive southwest to the Black Sea coast in hopes of cutting off and destroying the entire German southern wing. This was the movement Manstein had feared after the fall of Stalingrad, and it remained an ever-present danger.

But the balcony offered a wonderful bait as well. Manstein had proposed the plan after Stalingrad, and he now urged it on Hitler again. As soon as the Russians launched an attack southward, he said, all German forces on the Donetz and Mius should withdraw step by step, pulling the Red Army westward toward the lower Dnieper River around Dnepropetrovsk and Zaporozhye. At the same time, reserves should assemble west of Kharkov, and drive into the northern flank of the Russians as they advanced westward.

"In this way," Manstein asserted, "the enemy would be doomed to suffer the same fate on the coast of the Sea of Azov as he had on store for us on the Black Sea."

Hitler did not understand mobile warfare, or surrendering ground temporarily to give his forces operational freedom. He rejected Manstein's plan. He turned to the kind of brute force, frontal battle he did understand. Hitler resolved to attack the Kursk salient—a 150-mile-wide bulge that extended nearly a hundred miles into the German front north of Belgorod and Kharkov and south of Orel.

The idea for this attack (Operation Citadel) originated with Kurt Zeitzler, army chief of staff, and Günther von Kluge, commander of Army Group Center. They proposed to cut off the salient at its eastern base and destroy the Russian forces within it.

Manstein's Army Group South was to drive north with eleven "fast divisions" (panzer or panzergrenadier) and five infantry divisions, while Kluge's army group was to push south with six fast and five infantry divisions. Because of technical problems in getting new Tiger and Panther tanks into combat condition, Hitler advanced the date of Citadel to July 5, giving the Russians all the time they needed to prepare.

The Russians picked up evidence of the Kursk buildup from radio intercepts and a spy ring in Switzerland. They began to assemble overwhelming strength in and around the salient.

# RETREAT IN RUSSIA 1943

0 Miles 200 300

0 Kilometers 200 300

## OPERATION CITADEL

Lake Lagoda

Leningrad · Schlüsselburg

**LENINGRAD FRONT**

**VOLKHOV FRONT**

Lake Peipus · Luga

Lake Ilmen

Pskov

**NORTHWEST FRONT**

· Demyansk

**ARMY GROUP NORTH**

abandoned by Germans March 1943

Opochka ·

**LATVIA** · Velikiye Luki End 1942

**KALININ FRONT**

Belyy · · Rzhev · Klin

Dvina R.

Vitebsk · Vyasma

**WEST FRONT**

Moscow ★

Orsha · Smolensk · Kaluga

Berezina R.

· Minsk Mogilev · Kirov · Tula

Roslavl · · Poltava

Rogachev · Bryansk · Orel **BRYANSK FRONT**

Zhlobin ·

**ARMY GROUP CENTER**

Mozyr · Kursk ·

Chernigov · · Voronezh **VORONEZH FRONT**

Korosten · Sumy ·

Zhitomir · Kiev · Belgorod

Berdichev · Fastov **ARMY GROUP SOUTH**

Poltava · Kharkov · Don R.

Kremenchug · Izyum · Millerovo · **SOUTHWEST FRONT** · Stalingrad

Bug R. Lozovaya ·

Kirovograd · Dnieper R. Pavlograd · Donetz R.

Dniester R. Pervomaysk · Dnepropetrovsk · Krasnoarmeisk · Kamensk Don R.

Prut R. Krivoi Rog · Nikopol · Zaporozhye Stalino **ARMY GROUP DON**

Berislav · · Melitopol Mius R. · Rostov **SOUTH FRONT**

Kherson · Taganrog · Manych R.

· Odessa

Salsk · · Elista

**Sea of Azov**

**CRIMEA** Kerch Kuban R. **ARMY GROUP A**

Novorossiysk · · Armavir · Budenovsk

Tuapse · C a u c a s u s Pyatigorsk · Mozdok

**Black Sea** · Nalchik

### OPERATION CITADEL detail

Bryansk ·

**BRYANSK FRONT (Popov) July 12**

· Orel

AUG.18 Aug. 5

**ARMY GROUP CENTER (Kluge)**

JULY 5 July 5/10 German attacks

**CENTRAL FRONT (Rokossovsky)**

· Kursk

**VORONEZH FRONT (Vatutin)**

**ARMY GROUP SOUTH (Manstein)**

Aug. 4 July 5/15 German attacks

Belgorod · **STEPPE FRONT (Koniev) Aug. 14**

Kharkov ·

AUG.23 · Poltava **SOUTHWEST FRONT (Malinovsky)**

⟵ Russian attacks

⟶ German Attacks

Jeffrey L. Ward

### Legend

– – – Front lines end December 1942

- - - Front lines July 12, 1943

······· Front lines end December 1943

The only forceful opponent of the attack now became Heinz Guderian, whom Hitler had brought back in February 1943 as inspector of armored troops. At a conference on May 3–4, 1943, at Munich with Hitler and other generals, Guderian looked at aerial photographs showing the Russians were preparing deep defensive positions—artillery, antitank guns, minefields—exactly where the German attacks were to go in.

Guderian said Germany ought to be devoting its tank production to counter the forthcoming Allied landings in the west, not wasting it in a frontal attack against a primed and waiting enemy.

A few days later in Berlin, Guderian told Hitler: "It's a matter of profound indifference to the world whether we hold Kursk or not." Hitler replied: "You're quite right. Whenever I think of this attack my stomach turns over."

Meanwhile Guderian was having great problems with the new Panther tank, armed like the Tiger with a powerful 88-millimeter gun. Its track suspension and drive were not operating correctly, and optical instruments were unsatisfactory. He told Hitler on June 15 that the Panthers were not ready for battle, but by now Hitler had committed himself and turned a deaf ear.

In the Kursk salient the Russians barred likely avenues of approach with minefields and tank traps, built several lines of resistance, and converted important points into defensive bastions. Even if the Germans hacked their way through the minefields and broke the barriers, the Russians would have time to withdraw, and the Germans would gain little.

Hitler was committing the same error he had made at Stalingrad: he was going to attack a fortress, throwing away all the advantages of mobile tactics and meeting the Russians on ground of their own choosing. Besides that, he was concentrating his strength along a narrow front and gravely weakening the rest of the line, as he also had done at Stalingrad.

The Germans assembled 900,000 men, 10,000 cannons, 2,000 aircraft, and 2,000 tanks. The Russians marshaled 1.9 million men, 20,800 cannons, 2,000 aircraft, and 5,100 tanks.

Except for parity in aircraft, Hitler was risking his entire position in the east by attacking an enemy with more than twice his own strength. Even more ominous, the Russians had *not* stripped their other fronts to achieve this huge mass of men and weapons. They were assembling strong forces on either flank of Kursk, with the intention of breaking through and rolling up the German army, just as they had done on either side of Stalingrad.

✠          ✠          ✠

Hitler's plan was for Hermann Hoth's 4th Panzer Army on the south and Walter Model's 9th Army on the north to advance toward each other. The main thrust of 4th Panzer Army was to be delivered by 48th Panzer Corps and SS Panzer Corps. East of Kursk they were to meet 9th Army advancing south with 800 tanks.

In the south, 48th Panzer Corps, with 300 tanks and 60 assault guns in the "Gross Deutschland" Panzergrenadier and the 3rd and 11th Panzer Divisions, was to attack on the west, while, about ten miles to the east, SS Panzer Corps's three Waffen-SS divisions of about the same strength were to thrust along the railway line running north from Belgorod. M. E. Katukov's 1st Tank Army was waiting to block both corps.

The battlefield was mostly an open plain, covered with grainfields, broken by numerous valleys, small copses of trees, villages here and there, and a few rivers and streams. The ground rose slightly to the north, giving the Russians better observation.

The Germans had assembled their forces in secrecy, but the Russians knew their positions and approximate strength.

The battle opened on July 5 with a sharp artillery preparation and an air bombardment, using Stukas, new Focke-Wulf 190-A fighter-bombers, and new Henschel 129 B2 tank-killer aircraft. The Germans had mounted 30-millimeter automatic cannons on Stukas and Henschels, which could penetrate the thin armor on the tops of the T-34s.

But neither 48th Corps nor SS Panzer Corps was able to penetrate the Russian line. Not only was the entire area infested with mines, but Soviet guns shelled the panzers heavily, aircraft flew in and destroyed a number of tanks, and Russian armor occupied high ground and targeted German panzers.

The Russians had mastered new antitank tactics developed by the Germans. They distributed numerous "antitank fronts" all over a defended area. Each front had ten antitank guns under a single commander. The aim was to draw a German tank into a web of these guns, firing at it from several locations. The Russians fortified their antitank fronts with minefields and antitank ditches. Even after penetrating miles into Russian lines, the Germans found themselves in the midst of minefields and facing more antitank fronts.

To guard against these defenses, German armor advanced in a wedge (*Panzerkeil*), with the heaviest tanks in the spearhead. Tigers could break an antitank front, but Mark IVs could not, and *Panzerkeile* were generally able to advance only by delivering concentric tank fire on the AT guns. Even so, losses were often heavy.

On the north, Hoth's 9th Army had heavy going from the outset. Russian defenses were formidable, and the main hope of the Germans, ninety Tiger tanks made by Ferdinand Porsche (who had designed the Volkswagen automobile), had no machine guns. As Guderian wrote, they "had to go quail-shooting with cannons." The Tigers could not neutralize enemy rifles and machine guns, so German infantry was unable to follow them. Russian infantry, in no danger of being shot down, approached some of the Tigers and showered the portholes with flamethrowers, or disabled the machines with satchel charges. The Tigers were shattered, the crews suffered high losses, and Model's attack bogged down after penetrating only six miles.

The experience of 48th Corps demonstrated the kind of war now being fought in Russia. The corps could make little progress till July 7, when it finally broke through on both sides of a village (Ssyrzew), and advanced four miles. A "Gross Deutschland" battle group then moved north six miles and attacked a hill (243) that had been holding up 3rd Panzer Division on the left flank, but the battle group broke down in front of the hill.

On July 9, 3rd Panzer finally was able to swing to the west of the Russians blocking it, but was stopped by more enemy in a small forest four miles southwest of Hill 243 and three miles northwest of Beresowka village. "Gross Deutschland" Division evicted the Russians from Hill 243 with the help of a Stuka attack and, in a series of bitter engagements, drove the surviving Russian tanks into the wood.

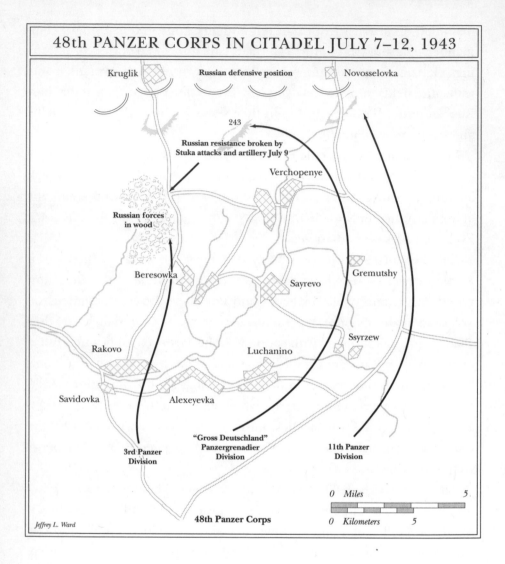

## 48th PANZER CORPS IN CITADEL JULY 7–12, 1943

Kruglik          Russian defensive position          Novosselovka

243

Russian resistance broken by
Stuka attacks and artillery July 9

Verchopenye

Russian forces
in wood

Beresowka                                    Gremutshy

Sayrevo

Rakovo                          Ssyrzew

Luchanino

Savidovka          Alexeyevka

"Gross Deutschland"
Panzergrenadier
Division

3rd Panzer
Division

11th Panzer
Division

Jeffrey L. Ward

**48th Panzer Corps**

0   Miles                    5

0   Kilometers        5

It looked as if the enemy on the left flank had been eliminated, and Otto von Knobelsdorff, the corps commander, ordered "Gross Deutschland" to turn north, hoping to break through, since Model's attack had collapsed. But the Russians counterattacked out of the wood and overran 3rd Panzer, forcing "Gross Deutschland" to turn back and rescue the division in new headlong attacks that finally drove the Russians out of the wood, but left the corps too weak to advance.

Meanwhile 11th Panzer on the corps's east flank was unable to do more than defend against repeated Russian tank attacks. SS Corps east of 11th

July 12, Markian M. Popov's Briansk Front launched an offensive st the Orel salient to the north of Kursk, and by August 5 he had ed the Germans entirely out of the salient.

On August 4, Nikolai F. Vatutin's Voronezh Front in the southern end the Kursk salient attacked 4th Panzer Army's weakened line, and cap- red Belgorod the next day. Exploiting the German exhaustion, Vatutin rove eighty miles in the next week, pushing toward the rear of Kharkov nd its communications with Kiev.

In the second half of August eighteen Soviet armies pressed westward on a front of 270 miles. The main thrust was against Army Group South, which faced forces three times the size of its own.

Against Army Group Center, Popov advanced from Orel on Bryansk, ousting the Germans in mid-September, while other Russian columns squeezed them out of Smolensk on September 25. German forces slowly fell back to a chain of bastion towns along the upper Dnieper—Zhlobin, Rogachev, Mogilev, and Orsha—and Vitebsk on the Dvina.

Farther south unrelenting Russian attacks forced the German armies to abandon Kharkov and withdraw to a new line from Zaporozhye to the Black Sea.

In late September, Russians seized Zaporozhye, and imperiled 1st Panzer Army holding the Dnieper bend, 6th Army holding the region between the Dnieper and the Sea of Azov, and 17th Army, which Hitler had finally ordered out of the Kuban peninsula, but had sent into the Crimea.

Late in October Russians attacked 6th Army, which withdrew to the lower Dnieper between Nikopol and Berislav, thus cutting off 17th Army in the Crimea, and threatening 1st Panzer Army.

Early in November, Russian forces along the Dnieper swung west of Kiev, and took the city from the rear. They were now more than 300 miles west of Kursk.

The Germans were unable to contain these advances, but Hitler rejected a plan that might have stymied the Russians. Immediately after Citadel, Rommel devised a method that would have worked: building a heavily mined defensive line perhaps six miles deep protected by every antitank gun the Germans could find. Russian tanks would bog down before such a line, and from then on would have to gnaw their way for-

Panzer at first also could do little but ward off tank at.
SS division chopped holes in the enemy front, advanc

On July 12, SS Panzer Corps's slugging match reac.
Station on the railway line, twenty-one miles past the jum,
penetration was dangerous, and Marshal Zhukov authorize
tack by 5th Guards Tank Army under P. A. Rotmistrov.

The resulting collision developed into the greatest tank b.
tory. SS Panzer Corps had about 400 tanks, the Russians twice
The surviving Tiger and Panther tanks with their 88-millimeter
and thick armor could engage the Russian tanks beyond the range
T-34s.

To close the distance to a point that the T-34s could be effective,
Russians launched an almost suicidal charge across the open, rolli
plain. In the terrible dust-shrouded melee that followed, the Germans los.
their long-range advantage, and Russian and German armored vehicles
fought it out in almost point-blank gun battles. Rotmistrov lost more than
400 of his tanks, but the Germans lost 320.

At the end of July 12 Prokhorovka was a graveyard of burned-out tanks,
but the Russians had stopped the German offensive. Tank losses had been
staggering. Not only had Porsche's Tigers failed, but the Panthers were
breaking down because of their drive problems and were easily set ablaze
because the oil and gasoline feeding systems were inadequately shielded.
Of eighty Panthers at the start, only a few remained.

Hitler summoned Manstein and Kluge to his headquarters in East
Prussia on July 13 and informed them that the attack must be called off
at once. The Allies had landed on Sicily, and troops had to be transferred
to the Mediterranean.

The Russian high command had done a superb job, yielding ground,
taking the strength out of the German attack with minefields and antitank
defenses. Though Russian tank losses were much greater than German,
the Russians still had a great superiority in armor, and pushed 4th Panzer
Army back to its start line by July 23.

✠　　　✠　　　✠

The strategic initiative now passed to the Russians. They did not relin-
quish it for the remainder of the war.

ward. Meanwhile the Germans could build more minefields and antitank screens behind.

But Hitler would not listen. When Guderian proposed such a line, Hitler asserted that his generals would think of nothing save withdrawal if he permitted defensive positions in their rear. "He had made up his mind on this point," Guderian wrote, "and nothing could bring him to change it."

As the year 1943 ended on the eastern front, the German army had been pushed well west of most points it had reached at the end of 1941 but was holding this line precariously. Everyone from field marshal to private knew the Russian juggernaut was poised to drive the Germans out of the Soviet Union and beyond in 1944.

# 20 THE ASSAULT ON ITALY

IF THE ALLIES HAD LANDED AIRBORNE TROOPS AT ROME AND MADE A SEA LANDing nearby, Kesselring would have been forced to evacuate all of the southern half of Italy.

Indeed, many of the Germans in the six divisions of H.-G. Vietinghoff's 10th Army in southern Italy might have had to surrender. Siegfried Westphal, Kesselring's chief of staff, said the two German divisions around Rome were too weak to eliminate the Italian divisions there and defend against an Allied attack as well. "One could hardly bank on saving the 10th Army from being cut off," he said. The Allies should have landed not at Salerno but at Civitavecchia, thirty miles north of Rome. "A combined sea and air landing would have taken the Italian capital inside seventy-two hours." That would have brought all Italy south of Rome into Allied hands.

Despite Allied command of the sea, Eisenhower dared nothing so bold as a strike at Rome, because it was beyond the reach of fighter aircraft. He also ignored recommendations that the Allies land on the heel of Italy, around Taranto and Brindisi, also beyond fighter cover, but where the Germans had no troops.

Instead, Eisenhower and Alexander ordered the main thrust by General Mark Clark's 5th Army around Salerno (Operation Avalanche) on September 9, 1943—55,000 troops in the initial landing, 115,000 more to follow.

Belatedly realizing that no Germans were anywhere close to Taranto, the Allies pulled the British 1st Airborne Division out of rest camps in Tunisia, piled the men onto warships (the only vessels now available), and hurried them to the port—with only six jeeps and no tanks, artillery, or heavy weapons. The "paras" met no resistance, but were unable to exploit their success.

Kesselring, confident the Allies would do nothing daring, concentrated his slender forces around Salerno. Vietinghoff sent just two infantry battalions to slow Montgomery's entire 8th Army in its step-by-step march up the toe of Italy from the Strait of Messina. Only two roads ran up the toe, one on either side of the mountainous backbone of the peninsula, and they were easily blocked.

Of 10th Army's six divisions, four had escaped from Sicily and were badly depleted in men and equipment. Vietinghoff sent the 15th Panzergrenadier and Hermann Göring Divisions to Naples to refit, the 1st Parachute Division to the east coast to defend Foggia, and the 29th Panzergrenadier Division around the toe of Italy to face Montgomery. His other two divisions were the 16th and 26th Panzer. But the 26th had no tanks and Vietinghoff sent it temporarily to block 8th Army. This left the 16th Panzer, his best force, but with only half the strength of an Allied armored division, possessing eighty Mark IV tanks and forty self-propelled assault guns. He placed it to cover the Gulf of Salerno.

The landing was made by the U.S. 6th Corps under Ernest J. (Mike) Dawley on the right, and the British 10th Corps under Sir Richard L. McCreery on the left.

McCreery's corps landed on a seven-mile stretch of beaches just south of Salerno near the main road (Route 18) to Naples. This road crossed the low Cava Gap. Capture of that gap was important to open a way to Naples and to block German reinforcements coming from the north.

In 10th Corps were the British 46th and 56th Infantry Divisions, two British Commando outfits, and three battalions of American Rangers. The Commandos and Rangers were to seize Cava Gap and Chiunzi pass on a neighboring route.

Dawley's corps struck the beaches twenty to twenty-five miles south of Salerno around the Sele River and Paestum. The untried U.S. 36th Infantry Division was to land, with the U.S. 45th Infantry Division in reserve.

The Allies knew the Germans were expecting the invasion at Salerno because a German radio commentator forecast it two weeks before it took place. Even so, General Clark counted on catching the Germans unawares

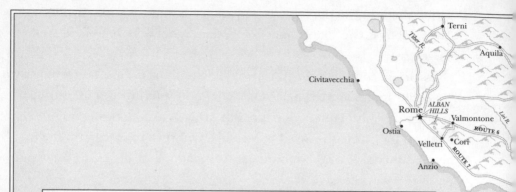

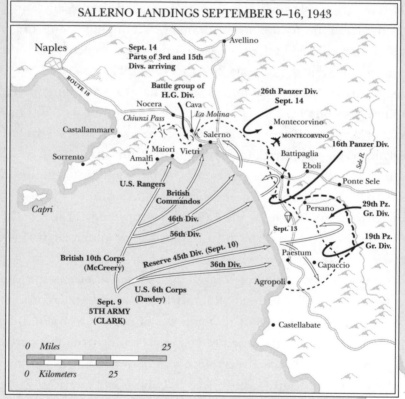

# SALERNO LANDINGS SEPTEMBER 9–16, 1943

Naples

Sept. 14
Parts of 3rd and 15th
Divs. arriving

ROUTE 18

Battle group of
H.G. Div.

Avellino

26th Panzer Div.
Sept. 14

Nocera

Cava

Chiunzi Pass

La Molina

Castallammare

Salerno

Montecorvino

MONTECORVINO

16th Panzer Div.

Maiori

Vietri

Battipaglia

Sorrento

Amalfi

Eboli

Sele R.

Ponte Sele

U.S. Rangers

British
Commandos

Capri

46th Div.

Persano

29th Pz.
Gr. Div.

56th Div.

Sept. 13

19th Pz.
Gr. Div.

British 10th Corps
(McCreery)

Reserve 45th Div. (Sept. 10)

36th Div.

Paestum

Capaccio

Agropoli

U.S. 6th Corps
(Dawley)

Sept. 9
5TH ARMY
(CLARK)

Castellabate

0   Miles           25

0   Kilometers      25

Palermo

*Jeffrey L. Ward*

Terni

Tiber R.

Aquila

Civitavecchia

Rome

ALBAN
HILLS

Valmontone

ROUTE 6

Ostia

Cori

Velletri

ROUTE 7

Anzio

Gaeta

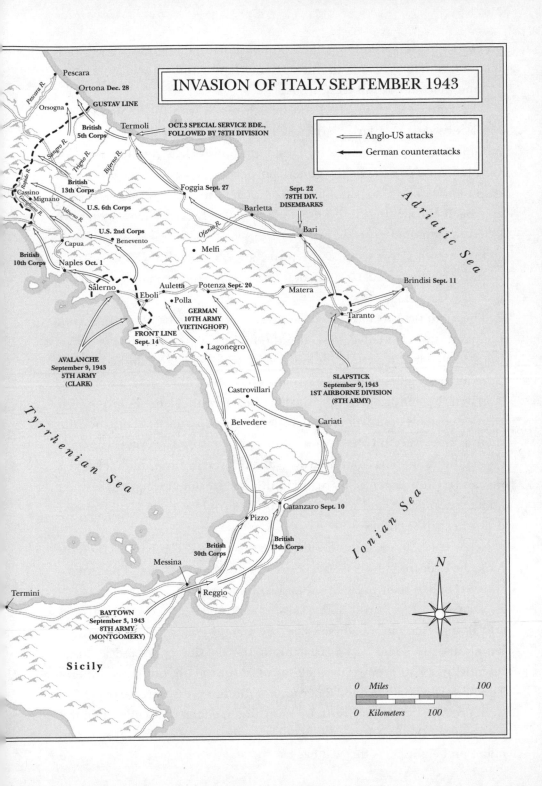

# INVASION OF ITALY SEPTEMBER 1943

Pescara

Ortona Dec. 28

Orsogna

**GUSTAV LINE**

**British 5th Corps**

Termoli

**OCT.3 SPECIAL SERVICE BDE.,
FOLLOWED BY 78TH DIVISION**

Pescara R.

Sangro R.

Trigno R.

Biferno R.

**British 13th Corps**

Rapido R.

Cassino

Garigliano R.

Mignano

Volturno R.

**U.S. 6th Corps**

Foggia Sept. 27

Barletta

**Sept. 22
78TH DIV.
DISEMBARKS**

*Adriatic Sea*

**U.S. 2nd Corps**

Capua

Benevento

Ofanto R.

• Melfi

Bari

**British
10th Corps**

Naples Oct. 1

Salerno

Eboli

Auletta

• Polla

Potenza Sept. 20

Matera

Brindisi Sept. 11

**GERMAN
10TH ARMY
(VIETINGHOFF)**

**FRONT LINE
Sept. 14**

Taranto

**AVALANCHE
September 9, 1943
5TH ARMY
(CLARK)**

• Lagonegro

**SLAPSTICK
September 9, 1943
1ST AIRBORNE DIVISION
(8TH ARMY)**

*Tyrrhenian Sea*

Castrovillari

Belvedere

Cariati

Catanzaro Sept. 10

• Pizzo

**British
30th Corps**

**British
13th Corps**

*Ionian Sea*

Messina

Reggio

Termini

**BAYTOWN
September 3, 1943
8TH ARMY
(MONTGOMERY)**

**Sicily**

N

### Legend

⟸ Anglo-US attacks
◂— German counterattacks

0  Miles  100

0  Kilometers  100

and forbade any preliminary naval bombardment, though the naval commander, American Vice Admiral H. Kent Hewitt, said, "It was fantastic to assume we could obtain tactical surprise."

The landing craft reached the British beach with little loss because McCreery, despite Clark's order, authorized a short but intense bombardment of beach defenses by naval guns and rockets (modeled on the German *Nebelwerfer*). On the American beaches, however, the divisional commander stuck to Clark's no-fire order. In the last stage of the approach, the landing craft came under a hail of fire, and many men were killed or wounded.

In the 10th Corps sector, American Rangers secured the Chiunzi pass within three hours, but German defenders stopped Commandos trying to grab the Cava Gap.

The main British landings south of Salerno met heavy resistance from the beginning and failed to secure the first-day objectives: Salerno harbor, Montecorvino airfield ten miles east of Salerno, and the road junctions at Battipaglia and Eboli, thirteen and sixteen miles east of the town.

When 36th Division troops hit their beaches, they encountered even heavier curtains of fire, plus numerous German air attacks that struck the men as they were on shore and coming on shore. The Americans got good gunfire support from destroyers that moved in close, and it checked thrusts by German tanks. By nightfall the American left wing had pushed about five miles inland to Capaccio, but the right wing was still pinned down near the beaches.

September 10 was quiet for the Americans, for 16th Panzer Division moved to confront 10th Corps, a greater strategic menace. The Americans expanded their bridgehead and landed most of 45th Division.

Meanwhile the British 56th Division captured Montecorvino airfield and Battipaglia, but was driven back by a counterattack of two German battalions and some tanks. That night the division mounted a three-brigade attack to capture the heights of Mount Eboli, but got nowhere. The 46th Division occupied Salerno, but did not press northward.

In the American sector, 45th Division advanced ten miles inland up the east bank of the Sele River, but a counterattack by a single German battalion and eight tanks threw it back.

By the end of the third day the Allies, now with the equivalent of four divisions on the ground, still held only two shallow bridgeheads, while the Germans possessed the heights and the approach roads.

By now 29th Panzergrenadier Division had arrived, plus a battle group of two battalions and twenty tanks from the Hermann Göring Division. On September 12, 29th Panzergrenadier with part of 16th Panzer thrust between the British and Americans and drove the British out of Battipaglia. The next day, the Germans evicted the Americans from Persano, forcing a general withdrawal. In some places German armored vehicles reached within half a mile of the beach. On the same day the Hermann Göring *Kampfgruppe* sealed off Cava Gap, broke through the British line above La Molina, and got almost to Vietri before Commandos stopped it.

By the evening of September 13 the situation was so grim that Clark stopped unloading supply ships, and prepared to reembark 5th Army headquarters, while asking that all available craft be made ready to evacuate 6th Corps. The order produced consternation at Allied headquarters and brought immediate help. Matthew Ridgway, commander of 82nd Airborne Division, dropped paratroops on the American sector that evening. On September 14, Eisenhower sent all available aircraft to attack German positions and their communications, a total of 1,900 sorties in one day. At the same time, warships commenced a powerful bombardment, hitting every target they could locate. The British 7th Armored Division started landing on the British bridgehead on September 15.

There was a lull on September 15 as the Germans reorganized their bombed and shelled units, and brought up some reinforcements, including the still-tankless 26th Panzer Division, and parts of the 3rd and 15th Panzergrenadier Divisions. Total German strength was only four divisions and a hundred tanks, however, while Clark had on shore on September 16 seven larger divisions and 200 tanks.

The same day the British battleships *Warspite* and *Valiant* arrived with a destroyer flotilla, and began bombarding targets a dozen miles inland with their heavy 15-inch guns.

September 16 was eventful in another way: Montgomery's 8th Army made contact in a fashion with Clark's 5th Army. A group of war correspondents got so exasperated with Montgomery's snail-like pace up the peninsula that they struck out on their own on minor roads and reached 5th Army across the fifty-mile stretch without meeting any Germans.

On the same day the Germans launched a renewed effort to drive the Allied bridgeheads into the sea. Combined artillery and naval gunfire, plus tanks, stopped the assaults, and Kesselring, seeing how close Montgomery was to 5th Army, authorized disengagement on the coastal front and gradual retreat northward.

First stage was withdrawal to the Volturno River, twenty miles north of Naples. As the Germans pulled away, a bomber disabled the *Warspite* with another of the new radio-guided gliding bombs.

Kesselring withdrew because 8th Army could move east of Salerno, and easily outflank the German positions, since Vietinghoff had only a small fraction of the combined forces of 5th and 8th Armies. Indeed, the Allies could have completely dislodged the German position in southern Italy by a swift strike up the east coast beyond Foggia to Pescara, where the main trans-peninsula road led to Rome.

But this was the sector of Bernard Montgomery, and it took him until September 20 merely to send a Canadian spearhead to Potenza, fifty miles inland from Salerno, a crossroads that opened the way through the mountains to the east coast. A hundred German paratroops blocked Potenza, causing Montgomery to mount a full brigade attack—that is, thirty times the strength of the German detachment—plus a huge air attack that killed 2,000 inhabitants of the town.

There were still virtually no German troops on the east coast, but the British 1st Airborne Division, which had landed at Taranto on September 9, had been able to take little advantage because it lacked arms and transportation. Using the half-dozen jeeps that had come on the warships, plus confiscated Italian vehicles, the paratroops occupied Brindisi and Bari, but that was all.

Even when transport and arms arrived beginning September 14, Montgomery's methodical, painstaking preparations still held the paras in check. The commander in the east, C. W. Allfrey, now reinforced with two more divisions, took until September 27 to send a small mobile force to occupy Foggia and the airfields there. Montgomery stopped any farther advance, though the only enemy element in front of Allfrey was the

1st Parachute Division with just 1,300 men at Termoli on the Biferno River, thirty miles northwest.

Early on October 3, a British Special Services brigade landed from the sea beyond Termoli, causing the German paratroops to withdraw. But Vietinghoff had already sent the 16th Panzer Division to the east coast, and early on October 5 it drove the British back to the edge of Termoli, then had to withdraw itself when attacked by the British 78th Division, also brought up to Termoli by sea.

The Germans disengaged and withdrew a dozen miles north to the next river line, the Trigno. But their counterattack had so shaken Montgomery that he paused for two weeks to shift his 5th Corps to the coast, moving 13th Corps into the mountainous interior. The 5th Corps did not break the Trigno position until November 3, when the Germans withdrew seventeen miles northward to the Sangro River.

Meanwhile Mark Clark's 5th Army slowly pushed up the west coast. It took three divisions and an armored brigade of the British 10th Corps a week to force passage over the hill barrier between Salerno and Naples, though the Germans employed only four infantry battalions. The breakthrough came on September 26, when the Germans withdrew, having carried out their mission of holding the line until comrades to the south had been able to pull back.

Because of broken bridges, 10th Corps did not reach Naples, twenty miles away, until October 1. The American 6th Corps came up abreast on the north. Clark had removed Dawley as corps commander because of poor performance and had replaced him with John P. Lucas. Clark's army sustained nearly 12,000 casualties (7,000 British, 5,000 American) reaching Naples—the penalty paid for choosing too obvious a place of landing.

Rain set in the first week of October, a month earlier than usual, and it was October 12 before the Allies attacked the Volturno River line, twenty miles northwest of Naples. They were held up by German counterstrikes long enough for Vietinghoff's main forces to withdraw to the next line of defense, fifteen miles northward—the Winter or Gustav line—along the Garigliano and the Rapido rivers, hinging on the Cassino defile, about twenty miles north of the Gulf of Gaeta. Above the town was Monte Cassino, where St. Benedict founded his monastery in 529, the parent house of Western monasticism and a center of arts and learning during the Middle Ages.

Bad weather and German demolitions slowed 5th Army's attack until November 5. Thereafter, German resistance was so severe that Clark was forced to pull his troops back after ten days. He was not ready to launch the next effort till the first week of December. By mid-November 5th Army had lost 12,000 Americans and 10,000 British.

✠          ✠          ✠

In Africa and Sicily Anglo-American forces had seen elements of a new kind of close combat that the German army had developed in Russia. But on the boot of Italy they came firmly up against it. The Germans saw in Russia that infantry actions were fought overwhelmingly at close range, 75 yards or less, and introduced the MP38 and MP40 "Schmeisser" machine pistol that fired high-velocity pistol bullets, giving heavy unaimed fire to blanket an area and suppress enemy resistance. The Russians introduced a different sort of weapon that achieved the same effect, the PPSh41 7.62-millimeter submachine gun (burp gun). Supported by fast-firing portable machine guns, the MG-34 and MG-42, the Schmeissers gave Germans mobility and high volume of fire. They never replaced all their standard medium-range bolt-action rifles (the Mauser Kar. 98k) or employed many of the next-generation automatic assault rifles (*Sturmgewehr*), but Schmeissers and MG-34s and MG-42s gave them high capacity to defend against attacks.

The British replaced in part their medium-range bolt-action rifle, the Enfield No. 4, with various submachine guns ("Sten guns") that fired the same 9-millimeter pistol cartridge as the Schmeisser, coupling them with the Bren gun, a reliable light machine gun. The Americans were slower to replace the M1 Garand semiautomatic medium-range rifle. Wherever possible they used the Thompson M1928 submachine gun, firing .45-caliber pistol ammunition, but this weapon was in short supply. Americans made do with their M1s, Browning Automatic Rifles (BARs), and light machine guns. It was late 1944 before they introduced the M3 submachine gun (grease gun) in large numbers to compete with the Schmeisser.

The Germans learned to exploit the weaknesses of Americans under fire for the first time. In such cases Americans had the tendency to freeze or to seek the nearest protection. All too often American infantry merely located and fixed the enemy, and called on artillery to destroy the defenders. Only after much experience in 1943 did American infantry learn that the best way to avoid losses was to keep moving forward and to close in rapidly on the enemy.

Tanks could not be used in the mountainous terrain of Italy in massed attacks as Rommel had done in Africa. In Italy tanks largely reverted to the infantry-support role that the British had envisioned for their Matildas and other "I" tanks at the start of the war. However, American tankers and infantry had little training in this role. Infantry and tanks could not communicate with each other. Infantry could not warn tankers of antitank traps and heavy weapons, and tankers could not alert infantry to enemy positions. Consequently, infantry had a tendency to lag behind tanks, and Americans did not work out the smooth coordination of tanks, infantry, and artillery that the Germans had developed long before in their battle groups or *Kampfgruppen*.

Similar problems developed in the use of tank destroyers (TDs), essentially 75-millimeter guns on open-topped tank chassis. TDs were designed to break up massed German panzer attacks. The Germans no longer massed tanks, but used them as parts of *Kampfgruppen*. American commanders slowly changed the use of TDs to assault guns to destroy enemy tanks and defensive positions with direct fire.

Finally, the Allies did a poor job of coordinating air-ground operations. Allied fighter-bomber pilots flying at 200 mph often could not distinguish between friendly and enemy forces on the ground. The pilots could not talk to ground units, and vice versa. This resulted in many cases of Allied aircraft bombing and strafing friendly forces. Consequently, Allied troops often fired on anything that moved in the sky. Only in the spring of 1944 did the U.S. Army Air Force deploy forward air controllers (FACs), using light single-engine liaison aircraft (L-5s) that could direct radio communication to aircraft and air-ground support parties at headquarters of major ground units. It was a bit late: the Germans had employed this system in the campaign in the west in 1940 to direct Stuka attacks on enemy positions.

✠        ✠        ✠

The idea of restricting Allied efforts to southern Italy had been forgotten. Eisenhower set his sights on Rome in a November 8 directive, and was thinking of driving on up at least to Florence and Livorno (Leghorn).

Because of slow Allied progress up the peninsula, Hitler decided to make a prolonged stand in Italy. He dissolved Rommel's army group in northern Italy, and gave Kesselring Rommel's divisions—though he sent four of the best to Russia and replaced them with three depleted divisions that needed to recover.

Kesselring also got the 90th Panzergrenadier Division which Hitler had sent to Sardinia. It had withdrawn to Corsica when the Italians surrendered, then to Livorno. Kesselring rushed it to the east coast to help check Montgomery's belated offensive, which finally developed on November 28.

Montgomery had been reinforced by the 2nd New Zealand Division, giving him five divisions and two armored brigades for the Sangro offensive. Meanwhile the Germans had formed 76th Panzer Corps to oppose 8th Army. This corps had received 65th Infantry Division, a raw and ill-equipped force of mixed nationalities, replacing 16th Panzer Division, being sent to Russia. Otherwise, the corps had only remnants of 1st Parachute Division and 26th Panzer Division, which was still en route to the Adriatic coast.

Montgomery intended to smash the Sangro line, drive to Pescara, get astride the highway to Rome, and threaten the rear of German forces holding up 5th Army.

The attack started under cover of an immense air and artillery bombardment. Montgomery had five soldiers to Kesselring's one, and 65th Division gave way, withdrawing behind the Sangro to the main line farther back. Here the division held on firmly, giving 26th Panzer and 90th Panzergrenadier Divisions time to come up. These reinforcements slowed the British to a crawl. It took till December 10 to cross the Moro River, eight miles on, and until December 28 for Canadians to clear Ortona, two miles beyond the Moro. Montgomery was checked at Ricco, halfway to Pescara. He had been forced into a stalemate by the end of the year, when he gave up his command to Oliver Leese, and returned to England to take over 21st Army Group in preparation for the cross-Channel invasion of Normandy.

Mark Clark's 5th Army had risen to ten divisions, but two of them, the British 7th Armored and the U.S. 82nd Airborne, were being withdrawn for the Normandy invasion. Kesselring now had four divisions facing Clark, with one in reserve.

Clark's offensive started on December 2, aiming to crack—in a headlong attack—the mountain barrier west of Route 6 and the Mignano Gap. He used 10th Corps and the new U.S. 2nd Corps under Geoffrey Keyes. In heavy attacks, supported by massive artillery bombardment, the Allies made some progress, but at heavy cost. By the second week of January 1944 the offensive had petered out, still short of the Rapido River and the forward edge of the Gustav line. Losses had risen almost to 40,000, far exceeding German casualties, plus 50,000 Americans who had become sick in the cold and wet struggle in the mountains.

Marshal Kesselring had the most insightful comment on Allied leadership in Italy:

> The Allied high command's dominating thought was to make sure of success, a thought that led it to use orthodox methods and material. As a result it was almost always possible for me, despite inadequate means of reconnaissance and scanty reports, to foresee the next strategic or tactical move of my opponent.

✠          ✠          ✠

By January 1944 Italy was already a secondary theater. German and western Allied attention was turning toward a direct confrontation on the beaches of northern France in the spring.

The Teheran conference between Churchill, Roosevelt, and Stalin in November 1943, immediately preceded by the Anglo-American conference at Cairo, confirmed the priority of Operation Overlord, along with Anvil, a supplementary landing in the south of France.

The role of Italy in Allied planning shrank to that of keeping as many German forces as possible from being moved to France. The Allied commander in Italy, Sir Harold Alexander, got only the task of capturing

Rome, and, later, of driving up to the Pisa-Rimini line. Therefore the terrible battles that followed in the winter and spring of 1944 had an anticlimactic air even as they were being fought.

It was well into January 1944 before 5th Army moved up to the Gustav line, which extended from the mouth of the Garigliano River on the west to Castel di Sangro in the center of the peninsula.

This barrier promised to be formidable, and the Allied commanders decided the easiest way to lever the Germans out of it and break their hold on Rome was to make an amphibious landing at Anzio, halfway between the Gustav line and Rome.

The plan was for Mark Clark's 5th Army to launch a direct assault against the Gustav line around January 20. Once the main advance got going, the U.S. 6th Corps was to land at Anzio. The hope was that German forces would have to turn back from the Gustav line to deal with the threat, thus weakening the line and making a breakthrough easier, thereby allowing 5th Army to link up with 6th Corps.

The campaign started well enough. The British 10th Corps forced a crossing of the Garigliano near its mouth on January 17–18, 1944, and formed a strong bridgehead around the town of Minturno. But the attack on January 20 by the U.S. 2nd Corps across the Rapido River a few miles south of Cassino proved a bloody failure. The aim was to swing around to the north and seize the abbey on Monte Cassino and the town of Cassino at its base. They dominated Route 6, the main highway between Naples and Rome, axis of the Allied advance.

The two leading regiments of the U.S. 36th Infantry Division were largely destroyed by German paratroopers. An attempted assault by the British 46th Division on the immediate left also failed.

On January 22 John P. Lucas's 6th Corps landed unopposed at Anzio (Operation Shingle). The initial forces were the U.S. 3rd and the British 1st Divisions, plus Commandos and Rangers, a parachute regiment, and two tank battalions. Lucas's job was to reach the Alban Hills south of Rome, and cut Routes 6 and 7, over which supplies reached the Gustav line.

Kesselring hadn't expected a lodgment at Anzio. An invasion farther north would have been much more dangerous. All he had in place was a battalion of the 29th Panzergrenadier Division, which was resting there.

But General Lucas was a cautious, pessimistic officer who moved with extreme slowness. In contrast, Kesselring reacted with great speed and skill. He told the forces on the Gustav line to stand firm, and switched the Hermann Göring Division and other elements to Anzio. Hitler, hoping a disaster at Anzio might deter a landing in France, told Kesselring he could call on all divisions in northern Italy and was sending two more divisions, plus two heavy tank battalions.

In eight days, Kesselring brought up elements of eight divisions to Anzio and set up a new army, the 14th, under Hans Georg von Mackensen, to contain it. Meanwhile Lucas—with Clark's approval—refused to advance until he had consolidated the beachhead. This might have been a blessing. Lucas and his subordinates were so super-cautious that a quick advance inland under their leadership might have led to disaster. They would have been easy targets for a German flank attack.

The first real attempt to push inland didn't start till January 30, and Germans already in place stopped it. The whole Anzio beachhead, only six miles deep by fifteen miles wide, was in range of German artillery, which promptly began to harass it. In addition, Luftwaffe aircraft made repeated bombing raids on the crowded Allied shipping around Anzio. Allied aircraft, operating out of the Naples area, were unable to stop these raids.

The Anzio beachhead—instead of being a lever to wrench the Germans out of the Gustav line—became a hemmed-in force in need of being rescued. As Winston Churchill commented, "I had hoped that we were hurling a wildcat onto the shore, but all we got was a stranded whale."

Mark Clark now decided to try to break the impasse at Cassino by attacking from the north side. On January 24, the U.S. 34th Division did that, assisted by a French four-division corps under Alphonse Juin, which joined 5th Army in January. It was hard going for the Americans against the German 14th Panzer Corps under Frido von Senger und Etterlin, and they were withdrawn February 11, exhausted and depleted.

A new corps under Lieutenant General Bernard Freyberg now came up, containing the 2nd New Zealand and 4th Indian Divisions (with combined British and Indian units).

Francis Tuker, commanding 4th Indian, urged an indirect approach on Cassino through the mountains to the north, a plan favored by the French. But Freyberg rejected the proposal, and Tuker, whose division drew the job of tackling Monte Cassino, asked that the historic monastery crowning the height be neutralized by aerial bombardment. There was no evidence the Germans were using the monastery. They had not even entered it, and General Senger had evacuated the monks and works of art. But the structure was a symbolic deterrent to the Allies, and Clark and Alexander authorized the operation.

On February 15, 1944, a tremendous attack dropped 450 tons of bombs that demolished the famous monastery. The Germans now felt they could occupy the rubble. Consequently, the attack actually increased the strength of their defenses. On two successive nights 4th Indian tried in vain to seize a knoll that lay between its position and Monastery Hill. On the night of February 18 the division made a third attempt. Fighting was desperate, and all the men reaching the knoll were killed. Later that night a brigade bypassed the knoll and moved directly toward the monastery, only to encounter a concealed ravine heavily mined and covered by German machine guns. Here the brigade lost heavily and had to retreat. Meanwhile 2nd New Zealand Division crossed the Rapido just below Cassino town, but German tanks counterattacked and forced it back. The direct attack on Cassino had failed.

On the Anzio front the Germans counterattacked on February 16, and on the next two days they threatened to reach the beaches and split the bridgehead in two. The Germans were held only by the desperate defense of the British 1st and 56th and American 45th Divisions. A new attitude appeared within the bridgehead when Lucian K. Truscott arrived, first as Lucas's deputy, then as his successor. The Germans tried once more on February 28, but Allied aircraft broke up the assaults, and on March 4 Mackensen stopped.

The Italian campaign was beginning to resemble the gruesome close-in battles on the western front in World War I, with losses just as great and gains just as minuscule.

On March 15, the Allies launched another direct attack on Cassino. The New Zealand Division was to push through the town, after which 4th Indian Division was to assault Monastery Hill. This time Cassino town was the main target. A thousand tons of bombs and 190,000 shells rained down on town and hill. As the bombers flew away and the cannon fire lifted, the infantry advanced.

"It seemed to me inconceivable," Alexander said, "that any troops should be left alive after eight hours of such terrific hammering." But they were. The 1st Parachute Division fought it out amid the rubble with the advancing New Zealanders. By nightfall two-thirds of the town was in Allied hands, while 4th Indian Division came down from the north and, the next day, got two-thirds of the way up Monastery Hill.

But that was the end. British tanks couldn't negotiate the craters made by bombs and shells, the Germans filtered in reinforcements, and the weather broke in storm and rain. On March 23 Alexander halted the operation. Once more stalemate had fallen on Cassino.

✠      ✠      ✠

The continued failures at Cassino demonstrated the basic mistake of the Allied strategy in Italy. Cassino was important because it barred entry to the valley of the eastward-flowing Liri River, the only route in this part of Italy that could accommodate Allied tanks, artillery, and vehicles. Route 6, the Naples-Rome highway, ran through it.

The Allies tried first to force a crossing of the Rapido a few miles south of Cassino, with the intention of swinging up and around the town and Monastery Hill. This had failed with heavy losses because the Rapido was fast-moving and German artillery could fire from valleys just west of Cassino.

The Allies had also tried to swing around Cassino from the north, but the Apennines in this region consist of rocky escarpments and deep ravines, which limited movement to small bodies of men supplied by mules.

Why did the Allies not swing entirely *around* Rome and the mountains and land farther up the Italian boot, either on the western or eastern coast? Allied sea power was overwhelming, and an invasion could have been made almost anywhere. It would have been easiest along the Adriatic coast, especially around Rimini or Ravenna in the great Po Valley of northern Italy, where there were no mountains to harbor German defenders, and the terrain would have been better for Allied tanks and other vehicles. But any strategic landing beyond major German troop dispositions—that is, beyond where a landing could be easily contested, not close by as Anzio was—would force an enemy withdrawal from points south.

Churchill was not a great strategist, but he saw the opportunity plainly. He telegraphed Alan Brooke on December 19, 1943: "There is no doubt that the stagnation of the whole campaign on the Italian front is becoming scandalous. . . . The total neglect to provide amphibious action on the Adriatic side and the failure to strike any similar blow on the west have been disastrous."

But the Allies had elected to conduct a straight-ahead, direct campaign right through the mountains of Italy, and at Cassino they experienced the bloody consequences of that strategy in full measure.

☩        ☩        ☩

In cooperation with British General H. Maitland Wilson, who had taken a new post as supreme commander, Mediterranean, in January 1944, Alexander developed another plan to break through the Gustav line. He shifted most of 8th Army westward to take over the Cassino–Liri Valley sector, leaving only a single corps on the Adriatic side of the Apennines. Clark's 5th Army, along with the French corps, assumed responsibility for the Garigliano River sector along the coast and the Anzio beachhead.

Alexander's plan was another brute-force effort, to be launched May 11. It called for 8th Army to crack through at Cassino, 5th Army to thrust across the Garigliano, and the Anzio force to break out toward Valmontone on Route 6. Alexander assembled sixteen Allied divisions along the Gustav line against six German divisions (with one in reserve). Twelve were lined up from Cassino to the mouth of the Garigliano, and four were close behind to exploit any breakthrough by thrusting up the Liri Valley in hopes of piercing a second defensive line, six miles in the rear, before the Germans could occupy it.

Three of 8th Army's nine divisions were armored. Because dry weather had come, the tanks would have far better going than in the wet and muddy winter. In the attack, a Polish Corps of two divisions was to tackle Cassino, while the British 13th Corps of four divisions was to advance about three miles south toward St. Angelo. The attack was supported by 2,000 guns, while all available Allied aircraft made heavy attacks on the German rail and road network.

The offensive opened at 11 P.M., May 11, with a massive artillery barrage. For the first three days the attack made little progress. The Polish Corps suffered heavily, and the American 2nd Corps on the coast and the British 13th Corps likewise had little to show for their efforts. However, General Juin's French corps, lying between the two, found only one division opposing its four, and made some progress in mountains where the Germans had not expected a serious thrust. On May 14 the French broke into the valley of the small Ausente River, and the German 71st Division fell back fast before them. This relieved pressure on 2nd Corps, and it began to move along the coast road after the German 94th Division. The two German forces were now separated by the roadless Aurunci Mountains. General Juin, sensing the opportunity, sent a division-sized force of Moroccan Goums, natives of the Atlas Mountains, across these mountains to break into the German rear.

The Moroccans pierced the Germans' second defensive line. The flank along the sea now collapsed, breaking the Gustav line, and the German paratroops at Cassino withdrew on May 17—leaving 4,000 Polish dead in the town and on the slopes of Cassino.

Alexander had ordered forces driving out of the Anzio beachhead to rush past the Alban Hills and block Route 6 at Valmontone, thus cutting off most of the German 10th Army. But Mark Clark wanted the Americans to be first into Rome. When, on May 25, the U.S. 1st Armored and 3rd Infantry Divisions from Anzio linked up with 2nd Corps at Cori, beyond Route 7 but ten miles short of Valmontone, Clark turned three American divisions north along Route 7 toward Rome, sending only one toward Valmontone. Three German divisions held up this division three miles short of Route 6.

Clark found he could not rush into Rome after all, for he was slowed by German resistance on the "Caesar line" of defenses just south of Rome. And 8th Army's armored divisions were unable to pin the retreating German divisions against the Apennines. They slipped away on roads through the mountains. It looked for a while that General Senger would be able to stop the Allies along the Caesar line, but the U.S. 36th Division pierced it at Velletri on Route 7 on May 30. Clark at once ordered a general offensive—2nd Corps took Valmontone and thrust up Route 6, while 6th Corps rushed along Route 7.

The Germans gave way, and the Americans entered Rome on June 4. Kesselring had declared it an open city in order to prevent destruction.

☦        ☦        ☦

Alexander's offensive had gained Rome but little else. The Americans lost 18,000 men in the operation, the British 14,000, and the French 10,000. The Germans sustained about 10,000 killed and wounded, but about 20,000 became prisoners of war. The Italian campaign had not proved a good investment for the Allies. They had committed two soldiers to every German. No Germans had been drawn away from northern France, though without Italy, German strength could have been increased there.

Churchill and Alan Brooke pushed for a campaign to drive into northern Italy, and press through the Ljubljana Gap into Austria, but General Marshall and President Roosevelt ruled instead for Operation Anvil (renamed Dragoon) on August 15—the invasion of southern France, to aid the Normandy operation.

The Italian campaign vanished from the front pages. The fighting was not over. The Allies slowly slogged their way northward. But the killing and the maiming that continued apace no longer played a decisive factor in the war.

# 21 NORMANDY

IRONICALLY, THE TWO GREATEST ARMORED COMMANDERS IN HISTORY—HEINZ Guderian and Erwin Rommel—clashed on the proper way to meet the Allied invasion of France. Adolf Hitler's response to that collision largely determined the outcome of the war.

Guderian came to his position from his experiences in the east with the Red Army, Rommel from his experiences in Africa with the western Allies. They proposed diametrically opposite solutions.

In February 1944 Guderian went to St.-Germain-en-Laye, just outside Paris, to visit Field Marshal Gerd von Rundstedt, commander in chief west, and General Leo Geyr von Schweppenberg, in charge of panzer training in the west. Together they came to agreement on handling armor.

Panzer and panzergrenadier divisions, Guderian wrote, "must be stationed far enough inland from the so-called Atlantic Wall so that they could be switched easily to the main invasion front once it had been recognized."

Guderian and Geyr proposed that the ten fast divisions Hitler had allocated to defend the west be concentrated in two groups, one north and the other south of Paris. Both officers recognized the immense superiority of Allied air power, and that it gravely affected German ability to shift armor. But they believed the problem could be overcome by moving at night.

When Guderian got back to supreme headquarters, he discovered that Rommel, who had taken over defense of the Atlantic Wall in November 1943 as commander of Army Group B, was stationing panzer divisions very near the coast.

To Guderian this was a fundamental error. "They could not be with-drawn and committed elsewhere with sufficient rapidity should the enemy land at any other point." When he complained to Hitler, the Fuehrer told him to discuss the matter with Rommel. Guderian hit a stone wall when he met Rommel at his headquarters at La Roche Guyon, a magnificent château west of Paris. Because of Allied air supremacy, Rommel said, there could be no question of moving large formations, even at night.

To Rommel the day of mobile warfare for Germany had passed, not only because of Anglo-American air power but because Germany had not kept up with the western Allies in production of tanks and armored vehi-cles—a result due more to the shortage of oil than to Allied bombing.

Implicit in Rommel's theory was that the Germans must guess right where the Allies were going to land. If German forces could not move, they had to be in place close to the invasion site. Rommel decided that the Allies would land at the Pas de Calais opposite Dover.

Rommel ruled out other landing places, especially because the Allies could provide greater air cover there than anywhere else. Rommel wrote Hitler on December 31, 1943, listing the Pas de Calais as the probable landing site. "The enemy's main concern," he wrote, "will be to get the quickest possible possession of a port or ports capable of handling large ships."

Guderian did not conjecture precisely where the Allies might invade. He thought they should be allowed to land and make a penetration, so that their forces could be destroyed and thrown back into the sea by a counteroffensive on a grand scale. This was in keeping with successful German movements in Russia. Although Rundstedt and Geyr accepted the idea, neither they nor Guderian had any idea how Anglo-American command of the air could restrict panzer movement.

Rommel did, and to him Guderian's proposal was nonsense. "If the enemy once gets his foot in, he'll put every antitank gun and tank he can into the bridgehead and let us beat our heads against it," he told General Fritz Bayerlein, commander of the Panzer Lehr Division.

The only way to prevent this, Rommel wrote, was to fight the battle in the coastal strip. This required operational reserves close behind the beaches that could intervene quickly. Bringing reserves up from inland would force them to run a gauntlet of Allied air power, and take so much time the Allies could organize a solid defense or drive farther inland.

Rommel set about building a fortified mined zone extending five or six miles inland. He also built underwater obstacles along the shore—including stakes ("Rommel's asparagus") carrying antitank mines, concrete structures equipped with steel blades or antitank mines, and other snares. But his efforts came too late to be fully effective, and they were concentrated in the Pas de Calais, though some work extended to Normandy.

Rommel and Guderian were both wrong, of course. The Allies were *not* bound to take the shortest route to seize the closest port. Rommel did not understand the vastness of Allied maritime resources, and he was not aware of British ingenuity in building two artificial harbors (Mulberries) which could serve as temporary ports. The Mulberries veiled the biggest secret of all: the Allies did *not* have to capture a port to invade the Continent. This made possible a landing at the least likely place still under the Allied air umbrella: the beaches of Normandy.

Guderian was wrong in his belief that the Germans could duplicate anything like the vast sweeping panzer movements they practiced in Russia. There the Luftwaffe generally had parity with the Red air force, and could achieve temporary local superiority to carry out a specific mission. In the west, Allied air power was overwhelming and permanent. In the winter of 1944, the Luftwaffe was virtually swept from the skies, primarily because of the American P-51 Mustang fighter. The Mustang surpassed all German fighters, yet the Luftwaffe was forced to challenge it since the P-51 was now escorting B-17 bombers in daylight raids over Germany. The Germans lost large numbers of fighters, and by March were reluctant to come up and engage the Mustangs.

Another reason Allied air power was decisive in France was that forests, rivers, and cities forced traffic along predictable arteries, which could be bombed and strafed, and bridges broken, unlike in Russia where panzers could often strike out across open plains.

The two generals should have sought a compromise. There *was* one: dividing the armor and placing one segment behind *each* of the invasion sites the Allies might choose, and making each segment available on call to Rommel or the commander of the invasion site directly ahead. Such a compromise would have answered most of Rommel's concerns, and it would have provided a partial answer to the mobile armored reserve Guderian wanted—in the form of the armor behind the sites *not* attacked by the Allies.

The actual number of potential invasion sites was three, and they could have been figured out by logic. The Allies would insist on heavy fighter coverage over the landing sites. The Allies were certain to land within the maximum range of their principal ground-support aircraft, Spitfires, P-38 Lightnings, and P-47 Thunderbolts, or about 200 miles from the main fighter bases in southeastern England. A strike into Holland would encounter hard-to-cross rivers and canals, and land below sea level that could be flooded. On the Brittany peninsula an invasion might be sealed off, and the French coast south of the Loire River was much too far. Both were beyond 200 miles of the English fighter bases.

This left just the Pas de Calais, the Cotentin peninsula of Normandy, and the beaches of Normandy as the only possible invasion places.

If Rommel, Guderian, Rundstedt, and Geyr had agreed that the invasion could strike one of these places, and none other, then allocation of armor equally to each of the three would have been sensible. Since Hitler had assigned only ten fast divisions to the defense of western Europe, it was imperative to decide *where* the landings might occur and locate armor at these places.

But this did not happen. Rommel persisted in believing, until a month or two before the landing, that the Pas de Calais was the only possible site. And since Guderian, Rundstedt, and Geyr believed otherwise, the final decision on where to locate the fast divisions fell to Adolf Hitler. He, in his characteristic indecisive and uncertain fashion, spread the ten panzer and panzergrenadier divisions from northern Belgium to the south of France.

Hitler refused to settle on even a *region* that the Allies might invade, let alone specific sites. In a meeting with senior commanders on March 20, 1944, he listed potential invasion places from Norway to southern France. In the final allocation, he stationed six fast divisions north of the Loire River, and four south of the river, three of them near the Spanish frontier or close to Marseilles along the Mediterranean coast.

Erich von Manstein had won the campaign in the west in 1940 by convincing Hitler to concentrate his armor. Now, at the moment of

Germany's greatest military peril, Hitler was *dispersing* his armor—all across the map. Furthermore, he kept a firm rein on most of these divisions, intending to direct the battle from Berchtesgaden.

If, instead, three or four fast divisions had been stationed directly behind the beaches at each of the potential sites, they very likely could have crushed any invasion on the first day.

From March 1944 onward Hitler had a "hunch" the invasion would come at Normandy, though he thought it would be only a diversion to the main assault on the Pas de Calais. He arrived at this hunch because Americans were concentrated in southwest England, thus were closer to Normandy, and because an exercise took place in Devon on a beach similar to Norman beaches. Rommel came around to the same belief, but, despite frantic efforts, it was too late to build adequate defenses along the Norman coast.

✠          ✠          ✠

Whether the landing on Normandy (Operation Overlord) was actually going to take place was the call of the three Allied leaders, not the generals. They did so at the Teheran conference in late November 1943.

Roosevelt was not as set on Overlord as Marshall, but if Stalin wanted it, he would demand it. Stalin still had the power to sign a cease-fire with Hitler. This was increasingly unlikely with the German retreat after Operation Citadel, but Roosevelt sought to avoid a separate peace at all costs. Beyond that, he was seeking a "constructive relationship" with Stalin after the war—a Soviet Union as a responsible member of the world community, not an agent of further disorder and war.

Consequently, at Teheran, when Stalin contested diversions in the Mediterranean that Churchill was seeking, Roosevelt announced he opposed any delay in the cross-Channel invasion. With that, the die was cast for Overlord.

Because American forces would predominate in an invasion of France, Roosevelt insisted that the commander be an American. Churchill had to accept, dashing the hopes of Alan Brooke to get the job. In partial compensation, Churchill arranged for British General Sir Henry Maitland Wilson to become supreme commander of the Mediterranean theater.

Early in December on his return from Teheran, FDR met Dwight Eisenhower at Tunis. The president was scarcely seated in the automobile when he said: "Well, Ike, you are going to command Overlord."

General Marshall had expected to receive this choicest of all commands, and Roosevelt had planned to give it to him. But he finally decided that Marshall could not be spared, telling him: "I could not sleep at ease if you were out of Washington."

Eisenhower, fifty-four years old, was probably the best possible choice. He was not a combat commander, but he was able to build consensus and cooperation among two quite different sorts of armies and officers. He quelled disputes and animosities by reason and with what Max Hastings called an "extraordinary generosity of spirit to his difficult subordinates."

Eisenhower secured British Air Chief Marshal Sir Arthur Tedder as his deputy. He had hoped to get General Alexander, whom the Americans liked despite his critical views of American soldiers, as British ground commander. But Alan Brooke favored Montgomery, and Churchill, deciding he needed Alexander in the Mediterranean, gave Montgomery the job. For American ground commander, Eisenhower selected Omar Bradley, a stable, discreet, but colorless fifty-year-old West Pointer. Because the slapping incidents in Sicily had revealed a serious character flaw in George Patton, Eisenhower refused to consider him for any post higher than commanding an army.

An enormous buildup commenced in southern England, and by the spring of 1944 much of the country had become a vast military encampment. Tank and vehicle parks covered thousands of acres. Most obvious were the troops who made up one French, one Polish, three Canadian, fourteen British, and twenty American divisions.

To permit rehearsal of landings with live ammunition, the British evacuated the entire population of a 25-square-mile region along the Devonshire coast between Appledore and Woolacombe. Great tented cantonments arose in the assembly areas. The initial American landing force comprised 130,000 men, with 1.2 million more to follow in ninety days. With them would go 137,000 wheeled vehicles, 4,200 fully tracked vehicles, and 3,500 cannons. Also assembled were prodigious amounts of supplies. Each American soldier in Normandy got six and one-quarter pounds of rations a day, each German three and one-third. On the other hand, a German rifle company's small-arms ammunition scale was 56,000 rounds, an American company's 21,000.

☩          ☩          ☩

British Lieutenant General Frederick Morgan, charged with drawing up an invasion plan, had put his finger on Normandy by the spring of 1943. The Pas de Calais defenses were too powerful, and the Germans might bottle up an invasion of Cherbourg and the Cotentin peninsula. This left only the beaches of Normandy within range of fighter cover. But the final decision came only when a British idea for two artificial harbors (Mulberries) turned out to be feasible, and work began apace.

If the Germans knew the Norman beaches were the site, they could build up overwhelming force there and smash the landing. It was imperative to deceive them into believing the main attack would come at the Pas de Calais, and that Normandy was only a feint or diversion.

Out of this arose the most brilliant Allied deception of the war (Operation Fortitude). The Germans had fingered Patton as the most aggressive, inventive, and determined general among the western Allies, and did not think the little matter of his slapping around a couple of enlisted men would make much difference. Patton, they were sure, would lead the assault forces into France. Therefore, when Eisenhower called him to Britain on January 22, 1944, and named him to command 3rd Army, counterintelligence spread the word that he was actually commanding the "1st U.S. Army Group" that would land in the Pas de Calais. The counterspies set up radio nets of this fictitious army group with lots of fake traffic and created the impression that a real army group was busily preparing for action. The Germans kept their strongest army, the 15th, to guard the Pas de Calais.

The Allies had decided to land at Normandy, but this was only the first step. Shortly after arriving in England on January 14, 1944, Eisenhower established the strategy to defeat Germany. He directed that after breaking out of Normandy the Allies were to advance on Germany on a broad front with two army groups—the British on the left, the Americans on the right. The British were to receive preference in order to capture the ports of Belgium, especially Antwerp, which were vital to build up supplies necessary to break into Germany, and to seize the Ruhr, the main center of German industry, which lay east of southern Holland along the Rhine around Düsseldorf, Duisburg, and Essen.

Eisenhower also ordered a massive bombing offensive against transportation centers in Belgium and France to reduce German ability to reinforce Normandy and to carry on a war in France. To minimize casualities among French and Belgian civilians, the Allies warned inhabitants in advance to move away from specific targets. The Allied aircraft did not target rail and road lines to Normandy alone, but bombed other sites, especially the Pas de Calais.

Sir Arthur Harris, chief of RAF Bomber Command, wanted to continue area or terror nighttime bombing of German cities, while Carl Spaatz, U.S. Strategic Air Forces commander, urged concentration on destroying synthetic fuel plants and refineries to immobilize German panzers, vehicles, and aircraft. However, Eisenhower overruled them.

Nevertheless, Spaatz's attacks on oil production facilities—which continued in the spring of 1944, and accelerated thereafter—slowed German motorized movements. By September 1944, German aircraft fuel production was only 10,000 tons, while the Luftwaffe's minimum monthly demand was 160,000 tons. These deficiencies reduced the menace of new German jet-engine fighters, now being introduced.

✠      ✠      ✠

General Morgan had come up with a limited plan for invading Normandy: an attack by only three divisions on a relatively narrow front. To Eisenhower this was fatally weak, and on January 21, 1944, at his first conference in London, he decided on a five-division assault on as wide a front as possible—60 miles—to reduce congestion when reinforcements came ashore.

The Americans were to land on the right, or west, on Utah and Omaha beaches, and go for Cherbourg, Brest, and the ports around the Loire estuary. In the final version, two U.S. airborne divisions (82nd and 101st) were to land at the base of the Cotentin peninsula to assist in securing it quickly. Also, because a lagoon was directly behind Utah beach, the paratroops were to prevent Germans from blocking the few causeways leading from the beach.

The British and Canadians were to land on the left in the vicinity of Caen, on Sword, Gold, and Juno beaches, and confront the main enemy body approaching from the east and southeast. The British 6th Parachute Division was to secure the high ground just east of Caen and the Orne River. The first objective, Caen, ten miles inland, was to be seized on the first day. All major roads funneled through this town. Then armored forces were to push southward to gain territory—especially around Falaise, 22 miles south of Caen—to make it difficult for German reserves to get past. Eisenhower set June 5, 1944, as D-Day.

The key to Normandy was Caen. Most German reserves would have to arrive from the south and southeast and go through Caen, even those headed for the American beachheads to the west.

Allied commanders knew from intelligence sources that the panzer divisions were being held in reserve, though they thought Rundstedt had control of them, not Hitler. Even so, they expected a delay before they were released to Rommel. This opened the window of opportunity the Allies needed to build strong beachheads. If they could hold on to the fifth day they would have fifteen divisions on shore, Bernard Montgomery, 21st Army Group commander and chief of land forces, told senior commanders on April 7, 1944. Even though he estimated the Germans could bring in six panzer divisions by that time, they would be unable to break up the lodgments. From that point on, Allied power would rise inexorably, making the outcome—the destruction of the German army in the west—inevitable.

✠          ✠          ✠

Selection of June 5, 1944, as D-Day was based on combinations of the moon, tide, and the time of sunrise. The Allies wanted to cross the Channel at night so darkness would conceal direction and strength of the attacks. They wanted a moon for the airborne drops, and they needed forty minutes of daylight ahead of the ground assault to complete bombing runs and preparatory naval bombardments. But the actual day of the attack would depend upon weather forecasts. Nevertheless, postponing the invasion beyond June 6 or 7 would involve rescheduling the entire operation and problems of enormous magnitude.

As the date approached, authorities cut off all of southern England from the rest of the country. No unauthorized person could go in either direction. Logistical officers charted every encampment, barracks, vehicle park, and unit. They scheduled movements of every unit to reach its embarkation point at the exact time the vessels were ready to receive it. The assault troops—the first wave of the invasion—went into cantonments surrounded by barbed wire to prevent any soldier from leaving once he'd learned his part in the attack.

As Eisenhower wrote, "The mighty host was tense as a coiled spring," ready to vault across the Channel in the greatest amphibious assault ever attempted.

On the morning of June 4, Eisenhower and his commanders met with the meteorologic committee, headed by RAF Group Captain J. M. Stagg. The news was not good. Stagg predicted low clouds, high winds, and strong waves on June 5. The naval commander, British Admiral Sir Bertram H. Ramsey, was neutral. Montgomery urged going on with the invasion on schedule. Tedder disagreed.

Eisenhower decided to postpone the invasion for one day. Since some vessels already had set out to sea, they had to be called back. Some in the Irish Sea had trouble gaining ports, refueling, and readying to move a day later.

At 3:30 A.M., June 5, a wind of almost hurricane force, along with sheets of rain, pounded Eisenhower's operational headquarters at Portsmouth on the south coast. At the naval center a mile away Captain Stagg had surprisingly good news: by the morning of June 6 a period of relative calm would ensue for about thirty-six hours. After that, the prospects were for more bad weather. The consequences of delay were so great that Eisenhower quickly announced his decision to go ahead with the invasion on June 6.

Orders went out at once. From the ports, 5,000 vessels put out to sea.

Winston Churchill informed Eisenhower that he was going to observe the invasion from a ship immediately off the Normandy shore. Eisenhower told him he could not do so. Churchill responded that he could name himself as a member of a ship's company, and Eisenhower couldn't stop him. King George VI heard about Churchill's scheme, and announced that if the prime minister felt it necessary to go, he, the king, felt it equally his duty to participate at the head of his troops. With that, Churchill backed down.

✠          ✠          ✠

On each of the five beaches—two American, two British, one Canadian— forces equivalent to one division were to land on D-Day. On each of the beaches, save Omaha, the defenders were static or garrison divisions, made up of older men or non-German volunteers, with no great enthusiasm and little or no battle experience.

Omaha was the sole exception. There on guard was the 352nd Infantry Division, a combat-toughened field force that had moved in three months before from service in Russia, a fact that had escaped Allied intelligence. One regiment of the 352nd was guarding the four miles of steep bluffs that rose behind the Omaha landing sectors. The other two regiments were a few miles inland at Bayeux. But one regiment of the 716th Division (a static force) had been incorporated into the command structure of the 352nd. Therefore, two full regiments were in place and waiting at Omaha.

The plan was for bombers to shatter the defensive positions on all five beaches in the first few minutes of daylight on June 6. Meanwhile, naval guns would bombard the beaches, while the landing craft approached.

Before any of this happened, however, the paratroops landed—16,000 Americans behind the Utah beaches at the base of the Cotentin peninsula; 8,000 British east of Caen.

The first paratroops came in by parachute and glider in the early hours in the dark. The foul weather and the inexperience of some transport pilots caused most of the Americans and British to be scattered far and wide of their objectives.

The British 6th Parachute Division, though suffering extreme losses in landings or because pilots veered from their assigned targets because of antiaircraft fire, nevertheless secured the area east of the Orne River, including the "Pegasus bridge" over the Caen canal, vital for linking traffic on the main coast road.

The job of the U.S. 101st Airborne Division was to take the four cause-

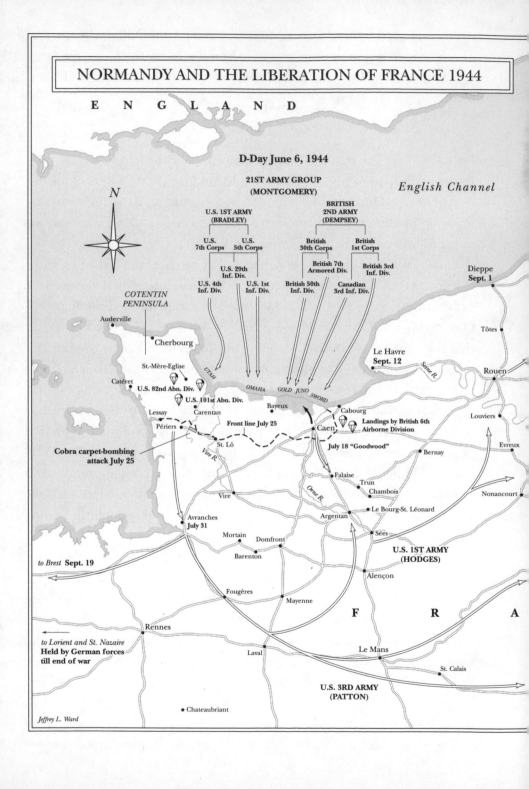

# NORMANDY AND THE LIBERATION OF FRANCE 1944

**E N G L A N D**

**D-Day June 6, 1944**

**21ST ARMY GROUP**
**(MONTGOMERY)**

*English Channel*

**U.S. 1ST ARMY**
**(BRADLEY)**

**BRITISH**
**2ND ARMY**
**(DEMPSEY)**

| U.S. 7th Corps | U.S. 5th Corps | British 30th Corps | British 1st Corps |

**U.S. 29th Inf. Div.**

**British 7th Armored Div.**

**British 3rd Inf. Div.**

| U.S. 4th Inf. Div. | U.S. 1st Inf. Div. | British 50th Inf. Div. | Canadian 3rd Inf. Div. |

**N**

*COTENTIN PENINSULA*

Auderville

Cherbourg

St.-Mère-Eglise

Catéret

**U.S. 82nd Abn. Div.**

**U.S. 101st Abn. Div.**

Lessay

Carentan

Bayeux

UTAH   OMAHA   GOLD   JUNO   SWORD

Dieppe
Sept. 1

Tôtes

Le Havre
Sept. 12

*Seine R.*

Rouen

Louviers

Cabourg

**Landings by British 6th Airborne Division**

Périers

**Front line July 25**

Caen

**July 18 "Goodwood"**

**Cobra carpet-bombing attack July 25**

St. Lô

*Vire R.*

Evreux

Bernay

Nonancourt

Falaise

Trun

Chambois

Le Bourg-St. Léonard

*Orne R.*

Vire

Avranches
July 31

Mortain

Domfront

Barenton

Argentan

Sées

**U.S. 1ST ARMY**
**(HODGES)**

*to Brest* **Sept. 19**

Alençon

Fougères

Mayenne

**F**          **R**          **A**

Rennes

*to Lorient and St. Nazaire*
**Held by German forces till end of war**

Laval

Le Mans

St. Calais

**U.S. 3RD ARMY**
**(PATTON)**

● Chateaubriant

*Jeffrey L. Ward*

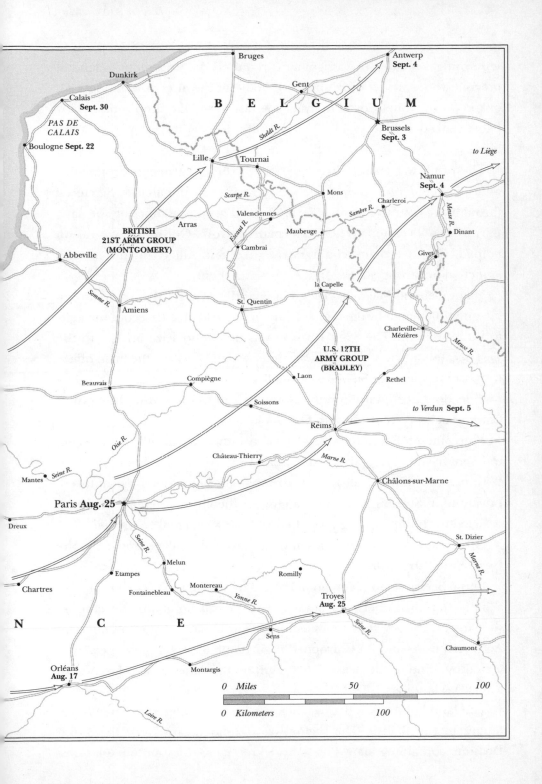

Bruges

Dunkirk

Calais **Sept. 30**

*PAS DE CALAIS*

Boulogne **Sept. 22**

Antwerp **Sept. 4**

Gent

**B  E  L  G  I  U  M**

*Sheldt R.*

Brussels **Sept. 3**

Lille
Tournai

*to Liège*

Namur **Sept. 4**

*Scarpe R.*

Mons

Charleroi

*Meuse R.*

Arras

**BRITISH 21ST ARMY GROUP (MONTGOMERY)**

Valenciennes

*Escaut R.*

Maubeuge

*Sambre R.*

Dinant

Cambrai

Givet

Abbeville

*Somme R.*

la Capelle

Charleville-Mézières

*Meuse R.*

Amiens

St. Quentin

Beauvais

Compiègne

Laon

**U.S. 12TH ARMY GROUP (BRADLEY)**

Rethel

Soissons

*to Verdun* **Sept. 5**

*Oise R.*

Reims

Château-Thierry

*Marne R.*

Mantes

*Seine R.*

Châlons-sur-Marne

Paris **Aug. 25**

Dreux

St. Dizier

*Seine R.*

Melun

*Marne R.*

Etampes

Montereau

Romilly

Chartres

Fontainebleau

*Yonne R.*

Troyes **Aug. 25**

**N         C         E**

Sens

*Seine R.*

Chaumont

Orléans **Aug. 17**

Montargis

*0   Miles            50            100*

*Loire R.*

*0   Kilometers            100*

ways leading to Utah beach; the task of the 82nd Airborne Division was to seize bridges inland. The assignments required the paratroops to land at precise drop zones. It didn't happen. Many of the aircraft were too high or too far off course, or were flying too fast to see the drop zones. Many pilots banked away to avoid antiaircraft fire, forcing the troopers to jump blind.

The result was chaos. Three-quarters of the paratroopers dropped so wide of their targets they never took any part in the attacks. Scattered through the countryside, they formed small groups, wandering for days, skirmishing occasionally with German patrols. Oddly the confusion helped. The Germans could not figure out Allied intentions and launched no strong attacks on the scattered men.

Major General Maxwell Taylor, commander of the 101st, could assemble only 1,000 men by the night of June 6, but was able to secure the exits to the causeways. The 82nd Division was unable to seize bridges to the west because much of the land was under water. However, the main objective was the village of St.-Mère-Eglise, five miles west of Utah beach, on a road leading northward into the Cotentin and southward to the town of Carentan and connection with Omaha beach.

Thirty men fell into the village itself, twenty of them right on the central square into the midst of the German garrison of a hundred men. Within a few minutes all the paratroops had been killed or captured. Private John Steele's parachute caught on the church steeple, where he dangled for hours, playing dead, before finally being taken prisoner.

Other 82nd Airborne men assembled outside the village, and drove the Germans out by dawn.

In the British sector, Montgomery held up the landing for an hour and a half after the Americans landed in order to bombard the landing sites for two hours, four times as long as at Omaha. Large numbers of American B-17s and B-24s dropped their bomb loads on the targets, protected by some of the nearly 5,000 fighters the Allies had committed to the D-Day landings.

The land behind the flat beaches was low, and offered no great challenges to the British. The sector was defended largely by the 716th Division, containing many Poles and Ukrainians, and it put up a lackluster defense. The only threat from the air was from two FW-190 fighters based at Lille that made a single bold sweep along the beaches, guns blazing, before banking away and returning to base. On a cliff west of Le Hamel on Gold beach on the west a unit of the 352nd Division mounted an 88-millimeter antiaircraft gun with a clear field of fire. A round struck a landing ship, wrecking its engine room and turning it broadside up on the beach. Eventually a tank carrying a heavy mortar lobbed a forty-pound "flying dustbin" into the 88's position and destroyed it. The British 50th Division, which landed at Gold, pushed four miles inland, but failed to capture the D-Day objective, Bayeux.

All across the British sector tanks fitted with flails moved up from the beaches, blowing up mines in their path. The tanks created lanes through which the infantry and vehicles could advance.

On Juno, the Canadian beach in the center, the Germans were waiting. Mines and shells sank many of the 306 landing craft. At Bernières, the 8th Canadian Brigade arrived ahead of its flail tanks. The assault regiment, the Queen's Own Rifles, lost half of one company killed in the 100 yards it had to traverse from sea to sea wall. The Canadians broke through by point-blank fire from a gunship and a quick assault through one point of the defenses, and the Germans withdrew. The Canadians penetrated about four miles inland.

At Sword, on the east, the British 3rd Division lost 28 of 40 tanks in pitching seas, but the remaining 12 knocked out German gun positions. The division overran the enemy, pushed four miles inland, and linked up with the 6th Parachute Division along the Orne River, but failed to take the D-Day objective, Caen.

General Miles Dempsey, commander of 2nd Army, landed 75,000 men on D-Day at all three beaches, plus 8,000 paratroopers, and suffered about 3,000 casualties, one-third of them Canadian.

Meanwhile, nearly forty miles to the west, the U.S. 4th Infantry Division landed on Utah beach. The advance bombing by the air force had achieved little because a heavy overcast obscured the target, and most of the bombs landed far to the rear. An hour-long naval bombardment, however, was highly effective.

Utah was defended by one regiment of the 709th Division, another nonmobile outfit made up of older men and volunteers from the Soviet Georgian republic. The defenders raked the landing craft that came within their field of fire, but quickly surrendered.

By the end of the day, 23,000 Americans had landed on Utah, and the division had pushed six miles inland. Total casualties were only 197.

✠          ✠          ✠

Omaha was utterly different. In the words of Omar Bradley, it was a nightmare. Before daylight, the invasion fleet, fearing shore batteries, anchored twelve miles off the coast. One of these batteries, at Pointe du Hoc, four miles west of the beaches, was reported to have six 155-millimeter guns with a range of 25,000 yards. Bradley had assigned two Ranger battalions to scale the high cliffs and destroy the guns.

Waves three to six feet high slapped the ships. Launching landing craft in darkness was difficult and dangerous. The "secret weapon" upon which the Americans were relying was the DD (for dual-drive) Sherman tank, equipped with canvas flotation gear and a boat screw. DDs were to be launched at sea and "swim" ashore to provide the troops instant artillery fire. Twenty-nine of the thirty-two DDs for the east sector were launched two and a half miles off the coast. All but two foundered, taking nearly all the crews to the bottom of the sea with them. Three others were landed directly on the beach. The seamen in charge of landing the thirty-two DDs on the western sector, horrified at what was happening, called off the sea launch and landed twenty-eight DDs directly on the beach, though only later—just two of the DDs intended to support the infantry made it ashore with the troops. Most of the amphibious DUKWs transporting 105-millimeter howitzers also foundered.

At 5:50 A.M. terrific salvos burst from the warships onto Omaha. The bombardment went on for thirty-five minutes. Meanwhile, beginning at 6 A.M., waves of B-24s dropped nearly 1,300 tons of bombs. The naval bombardment was partially effective, but the aerial bombardment was useless, falling well inland and missing the beach entirely.

The Omaha beach fortifications were formidable: three rows of underwater steel or concrete obstacles, most mined. The beach was two hundred yards wide with no cover. Beyond a low seawall were sand dunes and bluffs, cut by five draws the Americans intended to use as exits. All the draws were covered by German gun emplacements and the area between the seawall and cliffs was sown with mines.

At 6:30 A.M. the first waves of infantry, 1,500 men in 36 landing craft, hit Omaha: members of the 116th Regiment of the 29th Division and the 16th Regiment of the 1st Division, plus engineers to blow up underwater obstacles.

The Germans held their fire until the first wave of infantry hit the beaches. The initial burst of machine-gun fire came from a strongpoint only a quarter of a mile away from the lead craft. Others followed, creating a hurricane of fire. First out were men of the 116th on the west. As the ramps went down, they saw the shallows ahead whipped white by bullets. Men dropped dead or wounded as they lumbered forward in waist-deep water, creating a bloody surf that horrified everyone from the first moments. Other soldiers, seeing what was happening, tried to dive into deeper water and swim clear of the boats. But their heavy equipment dragged them down. Some drowned, others fought back to the surface. The survivors who dragged themselves ashore found no shelter, and some crawled back into the water for its scant protection. Within ten minutes every officer and sergeant had been killed or wounded. In Company A of the 116th, 22 men from one town—Bedford, Virginia—died, among them three sets of brothers.

The engineers were supposed to clear sixteen 50-yard-wide paths through the obstacles. But half the engineers were dead or wounded, and they managed to clear just one path in the first half hour. The landing craft bringing in the succeeding waves of troops crowded into this single corridor. As the ramps dropped, the men faced almost certain death or wounding. All along the beach landing craft sank or exploded as they hit mines or were struck by artillery.

Ashore, dead and wounded were scattered across the sand and shallows. The survivors lay in the sand or shallow water or crouched behind landing craft, hearing bullets clanging against the steel hulls. Howitzer shells blasted the beach and sent shrapnel flying. The DDs were knocked out, and the Americans had nothing to stop the murderous fire.

Four miles to the west, 225 men of the 2nd Ranger Battalion began scaling the cliffs of Pointe du Hoc to destroy the guns reported there. The Rangers shot rope ladders and rope-bearing grapnels onto the clifftop and started climbing, in the face of withering fire from above. A number of Rangers died, others blasted shelters and hand-holds in the cliff with their grenades. Meanwhile an American and a British destroyer moved in close and drove the enemy away from the top of the cliff with heavy fire. The Rangers hauled themselves up and discovered that the guns were not there. They had been moved back to an orchard. There the Rangers destroyed them.

DD tanks now began to come ashore. The novelist Ernest Hemingway, observing from a landing craft, saw two tanks start burning: "The first, second, third, fourth, and fifth waves [of infantry] lay where they had fallen, looking like so many heavily laden bundles on the flat, pebbly stretch between the sea and the first cover." Hemingway also witnessed the Germans hitting another tank: "I saw two men dive out of the turret and land on their hands and knees on the stones of the beach," he reported. "But no more men came out as the tank started to blaze up and burn furiously."

The only thing that saved the infantry on Omaha was the U.S. Navy. Twelve destroyers moved in close to the beach, ignoring shallow water and mines, and turned every possible gun onto the German positions on the bluffs. This intense fire diminished German resistance, and permitted the soldiers to slowly gain headway.

For six hours, Omaha was bloody chaos. The Americans held only a few yards of beach; the waves actually ran red with blood. Not until the principal commanders got ashore did the men begin to move toward the seawall and bluffs. Brigadier General Norman D. Cota, assistant commander of the 29th Division, strode calmly among the crouching soldiers. He yelled: "Two kinds of people are staying on this beach, the dead and those who are going to die. Now let's get the hell out of here."

Slowly, lone and mostly anonymous individuals of incredible heroism began to get things moving, creating breaches to open the draws to advance. In front of one such place, a lieutenant and a sergeant in the 16th Regiment took their lives in their hands and went up and found only barbed wire barred the way. The lieutenant returned to the GIs cringing behind a low shingle shelf on the beach. Standing with his hands on his hips, he said: "Are you going to lie there and get killed, or get up and do something about it?" Nobody moved, so the sergeant and the lieutenant blew the wire themselves. That gave the men courage enough to file through the gap and through a minefield.

There were many such events on June 6, 1944. By the end of the day the Americans had pushed out a patchwork of pockets over an area six miles long and two miles deep. Behind them, 3,000 Americans lay dead on Omaha beach.

✠          ✠          ✠

Early on June 6, German duty officers in Normandy began to get frantic calls that thousands of paratroops were landing. The officers raced to field telephones to report to higher quarters, and the whole machinery of command went into action.

Erwin Rommel was in Germany for his wife's birthday, assuming the bad weather would prevent an invasion any time soon, and his chief of staff, Hans Speidel, only reached him by phone at midmorning. Rommel at once started driving toward Normandy.

There was one panzer division within immediate striking distance of the beaches, the 21st, south of Caen. Two other divisions were fairly close: the Panzer Lehr in the vicinity of Chartres, and the SS Panzer Hitler Jugend just west of Paris. If they had moved at the first word of the invasion, they almost certainly could have smashed it, since the morning of June 6 was heavily overcast, and Allied fighter-bombers could not fly. But while Army Group B had control of the 21st Division, Hitler controlled the other two. Jodl refused to wake the Fuehrer, and questioned whether the Normandy landings were the main effort. It was 4 P.M. before the divisions were at last released.

The 21st Panzer had 150 tanks, 60 assault guns, and 300 armored troop carriers. Its commander, Edgar Feuchtinger, formed up part of his division to attack the British paratroops east of the Orne River in the morning, but got countermanding orders from 7th Army to attack west of the river. This caused delay and only a single battle group of fifty tanks and a battalion of panzergrenadiers launched the strike toward Sword beach about midday.

Around 9:30 A.M. the 1st Battalion of the British South Lancashires reached a point almost within sight of Caen when they encountered three antitank guns emplaced on a ridge. The South Lancs dug in and waited for the 65 tanks of the 185th Brigade, which were supposed to lead the midmorning attack toward Caen. For three hours the South Lancs sat there, while the tanks waited for the traffic jam on the Sword beach to clear.

Around 2 P.M. twenty Sherman tanks finally attacked the three AT guns, which withdrew, and the tanks' accompanying force, the Shropshire Light Infantry, pressed on toward Caen. Just short of the town it ran into dug-in infantry, and withdrew to Biéville, four miles north. This was the closest the Allies got to Caen for a month.

Meanwhile the 21st Panzer battle group skirted around west of the Shropshires and drove northward with the intention of splitting Juno from Sword, and destroying each beachhead in turn. The Germans reached the unguarded coast between the two beaches at 8 P.M.

Feuchtinger was sending another fifty tanks to reinforce this advance when overhead the panzers saw the largest glider-borne force in the war, 250 transports, coming to reinforce the 6th Airborne a few miles east. Feuchtinger assumed wrongly that the gliders were landing in his rear with the intention of cutting off the division, and he recalled all his tanks. This fortuitous appearance of the gliders ended the last chance the Germans had to smash the beachheads.

The Germans made another fundamental error: they sent the two closest panzer divisions in daylight toward the Normandy beaches. Rommel and Guderian had preached against this, saying that troops had to move at night. But OKW ordered 12th SS Panzer Hitler Jugend Division, west of Paris, to advance on Caen on the late afternoon of June 6. It did not complete its 75-mile journey until 9:30 A.M., June 7. Friedrich Dollmann, 7th Army commander, ordered Panzer Lehr Division, near Chartres, 110 miles from the front, to drive in daylight on June 7 toward Villers-Bocage, fifteen miles southwest of Caen, to block British movement in that direction. Fritz Bayerlein, Panzer Lehr commander, protested in vain.

Both divisions suffered heavy damage from Allied air attacks. Panzer Lehr, the only division in Normandy at full strength, lost 5 tanks, 84 self-propelled guns and half-tracks, and 130 trucks and fuel tankers. Because of the air attacks Panzer Lehr's tracked vehicles got separated from the wheeled units, and the division was unable to deliver an attack when it arrived, while SS Hitler Jugend had neither the time nor space to launch a coordinated assault by all its formations.

Nevertheless, the arrival of both panzer divisions stopped the rapid advance of the Allies out of Normandy. But these and other divisions were eaten up as they were committed piecemeal, and the moment passed when the German army could have thrown the Allies into the sea. Meanwhile Hitler held some of his strongest divisions at the Pas de Calais, still believing the Normandy invasion was a feint. From sites around the Pas, he also launched attacks on London, beginning June 12–13, with the V-1 jet-propelled cruise missile, and, in September, fired the first V-2 rocket-propelled ballistic missiles.

On June 10, Rommel proposed to Hitler that all armored forces in the line be replaced with infantry formations, and that armor be shifted westward to cut off and destroy the Americans in the lower Cotentin peninsula (7th Corps that had landed at Utah and the 82nd and 101st Airborne Divisions). But Hitler vetoed the plan, and the Germans were forced into a wholly defensive operation.

This led to a murderous battle, but the outcome was never in doubt. Overwhelming Allied power was building day by day. Before long the Allies would burst out of Normandy and roll over the German army.

# 22 THE LIBERATION OF FRANCE

ALL THE DISASTERS PREDICTED BY ERWIN ROMMEL FOR FAILURE TO MOVE UP forces in advance now came to pass. Practically every unit ordered to the battlefront suffered heavy damage. Reinforcements had to be thrown in as soon as they arrived, and their strength eroded rapidly. Battle losses ran 2,500 to 3,000 a day. Tank losses were immense, replacements few.

Allied aircraft destroyed the railway system serving Normandy and smashed anything moving on the roads in daytime. The supply system was so damaged that only the barest essentials reached the front.

As Hitler repeated his familiar order to hold every square yard, Rundstedt and Rommel went to Berchtesgaden on June 29 to talk with the Fuehrer.

Hitler's ideas for stopping the western Allies were utterly unrealistic. The navy was to attack the Allied battleships, but Admiral Dönitz pointed out only a few small torpedo and other light boats were available, and they could accomplish little. A thousand of the new Me-262 twin-engine, jet-propelled fighters were to wrest control of the air over Normandy. However, Anglo-American air attacks in the winter and spring of 1944 had virtually wiped out the pool of skilled German pilots. The Luftwaffe could produce only 500 crews, most of them ill-trained. Consequently, very few Me-262s, with a speed (540 mph) and armament (four 30-millimeter cannons) exceeding any Allied fighter, ever flew against the Allies.

Rundstedt and Rommel told Hitler the situation was impossible. How, Rommel asked, did Hitler imagine the war could still be won? A chaotic argument followed, and Rundstedt and Rommel expected to be ousted from their jobs.

Back at Paris on July 1, Rundstedt got Hitler's order that "present positions are to be held." He called Hitler's headquarters and told a staff officer he couldn't fulfill this demand. What shall we do? the officer asked. Rundstedt replied: "Make peace, you fools."

The next day an emissary from Hitler presented Rundstedt with an Oak Leaf to the Knight's Cross and a handwritten note relieving him of his post because of "age and poor health." Hitler replaced Rundstedt with Günther von Kluge, who at first thought the situation was better than it was. He changed his mind the moment he visited the front.

Rommel, to his surprise, remained at his post. About this time Rommel and his chief of staff, Hans Speidel, concluded that the Germans should commence independent peace negotiations with the western Allies. Their idea was to open the west to an unopposed "march in" by the British and American armies, with the aim of keeping the Russians out of Germany. Everything had been prepared and Kluge and others won over, when fate intervened on July 17: Rommel was severely wounded by a low-flying Allied aircraft near Livarot.

Three days later, on July 20, 1944, Colonel Claus von Stauffenberg, a leader of the secret opposition to Hitler, placed a bomb under a table where Hitler was meeting in his headquarters at Rastenburg, East Prussia. The bomb exploded, but Hitler survived. Immediately afterward, he replaced the army chief of staff, Kurt Zeitzler, with Heinz Guderian, who reported to Hitler at noon on July 21.

"He seemed to be in rather poor shape," Guderian wrote. "One ear was bleeding; his right arm, which had been badly bruised and was almost unusable, hung in a sling. But his manner was one of astonishing calm."

Hitler quickly recovered from the physical effects of the bomb. An existing malady, which caused his left hand and left leg to tremble, had no connection with the explosion. The attempt on his life had a profound effect on his behavior, however. Guderian wrote that "the deep distrust he already felt for mankind in general . . . now became profound hatred. . . . What had been hardness became cruelty, while a tendency to bluff became plain dishonesty. He often lied without hesitation. . . . He believed no one any more. It had already been difficult enough dealing with him; it now

became torture that grew steadily worse from month to month. He frequently lost all self-control and his language grew increasingly violent."

Hitler commenced a wave of terror against anyone suspected of a role
in the bombing plot. This led to numerous executions. On October 14,
1944, Rommel, recovering from his wounds at his home in Ulm, received
the option of a People's Court trial, which would have meant execution,
or taking poison and getting a state funeral—and no persecution of his
wife and son. Rommel chose poison.

✠      ✠      ✠

By June 27, the Americans had pushed the Germans out of the Cotentin
peninsula and seized Cherbourg (though the Germans damaged the port
and it took weeks to get it operating). Meanwhile, Montgomery's British
forces on the east had been unable to budge the Germans from Caen.
Danger arose that the Allies would be boxed into Normandy, especially as
a Channel storm June 19–23 severely damaged the Mulberries on the
Norman coast and drove 800 vessels up on the beaches.

Omar Bradley, commanding the U.S. 1st Army, began moving his
forces south to carry out the original plan of Overlord: breaking out to
Avranches at the base of the Cotentin peninsula, thereby opening the
door to capture of Brittany and the ports there by George Patton's 3rd
Army, to be committed at this time. These advances in addition would give
the Allies space for a massive turning movement that could sweep across
France to the German frontier.

Bradley lined up twelve divisions in four corps to crack through in a
massive frontal assault. Troy H. Middleton's 8th Corps and J. Lawton
Collins's 7th Corps on the west were to drive full speed down the west
coast of the peninsula to Avranches. Meanwhile Charles H. Corlett's 19th
Corps would seize St. Lô in the center, and Leonard T. Gerow's 5th Corps
at Caumont would "hold the hub of the wheel," in Bradley's words, protecting the right flank of the British 2nd Army.

Middleton's corps, on the extreme west, opened the attack on July 3.
But it failed completely. Collins's 7th Corps had no better luck the next
day, while 19th Corps made only meager gains around St. Lô.

To Bradley and his corps commanders the fault lay with the leadership within the American divisions, which in numerous cases was inadequate. Bradley replaced several commanders, but the great problem the Americans faced was the *bocage*—the hedgerow country of Normandy—which caught the Americans by complete surprise. Planners, solving problems of the landings, had paid little or no attention to the terrain just behind the beaches. No troops were taught how to deal with it.

Virtually the entire American sector—from the coast of the Cotentin to the line Caumont-Bayeux—was *bocage* country. In the British sector to the east the land was part *bocage* and part rolling countryside punctuated by hamlets and small woods. For centuries Norman farmers had enclosed their land in small fields by raising embankments three or four feet high. These banks were overgrown with dense shrubbery, brambles, hawthorn, and small trees. The hedgerows were intended as fences to hold livestock, mark boundaries, and protect animals and crops from sea winds. Each field had a gate to admit animals and equipment. Dirt tracks or sunken lanes ran between these hedgerows, permitting troops and weapons to move free from observation from the air or on the ground. The effect was to divide the terrain into thousands of walled enclosures.

The *bocage* proved to be ideal country for the Germans to defend. Antitank weapons—*Panzerfäuste*, or bazooka rocket tubes—and machine guns posted in the hedgerows could remain hidden until a tank was within fifty yards, destroy all but the heaviest tank with one shot, and stop the advance of infantry. In addition, tanks, assault guns, and 88-millimeter antiaircraft guns concealed in the *bocage* or villages could knock out any Allied tank up to 2,000 yards distant.

The Germans organized each field (mostly seven to fifteen acres) as a defensive stronghold, posting machine guns in the corners to pin down Americans advancing across in the open. They placed other automatic weapons in the hedgerows on the front and flanks of the attackers. Once they had stopped the attack, the Germans brought down preregistered mortar rounds on the field. Mortars caused three-quarters of American casualties in Normandy.

American artillery fire could not be used often, since the range was so close that rounds might land on Americans. This undermined the standard American method of fighting. Infantry habitually maneuvered to locate the enemy, then called on artillery to finish him off. Green infantry tended not to move at all under fire, but to seek the nearest cover or hug the ground.

The hedgerows also nullified the tanks' greatest advantages, mobility and firepower. Tankers were reluctant to operate within the confined spaces of the *bocage,* yet if they stayed on the main roads or lanes they made excellent targets. Commanders realized tanks had to get off the roads, but this forced them into the hedgerows.

Some way had to be found to break the impasse. Normal American practice had been for tanks and infantry to advance in separate echelons. In Normandy, astute commanders realized the two had to work together (thus recognizing at long last the *Kampfgruppe* system the Germans had perfected since 1940).

The 29th Infantry Division's method was one of the best. Developed in June and tested on July 11 east of St.-Lô, the 29th's system consisted of a four-phase operation. First, a Sherman M4A3 medium tank broke through enough vegetation in the center of a hedgerow to allow its cannon and machine gun to open up against the enemy-held hedgerow on the opposite side of the field. Meanwhile a 60-millimeter mortar crew lobbed shells behind the enemy hedgerow. Under intense covering fire of the tank's machine gun, a squad of infantry advanced in open formation across the field. As they closed on the enemy, the infantry tossed hand grenades over the hedgerow to kill or confuse the German defenders. Meanwhile, the Sherman tank backed away from its firing position, and an engineer team blew a hole in the hedgerow for the tank to drive through. The tank then rushed forward to assist the infantry in flushing any remaining enemy soldiers out of the hedgerow.

Although this and similar systems worked, the process was slow. Others were thinking of a faster and safer way to get Shermans through the hedgerows—since crashing through exposed the thin underside of the tanks to enemy fire.

Shermans equipped with bulldozer blades could do the job, but there were few such equipped tanks in the theater. Using explosives to break a hole in the hedgerow gave away the attack and served as an aiming point for German weapons. At last, individual soldiers came up with welded devices on the front of Shermans that could crack through the thickest hedgerow. In a prodigious effort, 1st Army welding teams produced 500 hedgerow cutters between July 14 and 25. By late July 60 percent of the army's Shermans were equipped with the device.

✠       ✠       ✠

Bradley, stymied by fierce German defense of the hedgerows, conceived a new plan of attack, which he named Cobra. He decided to focus the breakout around St.-Lô, spearheaded by Lawton Collins's 7th Corps. The key feature would be a massive air attack on the narrow front. When Collins broke through, the whole weight of 1st Army, now fifteen divisions, would be thrown into the assault.

Meanwhile Montgomery drew up plans for an offensive at Caen, codenamed Goodwood, to support Cobra. Montgomery launched Goodwood on July 18, preceded by a massive air attack by 1,700 heavy and 400 medium bombers. At first the British attack went well. Tanks advanced against the stunned German defenders. But bomb craters slowed the armor, and the Germans pulled themselves together and launched a counterattack. It gained no ground, but inflicted heavy losses on the British. On July 20, Montgomery called off the attack, having moved six miles south of Caen, but having lost 4,000 men and 500 tanks.

Bradley's Cobra plan was risky because aviators were not skilled in pinpoint strikes, and the operation called for saturation bombing of a rectangle three miles wide and one mile deep south of the east-west St.-Lô–Périers road. An error would bring bombs down on American troops.

Bradley did not want the aircraft to fly over American lines, and proposed that the planes approach on a course parallel to the St.-Lô–Périers road. On July 19 Bradley flew back to England to discuss the operation with top air commanders. They opposed a parallel approach, saying aircraft would be exposed longer to enemy antiaircraft fire and the approach would require hitting a one-mile-wide target, whereas a perpendicular approach would present a three-mile-wide target. But by the time he left, Bradley thought he had got their agreement. To minimize the chances of American troops being hit, Bradley withdrew them 1,500 yards north of the road.

Heavy rains caused postponement of Cobra until July 24. Cloud cover forced cancellation this day as well, but not before 400 bombers reached France and let go their bombs. To Bradley's horror, the bombers approached perpendicular to the American lines, not parallel. Many bombs fell on American positions, killing 25 and wounding 131. When Bradley complained, the air force brass claimed they had never agreed to a parallel approach. And they told Bradley they would not mount a second attack except in the same direction.

Bradley, having no choice, agreed, and the air assault went in on July 25: 1,500 heavy bombers, 380 medium bombers, and 550 fighter-bombers dropped 4,000 tons of bombs and napalm. Once more "shorts" caused American casualties, 111 dead, 490 wounded.

Collins threw 7th Corps's three divisions into the blasted terrain that the bombers had created. The Americans expected the Germans to be dazed and unable to fight. Instead, they met heavy resistance. Eisenhower, who had observed the bombings, flew back to England dejected, determined never again to use heavy bombers to support ground forces.

Despite the bitter resistance of a few Germans, the bombing had done great damage. Fritz Bayerlein, commanding Panzer Lehr Division, which received the brunt of the attack, wrote: "Units holding the front were almost completely wiped out." Tanks were overturned, artillery shattered, infantry positions flattened, and all roads destroyed. By midday the landscape resembled the moon. "There was no hope of getting out any of our weapons," Bayerlein wrote. "The shock effect was indescribable. Several of the men went mad and rushed dementedly around in the open until they were cut down by splinters."

Martin Blumenson wrote in his official history that one-third of the German combat effectives were killed or wounded, only a dozen tanks or tank destroyers remained in operation, and a parachute regiment attached to Panzer Lehr virtually vanished.

The difficulty of Collins's advance after the bombing was due to spirited response of the Germans, a matter of habit, and to the caution and hesitation of the Americans, accustomed to the slow-moving battle of the hedgerows.

But German opposition melted away. By the end of July 26 American armor had penetrated ten miles, and the next day went farther. "This thing has busted wide open," Leland Hobbs, commander of the 30th Infantry Division, exulted.

Collins enlarged the rupture, and kept moving south. On his right,

Middleton's 8th Corps broke through, and Middleton cut loose his armor. Once Middleton turned the corner at Avranches and headed into Brittany, George Patton's 3rd Army was to be activated. Meanwhile Bradley asked Patton to supervise 8th Corps. A Patton trademark appeared almost at once: two armored divisions pushed forward through the infantry, emerged at the head, and dashed rapidly to Avranches, 35 miles away. Eisenhower's judgment of Patton was being manifested: "an extraordinary and ruthless driving power at critical moments." The Germans retreated or surrendered.

The *bocage* had been bypassed. The German left flank had collapsed. Montgomery announced the only German hope was a staged withdrawal to the Seine River, and to disrupt it the Allies should swing their right flank "round toward Paris." This seemed to be turning into the kind of war that suited most Americans—wide open, hell-for-leather, with the horizon as the destination. George Patton, just the sort of general to lead such a campaign, was coming onto the scene. But Patton had to obey Omar Bradley, who was not at all a damn-the-torpedoes type. And no one was able to guess how Adolf Hitler would react.

✠          ✠          ✠

On August 1, Patton's 3rd Army was formally activated. Bradley moved up to command the 12th Army Group, and Courtney Hodges took over command of 1st Army. Altogether, the Americans had twenty-one divisions, five armored, sixteen infantry, nearly 400,000 men. Overwhelming power now faced the battered and outnumbered Germans.

Originally, Patton's army had been intended to clear Brittany. But the Germans had stripped this region of most troops, and Bradley told Patton to send only Middleton's 8th Corps to secure it. Middleton blazed through Brittany but failed to achieve the primary objectives—the major ports. The Germans withdrew into them. By the time the Americans had seized them, suffering huge losses, the need had long since passed.

Patton was by far the most inventive, venturesome, and action-oriented general on the Allied side. Shortly after he took command of 3rd Army, he recognized that a gigantic victory might be in the offing. The Americans were well south of Normandy, and the way was open for a massive strike east to the region or "gap" between Orléans and Paris, then to Paris, and from Paris down the right bank of the Seine to the sea, cutting off all German forces in Normandy.

But Patton had no authority to order such an offensive, and Montgomery, still in charge of land operations, believed the Germans would build a temporary new defensive line running generally south from Caen, through Mayenne, to Laval, possibly as far south as Angers, near the junction of the Loire and Mayenne rivers. He told Bradley to move up to this expected line on the south. On the north he ordered the Canadian 1st Army under Henry Crerar to strike south from Caen eighteen miles to Falaise on August 8, with the aim of cutting off the Germans,

Bradley directed Patton—who had only a two-division corps (the 15th) under Wade Haislip—to build a sixty-mile front along the Mayenne and take the towns of Mayenne, Laval, and Angers.

Patton instructed Haislip to seize Mayenne and Laval. And, since he still hoped to strike for the Orléans-Paris gap, told Haislip to be prepared to continue to Le Mans, a major town forty-five miles east of the Mayenne River. Haislip, whose policy was to "push all personnel to the limit of human endurance," captured Mayenne and Laval on August 5–6, and Patton got Bradley's permission to drive on to Le Mans.

✠          ✠          ✠

Adolf Hitler saw the Cobra breakout to Avranches in an entirely different fashion than either Montgomery or the German generals on the spot. They, too, favored withdrawal from Normandy, and from France.

Hitler had been fixed on holding all positions since Stalingrad. But in Normandy there was the additional concern that—if the Germans withdrew—the motorized Allied armies could swiftly outrun the Germans' horse-drawn transport. Also, where could the Germans retreat to? The Seine's meandering course offered no sound defensive line. The best line was the German West Wall along the frontier. But it had been neglected since 1940 and would require six to ten weeks to repair. Hitler ordered work to start at once, reasoning that the Germans should remain in Normandy at least till the West Wall was defensible. Finally convinced the Allies would not invade the Pas de Calais, he ordered forces there to Normandy.

Also, Hitler saw the possibility of a riposte. The German western flank now rested just east of the town of Mortain, twenty miles from Avranches, in the wooded highlands of "Norman Switzerland." On August 1, he ordered Kluge to strike from Mortain to recapture Avranches. This would anchor the German line on the Cotentin coast, and divide Patton's 3rd Army south of Avranches from Hodges's 1st Army north of it.

Kluge assembled four weak panzer divisions. Three were to roll through Mortain and the Americans defending it, and drive as far as possible. Once they lost their momentum, the fourth division was to go to the front and strike for Avranches.

Ultra intercepts of German messages informed Bradley of the intended attack shortly before it struck. He already had nearly five divisions in the area, and alerted them to the attack.

The blow hit Mortain in the early minutes of August 7. The U.S. 30th Division had occupied the town only hours before. Key to Mortain was Hill 317 just to the east. While German infantry struck at the hill, seventy panzers went around it, drove through the town, and headed west. By midday they had advanced six miles. But Allied aircraft forced the panzers into the woods. Fighting continued, but the Germans had no chance to break through the iron ring of defenses. Meanwhile the 700 Americans on Hill 317 stood their ground, helped by artillery concentrations and RAF Hurricanes and Typhoon fighter-bombers equipped with rockets.

Hitler charged Kluge with poor judgment, haste, and carelessness, and ordered the attack to continue with a larger force. Kluge was to transfer three panzer divisions from the British-Canadian front to thrust into the deep flank of the American advance (Patton's move toward Le Mans).

Kluge, who saw the situation far more clearly than Hitler, knew his attack had bogged down, and the best move was to retreat. He also saw something that terrified him: the German front now extended as a deep salient into the Allied line. Montgomery's two armies (British 2nd, Canadian 1st) and Hodges's 1st Army were on the north, while Patton's 3rd Army was sweeping toward Le Mans on the south. If it continued through the Orléans-Paris gap and beyond, it could encircle all German forces west of the Seine.

But Hitler's orders were unequivocal, and Kluge directed the three panzer divisions to pull out of the British-Canadian sector and head for Mortain during the night of August 7. At 11 P.M., Kluge learned of an immense aerial bombardment along the road from Caen to Falaise—heralding a major attack by the Canadian army. One of the three panzer divisions had already left the Falaise sector, but Kluge canceled orders for the other two. The Germans could not afford to lose Falaise.

The Canadian attack, made with two armored brigades, followed by infantry in armored personnel carriers (APCs), advanced three miles during the darkness, and by dawn August 8 had passed through the German lines. But here the advance came to a halt, though the way to Falaise lay open.

To get the attack started again, General Guy Simonds, 2nd Canadian Corps commander, brought forward his two armored divisions, one Canadian, the other Polish, and ordered them to advance on a narrow front to Falaise. The two divisions were inexperienced and were distracted by Allied bombers that dropped bombs short, killing 65, wounding 250. Meanwhile the Germans recovered, rebuilt a defensive line, and barred the way. The effort pushed forward a few miles, but collapsed on August 10—though the Allies had 600 tanks against 60 German tanks and tank destroyers. George Kitching, commander of the Canadian division (the 4th), blamed the Poles, who, he said, scarcely moved.

Adolf Hitler, having lost confidence in Kluge, was directing the battles from his headquarters in East Prussia. On August 9 he ordered tanks and antitank guns from the Pas de Calais to Falaise. This, he figured, would take care of the Canadian threat. Next he turned to the effort to capture Avranches. He wanted another attack, this time by six panzer divisions, while two other divisions were to bolster them.

German commanders called Hitler's order "pure utopia." Kluge could muster only 120 tanks at Mortain, half those in a single American armored division.

Because of Hitler's insistence, the German army remained fixed from Mortain on the west to the front facing the Canadians on the east. Conditions were ripe for a colossal encirclement and caldron battle. Haislip's troops were about to seize Le Mans. They then would be only seventy-five miles from the Paris-Orléans gap. Patton tried to convince Bradley to let Haislip go all out for the gap, and carry out his plan to liberate Paris and drive down the right bank of the Seine, surrounding all Germans west of the river. If successful—and there were few Germans to stop it—Patton's plan would end Germany's capacity to resist in the west in a matter of days.

But Bradley did not have the vision of Patton. And he was unwilling to take chances. He saw a lesser opportunity, with lesser potential gains. At Le Mans, Haislip was to turn north toward Alençon and Sées, and link up with the Canadians coming down through Falaise and Argentan—thereby cutting off the Germans to the west. This move might not destroy all the Germans in Normandy but it could dispose of many.

✠          ✠          ✠

Haislip captured Le Mans on August 8 and prepared to move north. He had received two new divisions, a green American infantry outfit (80th) that was to guard the town, and the French 2nd Armored Division, whose commander, Jacques Leclerc, was primarily interested in liberating Paris. But he snapped up Patton's offer to take part in the drive toward Argentan alongside the U.S. 5th Armored Division under Lunsford Oliver.

These two armored divisions, followed by two infantry divisions (79th and 90th), advanced halfway to Alençon on August 10, meeting virtually no resistance. On Haislip's left, however, there was a wide gap with no American forces—since Bradley did not want to move troops into it while the Germans still threatened around Mortain. This void offered an opportunity for a German counterattack into Haislip's flank.

Early on August 11, Kluge determined to pull back from Mortain and strike this flank. He had inflicted 4,000 casualties on the Americans, but had lost many men of his own and a hundred tanks. Hitler approved, and Kluge drew his troops away from Mortain.

Meanwhile Haislip reached the outskirts of Alençon on August 11 and designated Argentan, twenty-three miles north by road, as the next objective. Argentan was eight miles inside the British-Canadian sector, but that seemed no problem.

Early on August 12 Leclerc's armored division captured Alençon, while Oliver's 5th U.S. Armored Division pushed ahead to Sées, twelve miles along the road to Argentan. Ahead Argentan was defended only by a German bakery company, which was digging in at the southern edge of town.

Oliver's American tanks could have rushed down the Alençon-

Argentan highway and seized the town quickly, except that Leclerc, in defiance of orders, usurped the road for some of his own troops. When the Americans finally got to Argentan, it no longer was guarded by bakers but by three panzer divisions and at least seventy tanks, moved over by Kluge from Mortain.

Kluge's intended strike against Haislip's flank never came off because the Germans lost stocks of gasoline and other supplies near Alençon, but the panzers' possession of Argentan left open an important east-west highway. If the Germans lost Falaise and Argentan, only a narrow thirteen-mile gap without good roads would remain.

Haislip informed Patton on the evening of August 12 that he intended to strike at Argentan the next morning. But he pointed out that the farther he advanced the more extended he became, with few troops guarding his flank. If he captured Argentan, he was certain to stir up a fierce German response. Should he go on or not?

Patton opted for audacity. In a letter to his wife, Patton quoted Napoleon: *"L'audace, l'audace, toujours l'audace."* The game was worth the candle. After taking Argentan, Patton told Haislip, proceed to Falaise, make contact with the Canadians, and close the pocket.

But when Patton informed Bradley, he told Patton: "Nothing doing. You are not to go beyond Argentan."

Bradley's reasons were in part that Haislip's corps was strung out on a forty-mile line, and that Lawton Collins's 7th Corps, which he had ordered to shore up Haislip's left, could not arrive for a couple days.

But Bradley's principal aim was to avoid offending his Allies.

"Falaise was a long-sought British objective," he wrote, "and, for them, a matter of immense prestige. If Patton's patrols grabbed Falaise, it would be an arrogant slap in the face at a time when we clearly needed to build confidence in the Canadian army."

Montgomery instructed his chief of staff, Francis de Guingand, to "tell Bradley they [Haislip's corps] ought to go back." De Guingand wrote after the war that if Montgomery had invited the Americans to cross the army group boundary, they would have closed the Germans in a trap. But Bradley and Eisenhower didn't ask, either.

As Haislip reached the edge of Argentan, Germans reinforced the shoulders there and at Falaise, and nonessential elements began escaping through the gap. The field divisions were still in the pocket.

Montgomery ordered the Canadians to push on and take Falaise on August 14. But the effort got nowhere. To assist, he directed Dempsey's British 2nd Army to attack at the same time from the northwest—a move Bradley and Eisenhower likened to squeezing a tube of toothpaste from the bottom with no cap on. The effect could only press the Germans out of the pocket, not hem them inside where they could be destroyed.

Meanwhile, Bradley planned a new turning movement to block the Germans who had already escaped. He ordered an advance by 3rd Army to the northeast—Haislip's 15th Corps (cut to two divisions) to Dreux, fifty miles west of Paris; Walton Walker's 20th Corps to Chartres, fifty miles southwest of Paris; and Gilbert R. Cook's 12th Corps to Orléans, seventy miles south of Paris. The idea was to wheel around the supposedly retreating Germans. The operation got under way on August 14.

Bradley's shifting of Patton's entire army away from the pocket weakened the Argentan shoulder and made it easier for the Germans to keep the gap open. Bradley recognized his error on August 15, and he rushed to Patton's headquarters to call off the wheeling movement. But it was too late. Patton's three corps were almost at their destinations. Even so, on Bradley's orders, Patton stopped at the three cities.

The next day, August 16, German panzers hit 90th Infantry Division, now guarding the Argentan shoulder, a severe blow, but the division—which had performed poorly so far—held. On the same day the Canadian army finally captured Falaise, despite heavy aerial bombardment by Allied planes that inflicted 500 casualties on the Canadians and Poles.

But there was still a thirteen-mile gap between Falaise and Argentan, and it was swarming with Germans trying to get out. Montgomery suggested a new place to close the gap: Chambois, eight miles northeast of Argentan, and thirteen miles southeast of Falaise. Montgomery ordered Crerar to turn the Canadians through Trun to Chambois. The only forces Bradley had were in a provisional corps he set up to guard Argentan—90th Division, Leclerc's French armored division, and the untried 80th Infantry Division. Bradley called Leonard T. Gerow, from 1st Army, to command it.

The Falaise pocket now stretched east-west about forty miles, and was from eleven to fifteen miles wide. About fourteen divisions, at least 100,000 men, were inside. Roads were clogged, Allied aircraft struck at anything that moved, Allied artillery could reach any objective observers could point out. There was a desperate shortage of fuel, units were mixed up, communications erratic.

On the morning of August 15, Field Marshal von Kluge traveled toward the front. Four hours later he vanished. Search parties could not find him. No messages came in. Hitler was suspicious. Kluge had associated with some of the conspirators of the July 20 putsch, and the timing was incriminating. Just that day Americans and French (6th Army Group under Jacob L. Devers) had invaded the French Riviera on the Mediterranean (Operation Dragoon), and were moving quickly north against minuscule opposition. Hitler suspected Kluge was trying to surrender German forces in Normandy, or might be trying to negotiate a deal.

Around 10 P.M., Kluge turned up at the headquarters of Josef (Sepp) Dietrich of the 5th Panzer Army. Where had he been? He had spent the day in a ditch. An Allied plane had struck his auto and knocked out his radio. So many aircraft were about he had to remain where he was. This explanation, though truthful, did not allay Hitler's suspicions.

At 2 A.M., August 16, Kluge sent a message to Alfred Jodl, Hitler's operations chief, recommending evacuation at once. Only at 4:40 P.M. did Hitler authorize full withdrawal.

His decision stemmed from the invasion of southern France. Only skeleton German elements were now in this region, and were too weak even to smash French Resistance forces. Hitler decided to abandon southern France and Normandy. He hoped to mass forces in the Vosges Mountains west of the Rhine, and form a new line. The decision meant that 100,000 Germans around the Bay of Biscay in southwestern France had to start moving, mostly on foot, through the French interior toward Dijon. Harassed by Resistance groups and by Allied aircraft, many of these soldiers finally crossed the Loire and surrendered to the Americans.

Kluge sent out instructions for partial withdrawal. Starting that night, westernmost units pulled back to the Orne River (about ten miles west of Falaise). On the following night they were to cross to the eastern bank. Since the Germans had to move through the three-mile space between Le Bourg-St.-Léonard and Chambois, Kluge ordered the Americans driven off the ridge at Le Bourg, which gave observation over the route. After a back-and-forth struggle with 90th Division, the Germans seized the ridge on the morning of August 17.

Meanwhile Bradley met with Hodges and Patton to plan future movements. Bradley removed Patton's halt order and directed the two American armies to establish a line from Argentan, through Chambois and Dreux to the Seine.

Hodges's army was to seize Chambois and Trun and make contact with the British and Canadians. As divisions disengaged on the west with the retreat of the Germans, they were to swing around to the east between Argentan and Dreux. Meanwhile Patton's army was to seize Mantes, thirty miles downstream from Paris, and prevent the Germans from escaping.

Patton wanted to implement his old idea of blocking the German retreat: a broad sweep by three corps down the Seine to the sea. Patton's plan was by far the best proposed, and it would have eliminated the most capable and experienced German force in the west. Units still in the Pas de Calais, the Low Countries, and the south of France were less powerful altogether than the two German armies in Normandy. With these gone, the Allies could have rolled into Germany against feeble opposition.

But it was not to be. Martin Blumenson wrote: "Although the battle of Normandy remained unfinished, the two leading Allied commanders, Montgomery and Bradley, were already ignoring the main chance of ending the war. Prematurely, they looked ahead to a triumphal march to Germany."

Since Gerow decided he couldn't move on Chambois till August 18, Montgomery told Crerar it was essential to take Trun and go on four miles to Chambois. Both of Crerar's armored divisions, Canadian and Polish, jumped off on the afternoon of August 17, but met bitter resistance. By day's end they were still two miles from Trun.

Field Marshal Walther Model, who had achieved much success in Russia, arrived in Normandy early on August 17 to replace Kluge. That night the Germans in the pocket withdrew across the Orne. The operation went smoothly. During the early morning of August 18, forty-five cargo aircraft delivered gasoline to the forces in the pocket. The Germans planned to move the night of August 18 from the Orne across the Argentan-Falaise highway.

When Gerow's advance on Chambois commenced, he asked little of the French 2nd Armored Division, only using its artillery to help 80th Division seize the town of Argentan. Leclerc had already loudly signified to anyone who would listen that he wanted to liberate Paris, little else. The 80th, in its first fight, made no progress. The 90th Division and the Canadians both got within a couple miles of Chambois against desperate German resistance to keep the exit open.

That night the Germans renewed their withdrawal. Allied artillery fire rained down, but most got away to high ground just east of the Argentan-Falaise highway. The German pocket now occupied an area six by seven miles. A bolt hole about three or four miles wide remained open.

At midnight August 18 Model took command of the theater. Kluge, returning to Germany by automobile and, afraid he had been implicated in the July 20 murder plot, swallowed poison and died. Meanwhile the Germans in the pocket strained all their efforts to get out.

At last at 7:20 P.M., August 19, a company of the 90th Division met a Polish detachment in the midst of the burning village of Chambois. The gap had finally been closed. But the barrier was porous, and the Germans continued to flow through for two more days. Most got out.

⊕          ⊕          ⊕

On August 20, 5th Armored Division from Haislip's 15th Corps commenced a slow push through fog and rain from Mantes down the left or near bank of the Seine, assisted on the west by two divisions of 19th Corps. This was not Patton's sweep to the sea, but a laborious process aimed at clearing the river of the enemy. The Americans hit solid resistance and made little progress.

The next day, Montgomery and RAF Air Chief Marshal Sir Trafford Leigh-Mallory, in charge of Allied air support of the invasion, came to an astonishing conclusion: the Seine bridges had all been destroyed, the Germans were unable to cross, so the Allies didn't need to make any more aerial attacks on the river—despite the fact that the Germans had been moving back and forth across the Seine throughout the Normandy campaign. Thus, as the Germans streamed toward the Seine crossings, they were not harassed by Allied aircraft. Virtually all the Germans got across the river—it was not impassable after all. Using back roads and traveling at night, most of the Germans reached the frontier and began preparing a new defensive line.

Meanwhile on August 20, George Patton, aggravated at Bradley and Montgomery for letting the Germans slip through their fingers, turned his sights eastward—toward the final liberation of France and the invasion of Germany. He ordered an immediate, open-throttled advance on Melun, Montereau, and Sens, all towns a few miles southeast of Paris, using 20th Corps under Walton Walker, and 12th Corps, now under Manton Eddy (Gilbert Cook had high blood pressure). He told Eddy to forget about his flanks and advance fifty miles a day.

Walker's tanks got to Melun, Montereau, and Fontainebleau on the upper Seine on August 21, and kept going. Eddy liberated Sens and quickly moved on forty miles and captured Troyes. Everywhere the bridges were still intact, opposition nil.

In his diary, Patton wrote: "We have, at this time, the greatest chance to win the war ever presented. If they will let me move on with three corps, two up and one back, on the line of Metz-Nancy-Épinal, we can be in Germany in ten days. . . . It is such a sure thing that I fear these blind moles [Montgomery, Bradley] don't see it."

Actually, Bradley did accept Patton's plan, on August 25, and told him he could go east toward Metz and Strasbourg. The problem was not Bradley but availability of gasoline.

✠        ✠        ✠

With the Germans withdrawing from the lower Seine and Manton Eddy's corps already eighty-five miles southeast of Paris at Troyes, the French capital was ripe for the picking. However important the liberation of the City of Light was to the world, it was virtually empty of German combat troops, and Bradley wanted to bypass it. But on August 19 the Resistance rose in Paris, and challenged the German commander, Dietrich von Choltitz, who had received orders from Hitler to defend the city to the end, then destroy it. Immense pressure developed to get Allied troops into the city, and Bradley succumbed, sending in Leclerc's French 2nd Armored Division, followed by the U.S. 4th Infantry Division. When Hitler learned that Allied troops were entering the capital, he asked his staff: *"Brennt Paris?"* Is Paris burning? Choltitz did not burn Paris but signed an armistice with the Resistance.

The movement of the Frenchmen to the city set off wild celebrations, and, as Bradley remembered it, "Leclerc's men, nearly overwhelmed with wine and women, rolled and reeled into Paris on August 25." Two days later, Eisenhower, Bradley, and Gerow met Charles de Gaulle at Paris police headquarters, where de Gaulle had already set up his base. Eisenhower allowed Leclerc's division to remain in Paris to give de Gaulle a show of political strength, but when de Gaulle demanded a victory parade, Eisenhower resolved to make it clear that de Gaulle had received Paris by the force of Allied arms. He ordered the U.S. 28th Infantry Division to parade down the Champs-Elysées on August 29—and keep right on going eastward into action. Bradley remembered it a bit differently. He had refused to let Leclerc's division take part, he wrote, because Leclerc's men "had disappeared into the back alleys, brothels, and bistros."

✠          ✠          ✠

The senior Allied commanders had been talking about how to defeat Germany as fast as possible. Montgomery wanted both army groups to advance northeast in a "solid mass" of forty divisions toward Antwerp, Brussels, Aachen, and the Ruhr—with himself in command.

Bradley favored a twofold advance, Montgomery's army group northward and his army group northeastward through Nancy and Metz toward the Saar industrial region and central Germany. This was better tank country than Montgomery's route, which led over many rivers and canals. However, Montgomery's route lay through the Pas de Calais, where the V-1s were being fired on London, and the rumor was that the V-2s were about to be launched from there. Much of Allied airpower was challenging the V-1s instead of striking at German synthetic oil production, which was a major factor in Hitler's ability to continue the war. Also, Antwerp and Rotterdam, two great ports, were in this direction, and the Allies badly needed ship berths.

As a consequence, Eisenhower decided—over Patton's bitter opposition—that Hodges's 1st Army with nine divisions, plus a new airborne corps of three divisions under Matthew Ridgway, be allocated to

Montgomery, giving him twenty-five divisions, leaving Patton with fifteen divisions to advance toward the Saar.

Divisions were not the whole issue. A severe shortage of supplies was developing, since few ports were open, and, as the armies rushed toward Germany, distances increased by the day. Eisenhower allocated the lion's share to Montgomery. Hodges, for example, got 5,000 tons of supplies a day, Patton 2,000 tons.

Both the northern and the eastern thrusts commenced at once. By August 31 spearheads of Patton's army crossed the Meuse River at Verdun, and the next day patrols pushed unopposed to the Moselle River near Metz, thirty-five miles farther east. They were barely thirty miles from the Saar on the German frontier, and fewer than a hundred miles from the Rhine River. But Patton's main body had run out of gasoline, and did not move up to the Moselle till September 5. By that time the Germans had scraped together five weak divisions to hold the river line. Patton became stuck in an attack on the fortified city of Metz and nearby points, and got no farther.

Meantime the spearhead of Montgomery's British 2nd Army swept into Brussels on September 3, and the next day another armored force raced on to Antwerp and captured the docks undamaged. Antwerp also was fewer than a hundred miles from the Rhine and entry into the Ruhr, Germany's industrial heartland.

At this moment, the Germans had nothing to oppose Montgomery. As Basil H. Liddell Hart wrote: "Rarely in any war has there been such an opportunity." But here Montgomery failed. His spearhead paused to "refit, refuel, and rest," resumed its advance on September 7, but pushed only eighteen miles farther, to the Meuse-Escaut Canal, where the desperate defense of a few German parachute troops halted it.

By mid-September the Germans had thickened their defenses all along the front but were not strong anywhere. Montgomery, instead of intensifying a direct drive eastward through Belgium and southern Holland, now mounted a huge fourteen-division thrust northward (Operation Market-Garden) on September 17 to get over the Rhine at Arnhem, Holland, using the recently formed 1st Allied Airborne Army to clear the path. His aim, not approved by Eisenhower, was an end run around the Ruhr and a direct strike at Berlin.

But the massive rivers running through Holland imposed severe barriers, and British tanks had to follow a single causeway from Antwerp to Arnhem. The Germans checked the thrust before it reached its goal. A large part of the British 1st Airborne Division dropped at Arnhem—"a bridge too far" for the rest of the Allies to reach, as described in Cornelius Ryan's book of the same name. Here the British paras were cut off and forced to surrender, a struggle that became legendary for its heroism.

The failure of both Montgomery and Patton to breach the West Wall and get into the heart of Germany in September 1944 has been the center of a controversy that has raged ever since. Both sides claimed they could have won the war if only the other had not got the necessary gasoline.

Patton, when his fuel supplies were petering out, rushed into Bradley's headquarters "bellowing like a bull" and roared: "To hell with Hodges and Monty. We'll win your goddam war if you'll keep 3rd Army moving." Montgomery opposed any diversion of supplies to Patton, and his complaints became stronger after his thrust at Arnhem miscarried.

The truth is messier. German General Siegfried Westphal, who took over as chief of staff for the western front on September 5, wrote that the entire German line "was so full of gaps that it did not deserve this name. Until the middle of October, the enemy could have broken through at any point he liked with ease, and would then have been able to cross the Rhine and thrust deep into Germany almost unhindered."

A number of mistakes occurred. Patton attacked Metz and Nancy, when they should have been bypassed, and his forces should have swung north to Luxembourg and Bitburg, where there were few Germans. This, General Günther Blumentritt reported, would have resulted in the collapse of German forces on the front.

Montgomery's greatest single failure was his pause from September 4 to 7 after reaching Brussels and Antwerp, giving German paratroopers just enough time to organize a defense. The fault, wrote John North, official historian of the 21st Army Group, was a "war-is-won" attitude. Little sense of urgency prevailed among commanders during a vital two-week period in mid-September, and among the troops there was a strong inclination to go slow and avoid being killed.

Montgomery's lack of drive at this critical point illustrates that the best chance to finish the war quickly was lost when Patton's gasoline was shut off at the end of August, and he was a hundred miles closer to the Rhine than the British. He, far more than Montgomery, was capable of exploiting opportunity. Yet, as Westphal pointed out, a breakthrough almost anywhere still could have succeeded till mid-October, and neither Patton, Bradley, nor Montgomery saw it.

✠     ✠     ✠

Meanwhile on the eastern front, the Germans had experienced nothing but disaster. By January 1944, the Red Army had twice the men and tanks as the German army. The only possibility for Germany to avoid total defeat was immediate withdrawal to the 1941 frontier and construction of a deep mine-strewn defensive line studded with antitank guns, advocated by Erwin Rommel. Heinz Guderian and Erich von Manstein recommended a similar approach, but Adolf Hitler rejected any retreat not actually forced on him by the Red Army, and on March 30 ousted Manstein. Consequently, throughout 1944, German forces in the east conducted one pointless defensive stand and one retreat after another.

By the end of the year, the Soviets were on the Vistula River opposite Warsaw, had surrounded Budapest, driven the Germans out of southeastern Europe and all but a small part of the Baltic states, and forced Finland, Romania, Bulgaria, and Hungary out of the war. The Germans had lost a million men. As 1945 began, the Soviets were poised for the final assault on the Third Reich.

# 23 THE BATTLE OF THE BULGE

ON SEPTEMBER 16, 1944, AS WESTERN ALLIED FORCES WERE CLOSING AGAINST the West Wall or Siegfried line, Adolf Hitler met with his closest military advisers at his *Wolfsschanze*—Wolf's Lair—in East Prussia.

Alfred Jodl, Hitler's operations chief, reported that German troops withdrawing from southern France were forming a new line in the Vosges Mountains and on old forts in northeastern France. Other Germans were building new lines in Holland or falling back from Belgium into the West Wall.

There was one place of special concern: the mountainous, heavily forested Ardennes of eastern Belgium and northern Luxembourg. Here Americans were attacking, and the Germans had almost nothing to deter them.

Hitler sat erect and ordered Jodl to stop. After a long pause, Hitler announced: "I have made a momentous decision. I shall go over to the offensive, that is to say here, out of the Ardennes, with the objective Antwerp."

The Ardennes: the same region through which Hitler had sent his panzers in 1940, and had defeated France and thrown the British off the Continent in six weeks. The French and British hadn't thought the blow would come through there in 1940. Perhaps the Americans would be equally blind in 1944.

With this decision, made at the nadir of German fortunes in the west, Adolf Hitler set in motion a campaign that was a stunning surprise to Allied commanders, on a scale beyond their imagination. It was to be the greatest battle ever fought by Americans, involving more than a million men, precipitating a supreme crisis, and demonstrating the most telling failure in history of American military intelligence.

Hitler reasoned that a swift and overwhelming strike at Antwerp, a hundred air miles away, would cut off the British and Canadian armies in the Netherlands. This would compel them to surrender, ending Britain's participation in the war. The U.S. 1st and 9th Armies, also north of the Ardennes, would be trapped as well. The United States, left with half its army in Europe and fearful of Communist hordes sweeping in from the Soviet Union, might conclude a separate peace. Hitler then could turn all his resources against the Russians, and stop their advance. Hitler and the Nazi regime would survive.

It was a desperation move, betting everything on a single throw of the dice. Yet if Adolf Hitler continued on his present course, he and his regime would perish in short order. He had just enough strength left to make one final effort to alter the balance of power.

Hitler had faith that chance could bring fortuitous circumstances. His greatest hero was Frederick the Great of Prussia, who had held on against impossible odds in the Seven Years War 1757–1763 until the empress of Russia died and the coalition against him evaporated. If Hitler could seize Antwerp and destroy four British, Canadian, and American armies, it could happen again.

Hitler was already planning for the offensive on September 1, when he called Field Marshal Gerd von Rundstedt, stiff, formal and seventy years old, to his headquarters and asked him to return as commander in chief west. Rundstedt, as Charles MacDonald wrote, "was to most Germans the paragon of all that was good and right about the German officers corps." Hitler disliked him intensely, in part because he represented the class and elegance that Hitler lacked, and in part because, in private, he referred to Hitler as "the Corporal," the Fuehrer's rank in World War I.

Hitler needed a figurehead around whom Germans could rally, and Rundstedt, true to his soldier's creed of loyalty, agreed to serve. Hitler didn't tell Rundstedt what he had in mind. The field marshal was to defend in front of the West Wall as long as possible, then fall back on it. Everything depended on this defense, Hitler stressed. There was insufficient strength to strike offensively.

Having lied to his commander, Hitler ordered his propaganda chief,

Joseph Goebbels, to find somewhere the manpower to create fifteen new divisions with a new name, *Volksgrenadier*, and reinforce thirty-five existing ones. Goebbels did so: seventeen-year-olds, men in their mid-forties, transfers from the navy, Luftwaffe, and rear services, drafts from garrisons in Scandinavia. Hitler withdrew four SS panzer divisions from the line in the west to be refitted, and created a new headquarters, 6th Panzer Army, commanded by Josef (Sepp) Dietrich, an old crony, a bullish former butcher and sergeant in the First World War. Dietrich was hard driving, had little education, and relied on a brilliant assistant, Fritz Kraemer, for military advice.

✠          ✠          ✠

On the Allied side, there was no idea whatsoever of a threat through the Ardennes. Troy Middleton's 8th Corps was covering an eighty-mile stretch, most of the region. Two of his four divisions were raw and new, two recuperating from heavy losses in battles elsewhere. Talking with Middleton, Omar Bradley said: "Even if the German were to bust through all the way to the Meuse, he wouldn't find a thing in the Ardennes to make it worth his while."

Eisenhower and Bradley were more concerned with the failure of an offensive Bradley had undertaken to smash through to the Rhine, then swing north and encircle the Ruhr. Patton's 3rd Army was to drive through the Saar to Frankfurt, while, north of the Ardennes, Courtney Hodges's 1st Army and the new 9th Army under William Simpson were to thrust eastward from Aachen to Cologne and Bonn. Patton gained Metz on December 13, but was stopped cold at the Siegfried line short of the Saar. In the effort, Patton's army lost 27,000 men.

The 1st and 9th Armies tried to cross the Roer River and the Hürtgen Forest a few miles to the east of Aachen. Six American divisions were chewed up (35,000 men lost) in bitter close-in attrition battles in and around those dark woodlands in three months beginning September 12.

Meanwhile Jake Devers's 6th Army Group (U.S. 7th and French 1st Armies) reached Strasbourg and the Rhine on the east by December 15. But across the Rhine lay the Black Forest, no acceptable route to the heart of German power.

✠          ✠          ✠

The key to Hitler's plan was to strike at a time when bad weather would endure for a week, keeping Allied aircraft out of the sky for that period. He figured it would take his panzers that long to reach Antwerp.

The major obstacle was the Meuse River, just beyond the Ardennes. The first wave of tanks had to seize bridgeheads over it quickly. Then a second wave of panzers was to strike off for Antwerp, while infantry divisions fanned off north and south to protect the flanks of the salient.

The final plan was for the offensive (code-named *Herbstnebel*, or Autumn Mist) to be launched by twenty divisions, seven of them panzers, along a sixty-mile front from Monschau, twenty miles southeast of Aachen, to Echternach. Sepp Dietrich's 6th Panzer Army was to deliver the main effort—or *Schwerpunkt*—from Monschau to Losheim, fifteen miles south, exactly the place Erwin Rommel's 7th Panzer Division had driven through in the 1940 campaign. Dietrich was to cross the Meuse south of Liège, then head for Antwerp, while anchoring his northern flank on the east-west Albert Canal.

On Dietrich's left or south, Hasso von Manteuffel's 5th Panzer Army was to attack through and south of St. Vith, cross the Meuse at Namur, then wheel northwest, bypassing Brussels, and guard Dietrich's flank.

South of Manteuffel, Erich Brandenberger's 7th Army, primarily infantry, was to attack on either side of Echternach, move west, and peel off divisions to block movement from the south.

A plan for a converging attack by 15th Army around Aachen had to be dropped, since troops had to be sent east to meet Soviet pressure. Consequently, Hitler could not block the Allies from bringing down reserves from the north.

Nevertheless, if all went well, more than a million Allied troops would be surrounded. But how such a huge army was to be defeated, even if encircled, no one really knew.

Secrecy was mandatory. Hitler prohibited transmission by telephone, telegraph, or radio. The few let in on the plan signed a pledge of secrecy on the pain of death. Rundstedt was not brought into the picture until the late stages.

On October 21, Hitler called in Otto Skorzeny, the officer who had rescued Benito Mussolini from his captors in 1943. Hitler promoted him to SS lieutenant colonel and told him to form a special force to go in advance of the offensive. In the first wave, a company of English-speaking commandos, wearing American field jackets over their German uniforms and riding in American jeeps, was to rush ahead, cut telephone lines, turn signposts to misdirect reserves, and hang red ribbons to imply roads were mined. Second, a panzer brigade of 2,000 men in American dress was to drive through and seize the bridges over the Meuse.

The second wave never materialized. Army command failed to provide the American equipment needed. But the first wave had astonishing success. Forty jeeps got through, and all but eight returned. The few Germans who were captured created the impression that many sabotage bands were roving behind the front. MPs and other soldiers stopped every vehicle, questioning drivers to see if they were German. Traffic tie-ups created chaos, and hundreds of innocent Americans were arrested.

General Bradley himself had to prove his identity three times: "The first time by identifying Springfield as the capital of Illinois (my questioner held out for Chicago); the second time by locating the guard between the center and tackle on a line of scrimmage; the third time by naming the then current spouse of a blonde named Betty Grable. Grable stopped me but the sentry did not. Pleased at having stumped me, he nevertheless passed me on."

✠     ✠     ✠

Rundstedt was appalled when he learned of the offensive. "Available forces were far too small for such an extremely ambitious plan," he said. "No soldier believed that the aim of reaching Antwerp was really practicable."

If the Germans crossed the Meuse, both flanks would be vulnerable to a major counterstrike. All that would happen, Rundstedt predicted, would be a deep salient or bulge into the line, costly and indecisive. Field Marshal Walther Model, commander of Army Group B, shared Rundstedt's pessimism, but neither could get Hitler to change his plans.

To direct the offensive personally, Hitler moved his headquarters from East Prussia to his *Adlerhorst*—Eagle's Aerie—in the Taunus hills east of the Rhine near Bad Nauheim.

Hitler designated twenty-eight divisions for the offensive, twenty in the first wave with 250,000 men, a remarkable figure given Germany's defeats. The new soldiers were green, of course, without the thorough training of the splendid troops who had swept through the Ardennes in 1940. But there was a hard core of combat veterans and tough noncommissioned officers to stiffen the recruits, plus a number of officers seasoned in battle. The most serious problem was motor transport. No division had more than 80 percent of the vehicles it needed. Fuel was in short supply, and most stockpiles were east of the Rhine.

Even so, Hitler had assembled a thousand tanks for the opening wave in seven panzer divisions, and 450 for the follow-up force. Tactical aircraft were the weakest element: Hermann Göring found only 900, half the number the Luftwaffe deployed in 1940, and a fifth the number of bombers the Allies could throw into the battle. Göring delivered this quantity only on one day—after the ground battle had been decided.

There were many signs of a German buildup opposite the Ardennes in the German Schnee Eifel Mountains, duly reported by air reconnaissance and by Ultra intercepts. But American intelligence (G-2) officers at all levels failed to draw the correct conclusion. They detected German armor but thought it would be used to counterattack the Allied drive toward the Rhine and Ruhr. G-2 saw troop movements in the Eifels as efforts to meet American offensives north and south of the Ardennes. Finally, they believed fuel was so short and troop losses were so great that the German army was in no condition to mount an offensive.

When the attack opened, Bradley was utterly confounded. "Just where in hell has this sonuvabitch gotten all his strength?" he asked his chief of staff, Leven Allen, at 12th Army Group's tactical headquarters at Luxembourg City. And Eisenhower, who wrote that "I was immediately convinced that this was no local attack," nevertheless waited till the evening of the second day to alert the two divisions he held in reserve, the 82nd and 101st Airborne. Only then did they start moving to the scene.

⊹          ⊹          ⊹

Hitler set the attack date for December 16, 1944. Bad weather was predicted for days ahead, keeping Allied aircraft from flying. Snow covered the ground. Hitler originally ordered a three-hour preliminary bombardment, but Manteuffel argued that a short, concentrated preparation would achieve the same effect while lessening the Americans' alert. And rather than attack at 10 A.M., which Hitler planned, leaving fewer than

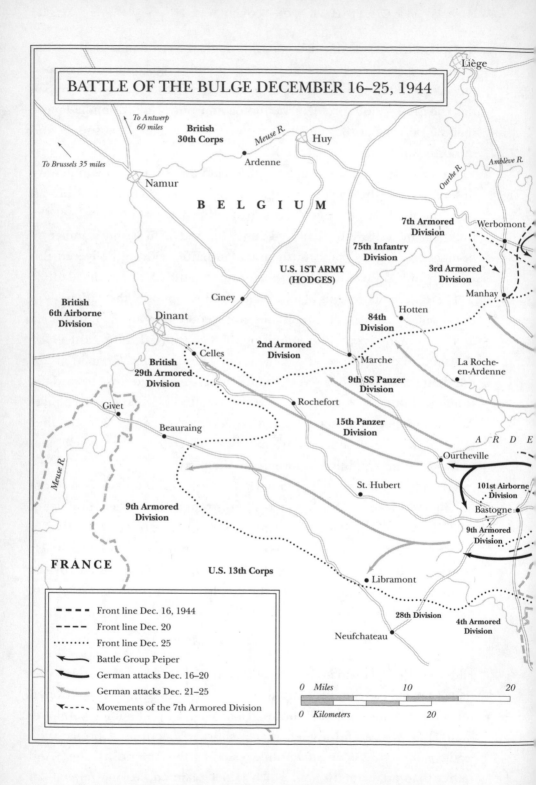

# BATTLE OF THE BULGE DECEMBER 16–25, 1944

*To Antwerp 60 miles*

**British 30th Corps**

Meuse R.

Huy

*To Brussels 35 miles*

Ardenne

Namur

Our the R.

Amblève R.

Liège

B E L G I U M

**7th Armored Division**

Werbomont

**75th Infantry Division**

**U.S. 1ST ARMY (HODGES)**

**3rd Armored Division**

Ciney

Manhay

**British 6th Airborne Division**

Dinant

Hotten

**84th Division**

Celles

**2nd Armored Division**

Marche

La Roche-en-Ardenne

**British 29th Armored Division**

**9th SS Panzer Division**

Givet

Rochefort

**15th Panzer Division**

A R D E

Beauraing

Ourtheville

St. Hubert

**101st Airborne Division**

**9th Armored Division**

Bastogne

**9th Armored Division**

**U.S. 13th Corps**

F R A N C E

Libramont

Meuse R.

**28th Division**

**4th Armored Division**

Neufchateau

- – – – Front line Dec. 16, 1944
- – – Front line Dec. 20
- ····· Front line Dec. 25
- ← Battle Group Peiper
- ← German attacks Dec. 16–20
- ← German attacks Dec. 21–25
- ◄–·–· Movements of the 7th Armored Division

0   *Miles*        10        20

0   *Kilometers*        20

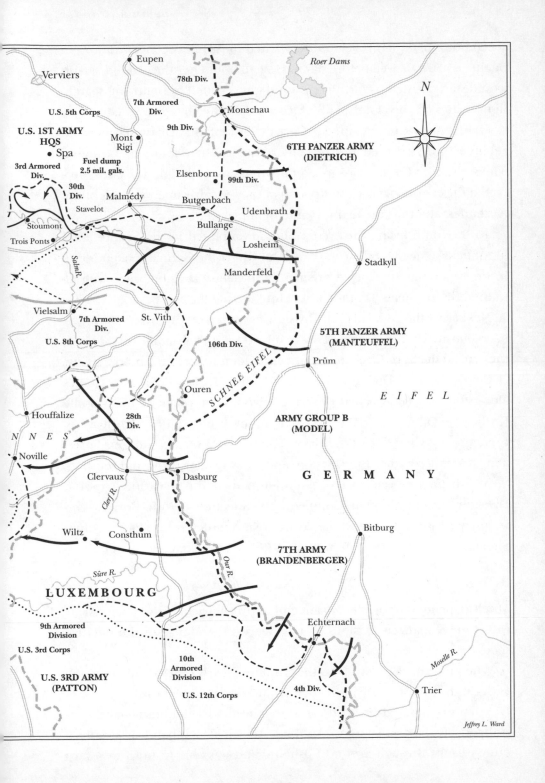

Eupen

Verviers

Roer Dams

*N*

78th Div.

U.S. 5th Corps

7th Armored Div.

Monschau

9th Div.

6TH PANZER ARMY
(DIETRICH)

U.S. 1ST ARMY
HQS

Spa

Mont Rigi

Fuel dump
2.5 mil. gals.

Elsenborn

99th Div.

3rd Armored Div.

30th Div.

Malmédy

Butgenbach

Stavelot

Udenbrath

Stoumont

Bullange

Trois Ponts

Losheim

Salm R.

Manderfeld

Stadkyll

Vielsalm

St. Vith

5TH PANZER ARMY
(MANTEUFFEL)

7th Armored Div.

106th Div.

U.S. 8th Corps

SCHNEE EIFEL

Prüm

Ouren

*EIFEL*

Houffalize

28th Div.

ARMY GROUP B
(MODEL)

*N N E S*

Noville

*G E R M A N Y*

Clervaux

Dasburg

Clerf R.

Bitburg

Wiltz

Consthum

7TH ARMY
(BRANDENBERGER)

Sûre R.

Our R.

**LUXEMBOURG**

Echternach

9th Armored Division

Moselle R.

U.S. 3rd Corps

10th Armored Division

4th Div.

Trier

**U.S. 3RD ARMY
(PATTON)**

U.S. 12th Corps

*Jeffrey L. Ward*

seven hours of daylight, Manteuffel wanted the artillery concentrations to begin at 5:30 A.M., well before dawn. Half an hour later the ground assault would start, assisted by "artificial moonlight" created by bouncing searchlight beams off the clouds. Hitler accepted all the changes.

On the American side, the 5th Corps's 99th Infantry Division, a new but reliable force, covered the region from Monshau south to Losheim. There the 14th Cavalry Group, equipped mainly with light weapons, protected the "Losheim Gap" itself—one of the few fairly open regions of the Ardennes, and thus the main avenue of approach.

To the south facing the West Wall and emplaced in the Schnee Eifel Mountains some five miles east of the Our River (the German-Luxembourg frontier) was the 8th Corps's green 106th Infantry Division, filled with ill-trained replacements assigned just before leaving the States.

Next came the 28th Infantry Division, a veteran outfit refitting after losing 5,000 men in the Hürtgen Forest. It held a twenty-five-mile sector along the Our to the Sûre River, about fifteen miles north of Luxembourg City.

Below the 28th Division, the 4th Infantry Division held twenty miles along the river (now called the Sauer) from Echternach to the Moselle River, then along the Moselle to a point twelve miles southeast of Luxembourg City. The 4th Division had suffered in the Hürtgen Forest almost as much as the 28th Division, and likewise was resting and refitting.

In 8th Corps reserve, Troy Middleton held the new 9th Armored Division, except Combat Command B, attached to 5th Corps's 2nd Infantry Division. In the whole corps area, Middleton had 242 medium Sherman tanks and 182 self-propelled (SP) guns or tank destroyers.

✠      ✠      ✠

Much depended upon the advance of Sepp Dietrich's 6th Panzer Army with four SS panzer divisions. It was nearest the Meuse in the decisive sector.

When the attack burst across the front lines early on December 16, the U.S. 99th Infantry Division below Monschau successfully blocked Dietrich's right-hand or northern punch around Udenbrath—and thus stopped his shortest route to Antwerp. Dietrich's left-hand or southern punch broke through around Losheim, and was able to push westward over the next two days against tough American resistance around Butgenbach and Elsenborn. But the 99th Division's resistance denied the Germans the northern shoulder they had planned to seize, and provided a base to press against them later.

Meanwhile 1st SS Panzer Division drove forward in an effort to outflank Liège from the south. The leading column, a battle group under SS Lieutenant Colonel Joachim Peiper with a hundred tanks, pressed forward, aiming for the Meuse crossing at Huy. At Malmédy on the way, it gained ignominy by massacring eighty-six American prisoners, as well as a number of Belgian civilians.

Peiper's group halted just east of Stavelot on December 18, but didn't grab the bridges over the Amblève there. Peiper also didn't go for a huge supply dump just to the north with 2.5 million gallons of fuel, or for Spa, a few miles farther on, where Hodges's 1st Army headquarters was located. American reinforcements reached Stavelot during the night and blew the bridges over the Amblève in Peiper's face the next day.

Peiper tried to detour down the river valley but Americans checked him at Stoumont, about six miles farther on. Peiper now learned that he was well ahead of the rest of 6th Panzer Army.

On Manteuffel's 5th Panzer Army front the attack got a good start. Storm battalions infiltrated into the American front, opening the way for the tanks, which advanced at 4 P.M. on December 16 and pressed forward in the dark with the help of "artificial moonlight."

Manteuffel's forces broke through in the Schnee Eifel against the 106th Infantry Division and 14th Cavalry Group. These forces covered the important road junction of St. Vith, some ten miles to the west. Two infantry divisions and a regiment of tanks of Walter Lucht's 66th Corps surrounded two regiments of the 106th and forced at least 8,000 men to surrender.

Farther south two panzer corps, Walter Krüger's 58th and Heinrich von Lüttwitz's 47th, attacked westward. The 58th crossed the Our River and drove to Houffalize, aiming at a crossing of the Meuse between Ardenne and Namur. The 47th was to capture the key road center of Bastogne—where six roads came together—and drive on to the Meuse south of Namur.

Outposts of the U.S. 28th Division delayed but could not halt the Germans crossing the Our, and by the night of December 17 they were approaching Houffalize and Bastogne—and the north-south road between them, which the Germans needed to develop their westward sweep.

In the extreme south, the 5th Parachute Division of Brandenberger's 7th Army got to Wiltz, a dozen miles west of the Our, but the 28th Division's right wing gave ground slowly, and 9th Armored and 4th Infantry Divisions checked the advance after it had gone four miles. By December 19, the southern shoulder of the German attack was being held firmly—and Patton's 3rd Army to the south would shortly be reinforcing it.

Meanwhile Manteuffel's pressure on St. Vith and Bastogne increased. The Germans made their first small attack on St. Vith on December 17. The next day the bulk of the U.S. 7th Armored Division arrived. Outlying villages fell to German assaults, while panzers outflanked St. Vith north and south.

By December 18, Lüttwitz's 47th Corps was closing on Bastogne with two armored divisions (2nd and Panzer Lehr), plus the 26th Volksgrenadier Division. But a combat command of the U.S. 9th Armored Division, plus engineers, had arrived to help defend the crossroads, and the 101st Airborne Division under Anthony C. McAuliffe reached Bastogne on the morning of December 19.

After the Germans were unable to rush the town against fierce defenses, the two panzer divisions swung around both sides of Bastogne, leaving the 26th Division with a tank group to reduce it. Thus Bastogne was cut off on December 20.

After finally realizing this was not just a small spoiling attack, Bradley ordered 10th Armored Division north and sent 7th Armored and 30th Infantry Divisions south. Thus, more than 60,000 fresh troops were moving, while 180,000 more were to be diverted over the next eight days.

The 30th Division struck Peiper's battle group, grabbed part of Stavelot, and, with the help of powerful blows by fighter-bombers, broke Peiper's links with the remainder of 6th Panzer Army. By December 19, Peiper, desperately short of fuel, found that the 82nd Airborne Division, plus some tanks, had arrived, turning the balance against him. The remainder of Dietrich's SS panzer forces were still stuck in the rear, with too few roads—and these interdicted by Allied aircraft—to get forward.

Peiper's battle group began to retreat on December 24 on foot, abandoning its tanks and other vehicles.

To the south, the U.S. 3rd and 7th Armored Divisions had barred Manteuffel's advance westward from St. Vith, where a strong German attack finally drove out the Americans with heavy losses. But a huge traffic jam permitted remnants of the 106th and 7th Armored Divisions to get away, and hindered Manteuffel's advance toward the Meuse.

Two major factors slowed the German advance: mud and shortage of fuel. Only half the artillery could be brought forward due to fuel lack. Foggy weather had favored the Germans on the opening days by keeping Allied aircraft on the ground. But clear skies came back on December 23, and Allied fighters and bombers commenced a terrible pummeling of the German columns.

On December 20 Eisenhower placed Montgomery in charge of all Allied forces north of the Bulge, including the U.S. 1st and 9th Armies. Montgomery brought the British 30th Corps (four divisions) west of the Meuse to guard the bridges.

Gaining command of two American armies was a great coup for Montgomery and a blow to Bradley, not helped when Montgomery arrived at 1st Army headquarters, as one British officer reported, "like Christ come to cleanse the temple." He made things worse at a press conference where he implied that his personal "handling" of the battle had saved the Americans from collapse, when actually he had done practically nothing. Montgomery also spoke of employing the "whole available power" of the British armies—a palpable lie heightened by the fact that he insisted he must "tidy up" the position first, and did not strike from the north until January 3. All the while 3rd Army was counterattacking toward Bastogne—spearheaded by the 4th Armored Division, following Patton's order to "drive like hell."

The 4th Armored, supported by the 26th and 80th Infantry Divisions, collided with the German 5th Parachute Division on the main north-south road. The paratroops had to be driven out of every village and block of woods. However, reconnaissance found there was less opposition on the Neufchâteau-Bastogne road leading northeast, and on December 25 Patton shifted the main attack to this line.

In Bastogne the situation remained critical. Repeated German attacks forced the Americans back, but never overwhelmed them. When Lüttwitz sent a "white flag" party on December 22 calling on the garrison to surrender, General McAuliffe replied: "Nuts!" Subordinate officers, seeing the baffled looks on the Germans' faces, translated it as "Go to hell!"

The next day better weather permitted Allied aircraft to drop supplies to the beleaguered troops. On Christmas Day the Germans made an all-out effort, but failed. Meanwhile the 4th Armored Division fought its way into the town at 4:45 P.M. on December 26. The siege was lifted.

A thin finger of Manteuffel's advance got within four miles of the Meuse, five miles east of Dinant at Celles, on December 24. But that was the high-water mark. The British 30th Corps had moved onto the east bank of the Meuse around Givet and Dinant, and fresh American forces were coming up to help.

Hitler had recognized his hope of capturing Antwerp was an illusion, and had shifted his goal to seizing crossings of the Meuse, releasing the 9th Panzer and 15th Panzergrenadier Divisions from reserve to help Manteuffel clear the approaches to Dinant between Celles and Marche. But the panzers were being severely harassed from the air, and after December 26 none could move during the day.

Meanwhile Lawton Collins's U.S. 7th Corps was converging on the threat. Collins had the 2nd and 3rd Armored Divisions and the 75th and 84th Infantry Divisions, and they slowly gained ground. On Christmas morning they recaptured Celles. The 9th Panzer Division arrived near the village on Christmas evening but could not shake the 2nd Armored Division in front of it.

Sepp Dietrich's 6th Panzer Army to the north tried to assist Manteuffel, but his panzer divisions made little impression on American defenses that now were strongly reinforced, with swarms of fighter-bombers on momentary call to strike anything moving.

Manteuffel wrote that his reserves were at a standstill for lack of fuel just when they were needed.

Hitler wanted to hold the positions in the Bulge, and insisted that Manteuffel capture Bastogne by cutting Patton's Neufchâteau-Bastogne corridor. But German attacks over three days, beginning December 30, failed.

It was obvious to Manteuffel that he could not hold the Bulge without Bastogne and could do nothing against Collins's determined advance on the west. He telephoned Jodl and announced he was moving his forces out of the nose of the salient. But Hitler, as usual, forbade any step back. Instead, he ordered another attack on Bastogne.

To demonstrate how determined he was to have Bastogne, Hitler risked what was left of the Luftwaffe to prevent Allied fighter-bombers from intervening in Manteuffel's efforts. Early on New Year's Day a thousand Focke-Wulf 190 and Messerschmitt 109 fighters came in at rooftop level over twenty-seven Allied airfields in Holland, Belgium, and northeastern France. The Germans destroyed 156 planes, 36 of them American, most of them on the ground or while trying to take off. These were heavy losses, but the Allies could replace them quickly. The Luftwaffe, however, lost 300 planes and as many irreplaceable pilots, the German air force's largest single-day loss in the war. It was the Luftwaffe's death blow.

Having failed to cut the corridor south of Bastogne, Manteuffel now struck from the north astride the Houffalize-Bastogne road, using four depleted and exhausted divisions which, between them, had only fifty-five tanks. The Germans got nowhere, just as Manteuffel had feared. He now pulled the forces off. The threat to Bastogne ended.

At last on January 8, 1945, Hitler agreed to a limited withdrawal from the tip of the Bulge. Inexorably, the retreat continued. By January 28, the German lines were back approximately where they had been when the offensive started.

Among 600,000 Americans eventually involved in the battle of the Bulge, casualties totaled 81,000, of whom 15,000 were captured and 19,000 killed. Among 55,000 British involved, casualties totaled 1,440, of whom 200 were killed. The Germans, employing close to 500,000 men, lost at least 100,000 killed, wounded, or captured. Each side forfeited about 800 tanks, and the Luftwaffe lost a thousand aircraft.

The Americans could make good their losses in short order, the Germans could not replace theirs. All that Adolf Hitler achieved at this terrible cost was to delay the Allied advance in the west by a few weeks. But it actually assured swift success for the Red Army advancing in a renewed drive in the east. In the end, the battle of the Bulge probably speeded up Germany's collapse.

# 24 THE LAST DAYS

THE RED ARMY HAD BEEN STALLED ALONG THE VISTULA RIVER IN POLAND SINCE autumn 1944. Its astonishing advances during the summer had come to a standstill because the vastly overextended Russian supply line finally snapped. Red Army commanders held up the final assault on Nazi Germany until the railways behind the front could be repaired and converted to the Russian wider-gauge track.

Once done, the Soviets accumulated abundant supplies along the entire front and reconstituted their armies. By early 1945 they had assembled 225 infantry divisions and twenty-two armored corps between the Baltic Sea and the Carpathian Mountains. Soviet superiority was eleven to one in infantry, seven to one in tanks, and twenty to one in artillery and aircraft. Most important was the great quantity of American trucks delivered to the Russians by Lend-Lease. Trucks transformed a large part of the Red Army into motorized divisions able to move quickly around the Germans, whose mobility was shrinking by the day due to extreme shortages of fuel.

When Heinz Guderian, army chief of staff, presented the figures of Soviet strength, Hitler exclaimed, "It's the greatest imposture since Genghis Khan! Who is responsible for producing all this rubbish?"

Hitler had not used the long stalemate in the east to build a powerful defensive line of minefields and antitank traps—such as Erwin Rommel had urged immediately after the battle of Kursk in 1943. His defensive system remained what it had been all along: each soldier was to stand in place and fight to the last round. He refused even a timely step back to avoid the full shock of a Soviet attack. The Russians were well aware of the hopeless weakness of Hitler's "hold-at-all-costs" policy, and were prepared to exploit it.

On December 24, 1944, Guderian met with Hitler and his staff and pleaded with them to abandon the Ardennes offensive and move every possible soldier eastward to shield against the Soviet attack.

The heart of continued German resistance, Guderian emphasized, was the industrial region of upper Silesia (about fifty miles west of Cracow around Katowice and Gliwice). The German armaments industry had already been moved there, and it was beyond the range of American and British bombers. The Ruhr, on the other hand, was paralyzed by bombing attacks.

"The loss of upper Silesia must lead to our defeat within a very few weeks," Guderian said.

It was no use. Hitler insisted that continued attacks in the west would eventually cripple the western Allies. Furthermore, he rejected Guderian's request to evacuate by sea the army group (of twenty-six divisions) now isolated in Courland in western Latvia. And while Guderian was en route back to his headquarters near Berlin, Hitler transferred two SS panzer divisions from the Vistula to Hungary with the task of relieving the siege of Budapest. This left Guderian with a mobile reserve of just twelve divisions to back up fifty weak infantry divisions holding a front 750 miles long.

"The eastern front is like a house of cards," Guderian told Hitler on January 9. "If the front is broken through at one point all the rest will collapse." But Hitler merely responded: "The eastern front must help itself and make do with what it's got."

Hitler also turned down requests of field commanders that German civilians be evacuated from East Prussia and other regions likely to be overrun by the Russians. He said evacuation would have a bad effect on public opinion.

✠        ✠        ✠

When the Soviet offensive burst across the Vistula on January 12, 1945, the Red Army commanders had their eyes set on Berlin, 300 miles west of Warsaw. This was to be the final drive to destroy Nazi Germany.

The first assault came by seventy Soviet divisions of I. S. Konev's 1st Ukrainian Front across the Vistula out of a bridgehead near Baranov, 120

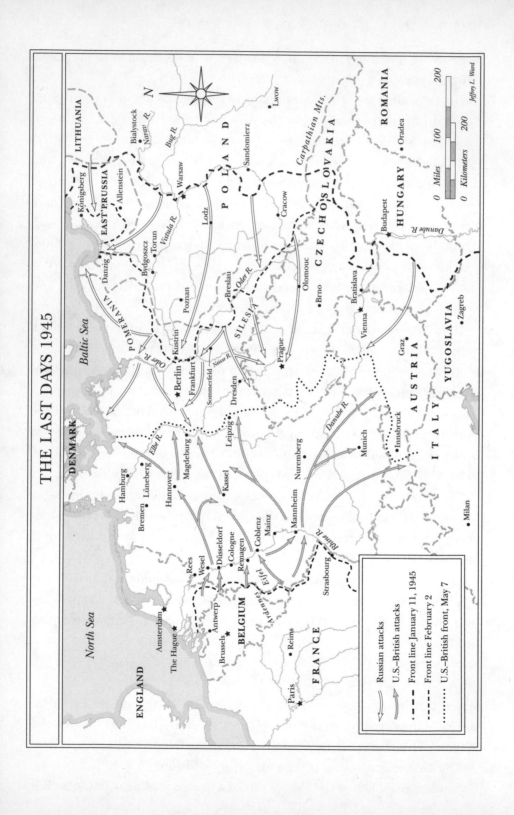

THE LAST DAYS 1945

ENGLAND

North Sea

Baltic Sea

N

LITHUANIA

Königsberg • Allenstein
EAST PRUSSIA

Bialystock
Narew R.
Bug R.

DENMARK

Hamburg
Bremen • Lüneberg
Hannover

Danzig
Bydgoszcz
Torun
POMERANIA

Warsaw

P O L A N D

Lodz

Poznan

Kustrin
★ Berlin
Frankfurt
Sommerfeld
Neisse R.
Dresden
Magdeburg
Leipzig
Kassel

Sandomierz

Cracow

SILESIA
Breslau
Oder R.

Olomouc
Brno

CZECHOSLOVAKIA

Prague ★

Lwow

ROMANIA

• Oradea

HUNGARY

Budapest ★

Danube R.

Bratislava

Vienna

AUSTRIA

Graz

YUGOSLAVIA

Zagreb

Elbe R.

Amsterdam
The Hague ★

Rees
Wesel
Düsseldorf
Cologne
Remagen

Antwerp
Brussels

BELGIUM

Ardennes
Eifel

Coblenz
Mainz
Mannheim

Nuremberg

Munich
Innsbruck

ITALY

Milan

Rhine R.

Danube R.

Strasbourg

Reims

F R A N C E

Paris ★

0 Miles 100 200

0 Kilometers 200

Jeffrey L. Ward

Russian attacks

U.S.–British attacks

Front line January 11, 1945

Front line February 2

U.S.–British front, May 7

miles south of Warsaw. Artillery pulverized the Germans, and in three days the Red soldiers had broken entirely through their defenses, captured Kielce, and were pouring over the Polish plain in an expanding torrent.

Two days later G. K. Zhukov's 1st White Russian Front burst out of bridgeheads around Magnuszev and Pulawy, 75 miles south of Warsaw, while K. K. Rokossovsky's 2nd White Russian Front stormed across the Narev north of Warsaw. Zhukov's divisions wheeled north to surround Warsaw, while Rokossovsky's troops blew apart the German defenses covering the southern approach to East Prussia, creating a breach 200 miles wide. Altogether 200 Soviet divisions were now rolling westward.

Chaos descended on the Nazi high command. Hitler, more and more ignoring reality, returned to Berlin on January 16 from his Eagle's Aerie east of the Rhine. The marble halls of the Chancellery were in ruins from bombing, but the underground bunker fifty feet below remained operational. At long last, Hitler decided that the armies in the west had to go over to the defensive to make forces available to stem the Russian tide. He immediatcly ordered 6th Panzer Army to move eastward.

Guderian was delighted, and planned to use the army to attack the flanks of the Soviet spearheads in Poland to slow their advance. He learned, however, that Hitler was sending 6th Panzer Army to Hungary to assist in relieving the siege of Budapest.

"On hearing this I lost my self-control and expressed my disgust to Jodl in very plain terms," Guderian wrote. But he could not change Hitler's mind.

On January 17 the General Staff operations section reported that Soviet forces were about to surround Warsaw, and proposed a new defensive line to the west. Guderian agreed, and ordered the small city garrison to withdraw at once. When informed, Hitler insisted that Warsaw be held at all costs. The garrision commander, however, ignored Hitler's command and withdrew his battalions. Hitler flew into a rage, and thought of nothing the next few days but how to punish the General Staff.

Guderian protested that he had made the decision, but Hitler replied: "No, it's not you I'm after, but the General Staff. It is intolerable to me that a group of intellectuals should presume to press their views on their superiors."

Hitler arrested a colonel and two lieutenant colonels in the operations section. Guderian demanded an inquiry, and two Gestapo agents interrogated him for days. These interrogations squandered Guderian's time and nervous energy at a time when a battle for life or death was being fought on the eastern front. Guderian got two of the officers released, but the third remained in a concentration camp till the end of the war.

On January 25 Guderian tried to get Foreign Minister Joachim von Ribbentrop to convince Hitler to seek an armistice on the western front, while continuing to fight the Russians in the east. Ribbentrop replied that he did not dare approach the Fuehrer on the subject. As Guderian departed, Ribbentrop said, "We will keep this conversation to ourselves, won't we?" Guderian assured him he would do so. But Ribbentrop tattled to Hitler, and that evening the Fuehrer accused Guderian of treason.

Meanwhile Russian forces continued to advance on all fronts, reaching the German frontier in Silesia on January 19, and soon overrunning upper Silesia. Zhukov's troops captured Lodz, bypassed Posen (Poznan), crossed the German frontier, and on January 31 reached the lower Oder River near Küstrin (now Kostryzh)—forty miles from Berlin. Only 380 miles separated the Russians from the advanced positions of the western Allies.

At the same time, Rokossovsky gained the southern gateway to East Prussia at Mlawa and drove on to the Gulf of Danzig, isolating German forces in East Prussia. These fell back into Königsberg (now Kaliningrad), where Russians besieged them.

The virtually unchecked advance of the Red Army set off the frantic flight of most German civilians toward the west. The flood of refugees jammed roads, created chaos, and made troop movements all the more difficult.

Hitler's final divorce from reality came now. With the Ruhr bombed into rubble and upper Silesia occupied, Albert Speer, Nazi armaments chief, sent a memorandum to Hitler that began: "The war is lost." Hitler read the first sentence and locked the memo in his safe. Speer requested a private interview to explain Germany's desperate straits. But the Fuehrer declined, telling Guderian: "I refuse to see anyone alone anymore. Any man who asks to talk to me alone always does so because he has something unpleasant to say to me. I can't bear that."

The Red Army was outrunning its supplies, and a thaw in the first week of February braked supplies further by turning roads into quagmires, while the ice broke up on the Oder, increasing its effect as an obstacle. Guderian scraped up what troops he could find. These stopped the Russians with only shallow bridgeheads over the Oder near Küstrin and Frankfurt-an-der-Oder.

Meantime Konev in Silesia extended bridgeheads north of Breslau (now Wroclaw), swept north down the left or western bank of the Oder, and on February 13 reached Sommerfeld (now Lubsko). This same day Budapest fell at last; Hitler's attempt to relieve it had failed. The surrender yielded 110,000 prisoners to the Russians. On February 15, Konev's troops advanced to the Neisse River, near its junction with the Oder, and came level with Zhukov's forces.

By the third week of February the front in the east was stabilized, with the aid of reinforcements brought from the west and the interior. The crisis posed by the Russian menace led to Hitler's decision that defense of the Rhine had to be sacrificed to holding the Oder.

Hitler diverted the major part of his remaining forces to the east, still believing that the western Allies were unable to resume the offensive because of losses in the Ardennes. He turned his V-1s and V-2s on Antwerp, in hopes of stopping the arrival of Allied supplies. In all, the Germans hurled 8,000 V-weapons at Antwerp and other targets, but the damage they did was negligible.

Eisenhower's armies, now eighty-five divisions strong, prepared to close in on the Rhine. Hitler refused to withdraw forces behind this river barrier. Consequently, the Allies had only to break through the thin crust of front-line defenses to open wide avenues of advance into the German rear.

Eisenhower, to the disgust of American senior commanders, assigned the main striking force to Montgomery's 21st Army Group in the north, adding the U.S. 9th Army to Montgomery's British 2nd and Canadian 1st Armies. Montgomery planned another of his meticulously slow, overwhelming assaults—this time over the Rhine in the vicinity of Wesel, opposite Holland.

Even so, Bradley's U.S. 1st and 3rd Armies were far stronger than the German forces facing them, and on March 7, 1945, George Patton's 3rd

Army broke through the Schnee Eifel Mountains east of the Ardennes and, in three days, reached the Rhine near Coblenz. The same day farther north the 9th Armored Division of 1st Army found a gap and raced through to the Rhine so quickly that the Germans did not have time to blow the railroad bridge at Remagen, near Bonn.

American engineers frantically cut every demolition wire they could find, while a platoon of infantry raced across the bridge. As they neared the east bank, two charges went off. The bridge shook, but stood. Tanks rushed over the span, and by nightfall the Americans had a strong bridgehead on the east bank.

When Hodges called Bradley with the news, Bradley responded: "Hot dog, Courtney, this will bust him wide open!"

Bradley told Hodges to pour every man and weapon possible across the bridge and strike for the heart of Germany. But Harold R. (Pink) Bull, Eisenhower's chief of operations, said no. "You're not going anywhere down there at Remagen," he announced. "You've got a bridge, but it's in the wrong place. It just doesn't fit the plan."

The "plan"—agreed to by Eisenhower—was for Montgomery to launch his grand attack at Wesel on March 24, three weeks later.

Bradley was furious, and finally got Eisenhower to approve a strike out of the Remagen bridgehead toward Frankfurt with five divisions. Meanwhile Patton cleared the west bank of the Rhine between Coblenz and Mannheim, cutting off all German forces still to the west by March 21. The Germans lost 350,000 men, the vast bulk of them captured.

On March 22, Patton's troops crossed the Rhine almost unopposed at Oppenheim, between Mainz and Mannheim. When the news reached Hitler, he learned that only five tank destroyers were available to contest the advance of an entire American army—and they were a hundred miles away.

The American advance east of the Rhine now became a procession. Columns spread out east, south, and north. Meanwhile Montgomery had completed his elaborate preparations. He had assembled twenty-five divisions, vast quantities of ammunition and supplies, and on the night of March 23 launched his attack after a tremendous bombardment of more than 3,000 guns, followed by waves of bombers. After daybreak two airborne divisions dropped ahead.

But there were only five weak and exhausted German divisions defending the thirty miles of the river where Montgomery crossed. They offered little resistance, and Allied losses were tiny.

Even so, Montgomery refused to sanction a general advance until he had massed twenty divisions and 1,500 tanks in the bridgehead. By this time American columns were fanning out all over central and southern Germany.

Hitler sacked Rundstedt for the last time on March 10, replacing him with Kesselring, and hunted for scapegoats for the collapse of resistance. A "Flying Special Tribunal West" tried and executed eight German officers who commanded the weak forces at Remagen. But despite these and other frantic efforts by Hitler to require every soldier to stand or die, Germans everywhere knew the end was near, and withdrew or surrendered. Only a few fanatic troops, mostly SS, resisted here and there.

Hitler now turned on his own people. On March 19 he issued an order that the entire German economy was to be destroyed—industrial plants, electric-generating plants, waterworks, gas works, bridges, ships, locomotives, food, clothing stores. His aim was to produce a "desert" in the Allies' path.

Albert Speer, Nazi armaments chief, immediately petitioned Hitler. "We have no right at this stage of the war to carry out demolitions which might affect the life of the people," he said. But Hitler, his own fate sealed, was not interested in the continued existence of the German people.

"If the war is lost," he told Speer, "the nation will also perish. . . . It will be better to destroy these things ourselves because this nation will have proved to be the weaker one."

The scales fell from the eyes of Speer. With superhuman efforts, Speer and a number of army officers, directly disobeying Hitler's orders at last, raced about the country to make sure the demolitions did not take place.

The end was now approaching. Montgomery's British and Canadian armies pushed north toward Bremen, Hamburg, and Lübeck on the Baltic. Simpson's U.S. 9th Army rushed past the Ruhr on the north while Hodges's 1st Army drove past it on the south. They linked up April 1 at Lippstadt, closing 325,000 Germans of Walther Model's Army Group B in the Ruhr pocket. The army group held out till April 18, when it surrendered. Model was not among the prisoners: he had shot himself.

During this period Hitler more and more lost contact with what was happening. While the western Allies were sweeping almost unopposed over Germany, Hitler focused his attention on recapturing the fortress of Küstrin on the Oder, complaining that the attacking general had not used enough ammunition in the artillery preparation. When Guderian angrily pointed out on March 28 that there *was* no more ammunition, Hitler relieved him, appointing Hans Krebs as chief of staff.

On April 12, President Roosevelt died unexpectedly, arousing wild hopes in Hitler that a miracle like that which saved Frederick the Great from defeat in the Seven Years War would be repeated. The death of the empress of Russia ended the coalition against Frederick.

The day before FDR died, the spearhead of 9th Army reached the Elbe River near Magdeburg in the heart of Germany. Berlin was only sixty miles away, and the road lay open.

Over the violent objections of Churchill and the British military chiefs, who wanted to beat the Russians to Berlin, Eisenhower halted the western Allies on the Elbe.

Berlin "was not the logical or the most desirable objective for the forces of the western Allies," Eisenhower wrote.

The Russians commenced their drive from the Oder shortly after the Americans reached the Elbe. This meant, to Eisenhower, that they would reach Berlin before the British and Americans could do so. Eisenhower and his staff were obsessed with Nazi reports that they would establish a "National Redoubt" in the mountains of southern Germany and conduct guerrilla warfare for years. Eisenhower also feared the Nazis were setting up an "underground army" of "Werewolves," composed of loyal followers of Hitler, to commit murder and carry out acts of terrorism.

The National Redoubt and the Werewolves existed only in the propaganda blasts of Joseph Goebbels. But Eisenhower and his staff fell for the ploy, and he directed the American armies into the southern mountains as fast as possible. American troops reached Nuremberg on April 16, Munich on April 30, and met troops of the U.S. 5th Army from Italy at the Brenner Pass between Austria and Italy on May 3. German resistance had collapsed in Italy and commanders had signed a surrender on April 29.

The Russians burst out of their bridgeheads on the Oder on April 16, and reached the suburbs of Berlin a week later. While several hundred thousand Soviet troops invested the city, others swept around it north and south, and on April 25 patrols of the 58th Guards Division met patrols of the U.S. 69th Division on the Elbe at Torgau, seventy-five miles southwest of Berlin. Adolf Hitler was cut off in Berlin. The death throes of the Third Reich had come.

✠        ✠        ✠

Hitler had planned to leave Berlin on April 20, his fifty-sixth birthday, for Obersalzberg in the Bavarian Alps. Most officials had already moved south, along with the Fuehrer's personal staff. But Hitler stayed, convinced that the Russians would suffer their greatest defeat trying to capture the German capital. But Himmler, Göring, and Ribbentrop got out. Hitler called for a counterattack that never came—and in fact existed only in the mind of the dictator. Hitler had fallen into a world of delusion.

On April 22, Jodl and Keitel reported that the Russians had broken through on the north and their tanks were now inside the city limits. Hitler completely lost control. This was the end, he shrieked. There was nothing but treason, lies, cowardice! All was over. He would stay in Berlin, and personally take over defense of the city.

Three defensive rings encircled the city, the last a small circle around the Chancellery and other main government buildings in the center. Forces included 9th Army, elements of 3rd and 4th Panzer Armies, and *Volkssturm* units of overage untrained men and Hitler Youth boys. Red Army forces occupied outlying areas of Berlin on April 21, and completely surrounded the city on April 25. The battle was largely a huge mopping-up operation. Russians destroyed pockets of resistance with artillery fire, or bypassed them until supplies ran out.

Only in the center around the government buildings was resistance fierce. The Russians abandoned efforts to overrun the center with tanks when German infantry were able to get close enough in the heavily built-up area to destroy armor with antitank weapons. The Russians also found it difficult to deploy artillery in the close confines of the city. They used cannons where they could, but relied mainly on mortars and rockets. Small combat teams cleared the center city block by block—300 blocks in all, every house or building taken by storm. It was a slow process, but thorough. Especially heavy fighting raged in the subway and underground communications facilities.

Before the fighting started, on April 15, Hitler's mistress for twelve years, Eva Braun, thirty-five years old, arrived in Berlin to join him in a wedding and her ceremonial death. Eva Braun was a simple woman with no intellectual pretensions, but she was determined to share Hitler's end.

So also was Goebbels and his wife. They and their six children (the oldest twelve years old) moved into the Chancellery bunker.

Hitler sorted out his papers, and sent one of his adjutants up to the garden to burn those he wanted destroyed. He ordered Keitel and Jodl to go south and take direct command of the remaining armed forces.

Meantime Göring arrived at Obersalzberg, and on April 23 sent Hitler a telegram proposing that he take over "total leadership of the Reich." Hitler responded that Göring had committed high treason. Martin Bormann, Hitler's sinister private secretary, got off a radiogram to SS headquarters in Berchtesgaden, and had Göring arrested. On April 28 Hitler received word through a BBC broadcast from London that Himmler was negotiating through Sweden to surrender all armies in the west to Eisenhower.

A few minutes later Hitler received word that the Russians were nearing the Potsdamerplatz, only a few hundred yards away, and would likely storm the Chancellery on the morning of April 30.

Hitler directed General Robert Ritter von Greim, whom he had named as Luftwaffe chief, along with Hanna Reitsch, a famous woman test pilot and admirer of Hitler, to leave the bunker, rally the Luftwaffe for a last attack on the Russians, and arrest Himmler as a traitor. Meanwhile he had Himmler's chief liaison officer, Hermann Fegelein, taken up to the Chancellery garden and shot.

Hitler also married Eva Braun, and drew up his last will and testament. These two documents reveal that Hitler had learned nothing from his errors and from the disasters he had brought upon the world. He denied he had wanted war in 1939, and claimed it had been brought on by foreign leaders who were "of Jewish origin or worked for Jewish interests." He placed the "sole responsibility" for all the deaths on the Jews.

Hitler held that honor required "a district or town" to be held "unto death," thus showing he had learned nothing from the disasters he himself had brought on at Stalingrad and other places he ordered defended to the last.

He expelled Göring and Himmler from the Nazi party and their offices, and appointed Admiral Karl Dönitz as president of the Reich and supreme commander, enjoining him to resist "international Jewry."

The time was now 4 A.M. on Sunday, April 29, 1945. Hitler called in Goebbels and others in the bunker to witness his signatures. He then drew up his will, handing over to his relatives any property he might possess, and adding: "My wife and I choose to die in order to escape the shame of overthrow or capitulation. It is our wish that our bodies be burned immediately."

Hitler now went to bed, exhausted. Above ground Russian artillery shattered buildings at point-blank range only yards from the Chancellery. A pall of smoke and dust hung over the city.

In the afternoon, news came in that Italian partisans had shot Mussolini and his mistress, Clara Petacci, near Lake Como and that their bodies had been strung up by their heels on lampposts in Milan. Soon thereafter, Hitler poisoned his favorite Alsatian dog, Blondi, and gave his two remaining women secretaries capsules of poison to take if they wished when the Russians broke in. About 2:30 A.M. on April 30 Hitler said good-bye in the dining area to twenty persons of the bunker staff, mostly women.

A bizarre event now took place. Tension had been building to such a height that several persons went into the canteen and began to dance. The party got so noisy that word came from the Fuehrer's quarters asking for quiet. But the partygoers, at last released from Hitler's control, frolicked all through the night.

At noon on April 30 word reached the bunker that the Russians were at the eastern end of the Tiergarten and had broken into the Potsdamerplatz. They were just a block away. Hitler's chauffeur, on orders from below, delivered 180 liters of gasoline to the Chancellery garden. Hitler fetched his bride, Eva, and they made their final good-byes to Goebbels and a few others.

Hitler and Eva retired to their rooms. Goebbels, Bormann, and a few others waited in the passageway. In a few moments they heard a revolver shot. They waited for a second shot, but none came. They entered the Fuehrer's quarters. Adolf Hitler's body sprawled on the sofa, dripping blood. He had shot himself in the mouth. Eva Braun lay beside him. She had taken cyanide poison, and had not used a pistol. It was 3:30 P.M. on Monday, April 30, 1945—twelve years and three months since Hitler had become chancellor.

As Russian shells screamed and exploded in the immediate environs, their bodies were brought to the garden above, and Adolf and Eva Braun Hitler were consumed in a funeral pyre.

☩        ☩        ☩

The Third Reich survived for seven days.

Early on the evening of May 1, Goebbels and his wife ordered a physician to give their children lethal injections. That done, they mounted the stairs to the garden. There, at their request, an SS orderly shot them both in the back of the head. SS men poured gasoline on their bodies and set them on fire, but the cremation was incomplete, and the Russians found the charred remains the next day.

Around 9 P.M. on May 1, about 500 survivors of Hitler's headquarters, mostly SS men, tried to get away, walking along the subway tracks from the station under the Wilhelmplatz, opposite the Chancellery, to the Friedrichstrasse railway station, then crossing the Spree River and slipping through the Russian lines to the north. A good many got through, but not Martin Bormann. He was either killed or took poison to avoid capture.

On March 4 the German high command surrendered to Montgomery all forces in northwest Germany, Denmark, and Holland. The next day Kesselring's Army Group G, comprising the armies north of the Alps, capitulated.

On May 5, Admiral Hans von Friedeburg, now navy commander, arrived at Eisenhower's headquarters at Reims, France, to negotiate a surrender. General Jodl came the next day, hoping to draw out proceedings long enough for hundreds of thousands of German troops and refugees to move west far enough to surrender to the western Allies instead of the Russians.

But Eisenhower would brook no delay, and at 2:41 A.M. on May 7, Friedeburg and Jodl signed Germany's unconditional surrender, effective at midnight May 8, 1945.

Himmler, captured by the British, bit down on a cyanide capsule and died. Nineteen of the worst Nazis were convicted at Nuremberg of war crimes. Seven drew prison terms, the remainder were sentenced to hang, including Ribbentrop, Keitel, Jodl, and Göring, though Göring cheated the hangman by two hours. Someone had slipped a poison vial into his cell, and he was dead when the guards came for him.

Germans were evicted from all the lands east of the Oder and from the Sudetenland. Germany lay in rubble with no government and scarcely any economy. Hitler's dreams of world dominance and *Lebensraum* had collapsed. Only the generosity of their former enemies in providing food and fuel kept the German population alive that summer and bitter winter of 1945–1946.

But the most terrible, costly war in history had ended. The world had finally rid itself of Hitler, Nazism, and the Third Reich.

# Notes

A note on the Notes: Some references cite only the last name of the author or editor. These works are cited in full in the Selected Bibliography. References not so listed are cited in full where they appear. Numbers refer to pages.

### Chapter 1: Germany's Opportunity for Victory

p. 2:    "after France fell." Kimball, 48.

p. 2:    "the European continent." Ian Kersaw in Finney, 132.

p. 3:    *"Schutzstaffel* or SS." Dahms, 332–38.

p. 4:    "or were murdered." This book focuses on the military and political decisions open to Germany in World War II. Nothing in it should be misunderstood as approval for what the Third Reich did in six years of pillage and genocide, carried out by Nazi authorities and private soldiers alike. This book seeks to explore how close we came to losing the war, and how close Adolf Hitler came to creating the unspeakable world he wanted. There is insufficient space to examine the Holocaust and other murderous programs Hitler and Nazi Germany pursued to the very last days of the war. There are many fine books on this aspect of Nazism. Two of the best are *Hitler's Willing Executioners* by Daniel Jonah Goldhagen, and an official German study of the *Einsatzgruppen,* or murder units, in eastern Europe from 1939 to 1942: *Die Truppe des Weltanschauungskrieges* (*The Troops of the War of Ideology*) by Helmut Krausnick and Hans-Heinrich Wilhelm. For human losses, see Zabecki, vol. 1, 32–34 (Paul J. Rose); Omer Bartov, *Hitler's Army,* 83–84.

p. 6:    "kinds of *vehicles."* Fuller, vol. 3, 379–81.

p. 7:    " 'had time to react.' " Rommel, 124.

p. 7:    "infantryman could walk." France had about 3,400 modern tanks, though not all were in organized tank units. Britain sent about 700 tanks to the Continent, mostly Mark VI light tanks, with 14-millimeter armor and armed with two machine guns, the rest Matildas, a powerful, slow (maximum speed 15 mph, but operating even slower) "infantry" tank with 70-millimeter main armor. Most were the Mark I version armed only with a machine gun, and only 50 were Mark IIs with a high-velocity two-pounder (40-millimeter) gun. On May 10, 1940, 2,300 French tanks had been formed into 51 battalions: 12 in three armored divisions, 12 in three light mechanized divisions, 27 in independent battalions. Each French battalion usually had 45 medium or light tanks, or 33 heavy tanks. The French deployed mostly infantry tanks with thick armor (34–60 millimeters), short range, and slow speed. Most had a good 37-millimeter gun, and some had an excellent high-velocity 47-millimeter gun. Either could pierce most German armor. See Goutard, 27–28; Zabecki, vol. 2, were a matter of life or death for Germany. Hitler abandoned the idea of a four-power alliance, and reached his final decision to attack the Soviet Union. "forced to cede to others." Close to midnight on November 11, 1940, thirty obsolete Swordfish torpedo bomber biplanes from the British aircraft carrier *Illustrious* sank one and heavily damaged two Italian battleships lying at anchor at Taranto. The British lost two aircraft, and eliminated Italy as a naval competitor in the Mediterranean. The air strikes proved that bombers could sink capital ships. The Japanese learned the lesson, and were the first to realize that thereafter aircraft carriers were to dominate naval warfare. See Zabecki, vol. 2, 1708–9 (Francesco Fatutta).

5: "for a hasty departure." Beginning January 19, 1941, small British forces struck from Sudan in the north and Kenya in the south to evict the Italians from their East African colonies of Ethiopia, Eritrea, and Italian Somaliland, and from British Somaliland, which they had occupied in 1940. The British were aided by Ethiopians who accompanied Emperor Haile Selassie, exiled by the Italians when they conquered Ethiopia in 1935–1936. The Italians had 160,000 native and 100,000 Italian troops, but they retreated before the much smaller British forces. By April 6, 1941, the British had occupied Addis Ababa, the Ethiopian capital, and most other important places in the colonies. The last Italian force surrendered at Gondar, Ethiopia, on November 27. The campaign demonstrated poor leadership by Italian officers and a tendency of Italian soldiers to surrender or run away.

p. 57: "680,000 troops in Romania." Romanian King Carol II was forced to abdicate in favor of his eighteen-year-old son Michael I, but General Ion Antonescu took control of the country and joined the Axis on November 27, 1940.

p. 59: "Yugoslavia from all quarters." *Das Deutsche Reich und der Zweite Weltkrieg*, vol. 3 (by Detlef Vogel), 417–84; Liddell Hart, *History of the Second World War*, 131–35.

## Chapter 6: Attacking the Wrong Island
p. 62: " 'in the Mediterranean.' " *Das Deutsche Reich und der Zweite Weltkrieg*, vol. 3, 487.
p. 63: " 'toward the Suez Canal.' " Ibid., 488.
p. 65: "actually in British lines." Liddell Hart, *The Other Side of the Hill*, 238–43.
p. 69: " 'not let the army down.' " Zabecki, vol. 1, 268 (Philip Green).
p. 70: " 'The day of parachute troops is over.' " Ibid., 138–39.

## Chapter 7: Rommel's Unappreciated Gift
p. 71: "elements of his corps arrived." *Das Deutsche Reich und der Zweite Weltkrieg*, vol. 3 (Bernd Stegemann), 615–30.
p. 71: " 'far as the eye could reach.' " Rommel, 101.
p. 72: " 'movement around the south.' " Ibid., 91.
p. 72: " 'according to his wishes.' " Schmidt, 77.
p. 73: " 'attempt to recover Benghazi.' " Alexander, 244; Rommel, 105.
p. 76: "the 'armored brigade' " A British brigade was made up of battalions and corresponded in size and function to a regiment in the German, American, and most other armies. The terminology grew out of the fact that most British soldiers were assigned to a regiment, which was not a tactical organization but the military home of its members. Individual battalions of this regiment were attached to brigades, but were generally called "regiments" instead of battalions.

1107–10, 1131–32 (Kenneth J. Swanson, Robert G. Waite, and John Dunn); Ellis, 88–89.
p. 8: "speed of only 240 mph." This was the 1938 model with a 490-mile range used in the 1940 campaign. In 1941 the Ju-87D came out with a 4,000-pound payload and a 950-mile range. The D-model saw heavy and successful service in North Africa and Russia.
p. 8: "on the battlefield." The German Wehrmacht (armed forces) were the first to develop close tactical or battle cooperation between aircraft and ground troops. A Stuka could drop a bomb within a hundred yards of any target designated by the ground forces. The Luftwaffe sent liaison officers to corps and panzer divisions to relay requests for support. In the campaign in the west, panzer forces could receive air support forty-five to seventy-five minutes after the request was made. See Corum, 271–75.

## Chapter 2: The Campaign in the West: 1940
p. 9: "east of Holland." Dahms, 162; *Das Deutsche Reich und der Zweite Weltkrieg*, vol. 2, 238–47 (Hans Umbreit).
p. 11: "the French army." Manstein, 100–102; Cooper, 198–200.
p. 11: " 'was inadmissible,' Manstein wrote." Manstein, 103–104.
p. 12: " 'of the German offensive.' " Ibid., 118.
p. 13: " 'had to say,' Manstein wrote later." Ibid., 121.
p. 15: "vulnerable to ground fire." Goutard, 32–37.
p. 16: "on only slightly inferior terms." Zabecki, vol. 2, 962, 964–66, 983–85 (Carl O. Schuster, Philip C. Bechtel).
p. 16: "could be moved forward." Kiesling, 140–42.

## Chapter 3: The Defeat of France
p. 20: "Walther von Reichenau's following 6th Army." Zabecki, vol. 2, 1471–72 (Kevin Dougherty); *Das Deutsche Reich und der Zweite Weltkrieg*, vol. 2, 285–87 (Hans Umbreit); Dahms, 166–69; English and Gudmundsson, 61.
p. 21: "to Antwerp, Belgium." The Allied land forces were divided into the 1st Group of Armies (Billotte), located between the English Channel and Montmédy, and including 7th Army (Giraud), the BEF (Gort), 1st Army (Georges Blanchard), 9th Army (André Corap), and 2nd Army (Charles Huntziger); the 2nd Group of Armies (Gaston Prételat) between Montmédy and Sélestat (thirty miles south of Strasbourg on the Rhine River), and including 3rd Army (Charles Condé), 4th Army (Edouard Réquin) and 5th Army (Victor Bourret); and the 3rd Group of Armies (Georges Besson) between Sélestat and Geneva, Switzerland, with 8th Army (Joanny J.M. Garchery) and 3rd Army (Robert Auguste Touchon).
p. 22: "to the German panzers." Goutard, 111–13.
p. 22: " 'Victory whatever the cost!' " Churchill, *The Second World War, Their Finest Hour,* 25–26.
p. 23: "in their thrust westward." Guderian's three divisions had 276 tanks each, Reinhardt's two divisions 218 each; Hoth's 5th Division had 324 tanks, his 7th Division 218; Hoepner's two divisions had 324 tanks apiece, and the 9th Division (detailed to Holland) 229: total 2,683. Of these, 640 were Mark Is, 825 Mark IIs, 564 Mark IIIs, and 654 Mark IVs. The Mark Is were inadequate for

combat and were relegated to reconnaissance. They weighed 6.5 tons, were armed with two machine guns, and had maximum armor 15 millimeters thick. The Mark IIs also were inadequate, weighed 10.5 tons, had only a 20-millimeter gun and 30-millimeter armor. The Mark IIIs carried a 37-millimeter gun and had 57-millimeter maximum armor. The Mark IVs mounted a short-barreled 75-millimeter gun and had maximum of 60-millimeter armor. All four models could travel at about 25 miles per hour. However, the tanks designated Mark IVs in the 6th, 7th, and 8th Panzer Divisions were Czech Skodas. They weighed 11.5 tons, could travel 21 miles an hour, had 25-millimeter maximum armor, and carried a 37-millimeter gun. See Goutard, 27; Chapman, 347; Zabecki, vol. 2, 1111–14, 1133 (Paul W. Johnson and Robert G. Waite).

p. 23: " 'think there is any danger?' " Chapman, 113.

p. 25: " 'guns had been abandoned.' " Ibid., 121.

p. 28: " 'boundless shores' (*Uferlose*)." Dahms, 171.

p. 28: "and seized Bouvellement." Guderian, 108.

p. 31: "attempted no further attack." Ellis, 90–98.

p. 32: " 'and protective movements.' " Liddell Hart, *The German Generals Talk*, 132.

pp. 33–34: " 'the liberation of the Old.' " Churchill, *The Second World War, Their Finest Hour*, 118.

p. 35: "51st Highland Division." Rommel, 44–67.

p. 35: " 'the back of its neighbor.' " Kimball, 51.

## Chapter 4: Hitler's First Great Error

pp. 36–37: " 'their finest hour.' " Churchill, *The Second World War, Their Finest Hour*, 225–26.

p. 38: "pick up low-flying aircraft." One of the greatest British feats in the war was breaking the German Enigma cipher machine's code by the Government Code and Cipher School at Bletchley, between Oxford and Cambridge. Radio intercepts of Enigma-encoded messages gave the Allies advance warning of many German actions, plans, and dispositions. A Berlin commercial company invented the Enigma machine, and the army adopted it in the late 1920s and other governmental agencies in 1933. The machine mechanically enciphered plain text messages by means of three cipher drums, or rotors, with twenty-six letters along the rims and a fourth stationary reflector or reversing cipher drum. Changing the connections of these four rotors gave almost infinite potential codes. The Germans regarded Enigma transmissions as unbreakable. Polish intelligence turned over one of these machines to the British in late July 1939. Mathematicians at Bletchley began a laborious process of breaking the codes based on the repeated sequence of letters an operator was obliged to preface messages with to show the receiving station how he had geared or set the machine. Luftwaffe keys were the first broken, but Gestapo keys were never broken. The Bletchley operation was code-named Ultra. Its first great victory was in the Battle of Britain, when Ultra was able to give key advance information on Luftwaffe operations to the RAF. See Zabecki, vol. 2, 959–60, 1290–91 (Alexander Molnar, Jr.); Keegan, *Second World War*, 163–64, 497–502; Ronald Lewin, *Ultra Goes to War: The Secret Story*, London: 1978.

p. 42: "role in deciding the war." Shirer, 775–82; Dahms, 211; Zabecki, vol. 2 (Robert G. Waite), 1405–9; Liddell Hart, *History of the Second World War*, 87–108.

p. 43: "to British Guiana (Guyana)." Hitler made a great [...] signed the Tripartite Pact between Germany, Italy, a[...] 27, 1940. The alliance was aimed at maintaining Ame[...] ing the prospect of a two-front war, against Germany a[...] against Japan in the Pacific. This threat increased [...] American leaders to arm the nation. But the pact encou[...] attack on the United States in the belief that in a two[...] would be unable to defeat the Japanese navy, leaving con[...] Japan. This decision probably cost Germany and Japan th[...] offer Japan the opportunity to exclude the United State[...] Pacific, the pact encouraged Japan to seize the colonies of B[...] the Netherlands in Southeast Asia (the so-called southe[...] diverted Japanese attention from its designs on Siberia, and [...] ity treaty with the Soviet Union in April 1941.

p. 44: "American entry into the war." Paul Kennedy points out that the [...] of the United States dwarfed that of every other nation. In 1938, [...] of its capacity idle because of economic depression, the United [...] duced almost 29 percent of the world's manufactured goods, m[...] that of Germany, whose factories were operating at maximum cap[...] the United States had three times the income of the entire British En[...] seven times that of France, four times that of Germany, and sixteen [...] Japan. In 1937, the United States possessed 41.7 percent of the entire [...] production potential. Germany's share was 14.4 percent, the Soviet [...] Britain's 10.2, France's 4.2, Japan's 3.5, and Italy's 2.5. See Kennedy, 3[...]

p. 44: "a peaceful solution." Kimball, 69–76; Zabecki, vol. 1, 108–9[...] Pierpaoli, Jr.).

## Chapter 5: The Fatal Turn to the East

p. 45: " 'the spring of 1941.' " Hitler's meeting occurred at Berchtesgaden i[...] *Berghof* (retreat) at Obersalzberg in the Bavarian Alps. All the top leade[...] the armed forces were there.

p. 45: "invaded Russia in 1812." Liddell Hart, *Strategy*, 236.

p. 48: "against the Soviet Union." *Das Deutsche Reich und der Zweite Weltkrieg*, vol.[...] 191–200; Shirer, 813–15.

p. 49: "if the United States entered." Shirer, 829; Kimball, 84.

p. 49: "never counsel Hitler correctly." *Das Deutsche Reich und der Zweite Weltkrieg*, vol. 3, 197.

p. 49: "than capture of London." Fuller, vol. 3, 413.

p. 53: "a single panzer division for Africa." Alexander, 237. Soviet Foreign Minister V. M. Molotov went to Berlin on November 12, 1940, to discuss a four-power entente and "delimitation of spheres of influence." Joachim von Ribbentrop, German foreign minister, outlined a remarkable proposal for Germany, Italy, Japan, and the Soviet Union to divide up Eurasia and Africa. But the plan had an air of unreality about it. Hitler had devoted large portions of *Mein Kampf* to describing his hatred of Communists and his desire to eradicate them. It is doubtful whether Joseph Stalin believed Hitler was serious. On November 26, he demanded a base in Bulgaria to secure control of the Dardanelles. This would place Romania under Soviet threat, and Romania's Ploesti oil fields

p. 76: "only a limited combat role." At this time the Mark III had a 50-millimeter gun with moderate velocity, while the Mark IV had a short-barreled 75-millimeter gun with relatively low velocity. Both had a top speed of about 25 mph. Neither gun could penetrate the 78-millimeter frontal armor of the British Matilda infantry tank, and had difficulty stopping the faster (30 mph) British Mark V cruiser tanks with 40 millimeters of frontal armor. Moreover, the British tanks were armed with a two-pounder (40-millimeter) gun with higher velocity and slightly better penetration (44 millimeters of armor at 1,000 yards) than the German tank guns. Since the German medium tanks had only 30 millimeters of frontal armor at this time, the two-pounder could often stop them.

p. 76: " 'That's your affair!' " *Das Deutsche Reich und der Zweite Weltkrieg,* vol. 3, 617.

p. 77: " 'at one stroke,' Rommel wrote." Rommel, 109.

p. 79: "the end of 1941." Fuller, vol. 3, 419.

p. 79: " 'would have been impossible.' " Rommel, 120.

## Chapter 8: Barbarossa

p. 82: "slightest threat to his dictatorship." In the purges, beginning in May 1937, at least 30,000 of the Red Army's 75,000 officers were imprisoned or executed, including the vast majority of senior officers. Another 10,000 were dismissed from the service. See Glantz and House, 11; English and Gudmundsson, 83.

p. 82: "Communist party agents in the army." These political officers had the power to veto commanders' orders during the revolutionary wars and disturbances in the 1920s and early 1930s. After 1934 Stalin withdrew this power, reimposed it during the purges, then withdrew it after the Finnish campaign. The commissars were restricted to political education of soldiers and ensuring political conformity among officers. See Keegan, *Second World War,* 177.

p. 82: "hobbled the German army." Hitler insisted that all generals understand no holds were to be barred. In March 1941 he laid down the law to the chiefs of all three services and key army field commanders. Halder's diary recorded Hitler's words: "The war against Russia will be such that it cannot be conducted in a knightly fashion. This struggle is one of ideologies and racial differences and will have to be conducted with unprecedented, unmerciful, and unrelenting harshness. All officers will have to rid themselves of obsolete ideologies. . . . I insist that my orders be executed without contradiction. The commissars are the bearers of ideologies directly opposed to National Socialism. Therefore the commissars will be liquidated. German soldiers guilty of breaking international law . . . will be excused. Russia has not participated in the Hague Convention and therefore has no rights under it." On May 13, 1941, Keitel issued a new order in the name of the Fuehrer, which limited courts-martial. Civilians suspected of criminal action were to be brought at once before an officer. This officer was to decide whether they were to be shot on the spot. In the case of offenses committed against enemy civilians by Wehrmacht members, prosecution was not obligatory, even where the deed was a military crime. See Shirer, 830–31.

p. 84: "have to defend all three." Liddell Hart, *Strategy,* 255.

p. 84: "along the Bug River to Smolensk." Army Group North had twenty infantry divisions, and three panzer and three motorized divisions, in the 18th Army under George von Küchler, 16th Army (Ernst Busch), and 4th Panzer Group (Erich Hoepner). Army Group Center had thirty-one infantry divisions, nine

panzer and seven motorized divisions, and one cavalry division in 9th Army
(Adolf Strauss), 4th Army (Günther von Kluge), 2nd Panzer Group (Heinz
Guderian), and 3rd Panzer Group (Hermann Hoth). Army Group South had
thirty infantry divisions, and five panzer and four motorized divisions, in 6th
Army (Walther von Reichenau), 17th Army (Karl Heinrich von Stülpnagel),
and 1st Panzer Group (Ewald von Kleist). Attached were the 3rd Italian Corps
of four divisions, a Hungarian corps, a Slovak division, and a Croatian regiment. To protect the right flank of Army Group South were the 11th Army
made up of Romanian and German forces, and the 3rd and 4th Romanian
Armies, nominally under the command of Ion Antonescu, the Romanian dictator. The Finns in the north had sixteen divisions (150,000 men), assisted by
four German divisions, two infantry, two motorized. In the German general
reserve were twenty-four infantry divisions, and two panzer and two motorized
divisions. See Fuller, vol. 3, 424.

p. 86:  " 'of armaments manufacture, Moscow.' " Guderian, 515. Hitler's entire
Directive 21 of December 18, 1940, is reprinted in Guderian, appendix 22,
514–16. The essential elements also are in Fuller, vol. 3, 421–24.

p. 87:  " 'were all grossly underestimated.' " Guderian, 261.

p. 88:  "enemy flanks to create caldrons." Count Alfred von Schlieffen, chief of the
German General Staff 1891–1905, sought to achieve modern Cannaes in
*Vernichtungskriege*, or "wars of annihilation." The aim was to avoid frontal
attacks by deep, concentric encircling movements around enemy flanks with
infantry armies to drive enemy forces into pockets where they had to surrender or be annihilated. Blitzkrieg was different. Its principal element was a deep
penetration through a narrow gap punched into the enemy's line. The aims
were to paralyze the enemy's ability to respond and to gain decisive objectives
far in the enemy's rear. As happened in the campaign in the west in 1940,
flanks remained only thinly guarded, or not at all, the speed of the panzer
advance acting to prevent enemy reaction. For an analysis of Cannae, see
Alexander, 45–48. For a summary of blitzkrieg and caldron battles, see Tarrant
5–7, 12–14, 31.

p. 89:  "and 2,770 aircraft." Shortage of oil was already severely restricting German
operations. There was only enough for a small fraction of transport to be
motorized, and this limited the number of mobile divisions. Most divisional
supply was delivered from railheads by horse and wagon. Fuel shortage to
some extent explains the lackadaisical German attitude regarding production
of tanks. After the campaign in the west in 1940, Hitler doubled the number
of panzer divisions but halved the number of tanks. In 1941 each panzer division (17,000 men) was authorized two or three panzer battalions, or 150–200
tanks, but divisions averaged only about 125. Motorized infantry divisions were
slightly smaller, but now were equipped with an armored battalion (about 50
tanks). The typical German infantry division had 15,000 men, in three regiments, plus four horse-drawn artillery battalions. See Glantz and House,
28–29; Liddell Hart, *Second World War,* 157–58; Fuller, 425; Guderian, 144.

p. 89:  "invisible to German intelligence." The Soviet field army, when the Germans
invaded, had six to ten divisions in two rifle corps, one incomplete mechanized corps, but little maintenance support. See Glantz and House, 36–41.

p. 90:  "were many more warnings." Ibid., 41–42; Shirer, 843–44; Keegan, *Second
World War,* 179–80.

p. 90:  " 'will be no war.' " Keegan, *Second World War,* 181.

p. 91:   "in the 1940 campaign." The tank division had 11,000 men in two tank regiments (375 tanks), one motorized rifle regiment, and reconnaissance, antitank, antiaircraft, engineer, and signal battalions. Most tanks were obsolete light models, but a few formations had the new KV-1 heavy and T-34 medium tanks, both vastly superior to the German Mark IIIs and IVs. The Red Army had about 1,800 of these new tanks when the war started. The T-34 weighed 26.5 tons and could travel at 31 mph (against the Mark IV's 25 tons and 25 mph), and had good armor (45-millimeter front, 40-millimeter sides). It carried a high-velocity 76-millimeter gun compared to the Mark IV's low-velocity 75-millimeter and the Mark III's medium-velocity 50-millimeter gun. The 47.5-ton KV-1 also carried a 76-millimeter high-velocity gun, but had 90-millimeter armor. Both tanks were impervious to almost all German weapons, except the 88-millimeter high-velocity antiaircraft gun. Russian mechanized forces were weakened by bad logistic support and poor radios, which made coordinated maneuvers almost impossible. Also, the number of motor vehicles in mechanized corps was extremely low. See Glantz and House, 36; Keegan, *Second World War*, 177; Liddell Hart, *Second World War*, 158; Zabecki, vol. 2, 1115–17 (Paul W. Johnson, Robert G. Waite).

## Chapter 9: Falling Between Two Stools

p. 92:   "and achieved air supremacy." Arguments that the Balkan campaign caused a fatal delay of six weeks in attacking Russia are incorrect. The campaign could not have commenced any earlier. Spring 1941 was exceptionally wet. The Bug River and its tributaries were still in flood stage well into May, and the ground nearby was swampy and almost impassable. See Fuller, vol. 3, 420; Guderian, 145.

p. 93:   "submission in a week." Only a day after the Germans invaded, Joseph Stalin caused the Supreme Soviet to establish the State Defense Committee, or GKO, with himself as chairman, with a Supreme Command, or Stavka, which he also dominated, placed under the GKO.

p. 93:   " 'blinded us for a few moments,' Guderian wrote." Guderian, 156.

p. 94:   " 'obedience and endurance.' " Liddell Hart, *Second World War*, 162.

p. 94:   "something that shortly did happen." On July 27, troops were read an order sentencing nine senior officers to death for being defeated. Others were shot in secret or committed suicide rather than face executioners. "Special sections" of the NKVD were deployed behind the lines to shoot deserters. On July 16 Stalin restored the "dual authority" of the political commissars—meaning once more they could overrule decisions of commanders.

p. 94:   " 'by an order of an officer.' " Bartov, *Hitler's Army*, 86.

p. 97:   " 'an attack toward Moscow.' " Guderian, 190.

p. 97:   "Ukraine and Crimea." Ibid., 198–200.

p. 98:   *"Rasputitsa* (literally 'time without roads')." Glantz and House, 80.

## Chapter 10: Failure Before Moscow

p. 101:  " 'unbounded determination to win.' " Kimball, 92.

p. 102:  "first meeting of the two leaders." At Placentia, FDR and Churchill agreed to the "Atlantic Charter," which reflected American ideals. It included Roosevelt's "Four Freedoms": freedom from want and fear, and freedom of worship and speech. Plans for a postwar international system remained vague. The charter called for "self-determination" of peoples to choose their form of government, but it didn't condemn colonies of the imperialist powers or Stalin's claims in eastern Europe. The charter also referred to "economic liberalism," calling for equal access for all to trade and raw materials, thus implicitly opposing closed trading blocs, including Britain's empire preference in commerce. See Kimball, 99–101, 205–6; Zabecki, vol. 1, 15–16 (Spencer Tucker).

p. 102: "convoys to Iceland." Britain had occupied Iceland on May 10, 1940. The United States took over protection of the island in April 1941 and sent in troops to guard it in July 1941.

p. 103: "request by generals for retirement." Goerlitz, 402–4.

p. 104: "clothing turning into rags." Keegan, *Second World War,* 198–99.

p. 105: " 'the situation was reversed.' " Guderian, 237.

pp. 105–106: " 'great wear to the engines.' " Ibid., 233–34.

p. 107: "with no loss to themselves." Glantz and House, 87.

p. 109: " 'very difficult to get out of.' " Mellenthin, 153.


## Chapter 11: To and Fro in the Desert

p. 110: " 'carried there at all costs.' " Churchill, *Second World War, The Grand Alliance,* 246.

p. 111: " 'tearing my tanks to bits.' " Liddell Hart, *Second World War,* 179.

p. 112: "never be allowed to reorganize." Rommel, 198–200.

p. 115: "conditions favorable to the British." Liddell Hart, *The Tanks,* vol. 2, 103.

p. 115: " 'smash them in detail?' " Ibid.


## Chapter 12: No Change in Strategy

p. 126: "supplies from America." Dahms, 342–43.

p. 126: "oil fields of Iraq and Iran." Rommel wrote that "in the summer of 1942, given six German mechanized divisions, we could have smashed the British so thoroughly that the threat from the south [Mediterranean] would have been eliminated for a long time to come. There is no doubt that adequate supplies for these formations could have been organized if the will had been there." See Rommel, 192.

p. 129: "won the Battle of the Atlantic." Dahms, 344–45.

p. 129: "the Caucasus oil fields and Murmansk." Ibid., 342.

p. 130: " 'clear away the problems involved.' " Rommel, 191–92.


## Chapter 13: The Drive to El Alamein

p. 131: "but he was turned down." Rommel, 203.

p. 132: "nearly won a total victory." On January 22, 1942, Hitler designated Rommel's force as Panzer Army Africa. In addition to Africa Corps (21st and 15th Panzer Divisions) and 90th Light Division, it included the Italian 20th Corps (Ariete Armored Division and Trieste Motorized Division), 21st Corps (Pavia, Trento, and Sabratha Infantry Divisions), and 10th Corps (Bologna and Brescia Infantry Divisions). Later the Italians committed another armored division, the Littorio. Only it and 20th Corps were motorized, and hence of any use in mobile warfare. The others had little organic transportation. See Ibid., 181, 195, 198.

p. 132: "moved 2nd Air Corps back to Russia." Ibid., 203fn; Dahms, 357.

p. 134: "be conducted offensively." Rommel, 194.

p. 134: " 'decided to strike first.' " Ibid., 193–94.

p. 136: " 'far as the eye could see.' " Lucas, 98–99.

p. 137: " 'to wherever danger threatened.' " Rommel, 208.

p. 138: " 'and use up their strength' " Ibid., 211.

p. 139: " 'strength at the decisive point?' " Ibid., 217.

p. 141: " 'given me one more division.' " Ibid., 232.


## Chapter 14: Stalingrad

p. 146: "and surrounded 6th Army." Stalingrad's main significance was to block oil from the Caucasus that Stalin had to have to stay in the war. Barge traffic from the Caspian to the Volga and northward became the main route for oil after the Germans broke the oil pipeline from the Caucasus at Rostov on July 23. Gunfire on the river was as effective in blocking barge passage as possession of Stalingrad itself. The Russians hurriedly laid a railway line west of the Caspian Sea from the oil fields at Baku to Astrakhan on the Volga. They also built a new rail line in the steppe from Astrakhan to Saratov, 250 miles northeast of Stalingrad, bypassing the city. In addition, the Russians sent 1,300 trucks a day over roads east of the Volga. When Averell Harriman asked Stalin if Russia needed more tanks, he answered that he'd rather have trucks. See Shirer, 909; Liddell Hart, *Second World War,* 247; Dahms, 370.

p. 147: "Baltic to the Black Sea." The army had suffered over a million casualties and received 800,000 replacements, but required 200,000 men to police the million square miles of Soviet territory Germany had occupied. See *Das Deutsche Reich und der Zweite Weltkrieg,* vol. 6, 778–85, 911–26. See also Theo J. Schulte, *The German Army and Nazi Policies in Occupied Russia* (Oxford, New York: Oxford University Press, 1989).

p. 147: "Halder wrote in his diary." Liddell Hart, *The Other Side of the Hill,* 296–98.

p. 147: "forces that had been surrounded." The German army survived the winter of 1941–1942 by holding key urban areas as bastions—Schlüsselburg, Novgorod, Rzhev, Vyasma, Briansk, Orel, Kursk, Kharkov, and Taganrog. Russians advancing around them could be cut off by flanking strokes from the strongholds. The German term for this process was *einigeln,* or to curl forces into a ball as *der Igel,* the hedgehog, does when it is threatened.

p. 149: "under Fedor von Bock." Walther von Reichenau had replaced Gerd von Rundstedt as army group commander, but he died of a heart attack in January 1942.

p. 149: "the oil fields of the Caucasus with four." Hitler assembled a million men in fifty-four divisions. In addition there were about 200,000 men in twenty allied divisions (six Hungarian, eight Romanian, and six Italian). The allied divisions were deficient in modern weapons and training. The main striking forces were 1,500 tanks in nine panzer and seven motorized (now designated panzer-grenadier) divisions. Also, cannons mounted on tank chassis (self-propelled guns) were coming on line. Unlike previous campaigns, *Schnellentruppen*—fast troops—were not concentrated, but divided among the five armies (2nd, 6th, 17th, and 1st and 4th Panzer). The panzer armies had three armored and two motorized divisions apiece, but also thirteen infantry divisions between them. All the infantry divisions relied on horse-drawn wagons and the legs of the sol-diers. There was thus a marked disparity in mobility between the fast troops and the foot-sloggers. The Soviets assembled about 1.7 million men in 81 rifle divisions, 38 rifle brigades, 12 cavalry divisions, and 62 tank and mechanized brigades in sixteen armies and four fronts. The Soviets had 3,400 tanks, 2,300 of them superior KVs and T-34s. See Tarrant, 30–32; Mellenthin, 144–59.

p. 149: " 'forces at Stalingrad to check it.' " Liddell Hart, *The Other Side of the Hill,* 214.

pp. 149–150: " 'able to exact a heavy toll.' " Mellenthin, 160.

p. 152: "of the entire city." On Soviet Lieutenant General V. I. Chuikov and his 62nd Army rested the defense of the city. Chuikov began with eight divisions. To neutralize German air and artillery superiority, he told his men to "hug" the Germans—remain so close that the enemy could not use air strikes or artillery without endangering his own men. The battle was fought out by small groups often separated by a single street or wall. German soldiers were in general bet-ter trained than Red soldiers, and by October had split Soviet defenses into four shallow bridgeheads, with front lines only 600 feet from the river front. The Reds resupplied and reinforced their troops at night by boats crossing the Volga. See Glantz and House, 122–23.

p. 153: " 'idiotic chatter' in his presence." Goerlitz, 418.

p. 153: "officers of the old German army." Ibid., 418.

p. 153: " 'through the adjacent fronts.' " Manstein, 302.

p. 154: "either side of Stalingrad." Stalin had divided his forces into twelve "fronts" under supreme headquarters or Stavka. These fronts usually had about four armies, which directly controlled attached divisions. There was no corps head-quarters. What the Russians now called corps were groups of tank and motor-ized brigades that actually were the size of divisions, controlled by the front commander. Stalin sent a senior general and staff from Stavka to direct several fronts involved in a single operation. The system had the advantage of reduc-ing intermediate headquarters and permitting fast movement of forces in fluid situations. It had the disadvantage of requiring commanders to direct large numbers of units. Stalin returned to army corps in the summer of 1943, before the system had been fully tested. See Liddell Hart, *Second World War,* 261; Glantz and House, 154.

## Chapter 15: Manstein Saves the Army

p. 157: " 'hundreds of miles of front.' " Manstein, 320.

pp. 157–158: "Luftwaffe Field Division arrived too late." The Luftwaffe Field Divisions were an invention of Hermann Göring, and they were a disaster. Göring formed them because the air force had far too many men for its few aircraft. He persuaded Hitler it was wrong to expose Nazi-indoctrinated air force men to reactionary army generals. He formed twenty-two Luftwaffe divisions, but the men had no training in ground combat, and the officers knew little of tac-tics or strategy. The divisions could only be used in static roles, and even here suffered extreme casualties and were largely ineffectual. See Goerlitz, 421.

p. 160: "forbidden 'by order of the Fuehrer.' " Manstein, 334.

p. 162: " 'risks in the military field.' " Ibid., 277.

**Chapter 16: The Western Allies Strike**

p. 165: "peace feelers in Stockholm." Dahms, 414.

p. 165: "invasions in the Mediterranean." FDR sent Marshall and Ernest J. King, U.S. Navy chief, to London July 18–24, 1942, with orders either to convince the British chiefs of staff to accept Sledgehammer or agree that the Americans fight in Africa, while extracting from the British a promise to plan for a cross-Channel invasion in 1943 (Operation Roundup). Roosevelt knew the British would reject Sledgehammer and agree at least to plan Roundup. The real purpose of the conference was to demonstrate to Marshall the true state of affairs. See Liddell Hart, *Second World War,* 312; Kimball, 152; Bryant, 341–45.

p. 166: "cross-Channel assault might not be necessary." Kimball, 166.

p. 166: "260 divisions actually in the field." *Das Deutsche Reich und der Zweite Weltkrieg,* vol. 6, 713.

p. 167: "same time as Oran and Casablanca." Churchill, *Second World War, Hinge of Fate,* 531–38.

p. 169: "French Admiral François Darlan, signed a cease-fire." The diplomatic jostling leading up to Torch was complicated, but it was only a sideline. The Americans were hoping the French could be convinced to give up without a fight or after token resistance; hence Roosevelt's insistence on the invasion looking like an American affair. FDR and Churchill refused to use Charles de Gaulle, chief of the Free French, because they didn't like him for his insistence on French rights at every turn, and because officers in Africa were loyal to Vichy, not him. They settled on General Henri Giraud, an army commander in 1940 who had escaped from a German prisoner-of-war camp. Giraud turned out to have few brains and much conceit, and wanted to be supreme commander of the invasion. Admiral Jean-François Darlan, a notorious collaborator with the Nazis, commander of all French armed forces and presumed heir to Henri Philippe Pétain, leader of Vichy France, happened to be in Algiers visiting a severely sick son when the Allies arrived, and, after tortuous negotiations, became the designated French head of government, while Giraud became commander of armed forces. Darlan called off French resistance but was assassinated December 24 by a disaffected young Frenchman. French forces in North Africa went over to the Allies and formed the nucleus of a large French army, which served with distinction later. But de Gaulle remained the true French leader, as confirmed by his wild reception by the people of Paris on liberation day, August 25, 1944. See Liddell Hart, *Second World War,* 317–21, 326–32; Kimball, 167–70, 173–75; Bryant, 414, 419, 423–30; *Das Deutsche Reich und der Zweite Weltkrieg,* vol. 6, 715–17; Blumenson, *The Duel for France,* 359–66.

p. 170: "arrow on French North Africa." On August 19, 1942, the British undertook a raid against Dieppe on the French Channel coast with two Canadian brigades, commandos, and tanks (Operation Jubilee). The aim was to test landing tactics and amphibious equipment. The raid was repulsed, with 3,400 casualties among the 6,100 men committed. The Dieppe failure was a propaganda victory for Germany, and it seemed to confirm Hitler's boasts about the impregnability of the European fortress. The Allies concluded that special assault methods and equipment had to be developed, cooperation between air, sea, and land forces improved, and that major seaports were too well protected to be assaulted. This led to building artificial harbors for the Normandy landings. See *Das Deutsche Reich und der Zweite Weltkrieg,* vol. 6, 710–11; Zabecki, vol. 2

(Paul Dickson), 1447–49; Dahms, 369–70; Kimball, 163; Robert Sherwood, *Roosevelt and Hopkins* (New York: Grosset and Dunlap, 1950), 626.

p. 173: "invasion of northwest Africa." Rommel, 192.

p. 175: "British mobile columns." Ibid., 327, 395.

p. 176: "to keep their weapons." Ibid., 358fn.

p. 176: " 'very great value,' Rommel wrote." Ibid., 396.

p. 177: " 'of nothing but jewelry and pictures.' " *Das Deutsche Reich und der Zweite Weltkrieg*, vol 6, 730–31; Rommel, 365–66.

p. 177: "secure from encirclement." On January 6, 1943, the Italian command asked Rommel to transfer a division to Tunisia to assist in the defense there. Rommel, eager to get his Africa Corps out of Libya, selected the 21st Panzer Division, but required it to leave all its tanks, guns, and other equipment, saying the division could be reequipped in Tunisia. See Irving, 257–58.

p. 177: " 'be it to the west or the east.' " *Das Deutsche Reich und der Zweite Weltkrieg*, vol. 6, 732.

p. 179: "armies, not the air forces." RAF nighttime attacks with incendiaries burned out large parts of the residential areas in the industrial Ruhr of western Germany, Cologne, and elsewhere. The greatest attacks were on Hamburg and Berlin. The Hamburg assault, which began July 24, 1943, created horrible firestorms that killed 32,000 people, made 900,000 homeless, and destroyed more than a quarter of a million houses and apartments. The Berlin assault began on November 19, 1943. Luftwaffe night fighters and antiaircraft defenses were readier for this threat, shooting down 492 aircraft and damaging 952 more so badly they had to be withdrawn from use. The 2,700 dead were far below the loss at Hamburg. Of 250,000 bombed-out Berliners, Joseph Goebbels evacuated many, and the remainder got emergency shelter. U.S. Army Air Force leaders believed B-17 bombers could deliver precision strikes on selected targets by flying in close formations or "combat boxes" that German fighters would be unable to penetrate. They were wrong. Losses were heavy. U.S. Army Air Force chief Henry H. (Hap) Arnold sent in Republic P-47 Thunderbolts to protect the bombers. The P-47s had only a short range (590 miles), however, and were unable to accompany the B-17s deep into Germany. The American theory had its first great tests on August 17, 1943, when German fighters shot down 36 of 183 B-17s on a raid against ball-bearing factories at Schweinfurt, and 24 of 146 bombers attacking the Messerschmitt works at Regensburg, both beyond the range of the P-47s. Production at both places continued. Eighth Air Force staged a second raid on Schweinfurt on October 14, 1943, using 291 B-17s. On the return flight, German fighters shot down 60 bombers, 17 crashed into the sea or in England, and 36 were damaged beyond repair—a single-day loss of 38 percent. Ball-bearing production was not interrupted. The cost was so great that doubts arose whether daytime bombing could be continued. However, Allied air commanders recognized the value of the North American P-51 Mustang fighter, which, with wing tanks, could reach a range of 2,200 miles, with a top speed (440 mph) comparable to the P-47, and higher than the top German piston-engined fighter, the Focke Wulf 190 (about 400 mph). P-51s did excellent service accompanying B-17s on deep raids into Germany. Even so, German industry was not paralyzed. Armaments minister Albert Speer transferred important industries to the east in 1942. Factories that had to remain were repaired quickly, large firms decentralized, and entire production branches transferred into caves, unused mines, and tunnels. Production actually increased. In 1943 Germany built 6,000 tanks (1942: 4,200) and 109,000 trucks and other vehicles (1942: 81,000); 36,500 cannons (1942: 23,500); 16,000 mortars (1942: 6,800); 4,180 antitank guns (1942: 1,300); and 4,400 88-millimeter antiaircraft guns (1942: 2,900); as well as 25,600 military aircraft (1942: 15,400). Most important, the destruction of German cities did not lead to a German collapse, as Sir Arthur T. Harris, chief of Bomber Command, had predicted. The German people began to identify their fate with that of the Nazi regime. See Dahms, 427–33; Crane, 93–119; Ronald Schaffer, *Wings of Judgment: American Bombing in World War II.*

p. 179: "to defeat the submarine menace." Early in 1943 Hitler replaced Erich Raeder with Karl Dönitz, his U-boat expert, as navy chief. A big reason for the Allied shipping losses in 1942 was the disruption of Magic intercepts because of a change in the naval code of German Enigma radio signals early that year. At the beginning of 1943 cryptologists at Bletchley, England, broke the code, but soon the Germans put a new roller in the Enigma machines and another blackout ensued. German naval intelligence had cracked the Allied code, leading to the greatest convoy battle of the war, which commenced on March 16, 1943. The fast convoy HX 229 caught up with the slower convoy SC 122 in the Mid-Atlantic. The two convoys, with nearly a hundred ships, ran into 38 waiting U-boats, which sank 21 freighters totaling 141,000 tons, at the cost of one submarine. This disaster set off extraordinary efforts. At Bletchley, Magic cryptologists broke the new Enigma code, while naval leaders at last solved the problem of the "black pit"— the Atlantic gap 600 miles wide not covered by air patrols that stretched from Greenland to the Azores. Here Dönitz concentrated his submarines, where they attacked convoys as they left air cover and broke off when they regained it. A conference in Washington called by Admiral Ernest J. King ordered escort carriers to shield convoys through the gap and stepped up use of B-24 Liberators to cover the gap from land. These measures, plus vastly improved radar (a 10-centimeter wavelength apparatus that could not be picked up by U-boats), broke the hold of the subs. In May, the Allies sank 41 U-boats, 24 by aircraft. With these catastrophic losses, Dönitz ended convoy battles until scientists could come up with defenses, but no one developed any. Germany had lost the "supply war." See Dahms, 421–24; Overy, 25–62; Liddell Hart, *Second World War,* 370–94.

## Chapter 17: Kasserine and the End in Africa

p. 183: "half the strength of the division." The Allies relied on Ultra intercepts, which seemed to point toward Fondouk, though observers on the spot noticed a German buildup at Faid. The concentration on Fondouk, Omar Bradley wrote, "came to be a near-fatal assumption." See Bradley and Blair, 127; Bradley, 25.

p. 184: "withdrawal to the Western Dorsals." Bradley, 25.

p. 184: "some of the supply dumps there." General Lucian Truscott described Fredendall as "outspoken in his opinions and critical of superiors and subordinates alike. . . . He rarely left his command post . . . yet was impatient with the recommendations of subordinates more familiar with the terrain and other conditions than he was." Omar Bradley wrote that Fredendall's command post "was an embarrassment to every American soldier: a deep underground shelter dug or blasted by two hundred engineers in an inaccessible canyon far to the rear, near Tebessa. It gave the impression that, for all his bombast and bravado, Fredendall was lacking in personal courage." See Bradley and Blair, 128.

p. 184: " 'uncertainty of command.' " Liddell Hart, *Second World War,* 405.

p. 185: " 'small private show of his own.' " Rommel, 401.

p. 185: " 'against the strong enemy reserves.' " Ibid., 402.

p. 187: "far lower tank losses." Blumenson, *Patton,* 181.

p. 187: "barred his return to Africa." Rommel, 418–19.

p. 188: "the defeat at Kasserine." Alexander's most damning indictment of Americans was in a letter to Alan Brooke: "They simply do not know their job as soldiers and this is the case from the highest to the lowest, from the general to the private soldier. Perhaps the weakest link of all is the junior leader who just does not lead, with the result that their men don't really fight." See Hastings, *Overlord,* 25.

p. 188: "attacks eastward, out of the mountains." Bradley and Blair, 141.

p. 188: "could find to oppose it." Omar Bradley agreed with Alexander, for he wrote that 2nd Corps "did not possess the force required for so ambitious a mission. Had we overextended ourselves from Gafsa to Gabès, we might have been seriously hurt on the flanks by an Axis counterattack." He also wrote: "Alexander was right, 2nd Corps was not then ready in any respect to carry out operations beyond feints." Bradley wrote that Patton and he accepted the corps's limitation "with good grace." However, a May 1943 German evaluation was much more complimentary. It said Americans had an ability to learn on the battlefield and would develop quickly into worthy opponents. See Bradley, 59–51; Bradley and Blair, 142; Liddell Hart, *Second World War,* 413, 415; Doubler, 28. Bradley's timidity shows a dramatic contrast with Rommel. One could scarcely doubt what Rommel would have done if he'd had four times as many men as the enemy placed firmly on the enemy's flank.

p. 189: "turn into a superb field commander." Bradley and Blair, 98–101, 139; Bradley, 43–45; Blumenson, *Patton,* 12, 17.

## Chapter 18: The Invasion of Sicily

p. 195: "cross-Channel invasion." Kimball, 214.

p. 196: "commanders in the Mediterranean." Churchill, *Second World War, Hinge of Fate,* 812–31.

p. 196: " 'the Messina bottleneck first.' " Bradley and Blair, 162–63.

p. 197: " 'an overwhelming victory.' " Ibid., 162; Liddell Hart, *Second World War,* 446.

p. 197: "the Allies invaded Sardinia." Liddell Hart, *Second World War,* 437–38.

p. 199: " 'surrenders were frequent.' " Ibid., 442.

p. 200: " 'on that goddamn beach.' " Kimball, 226. Churchill went ahead with a British-only effort to seize the Dodecanese Islands. The Germans beat the British to the islands, and the British failed badly, losing 4,500 men, 21 warships, and 113 aircraft. See ibid., 226–27; Michael W. Parish, *Aegean Adventures 1940–1943 and the End of Churchill's Dream* (Sussex, England: The Book Guild, 1993).

p. 201: "Badoglio announced surrender." Liddell Hart, *The Other Side of the Hill,* 356–57.

p. 203: "delivered him from disgrace." Blumenson, *Patton,* 209–18; Eisenhower, 179–83; Bradley, 160–62, 229; Bradley and Blair, 195–98, 201–2, 206–7, 218.

## Chapter 19: The Citadel Disaster

p. 204: "and fighting troops." Manstein, 443.

p. 204: " 'strongest fortress in the world.' " Mellenthin, 217.

p. 204: "mobilizing millions more." Dahms, 439–40.

p. 205: " 'begging to be sliced off.' " Manstein, 445.

p. 205: " 'on the Black Sea.' " Ibid., 446.

p. 205: "they needed to prepare." The original Tiger was a 56-ton machine mounting a high-velocity 88-millimeter cannon and 100 millimeters of armor, with a range of 87 miles. The 1944 model was several tons heavier with a slighter, longer range and shell-deflecting sloped sides on the turret like the Russian T-34. The Panther was first used in the Kursk battle. It was six tons lighter than the Tiger. It originally mounted an 88-millimeter gun, but later a 75-millimeter high-velocity cannon. Its range was 124 miles and it had 110-millimeter turret armor and 80-millimeter hull armor. Both were formidable weapons, and the Tiger was the best tank to come out of World War II.

p. 207: " 'my stomach turns over.' " Guderian, 306–9.

p. 207: "and 5,100 tanks." Dahms, 442.

p. 208: "SS Panzer Corps." The SS (*Schutzstaffel*, or protective staff) began in 1925 as Hitler's bodyguard, and under Heinrich Himmler expanded into many fields: intelligence (*Sicherheitsdienst* or SD); concentration camp guards; police, including the *Geheime Staatspolizei* (Gestapo or secret police); rulers of occupied territories; and the Waffen-SS or armed SS, which totaled 50,000 men in 1939 and 910,000 in 39 divisions in autumn 1944. SS divisions and corps were integrated into the *Wehrmacht* chain of command, and were generally directed by senior army generals. The Waffen-SS originally required volunteers to be of racially "pure Aryan" stock, but this provision disappeared in the late stages of the war. Although Waffen-SS units developed into effective fighting organizations, they were responsible for many atrocities, and were known for routine brutality. See Zabecki, vol. 1, 759–63 (Jon Moulton); 782–84 (Samuel J. Doss).

p. 209: "losses were often heavy." Mellenthin, 230–31. After Citadel, the Germans abandoned the *Panzerkeil* for the *Panzerglocke*, or tank bell. Superheavy tanks went to the center of the bell, medium tanks left and right, and light tanks behind ready for pursuit. The commander traveled behind the leading medium tanks, in radio contact with fighter-bombers, while engineers in armored vehicles just behind forward tanks were ready to clear gaps through minefields.

p. 209: " 'quail-shooting with cannons.' " Guderian, 311. At a demonstration on March 19, 1943, Guderian discovered the fatal flaw in Porsche's Tigers, but since Hitler was enthusiastic, Guderian had to use them. At this same event, Hitler and Guderian saw new armor plate "aprons" for the Mark III and IV panzers. These aprons or skirts hung loose about the flanks and rear of the tanks to cause antitank shells to detonate prematurely and not penetrate the main tank armor. The innovation was highly effective, leading the Russians to produce larger, high-velocity antitank guns and main tank guns. The T-34 gun was raised from 76 millimeters to 85 millimeters. See ibid.; Glanz and House, 162.

p. 212: "the size of its own." Manstein, 457.

**Chapter 20: The Assault on Italy**

p. 214: "Rome into Allied hands." Liddell Hart, *Other Side of the Hill*, 361–65.

p. 215: "forty self-propelled assault guns." Mark Clark in his memoirs, *Calculated Risk*, wrote the Germans probably had "about six hundred tanks at Salerno." See Clark, 199.

p. 218: " 'obtain tactical surprise.' " Linklater, 63.

p. 219: "ready to evacuate 6th Corps." Cunningham, 569; Liddell Hart, *Second World War,* 463.

p. 221: "with John P. Lucas." Eisenhower, 188.

p. 221: "obvious a place of landing." Liddell Hart, *Second World War,* 469.

p. 223: "attacks on enemy positions." Doubler, 13–21.

p. 225: " 'tactical move of my opponent.' " Liddell Hart, *Other Side of the Hill,* 364.

p. 227: " 'was a stranded whale.' " Churchill, *Second World War, Closing the Ring.* 488.

p. 228: "attack on Cassino had failed." Ibid., 500.

p. 229: " 'hours of such terrific hammering.' " Ibid., 506.

p. 230: " 'have been disastrous.' " Ibid., 429.


## Chapter 21: Normandy

p. 233: " 'once it had been recognized.' " Guderian, 328.

p. 233: "the other south of Paris." An eleventh division, 19th Panzer, was in southern Holland and would not be used unless the Allies invaded the Low Countries.

p. 234: " 'at any other point.' " Guderian, 329.

p. 234: " 'handling large ships.' " Ibid., 331; Rommel, 453. Another factor pointed to the Pas de Calais: Hitler's new revenge weapons, the V-1 unmanned jet bombers or cruise missiles, and the V-2 rocket-propelled ballistic missiles, were coming on line. The Allies were aware of them, and knew, because their range was limited, they had to be launched from around the Pas de Calais. The Germans believed the Allies would invade there to knock out the launch sites as quickly as possible.

p. 234: "commander of the Panzer Lehr Division." Rommel, 468.

p. 235: "extended to Normandy." Ibid., 454.

p. 237: "along the Norman coast." Liddell Hart, *Other Side of the Hill,* 391–92; Shulman, 112.

p. 237: "further disorder and war." Kimball, 238.

p. 238: " 'going to command Overlord.' " Eisenhower, 207.

p. 238: " 'his difficult subordinates.' " Hastings, *Overlord,* 29.

p. 239: "an American company's 21,000." Ibid., 34–35, 46.

p. 239: "work began apace." Churchill, *Second World War, Closing the Ring,* 72–76, 586–87; Eisenhower, 234–35.

p. 240: "especially the Pas de Calais." Eisenhower, 221–23, 225–29, 232–33; Bradley and Blair, 229–30.

p. 240: "fighters, now being introduced." Liddell Hart, *Second World War,* 606–12.

p. 241: "in the west—inevitable." D'Este, 76.

p. 241: "upon weather forecasts." Eisenhower, 239.

p. 242: "assault ever attempted." Ibid., 249.

p. 249: "among them three sets of brothers." Man, 46–48.

p. 250: " 'and burn furiously.' " Ibid., 52–54.

p. 250: " 'get the hell out of here.' " Bradley and Blair, 251.

p. 251: "were at last released." Liddell Hart, *Other Side of the Hill,* 405; Rommel, 474.

p. 253: "by all its formations." Rommel, 483; D'Este, 148, 162–63.

p. 253: "ballistic missiles." The V-1 had a range of 140 miles, a speed of 350 mph, an 1,800-pound warhead, and was accurate only within an eight-mile radius. Although the Germans launched 9,200 against England, antiaircraft fire and fighters destroyed 4,600. The V-2 had a range of 200 miles, a 2,200-pound warhead, and was less accurate than the V-1. However, it flew at 2,200 mph, beyond the speed of sound, and gave no warning. The Germans fired 1,300 V-2s against thirteen British cities. Later the Germans fired V-1s and V-2s against targets on the continent. The V-1s killed a total of 7,800 people and injured 44,400. The V-2s killed 4,100 and injured 8,400. See Zabecki, vol. 2, 1054–57 (Jonathan B. A. Bailey and Robert G. Waite).

p. 253: "wholly defensive operation." Rommel, 474–78.


## Chapter 22: The Liberation of France

p. 254: "talk with the Fuehrer." Rommel, 479–80.

p. 254: "most of them ill-trained." Guderian, 334.

p. 254: "against the Allies." Although Germany produced more than a thousand Me-262s, few ever got into the sky due to the quick work of Allied air forces. They bombed the refineries producing the special fuel for the jets, easily spotted the extended runways required for them to take off, and destroyed the Me-262s on the ground. See Shirer, 1099.

p. 255: " 'Make peace, you fools.' " Blumenson, *Battle of the Generals*, 100.

p. 255: "Allied aircraft near Livarot." Rommel, 485–86. Heinz Guderian wrote that on July 18, 1944, a Luftwaffe officer, whom he did not name, informed him that "Field Marshal von Kluge intended to arrange an armistice with the western powers without Hitler's knowledge, and that with this object in view was proposing shortly to establish contact with the enemy." See Guderian, 338.

pp. 255–256: " 'grew increasingly violent.' " Guderian, 341–42.

p. 256: "Rommel chose poison." Rommel, 503–6.

p. 256: "the British 2nd Army." Bradley and Blair, 269.

p. 257: "to deal with it." Michael D.Doubler, *Closing with the Enemy* (Lawrence: Kansas U. Press, 1944).

p. 257: "American casualties in Normandy." Ibid., 37–38.

p. 258: "soldiers out of the hedgerow." Ibid., 49–52.

p. 259: "equipped with the device." Ibid., 46.

p. 260: " 'cut down by splinters.' " Rommel, 489.

p. 260: "Panzer Lehr virtually vanished." Blumenson, *Breakout and Pursuit*, 240.

p. 260: "30th Infantry Division, exulted." Blumenson, *Battle of the Generals*, 145.

p. 261: " 'power at critical moments.' " Ibid., 147.

p. 262: "Mayenne, Laval, and Angers." In a side action, the 5th Infantry Division of Walton Walker's 20th Corps took both Angers and Nantes, thereby securing the Loire River line. Patton felt this operation was a diversion of strength, because there was little or no danger from Germans south of the Loire.

p. 263: "alerted them to the attack." Bradley and Blair, 291–92.

p. 264: " 'pure utopia.' " Blumenson, *Battle of the Generals*, 193.

p. 265: "Jacques Leclerc." Leclerc was the wartime pseudonym of Philippe François Marie de Hautecloque, a regular army captain who joined de Gaulle in 1940. He traveled through Chad to Libya and assisted Montgomery's army on the desert flank. He formed the 2nd Armored Division in North Africa in 1943 from assorted French and French Empire sources.

p. 266: " '*toujours l'audace.*' " Blumenson, *Battle of the Generals*, 216.

p. 266: " 'go beyond Argentan.' " Bradley and Blair, 298.

p. 266: " 'in the Canadian army.' " Ibid., 298.

p. 266: "the Germans in a trap." Blumenson, *Battle of the Generals,* 207.

p. 268: "surrendered to the Americans." Ibid., 227–28.

p. 269: " 'triumphal march to Germany.' " Ibid., 238.

p. 271: "a new defensive line." An RAF study, published in 1945, and located in the early 1990s by Michel Dufresne, revealed that the Germans had 270,000 men in the Falaise pocket and on the roads to the Seine on August 19, 1944. Another 50,000 men were elsewhere west of the Seine. Of these 320,000 men, 80,000 were lost in the last twelve days of August, while 240,000 arrived at the Seine and crossed, plus 28,000 vehicles and several hundred tanks. The principal means were sixty ferry- and boat-crossing sites, and three pontoon bridges at Louviers, Elbeuf, and near Rouen. Some crossed in small boats and rafts. The bulk of the crossings occurred at night. By September 1, all the Germans were across. See ibid., 259. Allied losses in the Normandy campaign were 200,000, two-thirds of them American. Bradley listed German losses at 500,000, but actual losses were probably about those of the Allies. German records showed total casualties in the west from June 1 to August 31 were 294,000. See Bradley and Blair, 304; Mellenthin, 283.

p. 271: " 'don't see it.' " Blumenson, *Battle of the Generals,* 255.

p. 272: "Is Paris burning?" Blumenson, *The Duel for France,* 360–61.

p. 272: " 'into Paris on August 25.' " Bradley and Blair, 309. A small French force, aided by civilians who hastily removed barricades, pushed through side streets from the south and actually reached the Hôtel de Ville shortly before midnight on August 24. See Blumenson, *The Duel for France,* 355.

p. 272: " 'back alleys, brothels, and bistros.' " Ibid., 359–66; Bradley and Blair, 309.

p. 273: "advance toward the Saar." Only half of Patton's army (two corps, Eddy's 12th and Walker's 20th) was available for immediate movement eastward. Troy Middleton's 8th Corps was still in Brittany, and Haislip's 15th Corps was deploying from Mantes. As a sop to Bradley, Montgomery got "operational coordination" of Hodges's army, but not "operational direction," which in theory remained with Bradley. See Bradley and Blair, 315, 318, 325.

p. 273: " 'such an opportunity.' " Liddell Hart, *Second World War,* 558.

p. 274: " 'if you'll keep 3rd Army moving.' " Ibid., 562.

p. 274: " 'into Germany almost unhindered.' " Westphal, 172–74.

p. 274: "forces on the front." Liddell Hart, *Other Side of the Hill,* 428.

p. 274: "avoid being killed." Liddell Hart, *Second World War,* 567; Bradley and Blair, 319.

p. 275: "the end of August." Bradley wrote that the Americans began running out of gasoline on or about September 1. See Bradley and Blair, 321.

## Chapter 23: The Battle of the Bulge

p. 276: " 'the objective Antwerp.' " Cole, *The Ardennes,* 2; MacDonald, 11. Another source for the battle is John S. D. Eisenhower, *The Bitter Woods: The Battle of the Bulge* (New York: Putnam, 1969; reprint New York: Da Capo, 1995).

p. 277: " 'the German officers corps.' " MacDonald, 21.

p. 278: " 'worth his while.' " Bradley, 454.

p. 280: " 'passed me on.' " Ibid., 467–69.

p. 280: " 'was really practicable.' " Liddell Hart, *Other Side of the Hill,* 447.

p. 281: "mount an offensive." MacDonald, 79.

p. 281: " 'sonuvabitch gotten all his strength?' " Bradley, 466.

p. 281: "he held in reserve." Eisenhower, 342.

p. 285: "massacring eighty-six American prisoners." On July 11, 1946, an American war crimes court convicted Peiper, Sepp Dietrich, and seventy-one other defendants, all former SS officers or soldiers. Peiper and forty-two others were sentenced to death. In time, attitudes changed due to a political climate more favorable to the Germans and the admission by the American prosecution that it had gained confessions by using hoods (as if the questioner was to be executed), false witnesses, and mock trials. None of the guilty were executed. All were ultimately paroled: Sepp Dietrich in 1955 and Peiper just before Christmas 1956. Peiper found Germany hostile to him, however, and moved to a village in Alsace. In the summer of 1976, two weeks after a sensational article about him appeared in the French newspaper *L'Humanité*, firebombs destroyed Peiper's house and killed the sixty-year-old former SS commander. See MacDonald, 216–23, 620–23.

p. 285: "help of 'artificial moonlight.' " Liddell Hart, *Other Side of the Hill*, 459.

p. 287: " 'Christ come to cleanse the temple.' " Bradley and Blair, 365.

p. 287: " 'drive like hell.' " Bradley and Blair, 365–67; MacDonald, 514–21; Liddell Hart, *Second World War*, 656–57; Montgomery, 275–82.

p. 288: " 'Go to hell!' " MacDonald, 511–13.

p. 288: " 'when they were needed.' " Liddell Hart, *Other Side of the Hill*, 463.

p. 289: "lost a thousand aircraft." MacDonald, 618.


**Chapter 24: The Last Days**

p. 290: " 'all this rubbish?' " Guderian, 382–83.

p. 291: " 'with what it's got.' " Ibid., 387–88.

p. 293: "change Hitler's mind." Ibid., 393.

p. 293: " 'views on their superiors.' " Ibid., 397.

p. 294: "accused Guderian of treason." Ibid., 401–2, 404–5.

p. 294: "all the more difficult." On February 4–11, 1945, Roosevelt, Churchill, and Stalin met at Yalta, a resort on the Crimean peninsula. With victory only months away, the sole topic was the postwar world, especially eastern Europe. Stalin insisted on an eastern frontier of Poland approximating the line dividing German and Soviet occupation zones after the defeat of Poland in 1939. To compensate, the three Allied leaders agreed to extend Poland's boundaries westward at the expense of Germany. The result established Germany's eastern frontier along the Oder and Neisse rivers, giving Poland Silesia, Pomerania, and southern East Prussia (Russia took over northern East Prussia, including Königsberg). Stalin also backed a Polish government set up by himself (the Lublin government). The western Allies supported the Polish government in exile in London, but, since Russia occupied Poland, could do little to advance its cause. See Zabecki, vol. 1, 50–51 (Philip Green); Kimball, 308–18.

p. 294: " 'I can't bear that.' " Guderian, 407; Shirer, 1097.

p. 296: " 'doesn't fit the plan.' " Bradley and Blair, 405–7.

p. 297: "did not take place." Shirer, 1103–5; Guderian, 422–24.

p. 298: "Eisenhower wrote." Eisenhower, 396–97.

p. 299: "defense of the city." Shirer, 1113.

p. 301: " 'be burned immediately.' " Ibid., 1123–27.

p. 302: "shot himself in the mouth." There is some evidence that Hitler bit down on a cyanide capsule and almost simultaneously fired a bullet through his head. See Rosenbaum, 79–80.

# Selected Bibliography

Addington, Larry. *The Blitzkrieg Era and the German General Staff.* New Brunswick, N.J.: Rutgers University Press, 1971.

Alexander, Bevin. *How Great Generals Win.* New York: W. W. Norton, 1993.

Barnett, Corelli, ed. *Hitler's Generals.* New York: Grove Weidenfeld, 1989.

———. *The Desert Generals.* Bloomington: Indiana University Press, 1982.

Bartov, Omer. *Hitler's Army.* New York, London: Oxford University Press, 1992.

———. *The Eastern Front, 1941–1945: German Troops and the Barbarization of Warfare.* New York: St. Martin's Press, 1986.

Bauer, Eddy. *Der Panzerkriege.* 2 vols. Bonn: Verlag Offene Worte, 1966.

Beaumont, Joan. *Comrades in Arms. British Aid to Russia 1941–1945.* London: Davis-Poynter, 1980.

Benoist-Méchin, Jacques. *Sixty Days That Shook the West: The Fall of France, 1940.* New York: G. P. Putnam's Sons, 1963.

Bessel, Richard, ed. *Life in the Third Reich.* New York: Oxford University Press, 1987.

Blumenson, Martin. *Breakout and Pursuit.* Washington, D.C.: Office of the Chief of Military History, 1961.

———. *The Duel for France.* New York: Houghton Mifflin, 1963.

———. *Patton: The Man Behind the Legend 1885–1945.* New York: William Morrow, 1985.

———. *Salerno to Cassino.* Washington, D.C.: Office of the Chief of Military History, 1969.

———. *Anzio: The Gamble That Failed.* Philadelphia: J. B. Lippincott, 1963.

———. *The Battle of the Generals: The Untold Story of the Falaise Pocket—The Campaign That Should Have Won World War II.* New York: William Morrow, 1993.

Blumenson, Martin. *The Patton Papers.* 2 vols. Boston: Houghton Mifflin, 1972, 1974.

Bradley, Omar N. *A Soldier's Story of the Allied Campaigns from Tunis to the Elbe.* New York: Henry Holt, 1951; London: Eyre & Spottiswoode, 1951.

Bradley, Omar N., and Clay Blair. *A General's Life: An Autobiography.* New York: Simon & Schuster, 1983.

Bryant, Arthur. *The Turn of the Tide, 1939–1943: A History of the War Years Based on the Diaries of Field-Marshal Lord Alanbrooke.* Garden City, N.Y.: Doubleday, 1957.

———. *Triumph in the West, 1943–1946.* London: Grafton Books, 1986.

Bullock, Alan. *Hitler, a Study in Tyranny.* London: Harper Perennial, 1971, 1991.

Butcher, Capt. Harry C. *My Three Years with Eisenhower.* New York: Simon & Schuster, 1946; London: Heinemann, 1946.

Chapman, Guy. *Why France Fell.* New York: Holt, Rinehart and Winston, 1968.

Churchill, Winston S. *The Second World War.* 6 vols. Boston: Houghton Mifflin, 1948–1954; London: Cassell, 1948–1954.

————. *The War Speeches of Winston S. Churchill.* Compiled by Charles Eade. 3 vols. Boston: Houghton Mifflin, 1953; London: Cassell, 1952.

Clark, Alan. *Barbarossa: Russian-German Conflict 1941–1945.* New York: Morrow, 1965; London: Hutchinson, 1965.

Clark, Gen. Mark. *Calculated Risk.* New York: Harper, 1950; London: Harrap, 1951.

Cole, Hugh M. *The European Theater of Operations: The Lorraine Campaign.* Washington, D.C.: Office of the Chief of Military History, 1950; reprint U.S. Army Center for Military History, 1984.

————. *The European Theater of Operations: The Ardennes: The Battle of the Bulge.* Washington, D.C. Office of the Chief of Military History, 1965; reprint U.S. Army Center for Military History, 1988.

Cooper, Matthew. *The German Army 1933–1945.* New York: Stein and Day, 1978.

Corum, James S. *The Luftwaffe: Creating the Operational War, 1918–1940.* Lawrence: University Press of Kansas, 1997.

Craig, Gordon A. *The Politics of the German Army 1640–1945.* New York: Oxford University Press, 1964.

Crane, Conrad C. *Bombs, Cities, and Civilians: American Airpower Strategy in World War II.* Lawrence: University Press of Kansas, 1993.

van Creveld, Martin. *Hitler's Strategy: The Balkan Clue.* Cambridge, U.K.: Cambridge University Press, 1973.

Cross, Robin. *Citadel: The Battle of Kursk.* London: Michael O'Mara Books, 1993; New York: Barnes & Noble, 1994.

Cunningham, Adm. Lord. *A Sailor's Odyssey.* London: Hutchinson, 1951.

Dahms, Hellmuth Günther. *Die Geschichte des Zweiten Weltkrieges.* München, Berlin: F. A. Herbig, 1983.

Dallek, Robert. *Franklin D. Roosevelt and American Foreign Policy, 1932–1945.* New York: Oxford University Press, 1979.

Dallin, Alexander. *German Rule in Russia.* New York: Macmillan, 1957; London: 1983.

*Das Deutsche Reich und der Zweite Weltkrieg.* Vols. 2–6. Produced by *das militärgeschichtlichen Forschungsamt.* Stuttgart: Deutsche Verlags-Anstalt, 1979–1983.

D'Este, Carlo. *Decision in Normandy.* New York: Harper Perennial, 1994.

Douhet, Giulio. *The Command of the Air.* New York: Coward-McCann, 1952; London: Faber, 1943.

Ehrman, John. *Grand Strategy.* Vol. 5. London: HMSO, 1956.

Eisenhower, Dwight D. *Crusade in Europe.* New York: Doubleday, 1948; London: Heinemann, 1949.

Ellis, John. *Brute Force: Allied Strategy and Tactics in the Second World War.* New York: Viking, 1990.

————. *The Sharp End: The Fighting Man in World War II.* New York: Scribner's, 1980.

Ellis, L. F. Major. *The War in France and Flanders, 1939–1940. History of the Second World War.* London: HMSO, 1953.

English, John A., and Bruce I. Gudmundsson. *On Infantry.* Westport, Conn.: Praeger, 1994.

Erickson, John. *The Soviet High Command: A Military-Political History.* New York: St. Martin's, 1962.

————. *The Road to Stalingrad.* London: Weidenfeld and Nicolson, 1975; New York: Harper & Row, 1975.

————. *The Road to Berlin.* New York: Harper and Row, 1983.

Eubank, Keith. *Summit at Teheran.* New York: William Morrow, 1985.

Feiling, Keith. *The Life of Neville Chamberlain.* London: Macmillan, 1946.

Finney, Patrick, ed. *The Origins of the Second World War.* New York: Oxford University Press, 1997.

French, David. *The British Way of Warfare.* London: Unwin Hyman, 1990.

Fuller, J. F. C. *A Military History of the Western World.* 3 vols. Reprint of 1956 ed. New York: Da Capo Press, n.d.

Gilbert, Martin. *The Second World War.* New York: Henry Holt, 1989.

Glantz, David M., and Jonathan House. *When Titans Clashed: How the Red Army Stopped Hitler.* Lawrence: University Press of Kansas, 1995.

Goerlitz, Walter. *History of the German General Staff.* New York: Praeger, 1953.

Goldhagen, Daniel Jonah. *Hitler's Willing Executioners: Ordinary Germans and the Holocaust.* New York: Alfred A. Knopf, 1996.

Goutard, Adolphe. *The Battle of France, 1940.* New York: Ives Washburn, 1959.

Greenfield, K. R., ed. *Command Decisions.* Washington, D.C.: Office of the Chief of Military History, 1960.

Guderian, Heinz. *Panzer Leader.* New York: E. P. Dutton, 1952.

Gudmundsson, Bruce I. *On Artillery.* Westport, Conn.: Praeger, 1993.

———. *Stormtroop Tactics.* Westport, Conn.: Praeger, 1989, 1995.

Halder, Gen. Franz. *Diaries.* Privately printed. Copyright Infantry Journal (U.S.A.), 1950.

Harrison, Gordon A. *Cross-Channel Attack. United States Army in World War II.* Washington, D.C.: Office of the Chief of Military History, 1950, 1977.

Hastings, Max. *Das Reich. Resistance and the March of the 2nd SS Panzer Division through France: June 1944.* London: 1981.

———. *Overlord: D-Day and the Battle for Normandy.* New York: Simon & Schuster, 1984.

———. *Victory in Europe: D-Day to V-E Day.* Boston: Little, Brown, 1985.

Hinsley, F. H., et al. *British Intelligence in the Second World War.* London: HMSO, 1979.

Horne, Alistair. *To Lose a Battle: France 1940.* Boston: Little, Brown, 1969; London: 1969.

Howard, Michael. *The Mediterranean Strategy in the Second World War.* London: Weidenfeld and Nicolson, 1968.

Howe, George F. *The Mediterranean Theater of Operations: Northwest Africa: Seizing the Initiative in the West.* Washington, D.C.: Office of the Chief of Military History, 1957.

Irving, David. *The Trail of the Fox: The Search for the True Field Marshal Rommel.* New York: E. P. Dutton, 1977.

Keegan, John. *The Second World War.* New York: Penguin Books, 1989.

———. *Six Armies in Normandy.* New York: Penguin Books, 1994.

Kennedy, Paul. *The Rise and Fall of Great Powers.* New York: Random House, 1987.

Kiesling, Eugenia C. *Arming Against Hitler: France and the Limits of Military Planning.* Lawrence: University of Kansas Press, 1996.

Kimball, Warren F. *Forged in War: Roosevelt, Churchill and the Second World War.* New York: William Morrow, 1997.

Kippenberger, Maj. Gen. Sir Howard. *Infantry Brigadier.* New York and London: Oxford University Press, 1949.

Knappe, Siegfried, and Ted Brusaw. *Soldat: Reflections of a German Soldier, 1936–1949.* New York: Orion Books, 1992.

Krausnick, Helmut, and Hans-Heinrich Wilhelm. *Die Truppe des Weltanschauungskrieges.* Stuttgart: Deutsche Verlags-Anstalt, 1981.

Levine, A. J. *The Strategic Bombing of Germany 1940–1945.* Westport, Conn.: 1992.

Lewin, Ronald. *Ultra Goes to War: The Secret Story.* New York: McGraw-Hill, 1978.

———. *The American Magic: Codes, Ciphers, and the Defeat of Japan.* New York: Farrar Straus Giroux, 1982.

Liddell Hart, Capt. Basil H. *The Defense of Britain.* London: Faber, 1939.

———. *The Other Side of the Hill.* London: Cassell, 1951. (Shortened version published as *The German Generals Talk*, New York: William Morrow, 1948.)

———. *The Tanks: The History of the Royal Tank Regiment and Its Predecessors.* 2 vols. New York: Praeger, 1959; London: Cassell, 1959.

———. *History of the Second World War.* New York: Putnam's, 1971.

Linklater, Eric. *The Campaign in Italy.* London: HMSO, 1951.

Lucas, James. *Battle Group: German Kampfgruppen Action of World War Two.* London: Arms and Armour Press, 1993.

———. *Panzer Army Africa.* San Rafael, Calif.: Presidio Press, 1978.

MacDonald, Charles B. *A Time for Trumpets: The Untold Story of the Battle of the Bulge.* New York: William Morrow, 1985.

Man, John. *D-Day Atlas.* New York: Facts on File, 1994.

von Manstein, Erich. *Lost Victories.* Chicago: Henry Regnery, 1958.

Martel, Lt. Gen. Sir Gifford. *An Outspoken Soldier.* London: Sifton Praed, 1949.

Matloff, Maurice, and Edwin M. Snell. *The War Department: Strategic Planning for Coalition Warfare.* Washington, D.C.: Office of the Chief of Military History, Department of the Army, 1957. Same title by Matloff for 1943–1944, Washington, D.C.: 1959.

McGuirk, Dal. *Rommel's Army in Africa.* Shrewsbury, England: Airlife Publishing, 1987.

von Mellenthin, F. W. *Panzer Battles.* Norman: University of Oklahoma Press, 1956.

Messenger, Charles. *The Art of Blitzkrieg.* London: Ian Allen, 1976.

*The Memoirs of Field-Marshal Viscount Montgomery of Alamein.* Cleveland: World Publishing, 1958.

Morison, S. E. *History of United States Naval Operations in World War II: Sicily-Salerno-Anzio, January 1943–June 1944.* Vol. 9. Boston: Little, Brown, 1954.

Müller, Rolf-Dieter. *Das Tor zur Weltmacht.* Produced by *das militärgeschichtlichen Forschungsamt.* Boppard am Rhein: Harald Boldt Verlag, 1984.

North, John. *North-West Europe 1944–1945: The Achievements of 21st Army Group.* London: HMSO, 1953.

Ogorkiewicz, Richard M. *Armoured Forces: A History of Armoured Forces and Their Vehicles.* New York: Arco Publishing, 1970.

Overy, Richard. *Why the Allies Won.* New York: W. W. Norton & Company, 1995.

———. *The Air War 1939–1945.* London: Papermac, 1980.

Playfair, Maj. Gen. I.S.O., et al. *The Mediterranean and the Middle East.* Vol. 3. London: HMSO, 1960.

Pogue, Forrest C. *George C. Marshall: Ordeal and Hope.* Vol. 2. New York: Viking, 1965. *George C. Marshall: Organizer of Victory.* Vol. 3. New York: Viking, 1973.

Postan, M. M., et al. *The Design and Development of Weapons.* London: HMSO, 1965.

Reynolds, Michael. *Steel Inferno: 1st SS Panzer Corps in Normandy.* New York: Sarpedon Publishers, 1997; Dell, 1998.

Rich, Norman. *Hitler's War Aims: The Establishment of the New Order.* London: W. W. Norton, 1974.

Rommel, Field Marshal Erwin. *The Rommel Papers.* Ed. B. H. Liddell Hart. New York: Harcourt, Brace, 1953; London: Collins, 1953.

Rosenbaum, Ron. *Explaining Hitler.* New York: Random House, 1998.

Roskill, Captain S. W. *The War at Sea.* Vol. 1. London: HMSO, 1954.

Schaffer, Ronald. *Wings of Judgment: American Bombing in World War II.* New York: Oxford, 1985.

Schmidt, Heinz Werner. *With Rommel in the Desert.* London: Harrap, 1951.

Seaton, Lt. Col. Albert. *The Russo-German War, 1941–1945.* New York: Praeger, 1970; London: Arthur Barker, 1970.

Shirer, William L. *The Rise and Fall of the Third Reich.* New York: Simon & Schuster, 1960.

Shulman, Milton. *Defeat in the West.* London: Secker & Warburg, 1986.

Spears, Sir Edward L. *Assignment to Catastrophe: Prelude to Dunkirk, The Fall of France.* New York: A. A. Wyn, 1955.

Speer, Albert. *Inside the Third Reich.* London: Macmillan, 1970.

Stewart, I. M. G. *The Struggle for Crete.* London: 1955.

Streit, Christian. *Keine Kameraden. Die Wehrmacht und die sowjetischen Kriegsgefangenen 1941–1945.* Stuttgart: Deutsche Verlags-Anstalt, 1978.

Sydnor, Charles. *Soldiers of Destruction: The SS Death's Head Division 1933–1945.* Princeton, N.J.: 1977.

Tarrant, V. E. *Stalingrad.* London: Leo Cooper, 1992.

Taylor, A. J. P. *The Origins of the Second World War.* London: 1963.

Tedder, Marshal Lord. *With Prejudice.* Boston: Little, Brown, 1967; London: Cassell, 1966.

Terkel, Studs. *The "Good War": An Oral History of World War Two.* New York: Pantheon, 1984.

Trevor-Roper, H. R. *Hitler's War Directives, 1939–1945.* London: Sedgwick, 1964.

———. *The Last Days of Hitler.* London: Collier, 1971.

Ueberschär, Gerd R., and Wolfram Wette, eds. *Unternehmen Barbarossa.* Paderborn: Ferdinand Schöningh, 1984.

Warlimont, Walter. *Inside Hitler's Headquarters.* San Rafael, Calif.: Presidio, 1994. 1962.

Webster, Sir Charles, and Noble Frankland. *The Strategic Air Offensive Against Germany 1939–1945,* vol. 1; *Preparation,* vol. 2; *Endeavour,* vol. 3; *Victory,* vol. 4. London: HMSO, 1961.

Westphal, Gen. Siegfried. *The German Army in the West.* London: Cassell, 1951.

Willmott, H. P. *The Great Crusade.* New York: Free Press, 1990.

Wilmot, Chester. *The Struggle for Europe.* New York: Harper, 1952.

Young, Desmond. *The Desert Fox.* New York: Harper, 1950.

Zabecki, David T., ed. *World War II in Europe: An Encyclopedia.* 2 vols. New York: Garland Publishing, 1999.

# Index

Aa Canal. *See* Bassée Canal
Acroma (Libya), 115, 135
Africa, 46, 48, 53, 187
  *See also* North Africa
Africa Corps, 117–19, 121, 123, 125, 135–37, 139–41, 143, 174, 175, 185, 186
Aircraft:
  Allied, 15, 223, 235
  British, 15–16, 38, 65
  French, 15
  German, 6–8, 15, 21, 38–40, 42, 65, 289
  Soviet, 92
  U.S., 179, 289
Aisne River, 34
Albania, 55, 60
Albert Canal (Belgium), 20
Alençon (France), 265
Alexander, Harold, 238
  and assault on Italy, 195, 199, 214, 225, 228–32
  in North Africa, 144, 184, 185, 188, 190, 191
Algeria, 37, 48, 166, 170
Algiers (Algeria), 167, 169, 170
Allen, Leven, 281
Allen, Terry, 189, 190
Allfrey, C. W., 220
Amiens (France), 30, 34
Anderson, Kenneth A., 169, 171, 172, 173, 183, 185
Antitank guns, 111, 112–13, 136, 209
Antwerp (Belgium), 21–22, 240, 272, 273, 276, 277, 279, 280, 284, 295
Anzio (Italy), 226–28, 230, 231
Archangel (Soviet Union), 50, 83
Ardennes (Belgium), 3, 11, 13, 22, 276–79, 281, 291
Argentan (France), 265–67, 270
Argentina, 47
Arnhem (Holland), 273–74
Arnim, Hans-Jürgen von, 173, 183–88, 190–92
Arras (France), 30, 31
Atlantic Conference (1941), 102
Atlas Mountains, 170
Attlee, Clement, 14

Attrition, 88–89, 97, 112
Auchinleck, Claude, 115, 116, 122, 134, 141–44
Avranches (France), 261–64
Azores islands, 47

Badoglio, Pietro, 199–201
Balck, Hermann, 25, 28, 158–59
Barbarossa campaign, 63, 76, 81–99, 102–9, 114
Bardia (Libya), 54
Barré, George, 171
Bassée Canal, 31, 32
Bastico, Ettore, 177
Bastogne (Belgium), 286, 287, 289
*Bataille conduite,* 16
Battipaglia (Italy), 218, 219
Battle of Britain, 38–41
Battle of Chancellorsville, 180
Battle of Kasserine, 180–87
Battle of the Atlantic, 129
Battle of the Bulge, 276–89
Bayerlein, Fritz, 234, 252, 260
Beda Fomm, 56, 113
Belgium, 3, 9–14, 30, 240
  invasion of, 1, 17
  King Leopold's surrender, 32
Benghazi (Libya), 55, 71, 73, 77, 125, 142
Berlin (Germany), 41, 298, 299, 316
Berlin-Moscow pact, 5
Bessarabia (Soviet Union), 43, 93
Bialystok (Soviet Union), 93, 95
Billotte, Gaston Harvé, 21
Bir Hacheim, 133, 135–39
*Blitzkrieg,* 5, 114, 310
Blumenson, Martin, 260, 269
Blumentritt, Günther, 274
*Bocage* country, 257–59
Bock, Fedor von, 11, 13, 31, 32, 84, 93, 96, 97, 104, 106, 107, 109, 149
Bohemia, 5
Bormann, Martin, 300–302
Bouillon (Belgium), 23
Bouvellemont (France), 28

Bradley, Omar, 190, 188, 274–75, 318
  and Allied invasion of France, 203, 238,
    248, 256–57, 259–67, 269, 271, 272
  and Battle of the Bulge, 278, 280, 281, 286,
    287
  in last days of war, 295, 296
Brandenberger, Erich, 279
Brauchitsch, Walter von, 11, 32, 46, 49, 76, 80,
    83, 87, 96, 97, 103, 107, 108
Braun, Eva, 300–302
Bren gun, 222
Brest (Soviet Union), 93
Britain:
  assault on Italy, 214–32
  attacks on French fleet, 37, 167
  Battle of Kasserine, 181, 183–87
  bombing of Germany, 178–79
  bombings over, 40–42
  on Crete, 61–69
  declaration of war, 5
  differences with U.S., 165
  Dunkirk sea lift, 33
  fleet, 132
  in Greece, 57, 60
  Hitler's turn away from, 2, 36
  in North Africa, 53–56, 72–73, 76–79,
    110–25, 131–44, 166–78, 181, 183–92
  political changeovers, 14
  RAF, 38, 40–42
  reliance on U.S., 2
  sanctions against Japan, 101
  survival of, 36–37
  U.S. backing, 37, 43–44, 102
British Expeditionary Force (BEF), 30–33
Brittany (France), 236, 256, 261
Broich, Friedrich von, 186
Brooke, Alan, 195–96, 230, 232, 237
Bryansk (Soviet Union), 105
Bucovina, 43
Budapest (Hungary), 291, 293, 295
Budenny, Seymon, 98, 99
Bulgaria, 50, 201, 307
Bull, Harold R. "Pink", 296

Caen (France), 241, 247, 252, 256, 259
"Caesar line," 231
Cairo (Egypt), 143
Calabria (Italy), 196
Caldron battles, 84, 86, 87, 88, 93–95, 96, 114
Canaris, Wilhelm, 47
Canary Islands, 47, 48
Cape Verde Islands, 47
Casablanca (Morocco), 167, 169
Caspian Sea, 83

Cassino (Italy), 226–31
Castellano, Giuseppe, 201
Caucasus (Soviet Union), 83, 87, 126, 129,
    145, 146, 150, 153, 162, 163, 313
Cava Gap, 215, 218, 219
Cavallero, Ugo, 132
Chamberlain, Neville, 5, 14
Chambois (France), 267, 269, 270
Chapman, Guy, 25
Cherbourg (France), 256
Chiunzi Pass, 215, 218
Choltitz, Dietrich von, 271–72
Churchill, Winston, 2, 14, 22, 45, 55, 57, 166
  alerting of Stalin to German invasion, 89
  and Allied invasion of France, 238, 242–43
  and assault on Italy, 195–96, 227, 230, 232
  Atlantic Conference, 102
  Casablanca conference, 178–79
  and Crete campaign, 63–64, 68
  "Germany first" policy, 127–28
  inspirational speeches, 33–34, 36–37
  in last days of war, 298
  Middle East and Egypt policy, 49, 52, 110,
    115, 144
  in Paris, 27
  Quebec conference, 199–200
  Teheran conference, 225, 237
  and U.S. aid to Russia, 100
Citadel. *See* Operation Citadel
Clark, Mark, 214, 215, 218, 219, 221, 222,
    225–28, 230, 231
Clausewitz, Karl von, 88
Cojeul River, 31
Collins, J. Lawton, 256, 259, 260, 266, 288
"Commissar order," 94
Communism, 2, 5, 43, 194, 309
Cook, Gilbert R., 267, 271
Corap, André, 26
Corlett, Charles H., 256
Corsica, 170, 224
Cota, Norman D., 250
Creagh, Michael, 56
Crerar, Henry, 262, 267, 269
Crete, 61–70, 79
Crimea, 97, 98, 103–4, 147
Croats, 59
Crocker, Joe, 191
Cruewell, Ludwig, 117–19, 122, 123, 135
Cunningham, Alan, 115–17, 121–22
Cunningham, Andrew, 68, 69
Czechoslovakia, 4–5

Dakar (Senegal), 48, 50
Daladier, Edouard, 5, 13–14, 27

François, 169, 171, 315
nest J. "Mike," 215, 221
243, 247
ve) Sherman tank, 248, 249, 250
arles, 29, 35, 48, 272
s, 247

72, 73, 75, 112, 134
268, 278
170, 315
pp," 268, 278, 279, 284,

h, 252
ne), 86, 103
, 317
52, 154

213

–33

r,

, 171

79, 115, 141–43
. 111–13, 119,

–74, 278,                  9–40, 272–73
                           , 238–42, 260,
09
4                          281, 287
                           , 214, 219, 224
                           98, 303
5–97,                      , 173, 183,

                           , 169

2–13

Fort Capuzzo, 111, 117, 120
40-millimeter antitank gun, 113
France, 9, 16, 194, 195
    Allied invasion of, 233–53
    British attacks on ships, 37, 167
    declaration of war, 5
    defeat of, 1, 17–35
    fleet, 37, 167, 170–71
    liberation of, 254–75
    political unrest in, 13–14
    Vichy government, 37, 48
Franco, Francisco, 46–47, 49, 55
Fredenall, Lloyd, 167, 180, 183, 184, 186, 188, 317
Frederick the Great, 277, 298
French North Africa, 48, 50, 166–73, 180–93
    *See also* Algeria; Morocco; Tunisia
Freyberg, Bernard Cyril, 64, 67, 68, 227
Friedeburg, Hans von, 302–3
Fuller, J.F.C., 7

Gamelin, Maurice, 13, 14, 21, 27
Gandhi, Mohandas K., 51
Gasoline. *See* Oil
Gazala line, 133–35, 138, 139
Geisler, Hans, 71
Gembloux (France), 22, 30
George II (king of Greece), 60
George VI (king of England), 243
Germany:
    Allied advance on, 272–75, 290–303
    Allied bombing of, 178–79
    assault on Italy, 214–32
    attack on Crete, 61–70
    Barbarossa campaign, 63, 76, 81–99, 102–9
    Battle of the Bulge, 276–89
    campaign in West, 9–16
    defeat of France, 17–35
    fatal turn to East, 45–60
    land to produce food, 3
    last days, 290–303
    in North Africa, 52–57, 71–80, 110–25,
        131–44, 168, 170–78, 180–93
    Operation Citadel, 204–13
    opportunity for victory, 1–8
    6th Army's defeat, 156–64
    U-boats, 129, 179, 317
Gerow, Leonard T., 256, 267, 269, 270, 272
Geyr von Schweppenberg, Leo, 233, 234, 236
Gibraltar, 46–48, 49, 50, 53, 55, 167
Giraud, Henri, 21, 315
Godwin-Austen, A.R., 115
Goebbels, Joseph, 278, 298, 300–302
Goerlitz, Walter, 103

Golikov, F.I., 155
Göring, Hermann, 33, 37–38, 40, 41, 155, 176–77, 281, 299–301, 303
Gort, Lord, 21, 30
Gott, W.H.E. "Strafer," 133, 143
Grants (tanks), 133
Graziani, Rodolfo, 52–54, 62
Greece, 55, 57–60, 76, 78, 79, 166, 197
Greenwood, Arthur, 14
Greim, Robert Ritter von, 300
Guderian, Heinz, 255, 275
  and Allied invasion of France, 233–36, 252
  and Barbarossa campaign, 84, 87, 93, 95–99, 102, 106–9
  and campaign in West, 11–13, 16
  and defeat of France, 22–26, 28–32, 34–35
  in last days of war, 290, 291, 293–95, 298
  and Operation Citadel, 207, 209, 213
  panzer arm, 5, 7, 16
Guingand, Francis de, 266
Gustav line, 221, 225–27, 230
Guzzoni, Alfredo, 197

Hafid Ridge, 111
Hague, The (Holland), 17
Haislip, Wade, 262, 265–67, 270
Halder, Franz, 11, 46, 49, 63, 69, 76, 80, 83, 87, 96, 97, 103, 108, 129, 145, 147, 149, 150, 153
Halfaya Pass, 110, 111, 116, 121, 122, 124, 141
Halifax, Lord, 14
Hamburg (Germany), 316
Hannibal, 88
Harmon, Ernest N., 190
Harris, Arthur, 240
Hastings, Max, 238
Hemingway, Ernest, 250
Hewitt, H. Kent, 218
Heydrich, Reinhard, 3
Himmler, Heinrich, 3, 299–301, 303, 319
Hitler, Adolf:
  and Allied invasion of France, 233, 234, 236–37, 251, 253–55, 262–65, 268, 271–72
  appeasement of, 5
  attack on Crete, 61–70
  attempt on life, 255–56
  campaign in West, 9
  death, 301–2
  declaration of war on U.S., 108
  and Dunkirk, 32–33
  errors in North Africa, 48, 49, 52, 53, 170, 173, 175–78, 187–88
  errors in Stalingrad campaign, 145–55

failure to appreciate Rommel's achie[vements], 79, 132
fallacies in Russia campaign, 81–99
fatal turn to East, 45–60, 194
first great error, 36–44
focus on destruction of Jews, 2–3
focus on destruction of Soviet Union, 45, 49, 52, 53, 127, 130, 194, 275, [?]
Gibraltar plan, 46–48
Hendaye talks, 55
inability to conceive strategic plan, 9[?]
and invasion of Sicily, 197
last chance to change direction, 129[?]
last days, 290–303
madness, 4, 145, 150
and Mediterranean arena, 132
and Operation Citadel, 204–5, 211, [?]
opportunity for victory, 1–8
plans for Italy, 200, 201, 224, 227
refusal to free 6th Army, 156–64
refusal to heed Rommel and Raede[r], 126–27, 130
rescue of Mussolini, 201–2
and Rundstedt, 277, 297
seizure of Corsica, 170
turn away from Britain, 2, 45
victories before 1940, 4–5
Hobbs, Leland, 260
Hodges, Courtney, 261, 263, 269, 27[?], 285, 296, 297
Hoepner, Erich, 13, 20, 21, 86, 105, [?]
Holland, 9, 13, 14, 17, 20, 236, 273–7[?]
Hooker, Joe, 180
Hopkins, Harry, 100–101, 102
Hoth, Hermann, 13, 23, 34, 84, 93, 9[?], 102, 105, 149, 151, 154, 208, 209[?]
Hube, Hans, 152, 200
Hubicki, Alfred, 13
Hull, Cordell, 101
Hungary, 50, 291, 293
Huntziger, Charles, 23
Hürtgen Forest, 278, 284

Iceland, 102
India, 51
Indochina, 101
Iraklion (Crete), 64, 67, 68
Iran, 50, 51, 88, 102, 126
Iron ore, 6
Italy, 35, 128, 132, 166, 170, 179
  assault on, 214–32
  capitulation to Allies, 201
  Hitler's plan to take over, 200

invasion of Greece, 55
in Libya, 46, 53, 56, 62, 71–72
offensive into Egypt, 52–55
weak performance of soldiers, 181, 199

Jackson, Stonewall, 180
James, William, 35
Japan, 44, 87, 127, 307
drive toward war, 101–2
Pearl Harbor attack, 108
Jews:
Hitler's focus on destruction of, 2–3
in Soviet Union, 82
Jodl, Alfred, 45, 46, 49, 62, 80, 97, 251, 268, 276, 289, 299, 300, 302, 303
Jomini, Antoine-Henri, 109
Juin, Alphonse, 227, 231
Juno beach, 241, 252

*Kampfgruppen*, 27, 114, 139, 223, 258
Kasserine. *See* Battle of Kasserine
Katukov, M. E., 208
Katyusha rocket launchers, 108
Keitel, Wilhelm, 49, 62, 80, 299, 300, 303
Kesselring, Albert, 170, 172, 186, 197, 201, 214, 215, 220, 224–27, 232, 297, 302
*Kesselschlachten*. *See* Caldron battles
Keyes, Geoffrey, 225
Khania (Crete), 64–67, 69
Khora Sfakion (Crete), 69
Kiev (Ukraine), 86, 96–99, 102–4
Kirchner, Friedrich, 157
Kirponos, Mikhail P., 90, 92, 98, 99
Kitching, George, 264
Kleist, Ewald von, 13, 23–24, 27–29, 32, 34, 59, 86, 92, 95, 98–99, 149, 150
Kluge, Günther von, 95, 205, 211, 255, 263–66, 268, 270
Knobelsdorff, Otto von, 158, 210
Koch, Walter, 20, 171, 172
Koenig, Pierre, 139
Konev, Ivan S., 104, 291, 295
Kraemer, Fritz, 278
Krebs, Hans, 298
Krüger, Walter, 285
Küchler, Georg, 21
Kursk (Soviet Union), 204, 205, 207, 208

Lang, Rudolf, 189
Laon (France), 29
Latvia, 43, 95, 291
Laval (France), 262
Leadership, 180–81

*Lebensraum*, 3, 49, 52, 82, 303
Lebrun, Albert, 14
Leclerc, Jacques, 265–66, 267, 270–72
Lee, Robert E., 180
Leeb, Wilhelm von, 15, 84, 96, 97, 103, 109
Leese, Oliver, 224
Leigh-Mallory, Trafford, 270
Le Mans (France), 262–65
Lemelsen, Joachim, 94
Lend-lease program, 44, 100, 290
Leningrad (Soviet Union), 6, 83, 96, 97, 102, 103, 109
Leopold (king of Belgium), 32
Libya, 46, 53, 54, 56, 57, 61, 62, 64, 71–80, 115, 131, 177
Liddell Hart, Basil H., 7, 273
Liebenstein, F. K. von, 183, 184, 200
Liri River, 229
List, Wilhelm, 29, 59, 60, 150, 153
Lithuania, 43
Livorno (Italy), 224
Löhr, Alexander, 64, 67, 68
London (England), 41, 42
Longwy (France), 23
Lucas, John P., 221, 226–28
Lucht, Walter, 285
Luftwaffe, 15, 21, 36–42, 92, 155, 235, 254, 289
Lüttwitz, Heinrich von, 285, 286
Luxembourg, 1, 14

Maas River. *See* Meuse River
Maastricht (Holland), 20
MacDonald, Charles, 277
Machine guns, 222
Mackensen, Hans Georg von, 227, 228
Madagascar, 167
Magic (decoding program), 101
Maginot Line, 9, 10, 15, 21, 34, 35
Maleme (Crete), 64–67
Malta, 46, 50, 61–63, 76, 79, 131, 132, 142
Manstein, Erich von, 3, 10–13, 23, 32, 103–4, 236, 275
attempts to relieve, 6th Army, 155–64
on Hitler, 162
and Operation Citadel, 204–5, 211
Stalingrad campaign, 145–47, 153
Mantes (France), 269
Manteuffel, Hasso von, 192, 279, 281, 284–89
Mareth line, 181, 187, 188, 189, 190
Marshall, George C., 128, 165–67, 195, 196, 200, 232, 237, 238
Matildas (tanks), 30, 31, 54, 55, 111, 112
Mayenne (France), 262

McAuliffe, Anthony C., 286, 288
McCreery, Richard L., 215, 218
Mediterranean arena, 46–49, 63, 79, 126, 132, 142, 166, 179, 194–95
Mehdia (Morocco), 169
*Mein Kampf* (Hitler), 3, 307
Mellenthin, Friedrich-Wilhelm von, 149, 204
Mersa Matruh (Egypt), 142–43
Mers-el-Kebir battle, 37
Messe, Giovanni, 178, 188, 190, 191
Messerschmitt fighter, 15–16, 21, 38–40
Metaxas line, 60
Metz (France), 272, 273, 274, 278
Meuse River, 1, 10–13, 20, 22–27, 279, 280, 284, 288
Middle East, 49–51, 53, 64, 127, 141
Middleton, Troy, 256, 261, 278, 284
Minsk (Soviet Union), 93, 95, 99
Model, Walther, 269, 270, 280, 297–98
Molotov, Vyacheslav, 90, 147, 307
Monte Cassino, 221–22, 226–28
Montgomery, Bernard:
    and Allied invasion of France, 238, 241, 246, 256, 259, 261–63, 266–67, 269–71
    and assault on Italy, 215, 219–21, 224
    and Battle of the Bulge, 287
    command of 8th Army, 144, 174
    and invasion of Sicily, 195, 197, 199
    in last days of war, 295–97, 302
    and march toward Germany, 272–75
    in North Africa, 169, 174–75, 178, 181, 183, 187–92
Monthermé (France), 23, 25, 26
Moravia, 5
Morgan, Frederick, 239, 240
Morison, Samuel Eliot, 196
Morocco, 48, 50, 166, 167, 169
Mortain (France), 263–65
Morzik, Fritz, 155
Moscow (Soviet Union), 83–84, 86–87, 95–99, 104–8
Motorized units, 72, 112, 132–33, 262, 290
Mozhaisk line, 106
Msus (Libya), 78
Mulberries, 235, 239, 256
Munich conference (1938), 4–5
Murmansk (Soviet Union), 50, 126, 129
Mussolini, Benito:
    death, 301
    declaration of war on U.S., 108
    and drive through Suez, 49
    Hitler's desire to keep him in war, 132
    invasion of Greece, 55

and North Africa, 53, 56, 61, 62, 131, 173, 176, 177, 187, 188
    ouster by Italians, 199, 200
    rescue by Hitler, 201–2
Mustang fighter, 179, 235

Nancy (France), 272, 274
Naples (Italy), 196, 215, 221, 227
Napoleon, 109, 118, 181, 266
Narvik (Norway), 6
Neame, Philip, 73, 76, 77, 78
*Nebelwerfer*, 186, 218
Nehring, Walter, 135–36, 171, 172–73
Netherlands. *See* Holland
Normandy, 203, 233–53, 256–58, 261, 268–70
Norrie, C.W.M., 116–18, 120, 134
North, John, 274
North Africa, 49, 52–57, 71–80, 110–25, 127, 131–44, 174–78
    *See also* French North Africa; Rommel, Erwin; *specific countries*
Norway, 6, 14, 50
Nuremberg trials, 303
Nye, Archibald, 197

O'Connor, Richard, 53–55, 57, 73, 78
Odessa (Soviet Union), 93
Oil, 50–51, 87, 102, 126, 129, 145, 150, 240, 272–74, 290, 310, 313
Oise River, 29
Oliver, Lunsford, 265
Omaha beach, 240, 243, 248–51
Operation Anvil, 225, 232
Operation Autumn Mist, 279
Operation Avalanche, 214
Operation Axis, 200
Operation Barbarossa. *See* Barbarossa campaign
Operation Battleaxe, 111, 114
Operation Bolero, 195
Operation Citadel, 194, 204–13, 237
Operation Cobra, 259, 262
Operation Crusader, 115
Operation Dragoon, 232
Operation Fortitude, 239
Operation Goodwood, 259
Operation Gymnast, 128, 166
Operation Husky, 195, 196, 197
Operation Mercury, 63
Operation Overlord, 195–96, 200, 225, 237, 256
Operation Roundup, 195
Operation Sea Lion, 37, 41, 42, 93
Operation Shingle, 226

Operation Sledgehammer, 165
Operation Torch, 166, 315
Operation Typhoon, 104
Operation Winter Tempest, 159
Oran (Algeria), 167, 170
Overlord. *See* Operation Overlord

Panthers (tanks), 207, 211
Panzer divisions, 7, 15, 89, 204, 233
Paris (France), 271–72
Pas de Calais (France), 234–37, 239, 240, 253,
    262, 269, 272
Patton, George S. Jr.:
    and advance on Germany, 272–75
    and Allied invasion of France, 239, 256,
        261–67, 269, 271
    and Battle of the Bulge, 278, 286, 288
    in Italy, 197, 199, 202–3
    in last days of war, 295, 296
    in North Africa, 167, 169, 188–92
    slapping incidents, 202–3, 238
Paul (prince of Yugoslavia), 59
Paulus, Friedrich, 150, 152, 154–55, 160, 163
Pavlov, Dimitri G., 99
Pearl Harbor, 44, 108, 127
Pearson, Drew, 203
Peiper, Joachim, 285, 286, 323
Petacci, Clara, 301
Pétain, Marshal Henri Philippe, 27, 35, 37,
    49, 55
Peter (prince of Yugoslavia), 59
Petroleum. *See* Oil
Ploesti oil fields, 97, 98, 196, 307
Poland, 3, 112, 290, 293
Popov, Markian M., 212
Porsche, Ferdinand, 209
Potenza (Italy), 220
Purple (encoding machine), 101

Qattara Depression, 142
Quadrant conference, 199–200

Radar, 38–40
Raeder, Erich, 45, 47–49, 52, 53, 62, 63, 79,
    126–27, 129, 130
Ramsey, Bertram H., 242
*Rasputista*, 106
Red Army, 82–84, 87–91, 127, 152, 156–57,
    194, 205, 290, 294, 295, 311
Reichenau, Walther von, 20
Reinhardt, Georg Hans, 13, 23, 25, 26, 31, 32,
    59
Reitsch, Hanna, 300
Remagen bridge, 296, 297

Rethimnon (Crete), 64, 67, 68, 69
Reynaud, Paul, 14, 27, 35
Rhine River, 295–96
Rhodes, 200
Ribbentrop, Joachim von, 59, 294, 299, 303,
    307
Richthofen, Wolfram von, 65, 67, 68
Ridgway, Matthew, 219, 272
Ringel, Julius, 68, 69
Ritchie, Neil, 122, 125, 134–35, 137, 138, 140,
    141
Rocket launchers, 108, 186
Roer River, 278
Rokossovsky, K. K., 293, 294
Romania, 43, 50, 57, 307
Rome (Italy), 200–201, 214, 226, 229, 231–32
Rommel, Erwin, 63, 275, 290
    on Africa as "lost cause," 130
    and Allied invasion of France, 233–37, 241,
        251–55
    Battle of Kasserine, 180–87
    on blitzkrieg warfare, 7
    death, 256
    and defeat of France, 23, 25, 26, 29–31, 35
    defeat/retreat in Africa, 143–44, 173,
        175–76
    on Göring, 177
    in Italy, 201
    method for Operation Citadel, 212
    on Mussolini, 187
    in North Africa, 56–57, 71–80, 110–25,
        131–44, 169, 173–78, 180–87, 193
    request to Hitler to change strategy,
        126–27
Roosevelt, Franklin D., 2, 35, 108, 232, 238
    aid to Russia, 100, 102
    Atlantic Conference, 102
    backing of Britain, 37, 43–44
    Casablanca conference, 178–79
    death, 298
    decision to fight Germany, 165–66
    demand for unconditional surrender, 179
    and North Africa, 166, 167
    Quebec conference, 199
    sanctions against Japan, 101–2
    and Stalin, 102, 165, 166, 237
    Teheran conference, 225, 237
Rosenberg, Alfred, 82
Roslavl (Soviet Union), 96
Rostov (Soviet Union), 103, 146, 149, 150,
    156, 159, 161, 163
Rotmistrov, P.A., 211
Rotterdam (Holland), 17, 272
Royal Air Force (RAF), 38, 40–42

Rundstedt, Gerd von, 10, 11, 27–29, 31, 32, 86, 96, 97, 103, 109, 233, 234, 236, 241, 254–55, 277, 279, 280, 297
Ryan, Cornelius, 274
Ryder, Charles W. "Doc," 169

Safi (Morocco), 169
St. Lô (France), 256, 259
St.-Mère-Eglise (France), 246
St. Petersburg. *See* Leningrad
Salerno (Italy), 195, 214–18
Saloniki (Greece), 60
Sardinia, 197
Scheldt River, 22, 30
Schlieffen plan, 9
Schmeisser machine pistol, 222
Schmundt, Rudolf, 13, 71
*Schnellentruppen*, 93
*Schwerpunkt*, 13, 22
Sedan (France), 11, 13, 21–26
Seine River, 269, 270–71, 322
Senger und Etterlin, Frido von, 227, 228, 231
Serbs, 57, 59
Sevastopol (Soviet Union), 104, 147
Shah Reza Pahlevi, 102
Sherman tank, 248, 249, 250, 258–59
Siberia (Soviet Union), 87
*Sichelschnitt*, 13
Sicily, 170, 179, 192, 195–99
Sidi Barrani (Egypt), 52, 53, 54
Sidi Rezegh airfield (Libya), 116–19
Siegfried line, 276, 277, 278
Silesia, 291, 294, 295
Simonds, Guy, 264
Simovic, Dusan, 59
Simpson, William, 278
Sirte (Libya), 71
Skorzeny, Otto, 200, 201, 279
Slavs, 82
Slovenians, 59
Smith, Walter Bedell, 201
Smolensk (Soviet Union), 95
Sollum Pass, 110, 111, 116, 121, 141
Somerville, Sir James, 37
Somme River, 10, 34, 35
Sorge, Richard, 101, 106
Soviet Union:
  and Baltic republics, 43
  Barbarossa campaign, 63, 76, 81–99, 102–9, 114
  Hitler's focus on destruction of, 2–3, 45, 49, 52, 53, 127, 194, 309
  industry, 100

  invasion of Finland, 6
  in last days of war, 290, 291, 294, 295
  oil fields, 50–51
  Operation Citadel, 204–13
  roads, 89
  Stalingrad, 145–60
  sufferings of people, 81–82
  U.S. aid, 100, 102
Spaatz, Carl, 240
Spain, 46–47, 50, 167
Speer, Albert, 294, 297
Speidel, Hans, 251, 255
Sponeck, Theodor von, 17
SS operations, 319
Stagg, J. M., 242
Stalin, Joseph, 2, 51, 52, 84, 87, 151
  and Baltic republics, 43
  and German invasion, 88–92, 95, 96, 98, 99, 101, 105, 106, 109
  purges of 1930s, 82
  system of "fronts," 314
  Teheran conference, 225, 237
  and U.S., 102, 165, 166
Stalingrad (Soviet Union), 145–60
Stauffenberg, Claus von, 255
Steele, John, 246
Steinhardt, Laurence, 90
Sten gun, 222
Stimson, Henry L., 128
Stonne ridge (France), 26
Strait of Messina, 196–97, 201
Strategic-bombing theory, 41–42
Strauss, Adolf, 109
Student, Kurt, 17, 64, 67, 69, 197, 201
Stuka dive-bomber, 8, 21, 24, 40, 114, 152, 223
Stülpnagel, Karl Heinrich von, 109
Stumme, Georg, 59, 174
Submarines, 129, 130, 179
Suda Bay (Crete), 64–69
Sudetenland, 5
Suez Canal, 46, 48, 49, 53, 79, 110
Sun Tzu, 81
Support groups, 113–14
Sweden, 6
Sword beach, 241, 252

Tank destroyers, 223
Tanks, 114
  Allied, 15
  British, 30, 31, 54–56, 111, 133, 139, 304, 309
  French, 25, 29–30, 304

German, 6–8, 11, 32, 121, 207, 211, 305–6
Italian, 54–56, 76, 131
Operation Crusader, 115
Soviet, 147, 311
U.S., 223, 248, 250, 258–59
World War I, 7
Taylor, Maxwell, 246
Tebessa (Tunisia), 183, 184, 185
Tedder, Arthur, 238, 242
Teheran conference (1943), 225, 237
Thoma, Wilhelm von, 53, 56, 174, 175
Thompson submachine gun, 222
Tigers (tanks), 209, 211
Timoshenko, Semen, 99, 147, 151
Tobruk (Libya), 54, 78, 79, 110, 115–18, 123, 139, 141
Trident conference (1943), 195
Trigh Capuzzo, 134–37
Tripartite Pact, 57, 307
Tripoli (Libya), 56, 57, 71, 72, 142, 177–78
Trun (France), 269
Truscott, Lucian K., 228, 317
Tuker, Francis, 227
Tunis (Tunisia), 170, 172
Tunisia, 48, 166, 167, 170–73, 181–88
Turkey, 48, 50, 64

U-boats, 129, 179, 317
Ukraine (Soviet Union), 83, 86–87, 92, 97, 98
United States, 51, 97
   aid to Russia, 100
   armed forces, 43
   assault on Italy, 214–32
   backing of Britain, 37, 43–44, 102
   Battle of Kasserine, 180–81, 184, 186
   Battle of the Bulge, 276–89
   bombing of Germany, 178–79
   differences with Britain, 165
   entry into war, 126, 307
   "Germany first" policy, 127–28

invasion of Sicily, 195–99
isolationism, 2
in North Africa, 166–70, 180–81, 184, 186, 188–93
Utah beach, 240, 246, 247–48, 253

*Valiant* (battleship), 219
Vatutin, N. F., 154, 212
Vichy government, 37, 48
Victor Emanuel (king of Italy), 199, 201
Vietinghoff-Scheel, Heinrich-Gottfried, 196, 214, 215, 220, 221
Vistula River, 290, 291
Volga River, 145, 150, 151
*Volksgrenadier*, 278
Vyazma (Soviet Union), 105

Walker, Walton, 267, 271
Ward, Orlando, 189–90
War of attrition, 88–89, 97, 112
Warsaw (Poland), 293
*Warspite* (battleship), 219, 220
Wavell, Archibald, 46, 52, 55, 57, 60, 63, 64, 68, 69, 73, 76, 77, 110, 111, 115
Weichs, Maximilian von, 59, 109
Welles, Sumner, 89
Wenzel, Helmut, 20
Westphal, Siegfried, 214, 274, 275
West Wall. *See* Siegfried line
Weygand, Maxime, 27, 34
Wietersheim, Gustav von, 13, 26, 27, 153
Wilson, H. Maitland, 230, 237
Witzig, Rudolf, 20, 171, 172
World War I, 3, 7, 9

Yugoslavia, 57–60, 78, 79

Zeitzler, Kurt, 153, 157, 205, 255
Zhukov, Georgy, 103, 106, 107, 152, 211, 293–95
Ziegler, Heinz, 184

# About the Author

Bevin Alexander was born in 1928 in Gastonia, North Carolina. He graduated in 1949 from the Citadel in Charleston, South Carolina, with a bachelor's degree with honors in history and worked as a journalist for *The Charlotte Observer*. He commanded the 5th Historical Detachment in the Korean War from 1951 to 1952. This detachment was a research organization that served in the combat zone, charged with producing battle studies for the Department of the Army. These battle studies are now lodged in the National Archives and form basic original sources of the history of the war. Alexander later graduated from Northwestern University, Evanston, Illinois, in 1954 with a master's degree with distinction. He worked as a journalist for the *Richmond Times-Dispatch*, was on the president's staff at the University of Virginia in charge of all university information programs, and now teaches history at Longwood College in Farmville, Virginia. He has three sons—two lawyers and an engineer. He lives near Richmond, Virginia.